Forschungs-/Entwicklungs-/Innovations-Management

Edited by

H. D. Bürgel (em.), Stuttgart , Germany
D. Grosse, Freiberg , Germany
C. Herstatt, Hamburg, Germany
H. Koller, Hamburg, Germany
C. Lüthje, Hamburg, Germany
M. G. Möhrle, Bremen, Germany

W0079503

Die Reihe stellt aus integrierter Sicht von Betriebswirtschaft und Technik Arbeits-ergebnisse auf den Gebieten Forschung, Entwicklung und Innovation vor. Die einzelnen Beiträge sollen dem wissenschaftlichen Fortschritt dienen und die For-derungen der Praxis auf Umsetzbarkeit erfüllen.

Edited by

Professor Dr. Hans Dietmar Bürgel
(em.),
Universität Stuttgart

Professorin Dr. Diana Grosse vorm. de
Pay,
Technische Universität Bergakademie
Freiberg

Professor Dr. Cornelius Herstatt
Technische Universität
Hamburg-Harburg

Professor Dr. Hans Koller
Universität der Bundeswehr Hamburg

Professor Dr. Christian Lüthje
Technische Universität Hamburg-
Harburg

Professor Dr. Martin G. Möhrle
Universität Bremen

Till Albert

Measuring Technology Maturity

Operationalizing Information
from Patents, Scientific
Publications, and the Web

 **Springer** Gabler

Till Albert
Bremen, Germany

Dissertation Universität Bremen, 2015

Forschungs-/Entwicklungs-/Innovations-Management
ISBN 978-3-658-12131-0   ISBN 978-3-658-12132-7 (eBook)
DOI 10.1007/978-3-658-12132-7

Library of Congress Control Number: 2016930681

Springer Gabler

Printed on acid-free paper

Springer Gabler is a brand of Springer Fachmedien Wiesbaden
Springer Fachmedien Wiesbaden is part of Springer Science+Business Media
(www.springer.com)

Foreword

Many companies are confronted with the necessity to evaluate technologies in a valid and robust manner. This necessity arises from the dynamic character of the contemporary business environment, which is marked by globalization, fast technological changes (especially in informatics) and the current demographic shift. In the context of technology evaluation, the metaphor of technological 'maturity' (analogous to biological maturity) and related typologies of maturity are quite commonly used. Often, these maturity typologies are defined by in-house specialists, and this involves a number of drawbacks, namely the specialists' subjective points of view, a lack of expertise concerning 'distant' technologies, a limited assessment of the dynamics of maturity development, and a merely sporadic monitoring of significant technologies.

These are the docking points for Till Albert's dissertation, which focuses on the (semi-) automatic assessment of the maturity levels of different technologies. Thus, he addresses a topic of high economic relevance in theoretical as well as empirical terms. The strengths of his approach become obvious in the following aspects: Referring to the model developed by Sommerlatte & Dechamps, the author consistently bases his argumentation on a viable theoretical concept. Through operationalization of the said model he manages to derive measurable indicators of technological maturity. By means of an impressive data-set which he skillfully assembles for various data storage technologies, he subsequently demonstrates the applicability of these indicators, comparing his semi-automatically obtained results with those of a simultaneously executed Delphi-survey.

The product of all this is a valuable tool which serves the abovementioned purpose very well. And the fact that Till Albert never fails to be self-critical in pointing out the limitations of his work also deserves recognition.

The presented text may be helpful for corporate experts who intend to automate and thereby improve the monitoring of technologies. It is also of use to people who are scientifically concerned with technology management and therefore take an interest in the dynamics and positioning of technologies. Research institutes working on studies on technology bundles are also likely to benefit from Till Albert's elaborations. I wish him all the best for a wide dissemination of his work.

Bremen, August 2015   Prof. Dr. habil. Martin G. Möhrle

Preface

The idea for this work originated from my work for the Future Research department at the Volkswagen AG and in the context of my startup Mapegy GmbH. Both enterprises depend heavily on current technological developments and are therefore permanently looking for ways to detect and assess technological trends as early as possible.

Volkswagen's future research department was organized as a model kit with different tools, each suitable to examine elements of the STEEP methodology. I was a member of the Technology Foresight team and I used diverse mostly quantitative methods to consult other departments in strategic questions of technology and innovation management. All of the studies were generated from publicly available data such as patents, scientific and press publications, as well as internet based media such as blogs or social networks.

Since the data is publicly available and strategic technology and innovation management questions are being asked not only in the automotive industry, at one point my colleague Dr. Peter Walde and I founded the company Mapegy GmbH in order to provide the same service to a larger audience. Mapegy generates automated reports from large volumes of data. Among other things these reports can determine technological trends, estimate a firm's technology strategy, or rank inventors regarding their attribution to a certain field of research.

I am glad I was able to put my professional knowledge to use in this work. At the same time, however, I was also able to pick my own subject rather than focusing on topics based on the strategic relevance for my clients. Deadlines were not as time critical, which allowed me to set my own scientific standards very high. I embraced this freedom very much, and used it to work with people whose company I enjoy very much.

I would like to thank my parents Sabine and Bernd Albert and my girlfriend Linn for emotional support. My academic mentor and "Doktorvater" Professor Dr. Martin G. Möhrle for providing valuable input throughout all stages of the writing process as well as for high frequency supervision, especially during the late stages of the dissertation. He is a great person. Reviewers and examiners of the final dissertation, Prof. Dr. Martin Kloyer, Dr. Iciar Dominguez Lacasa, Dr. Lothar Walter, as well as Prof. Dr. Jens Pöppelbuß for his willingness to help. My dear colleague Jens Potthast for helping me with major coding, soft- and hardware challenges and struggles. Christopher Perkins for cross-reading the manuscript and improving readability and intelligibility. Steffen Cords for being a valuable sparring partner concerning mathematical and statistical thoughts.

Berlin, August 2015   Till Albert

Table of Contents

Table of Contents.. IX

Abbreviations.. XIII

Figures.. XV

Tables.. XXIII

1   Introduction... 1

2   Measuring Technology Maturity: Theoretical Aspects...................... 9

2.1 Details of the Sommerlatte & Deschamps Strategic Technology
Management Approach and Maturity Model..................................... 10

2.1.1 Benefits of a Firm-Wide Technology Strategy 11

2.1.2 Reconstruction of the Sommerlatte and Deschamps Approach............. 15

2.1.3 Newly Enabled Capabilities to Assess Technology Maturity
Automatically as a Functional Option to Improve the S&D Approach in
General and the S&D Model in Particular 30

2.1.4 Technology Management Office as a Structural Option to Improve the
S&D approach.. 34

2.2 Defining Basic Terms and Mechanisms of Technology Maturity and
Developing a Characterization and Operationalization Framework for
Theoretical Technology Maturity Models... 35

2.2.1 Delineating Technologies as the Objects of Maturity Measurement........ 36

2.2.2 Developing a Framework for Maturity Model Characterization 41

2.2.3 Profiles of Selected Popular Models 51

2.3 Operationalizing Theoretical Technology Maturity Indicators 61

2.3.1 The Typology of Grupp and Options for More Indicators.......... 62

2.3.2 Information Scattering in Different Text Media 66

2.3.3 Identifying Text Media Suitable for Informetric Analyses 69

2.3.4 Deriving Relevant Indicator Values 85

2.3.5 Employing and Combining Indicators 102

3   Designing an Empirical Analysis 115

4   Execution and Results of the Empirical Analysis 121

    4.1 Issue Identification 121

    4.2 Using the Delphi Method for Letting Experts Typify Technology Maturity 124

    4.3 Selection of Data Sources 129

    4.4 Search Refinement, Data Retrieval, and Data Cleaning 134

    4.5 Basic Analyses 137

        4.5.1 Absolute Invention Count per Year 137

        4.5.2 Absolute Scientific Publication Activity 140

        4.5.3 Absolute Web Search Queries in Google Trends 140

        4.5.4 Juxtaposition of Absolute Document Frequencies for Technology
        Application, Paradigms, and Generations for Recall Estimations 141

    4.6 Methodological Triangulation 143

        4.6.1 Magnetic Tape as a Case Where Data is Available for the Later
        Maturity States Only 145

        4.6.2 Compact Disc as a Case Where Data is Available for All Maturity
        States 148

        4.6.3 Blu-ray as a Case Where Data is Available for the Earlier Maturity
        States Only 151

    4.7 Advanced Analyses.. 154

        4.7.1 Overview of Contestant Indicator Sets and Their Data Requirements ... 154

        4.7.2 Considering Indicator Biases 166

        4.7.3 Compiling Activity Indicator Values for a Technology by Example of
        the MiniDisc Technology 167

        4.7.4 Assigning Activity Indicator Observations to States of Maturity and
        Determining the Distribution of Observations Across These States 171

        4.7.5 Comparing Hypothetical to Actual Indicator Behavior 176

        4.7.6 Using a Linear Discriminant Analysis to Gauge the Maturity
        Classification Performance of the Activity Indicators..................................... 189

        4.7.7 Using a Linear Discriminant Analysis to Gauge the Maturity
        Classification Performance of the Patent Meta Data Indicators 226

4.8 Representation, Interpretation, and Utilization of the Advanced Analysis Results 235

4.8.1 Applying the S&D Model to Hard Disc Technology 237

4.8.2 Applying the S&D Model to NVRAM Technology 238

4.8.3 Applying the S&D Model to ReRAM Technology 239

4.8.4 Checking the Reaction Time and Precision of Activity Indicators on Optical Disc Technologies: DVD, Blu-ray, and HD-DVD 239

5   Measuring Technology Maturity: Conclusions...243

5.1 Quality Criteria and Limitations...245

5.2 Directions for Future Research..249

Bibliography...251

Annex A: Delphi Questionnaire and Information Basis 275

Annex B: Technology Search Strategies for Different Text Media Databases 286

Annex C: R-Code of Statistical Analyses Performed in the Scope of the Approach in this Book..288

Abbreviations

ANOVA	Analysis of Variance
CPC	Cooperative Patent Classification
DWPI	Derwent World Patent Index
HR	Human Resources
IP	Intellectual Property
IT	Information Technology
IPC	International Patent Classification
LDA	Linear Discriminant Analysis
NGO	Non-Governmental Organization
OEM	Original Equipment Manufacturer
PCT	Patent Cooperation Treaty
R&D	Research and Development
SWOT	Strengths, Weaknesses, Opportunities, Threats
S&D	Sommerlatte and Deschamps (authors of the S&D technology maturity model)
TMO	Technology Management Office
USPTO	United States Patent and Trademark Office

Figures

Fig 1.1 Possible levels of increasing operationalization of maturity models from left to right, described in detail in section 2.2.2.1 2

Fig. 2.1 Hierarchical view of the technology strategy according to ZAHRA et al. (1999). The arrows stand for factors of the former element directly influencing the latter 12

Fig. 2.2 Technology as a component of competitive strategy according to ZAHRA et al. (1999) 13

Fig. 2.3 Technology management on different management levels according to SOMMERLATTE & DESCHAMPS (1986) 14

Fig. 2.4 A variation of the originally strictly sequential approach for strategic technology management by SOMMERLATTE & DESCHAMPS (1986) 16

Fig. 2.5 Typical coincidence between maturity state and strategic relevance of a technology according to SOMMERLATTE & DESCHAMPS (1986).........................20

Fig 2.6 Internal and external technological resources connected to the relative technological position of a business unit according to the interpretation of the resource-based view of SOMMERLATTE & DESCHAMPS 21

Fig. 2.7 Technology strategies in emergence to early growth (left) and late growth to early maturity (right) as a subject to technological and competitive position of a firm according to SOMMERLATTE & DESCHAMPS (1986). Along with increasing maturity of a technology, the competitive and technological position requirements for more comprehensive technology strategies also increase..24

Fig. 2.8 Technology strategy options as a subject to competitive position of a firm and technology maturity state according to SOMMERLATTE & DESCHAMPS (1986)...25

Fig. 2.9 Technology risk matrix depending on the extent of dependent business and insecurity of technology strategy according to SOMMERLATTE & DESCHAMPS 29

Fig. 2.10 Risk categories adapted from SARTOR & BOURAUEL (2012) 30

Fig. 2.11 The difference between phases and states illustrated on the basis of the life of mammals and technologies. Boxes represent intervals of time with relatively steady conditions whereas ovals represent events or relatively short time intervals with rapidly changing conditions. Source: own figure, compare e.g. TANNER (1990) 38

Fig. 2.12 Linear model by WATTS & PORTER (1990) as interpreted by MARTINO (2003) 39

Fig. 2.13 Elements of theoretical technology maturity models and their operationalization 43

Fig. 2.14 Reflective and formative constructs and their main components, construct, indicators and error terms in comparison 49

Fig. 2.15 Total granted US patents 1970-2012 75

Fig. 2.16 Scientific literature published by ScienceDirect 1970-2012 77

Fig. 2.17 Web search queries in millions in Google Trends 1998-2012 based on data from the website Statistic Brain, which were collected from different sources (Statistic Brain 2013). The count of web search queries increased at a high rate throughout the entire period covered by the data. Absolute search query volume for the years 2001-2006 is unfortunately not available. The 4 million queries in the year 1998 and the 22,000 million queries in 2000 are too low to be displayed 80

Fig. 2.18 Activity indicator - publication activity over time 87

Fig. 2.19 Meta data of a document may serve as information basis for meta data indicators 88

Fig. 2.20 A document pointing to another relevant document by citing it may be the information basis of a network indicator 89

Fig. 2.21 Full text analyses may encompass substantial additional data evaluation 90

Fig. 2.22 Different ideal indicator development shapes 94

Fig. 2.23 Location parameters of a function 95

Fig. 2.24 Scale parameters of a function 96

Fig. 2.25 Shape parameters of a function 96

Fig. 2.26 Alternative interpretations for multimodal indicator development 97

Fig. 2.27 Example of function behavior which is unfit as an indicator 104

Fig. 2.28 Example of indicator behavior which allows for recognition of the latter out of two transitions between states 104

Fig. 2.29 Example of indicator behavior which allows for recognition of the former out of two transitions between states 105

Fig. 2.30 Example of indicator behavior which allows for recognition of two consecutive transitions between states 105

Fig. 2.31 Linear model as interpreted by Martino (2003)..................................... 108

Fig. 2.32 Indicator development throughout the information diffusion process with the publication activity functions of the text media A, B, C, D, and E........ 109

Fig. 2.33 Schematic flow chart of a supervised learning approach 111

Fig. 2.34 An example of 5-fold cross validation... 113

Fig. 3.1 Analysis design flow chart.. 116

Fig. 4.1 Steps of the Delphi Method as described e.g. by HSUEH (2013) 125

Fig. 4.2 International patent family applications connected to data storage technology (search strategies for technology paradigms from table 4.5 combined) as covered by Thomson Innovation in the years 1970 – 2012, assigned to years by application date 138

Fig. 4.3 US issued patents connected to data storage technology (search strategies for technology paradigms from table 4.5 combined) as covered by the USPTO in the years 1970 – 2012, assigned to years by issue date 138

Fig. 4.4 Absolute scientific journal publication count connected to data storage technology during the years 1970-2012, assigned to years by publication date 140

Fig. 4.5 Relative web search query volume for the term "data storage" in Google Trends between 2004 and 2012 141

Fig. 4.6 6090 US patent grants connected to the magnetic tape data storage technology as a fraction of all data storage technologies between 1976 and 2012... 145

Fig. 4.7 398 scientific publications connected to the magnetic tape data storage technology as a fraction of all data storage technologies between 1976 and 2012... 146

Fig. 4.8 Web search queries connected to the magnetic tape data storage technology between 2004 and 2012... 147

Fig. 4.9 US patent grants connected to the compact disc technology as a fraction of all data storage technologies between 1976 and 2012................. 148

Fig. 4.10 Scientific publications connected to the compact disc technology as a fraction of all data storage technologies between 1976 and 2012. 149

Fig. 4.11 Web search queries connected to the compact disc technology between 2004 and 2012. 150

Fig. 4.12 US patent grants connected to the Blu-ray technology as a fraction of all data storage technologies between 1976 and 2012. 151

Fig. 4.13 Scientific publications connected to the Blu-ray technology as a fraction of all data storage technologies between 1976 and 2012. 152

Fig. 4.14 Web search queries connected to the Blu-ray technology between 2004 and 2012. 153

Fig. 4.15 Overview of Haupt et al.'s meta data Indicators (Haupt et al. 2007) and activity indicators presented in section 2.3.4.2 (compare JÄRVENPÄÄ et al. (2011), MARTINO (2003), and WATTS & PORTER (1997)), which will be used to assess technology maturity in this analysis 155

Fig. 4.16 Data collection for backward patent citations indicator 159

Fig. 4.17 Data collection for immediacy of citations indicator 161

Fig. 4.18 Determining the dependent claims count is possible by first identifying independent claims and deducing their count from the total claims count 162

Fig. 4.19 Data collection for prior applications count indicator 163

Fig. 4.20 Data collection for examination duration indicator 164

Fig. 4.21 Data collection for forward patent citations indicator.............................166

Fig. 4.22 Absolute US patents count relevant for the minidisc technology by issue date in the years 1976-2012 168

Fig. 4.23 Fraction of US patents relevant for the minidisc technology of all data storage technology US patents by issue date in the years 1976-2012 168

Fig. 4.24 Slope of data storage US patents relevant for the minidisc technology by issue date in the years 1976-2012 168

Fig. 4.25 Absolute international patents count relevant for the minidisc technology by application date in the years 1976-2012 169

Fig. 4.26 Fraction of data storage international patents relevant for the minidisc technology of all data storage technology international patents by application date in the years 1976-2012 169

Fig. 4.27 Slope of data storage international patents relevant for the minidisc technology by publication date in the years 1976-2012 169

Fig. 4.28 Absolute scientific publications count relevant for the minidisc technology by publication date in the years 1976-2012 170

Fig. 4.29 Fraction of data storage scientific publications relevant for the minidisc technology of all data storage technology scientific publications by publication date in the years 1976-2012 170

Fig. 4.30 Slope of data storage scientific publications relevant for the minidisc technology by publication date in the years 1976-2012 170

Fig. 4.31 Fraction of data storage web search queries relevant for the minidisc technology by query date in the years 1976-2012. The 100% value is determined by the relatively highest weekly value as provided by Google; the yearly values are the arithmetic middle of all weekly values in the corresponding year.. 171

Fig. 4.32 Slope of data storage web search queries relevant for the minidisc technology by query date in the years 1976-2012 171

Fig. 4.33 Transformation of all indicator value sets from technology-and-year-based to a maturity-based assignment. Still, each indicator value set consists of six or eight indicator values: the fraction and slope of international and US patents, scientific publications, and, if applicable, web search queries 172

Fig. 4.34 Fraction of data storage US patents relevant for the minidisc technology with the starting point of the curve in the year 1976 marked with a dashed line and the top point of the curve in the year 1993 marked with a dashed and dotted line. It is important to note that the actual starting point of the curve may lie before the year 1976 187

Fig. 4.35 Fraction of data storage international patents relevant for the minidisc technology with the starting point of the curve in the year 1979 marked with a dashed line and the top point of the curve in the year 1999 marked with a dashed and dotted line... 188

Fig. 4.36 Fraction of data storage scientific publications relevant for the minidisc technology with the starting point of the curve in the year 1981 marked with a dashed line and the top point of the curve in the year 1992 marked with a dashed and dotted line... 188

Fig. 4.37 Data storage web search requests relevant for the minidisc technology with the starting and top points of the curve in the year 2004 188

Fig. 4.38 Setup of statistical tests for normality (left side) and homoscedasticity (right side) which assures that data which does not comply with the assumptions of parametric analyses is treated with due caution. The tests are arranged with decreasing sensitivity 191

Fig. 4.39 Boxplots of all activity indicator values of all technologies by maturity state between 2004 and 2012 to display spread and distribution. The indicator values are grouped by maturity states to make visible the difference between the groups and get an idea about normality and homoscedasticity. The group names are coded as follows: 0 – pre-existence, 1 – emergence, 2 – growth, 3 - saturation, 4 – decline 197

Fig. 4.40 Boxplots of all activity indicator values of all technologies by maturity state between 1976 and 2012 to display spread and distribution. The indicator values are grouped by maturity states to make the difference between the groups visible and give an idea about normality and homoscedasticity. The group names are coded as follows: 0 – pre-existence, 1 – emergence, 2 – growth, 3 - saturation, 4 – decline 198

Fig. 4.41 Schematic sample data configuration for indicator selection based on the random forest approach 215

Fig. 4.42 Misclassification rates for different indicator set sizes based on reverse indicator elimination with random forests for the data in the time period between 2004 and 2012 (grey squares) and between 1976 and 2012 (black dots) 217

Fig. 4.43 Schematic sample data configuration for the linear discriminant analysis 221

Fig. 4.44 Boxplots of all meta data indicator values between 1976 and 2012 by maturity state to display spread and distribution. The indicator values are grouped by maturity states to make visible the difference between the groups and get an idea about normality and homoscedasticity. The group names are coded as follows: 0 – pre-existence, 1 – emergence, 2 – growth, 3 - saturation, 4 – decline 232

Fig. 4.45 Hard disc maturity state classification values for the years 2006 and 2012 based on the activity indicator based technology maturity model including web search data 237

Fig. 4.46 NVRAM maturity state classification values for the years 2006 and 2012 based on the activity indicator based technology maturity model including web search data...238

Fig. 4.47 ReRAM maturity state classification values for the years 2006 and 2012 based on the activity indicator based technology maturity model including web search data...239

Fig. 4.48 DVD maturity state classification values for the years 2006 through 2012 based on the activity indicator based technology maturity model including web search data...240

Fig. 4.49 Blu-ray maturity state classification values for the years 2006 through 2012 based on the activity indicator based technology maturity model including web search data...241

Fig. 4.50 HD-DVD maturity state classification values for the years 2006 through 2012 based on the activity indicator based technology maturity model including web search data...242

Tables

Table 1.1 Linking elements of the research question to sections of this book 8

Table 2.1 Alternative technology strategies by activity and technology spectrum of the BU adapted from SOMMERLATTE & DESCHAMPS (1986) 22

Table 2.2 Application, paradigms, and generations of music storage according to TAYLOR & TAYLOR (2012) 37

Table 2.3 Chronological overview of influential technology maturity models 52

Table 2.4 Delineating the S&D technology maturity model 59

Table 2.5 Latent variables of the S&D technology maturity model and their expected development during maturation adapted from SOMMERLATTE & DESCHAMPS (1986) 60

Table 2.6 Indicator typology based on GRUPP (1997) 63

Table 2.7 S&D model's latent variables according to the GRUPP typology. The bold letters represent the S&D model's latent variables of table 2.5, the numbers are GRUPP'S indicator types as defined in table 2.6 above 64

Table 2.8 Innovation and information diffusion core aspects juxtaposed (Sources: see table) 67

Table 2.9 Characteristics of patents as a text medium 76

Table 2.10 Characteristics of scientific literature as a text medium.......................78

Table 2.11 Characteristics of web search queries as a text medium 81

Table 2.12 Latent variables of the S&D technology maturity model split up into new factors which can be operationalized and their expected development during maturation 82

Table 2.13 Different text media help with the analysis for different factors of the S&D model hypotheses 85

Table 2.14 Different factors of the S&D model hypotheses require different indicator types to evaluate the text media...91

Table 2.15 Overview of expected behavior of S&D model factors which can be operationalized with help of activity indicators...103

Table 2.16 Possible indicator behavior for two consecutive maturity state transitions. A "+" means the indicator rises significantly from two former to the latter, a "-" means the indicator decreases, and a "0" means it remains at a similar level before and after the transition... 106

Table 2.17 Possible indicator behavior for three consecutive maturity state transitions 106

Table 2.18 Indicator curve point progression hypothesized in different approaches: J (Järvenpää 2009), P (Watts & Porter 1997), M (Martino 2003) 110

Table 3.1 The nine-step data analysis process by (Porter & Cunningham 2005, p.323) serves to structure the data-driven analysis 115

Table 3.2 The advanced analyses comprise several analyses to check whether the data fulfills the necessary properties for the machine-learning based analysis to work properly, other analyses to prepare the data for the machine-learning approach as well as to actually conduct it 118

Table 4.1 Generations and corresponding paradigms of the analyzed data storage technologies.. 123

Table 4.2 Overview of data storage technologies and expert assigned maturity states in the time period between 1976 and 2012. The progression of maturity states is pre-existence → emergence → growth → saturation → decline. The years in the table mark the first year during which a technology changes from the antecedent technology state to the one in the observed column 127

Table 4.3 Distribution of maturity states for all technologies during the years 1976 - 2012 128

Table 4.4 Distribution of maturity states for technologies which change maturity state during the years 2004 - 2012 128

Table 4.5 Technology search strategies for the USPTO data is based on a mixed strategy of classifications and keywords. It looks similar for the other databases.. 134

Table 4.6 Absolute document counts for technology application and paradigms as an upper boundary for recall estimations of technology generation searches.. 142

Table 4.7 Selection of maturity state indicators derived from the S&D model based on different media types as described in sections 2.3.3.4 and 2.3.4 (operationalization) 144

Table 4.8 Observation count and median values of activity indicator values for all technologies by maturity state between 2004 and 2012 173

Table 4.9 Observation count and median values of activity indicator values for all technologies by maturity state between 1976 and 2012 174

Table 4.10 Distribution of maturity states for technologies which change maturity states during the time period 2004-2012 based on activity data indicators 175

Table 4.11 Distribution of maturity states for technologies which change maturity states during the time period 1976-2012 based on activity data indicators 175

Table 4.12 Mean fraction international patents indicator values for each technology, grouped by maturity state. 177

Table 4.13 Mean fraction of international patents indicator values (collected at time of patent application) for all technologies with observations of the emergence, growth, and saturation maturity states during the time period between 1976 and 2012, grouped by maturity state, rescaled to values between 0% and 100% 178

Table 4.14 Mean fraction of US patents indicator values (collected at the time of patent grant) for all technologies with observations of the emergence, growth, and saturation maturity states during the time period between 1976 and 2012, grouped by maturity state, rescaled to values between 0% and 100% 179

Table 4.15 Mean fraction of scientific publication indicator values for all technologies with observations of the emergence, growth, and saturation maturity states during the time period between 1976 and 2012, grouped by maturity state, rescaled to values between 0% and 100% 180

Table 4.16 Mean slope of international patents indicator values (collected at the time of patent application) for all technologies with observations of the emergence, growth, and saturation maturity states during the time period between 1976 and 2012, grouped by maturity state, rescaled to values between 0% and 100% 181

Table 4.17 Mean slope of US patents indicator values (collected at the time of patent grant) for all technologies with observations of the emergence, growth, and saturation maturity states during the time period between 1976 and 2012, grouped by maturity state, rescaled to values between 0% and 100% 182

Table 4.18 Mean slope of scientific publications indicator values (collected at time of publication) for all technologies with observations of the emergence, growth, and saturation maturity states during the time period between 1976 and 2012, grouped by maturity state, rescaled to values between 0% and 100% 182

Table 4.19 Comparison of smallest (minmax) and largest (maxmax) maximum values for different technologies by indicator and the ratio between smallest and largest value, based on data collected between 1976 and 2012 184

Table 4.20 Comparison of technology definition sizes: maximal indicator values of all maturity states for each technology by overall maximum indicator value 185

Table 4.21 R&D states defined by (Watts & Porter 1997) and typical sources which are hypothesized to rise during these states as well as activity indicators which are based on related sources 186

Table 4.22 Indicator curve point progression hypothesized in different works, transferred to media used in the approach in this book as displayed in table 2.18: **J** (Järvenpää 2009), **P** (Watts & Porter 1997), **1** always true, **0** always false 187

Table 4.23 Years of starting and top curve points for fraction indicators of different media. The order of the columns is arranged to fit the hypothesized order of media activity...189

Table 4.24 Arithmetic mean and standard deviation (SD) of all indicator values in the time periods between 2004-2012 and 1976-2012 192

Table 4.25 Significance level codes..192

Table 4.26 Results of Box's M homogeneity of variance-covariance matrices test for the activity indicators in the time periods of 2004-2012 and 1976-2012 193

Table 4.27 Results of the Shapiro-Wilk normality test for the activity indicators in the time period of 2004-2012...194

Table 4.28 Results of the Shapiro-Wilk normality test for the activity indicators in the time period of 1976-2012...194

Table 4.29 Results of Levene's homoscedasticity test for each separate activity indicator for the time period of 2004-2012 195

Table 4.30 Results of Levene's homoscedasticity test for each separate activity indicator for the time period of 1976-2012 195

Table 4.31 An ANOVA for different regression window sizes for the activity slope indicators shows that different indicators work best with different regression windows 199

Table 4.32 A non-parametric Kruskal-Wallis test with different regression window sizes for the activity slope indicators shows that different indicators work best with different regression windows 200

Table 4.33 Zero and near zero variance indicator values in the data from between 2004 and 2012 204

Table 4.34 Zero and near zero variance indicator values in the data from between 1976 and 2012 204

Table 4.35 Correlations between indicators according to Pearson's correlation coefficient, using the data from the time between 2004 and 2012. High correlations > .75 are marked by a grey shading 205

Table 4.36 Correlations between indicators according to Pearson's correlation coefficient, using the data from the time between 1976 and 2012 205

Table 4.37 Pairwise Mann-Whitney-Wilcoxon tests between maturity states x and y (The states are coded as follows: 0 – pre-existence, 1 – emergence, 2 – growth, 3 - saturation, 4 – decline) for the time period between the years 2004 and 2012. Test results reported include the p-value, Bonferroni-corrected significance level (8 comparisons), W-score, effect size r, and z-score 207

Table 4.38 Pairwise Mann-Whitney-Wilcoxon tests between maturity states x and y (The states are coded as follows: 0 – pre-existence, 1 – emergence, 2 – growth, 3 - saturation, 4 – decline) for the time period between the years 1976 and 2012. 209

Table 4.39 Bonferroni-corrected significance levels of pairwise Mann-Whitney-Wilcoxon tests between maturity states (The states are coded as follows: 0 – pre-existence, 1 – emergence, 2 – growth, 3 - saturation, 4 – decline) for the time period between the years 2004 and 2012 211

Table 4.40 Bonferroni-corrected significance levels of pairwise Mann-Whitney-Wilcoxon tests between maturity states (The states are coded as follows: 0

– pre-existence, 1 – emergence, 2 – growth, 3 - saturation, 4 – decline) for
the time period between the years 1976 and 2012 211

Table 4.41 Relevant results of Kruskal-Wallis tests on each indicator for
discriminating between maturity states for the time period between the years
2004 and 2012 212

Table 4.42 Relevant results of Kruskal-Wallis tests on each indicator for
discriminating between maturity states for the time period between the years
1976 and 2012 213

Table 4.43 Misclassification rates for different indicator set sizes based on
reverse indicator elimination with random forests for the data in the time
periods between 2004 and 2012 as well as between 1976 and 2012 with the
full set marked grey and the best set marked by a black frame. Set sizes
larger than the full set result from inclusion of dummy indicators 217

Table 4.44 Classifier for five maturity state groups and activity indicators in the
time span from 2004 to 2012. The values in the table represent indicator
weights. The column sum of the indicator values times the corresponding
weights represent the classification score of each maturity state. The column
sum which produces the highest score determines the maturity state............222

Table 4.45 Classifier for five maturity state groups and activity indicators in the
time span from 1976 to 2012..223

Table 4.46 Confusion matrix of the activity indicator based technology maturity
model based on data from between 2004 and 2012 223

Table 4.47 Confusion matrix of the activity indicator based operationalized
technology maturity model based on data from between 1976 and 2012 224

Table 4.48 Misclassification rates for different regression windows and indicator
sets 225

Table 4.49 Results of Box's M homogeneity of variance-covariance matrices test
for the meta data indicators 229

Table 4.50 Results of Levene's homoscedasticity test for each separate meta
data indicator 230

Table 4.51 Distribution of maturity states for technologies which change maturity
states during the time period 1976-2012 based on meta data indicators 233

Table 4.52 Distribution of maturity states for the equal size sample approach 233

Table 4.53 Classification function parameters for five maturity state groups in the time span from 1976 to 2012 as determined by an LDA. The rows represent factors for the patent meta data indicator values which were calculated according to HAUPT et al.(2007) and the columns represent the factors for maturity state equations. The sum of all indicator values each multiplied by the corresponding factors for an entire row add up to the corresponding maturity state score. The maturity state with the highest score is selected as the current maturity state of the analyzed technology 234

Table 4.54 Confusion matrix of the patent indicator based operationalized technology maturity model with the backward citation indicators considered in combination based on data from between 1976 and 2012 235

Table 4.55 The hard disc technology is located in the saturation state at the brink of the decline state 238

Table 4.56 NVRAM recently left the growth state and is now in the saturation state 238

Table 4.57 ReRAM was just recently introduced as a technology and is now in the emergence state..239

Table 4.58 The DVD technology has moved to the decline state and can now be regarded as obsolete...240

Table 4.59 The Blu-ray technology is shifting back and forth between the growth and saturation states 241

Table 4.60 The HD-DVD technology has lost the battle against the Blu-ray technology and is now in the decline state...242

Table 5.1 Important quality criteria for the approach presented in this book, compare STEINKE (2004) and PIPINO et al. (2002)...245

1 Introduction

Once a new technology rolls over you,
if you're not part of the steamroller,
you're part of the road.
(Brand 1987, p.22)

Nowadays, requirements for successfully managing a firm are different from what they were some 30 years ago. Many conditions have changed: The ongoing globalization increases the complexity of management decisions, which increasingly have to take into account globally dispersed customer groups, sources of innovation, and manufacturing capability (Teece 2007). New technologies are developed at an increasing speed (Kurzweil 2005, pp.24–43). Market boundaries are blurred, market players (i.e. buyers, suppliers, competitors, complementers) are ambiguous and shifting (Eisenhardt & Martin 2000, p.1111). Paradoxically, at the same time, new communication technologies are making markets more transparent (Shuen & Sieber 2009; Sher & Lee 2004), causing profit margins to decline. This increasing speed and complexity is leading to an innovation-based competition and the "creative destruction" of existing competences. Market success is reserved for the quickest and most innovative firms (Burgelman et al. 2009, pp.113–129).

New opportunities arise from this, especially for more dynamic firms. They are not short of ideas, but most lack the ability to determine an idea's value in a systematic, timely, and cost-effective way. How can a firm with its limited resources (physical, human, and organizational assets) make the best out of this situation? A good way is to align available resources to new opportunities quickly. This is postulated in dynamic capabilities theory (Teece et al. 1997; Teece & Pisano 1994). TEECE originally identified two core capabilities: a) the means to enable timely responsiveness and b) the management capability to coordinate and redeploy internal and external competences (Teece & Pisano 1994, p.1). This elaboration is about these competences: improving firm-level success by scanning the environment, evaluating markets and competitors, and thereby gaining the ability to reconfigure and transform ahead of competition (Teece et al. 1997, p.521).

But which technology presents an opportunity and should, in the words of Stewart BRAND, be machined with a dedicated steamroller (Brand 1987, p.22)? Timing is an important aspect as investing in a new technology too early will bind resources while not leading to an immediate advantage over competitors. Investing in a new technology too late, however, may cause market competitors to have built up significant "first mover" advantages which are hard to catch up (Christensen 2013). Many firms start developing a new technology too late and rely on old technology instead (Christensen 2013; Foster 1986, p.103). Recent examples can be found e.g. in the field of photography and mobile communication: Leica, Kodak, Nokia, Research In Motion (RIM).

Estimating a technology's maturity with high precision is not trivial. It takes skilled personnel and thus implies high (opportunity) cost. At the same time the R&D departments of technology driven firms often develop diverse technologies and employ many technology experts. Those in charge of allocating budget to technologies often lack in-depth-knowledge of single technologies and depend on expert assessment. Technology experts responsible for developing certain single technology know about this technology's maturity, but lack strategic overview of all technologies. Valuations from different experts are difficult to compare and it can be hard to find an expert who is knowledgeable in each relevant technology.

An expert-independent, yet precise approach to determine technology maturity and derive appropriate management advice from it would be opportune. Still, not every firm has adapted the use of technology maturity models, despite the myriad of models that exist for this purpose, each with its own strengths and weaknesses. Many weaknesses are due to the lack of operationalization of these models. To get a rough overview of different types of models, they will be typified according to their operationalization level as shown in figure 1.1.

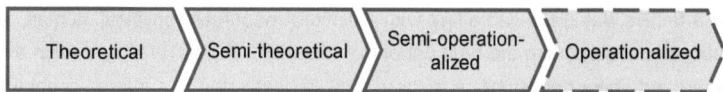

Fig 1.1 Possible levels of increasing operationalization of maturity models from left to right, described in detail in section 2.2.2.1

Many models are of the **theoretical** type and are based on theoretical considerations only. These do not provide the means to unambiguously determine the current state of maturity of a technology. Typical examples are the Dominant Design model by ABERNATHY & UTTERBACK and the Hype Cycle by LINDEN & FENN (Linden & Fenn 2003; Fenn 1999; Abernathy & Utterback 1978). These models therefore must rely on subjective interpretation and struggle with imprecision.

Semi-theoretical models provide actual indicators (model factors which can be measured) to a certain extent and describe their development during different maturity states or at least name states of maturity during which their activity rises. However, not all factors are usually represented by indicators. A typical example is the model by SOMMERLATTE & DESCHAMPS (Sommerlatte & Deschamps 1986). Still, models of this type typically require someone to interpret whether a certain value is "high" or "low", which is hardly possible beforehand or with otherwise incomplete information.

Semi-operationalized models do in fact provide indicators for all model factors, but do not provide generic rules with which a technology's maturity can be determined based on the values the indicators take on. Three types should be differentiated.

- Many semi-operationalized models rely on the so-called s-curve model by FOSTER (Foster 1986). The s-curve describes a typical s-shaped development of the performance gains of a technology. To get an idea of a technology's maturity, the current and the theoretically possible technology performance are compared. However, the relevant technology performance parameters are different even for closely related technologies. This makes these models laborious and strongly restricts their general use.

- The same technology specificity is true for Technology Readiness Level (TRL)-type models, which can be considered a type of project maturity model rather than a technology maturity model (European Space Agency 2012; Mankins 2009). As maturity indicators they describe precise project milestones rather than providing metric indicators.

- Another type of semi-operationalized model tries to overcome the effort of having to re-define relevant performance measures for each new technology by using generic measures such as patent-based indicators. Typical examples are the models by HAUPT, KLOYER & LANGE or WATTS & PORTER (Haupt et al. 2007; Watts & Porter 1997).

These models all provide indicators which produce significantly different values for separate states of maturity, which can be and has been tested in empirical analyses. What they lack thus far is a set of generic rules for determining the technology maturity of a yet unknown technology.

Operationalized models, which are actually able to determine a technology's maturity state based on a generic set of rules, are rare. Two kinds can be observed to date.

- One kind assigns activity of a certain indicator to a certain maturity state. An example is the model by WATTS & PORTER, who hypothesize that a rise in publication activity in a certain media type directly reveals the current maturity state of a technology (Watts & Porter 1997), for example, a rise in the publications of patents marks the technology application and is followed by a rise in the publications of press articles, which marks the social impact. JÄRVENPÄÄ et al. tested the hypotheses empirically (Järvenpää et al. 2011; Järvenpää 2009; Järvenpää & Mäkinen 2008b; Järvenpää & Tapaninen 2008); however, many of the empirical tests did not produce the expected results. Some came to sound conclusions but are effectively based on anecdotal evidence and cannot be inductively used for theory building (one technology; subjective interpretation); in neither case was a universal (mathematical) model the result. An important finding is that the model has to cope with a problem which arises from the fact that technologies have different drivers. An easy delineation distinguishes those technologies that are developed to meet a market demand (market pull) and those which originate from science (technology push). While for the latter the expected sequence technology "application" → "social impact" may be reasonable, the opposite sequence would be true for the former.

- A second kind of operationalized model is presented by GAO et al. and generates promising results (Gao et al. 2013). It combines a total of 13 patent-based indicators, among others those defined in the approach by HAUPT et al., with help of a k-nearest-neighbor machine-learning approach (Haupt et al. 2007). Still, several concerns arise regarding its robustness and universality, and, in addition, its precision remains vague.

In summary this results in different criticism for different model types:

1. All models have in common the lack of a defined level of technology aggregation (Taylor & Taylor 2012; Tiefel 2008; Höft 1992; Dhalla & Yuspeh 1976, p.103).
2. Due to the different technology drivers, unconsidered use of the models brings severe danger of misinterpretation (Grantham 1997; Höft 1992; Dhalla & Yuspeh 1976).
3. The operationalized models focus on operationalization aspects but do not provide theoretical foundation or strategic technology management advice (Höft 1992).
4. For the theoretical models an objective empirical analysis is impossible because their concepts cannot be measured (Tiefel 2008). Therefore all theoretical and many semi-operationalized models have no or insufficient empirical validation (Tiefel 2008; Höft 1992; Dhalla & Yuspeh 1976).
5. None other than the operationalized models describes a clearly defined pattern of their indicators during the maturity states (Taylor & Taylor 2012; Grantham 1997; Höft 1992; Dhalla & Yuspeh 1976; Patton 1959).

6. None other than the operationalized models describes a clear delineation of states or an approach for an unambiguous estimation of the current state (Höft 1992; Dhalla & Yuspeh 1976, p.104).
7. None other than the model by GAO et al. determines the maturity state as a combination of different indicators (Gao et al. 2013).
8. None other than the model by GAO et al. tests the general applicability of their model on a yet unknown technology (Gao et al. 2013).
9. Thus, none other than the model by GAO et al. is able to judge its classification performance (Gao et al. 2013).

An improved technology maturity model deals with some of this criticism. The research question of this book is therefore:

How should an approach be constructed with which existing theoretical maturity models can be operationalized to allow for valid, reliable, objective and useful statements regarding the maturity of a technology?

Taking into account the 9 points of criticism from above, this research question consists of several elements:

1. What is a sensible approach to technology definition and what is a sensible level of aggregation for technologies?
2. How should a model consider the fact that different technologies may originate from different drivers such as market pull and technology push?
3. How should an operationalized model provide strategic technology management advice?
4. What is a viable and sensible approach for operationalizing an existing theoretical technology maturity model to be able to test its assumptions empirically?
5. Do theoretical factor behavior hypotheses and actual indicator development of the operationalized model correspond?
6. How can each maturity state be recognized with a high precision?
7. What is a good way of combining different indicators and which ones should be considered?
8. How can the maturity information be deduced from the indicator values to estimate the technology maturity of a yet unknown technology?
9. How well does an operationalized model perform regarding maturity assessment?

The approach to responding to the research question and especially these 9 points of criticism is to operationalize the SOMMERLATTE & DESCHAMPS semi-theoretical technology maturity model (S&D model) (Sommerlatte & Deschamps 1986, pp.37–76) as an example because of its popularity. It is one element of an elaborate approach (S&D approach) which describes how to use technology maturity information for strategic technology management.

This approach responds to the nine elements of the research question mentioned above as follows:

1. The S&D approach was criticized for not providing rules regarding what a technology is. To establish such rules for the approach in this book, an approach described by TAYLOR & TAYLOR was used, which differentiates between the problem to be solved (the "technology application"), the technological mechanism that is used to solve the problem (the "technology paradigm"), and the actual solution (the "technology generation")(Taylor & Taylor 2012).

2. The different nature of different technologies is taken into account by relying on a broad information basis and using separate information sources in combination. Where in most approaches such as the ones by HAUPT et al. or GAO et al. a certain type of media is used exclusively (Gao et al. 2013; Haupt et al. 2007), the approach in this book uses several different media types. To keep the resulting operationalized technology maturity model open for new data sources, an operationalization mechanism is designed in a way to make it compatible with most media types. Instead of linking activity in one of these media types directly to a particular maturity state, as proposed originally in WATTS & PORTER, the interplay of indicators is considered (Watts & Porter 1997). This allows for the technology maturity to be determined according to a more complex set of rules which works for technologies that originate from different drivers.

3. To gain strategic technology management advice from an operationalized technology maturity model, it was deemed appropriate to operationalize an existing model which is part of an approach featuring such strategic technology management advice. In this case, this is the S&D approach and its technology maturity model (Sommerlatte & Deschamps 1986, pp.37–76).

4. Several of the factors of the S&D model are operationalized by an operationalization mechanism which can be used with most media types. The resulting indicators can be compared to the ones in approaches such as by JÄRVENPÄÄ et al. (Jarvenpää et al. 2011, Järvenpää 2009; Järvenpää & Mäkinen 2008b; Järvenpää & Tapaninen 2008), except that they intend to eliminate some of their shortcomings.

5. To test the operationalized model, an empirical analysis is designed and performed. The S&D model makes certain assumptions concerning the activity during different maturity states of a technology (Sommerlatte & Deschamps 1986, p.53), which can be tested with the operationalized model.

6. The question of how the maturity information is deduced from the indicator values is met by a linear discriminant analysis (LDA) as the basis of a supervised machine-learning approach, which determines distinct indicator patterns during the different technology maturity states.

7. The important indicators are chosen with reverse feature selection based on random forests. These are then combined based on the results of the LDA, which weights each indicator during each state of maturity.

8. A selection of twelve different technologies is used to train the LDA and generate a generic classifier, which is able to determine the maturity of a yet unknown technology.

9. To determine the performance of this analysis, the share of wrong classifications which results from it is compared to the share of wrong classifications which result from an LDA-based analysis with the elaborate patent indicators described in HAUPT et al. (Haupt et al. 2007).

The detailed discussion of these elements of the research question is located in the corresponding sections of this book listed in table 1.1.

This book provides several examples of how the relevant maturity related information can be communicated to the management intuitively. It concludes by pointing out advantages and shortcomings of the approach and providing possible future research.

Table 1.1 Linking elements of the research question to sections of this book

Element of the research question	Section
1. Rules for technology delineation, based on TAYLOR & TAYLOR (2012)	0 - Delineating Technologies as the Objects of Maturity Measurement
2. The interplay of different media and "information diffusion"	2.3.2 - Information Scattering in Different Text Media
3. Operationalization of the S&D technology maturity model	2.3.3.4 - Linking Information Contained in Text Media with Hypotheses of the S&D model
4. Presentation of a generic indicator mechanism	0 - Deriving Relevant Indicator Values
5. Empirical analysis of S&D model assumptions	4.7.5 - Comparing Hypothetical to Actual Indicator Behavior
6. Determining indicator patterns during different maturity states with help of an LDA	4.7.6 - Using a Linear Discriminant Analysis to Gauge the Maturity Classification Performance of the Activity Indicators
7. Selection of indicators	4.7.6.3 - Thoughts on Indicator Selection and Model Reduction
8. Presentation of the twelve sample technologies	4.1 - Issue Identification
9. Determining the indicator's performance	4.7.6 - Using a Linear Discriminant Analysis to Gauge the Maturity Classification Performance of the Activity Indicators

2 Measuring Technology Maturity: Theoretical Aspects

It is the goal of this book to propose an approach with which existing theoretical technology maturity models can be operationalized to allow for valid, reliable, objective and useful statements regarding the maturity of a technology. When it is part of a strategic technology management approach, such a model can be used to obtain strategic advice based on the values of certain indicators. There are plenty of different such approaches, but within the scope of this book only one will be operationalized as a proof of concept. Thus a suitable technology maturity model needs to be selected which ideally is part of a useful strategic technology management approach. There is no standard nomenclature for such models, so a working definition of key concepts needs to be established. And for the operationalization approach to be universal, a suitable operationalization mechanism is necessary.

One particularly integrative (semi-)theoretical technology maturity model by SOMMERLATTE & DESCHAMPS from the year 1986 (Sommerlatte & Deschamps 1986, pp.37–76) is described in detail in section 2.1. The model was chosen mainly for two reasons: for its relatively well-defined maturity states and for its popularity. The well-defined maturity states made it well-suited for operationalization in the first place. And the popularity of the model led to many subsequent approaches relying on it and providing relevant improvements until this day such as different approaches by ALBERT et al., GAO et al., HAUPT et al., HÖFT and ERICKSON et al. (Albert et al. 2015; Gao et al. 2013; Albert et al. 2011; Haupt et al. 2007; Haupt et al. 2004; Höft 1992; Erickson et al. 1990). This section also discusses recent developments which may aid in an improved use of the S&D approach but have not yet been integrated. Section 2.2 sets out to define working definitions for key concepts in technology maturity, create a technology maturity model typology, and compare the model from the previous section 2.1 to other models which address the same subject with different means. As a result, the strengths and weaknesses of each model can be identified much more easily. And finally, section 2.3 offers thoughts on how the weaknesses of the model described in section 2.1 can be tackled, and especially what a suitable operationalization approach could look like. It presents an operationalization mechanism which is designed in a way to make it compatible with most media types and thus can help operationalize model factors of other theoretical technology maturity models, too.

2.1 Details of the Sommerlatte & Deschamps Strategic Technology Management Approach and Maturity Model

In the 1980s, two employees of the strategic consultancy Arthur D. Little published a widely noticed book on strategic technology management (Sommerlatte & Deschamps 1986, pp.37–76). The book contains a structured 8-step approach (henceforth "S&D approach") to determine firm-internal needs and resources and align them with external conditions, very much in line with the concept of dynamic capabilities. Strategic handling options are pointed out for a set of common scenarios to give managers an overview of opportune behavior. The S&D approach features a set of components widely received with great interest. Still today, as this book will show, a section describing a technology maturity model (henceforth "S&D model") is regularly referenced in the pertinent literature. However, some components of the approach, especially those connected to assessing technology maturity, require detailed analyses: for each relevant technology, field experts have to be schooled in a complex system outside of their original expertise. Large quantities of hard-to-access data from multiple sources need to be processed. This may effectively have rendered part of the approach for which these are required impossible to implement on a larger, firm-wide scale.

The S&D approach was put forward ahead of its time for several reasons. The information technology had not been developed to a level that permitted it to sufficiently assist management in several of the tasks deemed necessary. Much has changed since 1986. According to a conservative approximation with a carefully recalibrated Moore's law (Kurzweil 2005, p.65; Kanellos 2003; Moore 1965), between the years 1986 and 2015 computer processing speed and memory capacity has increased by a factor of

$$2^{\frac{(2015\ -\ 1986)\cdot 12\ months}{20\ months}} \approx 174,000.$$

Moreover, computer literacy among managers has greatly increased and the necessary data is available digitally and at low cost. Furthermore, new discoveries in strategic intellectual property (IP) management such as the open paradigm or a modification of the project management office in the form of a technology management office can add to the approach.

The development of the past 30 years could not have been assumed at the time the S&D approach was put forward. Several functional and structural aspects of the approach have therefore been rendered obsolete today. At the same time it has not lost its conceptional ideas and may even be more relevant than ever before. Even though relevant data sources have been identified, what is now missing is a way to integrate current computer capabilities into the approach.

The following sections will therefore respond to the question, what parts of the S&D approach need reconsideration and how they can be transferred to the state of the art. The next section 2.1.1 presents the functional components of the original S&D approach, featuring useful realization techniques of more recent years in section 2.1.2, effectively disclosing and grouping improvement potential of the year 1986 S&D approach to identify the main drawbacks of the model and make it fit for the current management world. Later on, it will focus on newly enabled capabilities to assess technology maturity automatically as a functional option in section 2.1.3 and focus on a technology management office as a structural option in section 2.1.4.

2.1.1 Benefits of a Firm-Wide Technology Strategy

The objective of the S&D approach is to create a technology strategy well appropriate for a firm. The technology strategy of a firm is its overall plan concerning the objectives, principles and tactics relating to use of technologies. It is defined with a persisting competitive advantage and the long-term success of the firm in mind (Floyd & Wolf 2010). The technology strategy provides general rules for managing technologies deemed relevant for the firm. The S&D approach is based on a strategic management framework made popular by PORTER in the 1980s called the market-based view (Porter 2004; Porter 1980). The goal of this view is to achieve a sustainable competitive advantage on top of the internal capabilities by incorporating forces of the market into a firm's business and competitive strategy. A technology strategy is a component of such a business and competitive strategy which is essentially built from parameters dictated by external environment and internal capabilities and skills with the competitive advantage in mind (See figure 2.1 for the position of the technology strategy in the strategic setup of a firm). Little has changed regarding the elements as displayed in figure 2.1.

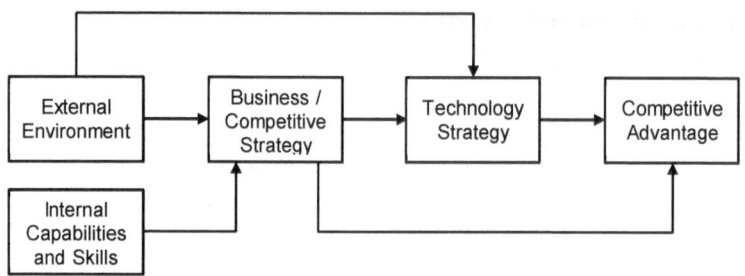

Fig. 2.1 Hierarchical view of the technology strategy according to ZAHRA et al. (1999). The arrows stand for factors of the former element directly influencing the latter

However, due to an increased pace at which new technologies and products are being developed, the original goal of the market-based view to achieve a sustainable competitive advantage has been rendered obsolete. Instead a sheer competitive survival must be aimed for, which can be achieved only through dynamically mixing and matching internally and externally sourced competences and resources (Shuen 2008, p.162). This new goal is approached by the dynamic capabilities view, which better reflects contemporary business realities and therefore replaces the market-based view of the original S&D approach in the sections, where applicable. *"Accordingly, companies and their executives should coordinate their technological and competitive choices in order to achieve superior performance. Companies need strategies that capitalize on the synergy between their technology and other resources"* (Zahra et al. 1999). An according integrated view on the competitive advantage of the firm would thus not be hierarchical. Instead it would focus on the available resources, as in figure 2.2.

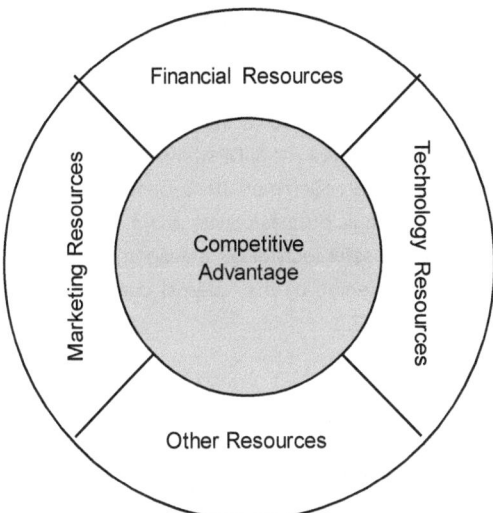

Fig. 2.2 Technology as a component of competitive strategy according to ZAHRA et al. (1999)

In either way, the technology has a direct impact on the competitive advantage of a firm. Since it is intended to remain unchanged over a long period of time, it should be built with care. The competitive advantage resulting from a good technology strategy influences a number of different business characteristics. The following advantages are the most obvious (Burgelman et al. 2009, pp.113–129; Zahra et al. 1999; Sommerlatte & Deschamps 1986):

- Cost decrease (economies of scale)
- No doubling of development
- Increased transparency (for all strategic business units and board)
  - o Objectives and scope
  - o Internal capabilities
  - o External forces
  - o Opportunities
  - o Threats
- Precise instructions
- Reaction time improvement
- Increased dynamic capabilities

Since it has such a great impact on a firm's success, and since it requires a general overview of the firm and its competitive environment, it is the task of the executive board (and its staff) to draw up a technology strategy which serves the business units of the firm. In a large firm, the executive board is unable to implement and maintain this strategy on its own. For this reason, SOMMERLATTE & DESCHAMPS identify three layers at which the technology must be managed (Sommerlatte & Deschamps 1986, p.39): 1.) the executive board itself, 2.) its strategic business units, and 3.) the product-market-combinations (see figure 2.3). A successful technology management requires feedback from all these layers. This is represented by the "internal capabilities and skills" box in figure 2.1 and the arrows in figure 2.3.

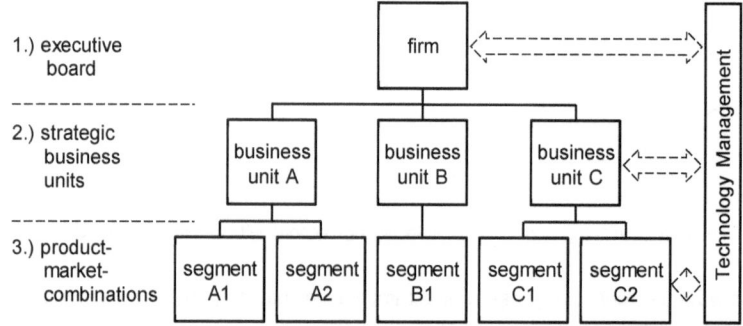

Fig. 2.3 Technology management on different management levels according to SOMMERLATTE & DESCHAMPS (1986)

Obviously, as can be seen in the "external environment" box in figure 2.1 above, the technology strategy is not limited to factors inside the firm. It is therefore essential to consider certain information from outside the firm as well. The following aspects need to be integrated into a viable technology strategy and will be described in greater detail in the subsequent sections (Sommerlatte & Deschamps 1986):

- The **maturity state of a technology** is an industry-independent judgment of the current and hypothetical performance of a technology. There are various interpretations what performance parameters are, as will be discussed in subsequent sections (Sommerlatte & Deschamps 1986, p.52).
- The **maturity state of an industry** reflects the degree of an industry's stability concerning factors such as growth rate, market saturation, intensity of product changes, competitor count, buying habits, and market share. A technology can be commercialized in different industries and an industry usually is based on

commercialization of different technologies (Sommerlatte & Deschamps 1986, pp.12–13).

- The **competitive position of a firm** is its business performance in comparison to other firms in the same industry. It depends on the market share of the firm, its relative cost structure, and internal factors which influence current strengths and weaknesses. (Sommerlatte & Deschamps 1986, p.15).

- The **technological position of a firm** depends on its capability of employing a technology to its advantage in comparison to other firms in the same industry. It thus depends on the firms know-how in key and pacing technologies as well as the availability of technological resources. This is an interpretation of the definition intended by SOMMERLATTE & DESCHAMPS, which unfortunately contains a self-reference (Sommerlatte & Deschamps 1986, p.57).

- The **strategic relevance of a technology for that industry** is the importance of that technology in comparison to other technologies for commercialization in that industry (Sommerlatte & Deschamps 1986, pp.50–52).

2.1.2 Reconstruction of the Sommerlatte and Deschamps Approach

The last section 2.1.1 presented the benefits of a firm-wide technology strategy, offered the market-based view and the more resource-focused dynamic capabilities view as theoretical foundation of technology strategy considerations, and collected competitive advantages which result from a well-defined technology strategy as well as important aspects from outside of a firm that should be integrated into a technology strategy.

The goal of this section is to reproduce the original 1986 S&D approach for strategic technology management, point out its weaknesses, and then successively "rejuvenate" it to incorporate relevant recent findings in each of the steps. The main point of action for rejuvenation lies in harnessing interim development of information technology into the process, facilitating implementation of the model's functional elements. The main effect can be expected for evaluation of independent external information as necessary for technology maturity.

The original S&D approach is described by SOMMERLATTE & DESCHAMPS (Sommerlatte & Deschamps 1986, p.76). It takes on all important interfaces mentioned in section 2.1.1 above and proposes an order for collecting and processing the relevant information and putting the outcomes to use. This section is built up according to the S&D approach for developing a technology strategy displayed in figure 2.4, each step representing a sub-section of this section:

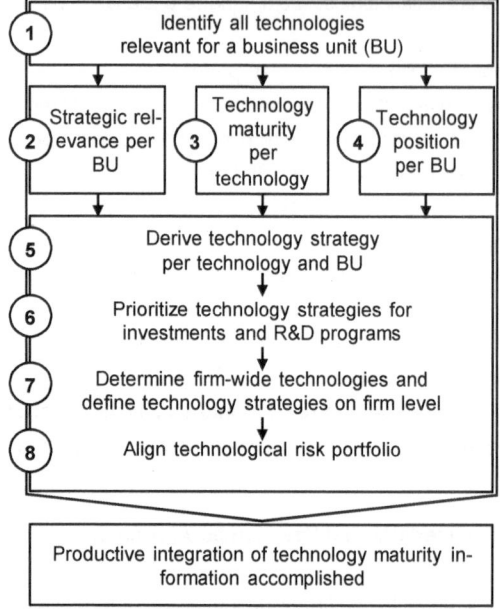

Fig. 2.4 A variation of the originally strictly sequential approach for strategic technology management by SOMMERLATTE & DESCHAMPS (1986)

Steps 1 and 2 were originally integrated and have been separated to display better the possible parallel evaluation of steps 2 through 4. Parallelization allows an increase in the speed of the approach, especially when it is automated such as described in section 2.1.3.

2.1.2.1 Identifying all Technologies per Business Unit

A business unit typically needs to employ multiple technologies to work. Therefore, a first step in the technology strategy building process comprises the identification of all relevant technologies. Not only are those technologies which are directly used within a business unit relevant, but also those which the competition develops and uses (Sommerlatte & Deschamps 1986, pp.48–49) and such which could potentially be used and thus are possibly relevant for future strategy development. The Open Paradigm (Chesbrough 2005) is worth mentioning in this context: in the traditional or *closed innovation process,* inputs come from internal and some external sources – customer inputs, marketing ideas, marketplace information or strategic planning inputs. Then, the R&D organization proceeds with the task of inventing, evolving and perfecting technologies for further development, immediately or at a later date (Docherty 2006). By contrast, in open innovation, *firms look inside-out and outside-in, across all three aspects of the innovation process*, including ideation, development, and commercialization. In doing so, much more value is created and realized throughout the process (Cooper 2009). Thus, on top of an "inventory" collection of all technologies already present, as suggested in the S&D approach, a scanning which is meant to discover new subject areas, developments and potential surprises is a suitable tool for this purpose (Pillkahn 2008, p.95)

It is necessary to evaluate the interdependence of the relevant technologies (Burgelman et al. 2009, pp.690–705). Some technologies can be developed autonomously, some may depend on other technologies in the same product (Sommerlatte & Deschamps 1986, p.49). The S&D approach does not propose an exact method to survey this interdependence, but a basic system dynamics causal loop diagram (Palm 2014) is probably sufficient to understand, discuss, and communicate the technological environment. If a more thorough understanding of the interdependence becomes necessary, e.g. because there are many external influences to consider, technology roadmapping and related techniques may become a solution to establish the necessary overview (Moehrle et al. 2013; Lizaso & Reger 2004). It is possessing knowledge about this interdependence which helps the management to understand a technology's strategic relevance for each BU in the next step.

2.1.2.2 Determining Technology's Strategic Relevance per Business Unit

A technology's strategic relevance for a BU depends on two main factors:

- Impact on product and service performance parameters (market advantages)
- Impact on production and servicing process (cost advantages)

The strategic relevance must also be seen in relation to the capabilities of market competitors. SOMMERLATTE & DESCHAMPS therefore distinguish between the following strategic relevance categories (Sommerlatte & Deschamps 1986, pp.50–52):

Base Technologies

Base technologies are technologies a firm has to master in order to participate in the industry. They are the foundation of most all products and without them the industry would not exist. They are of elemental importance. However, there are limited opportunities to use them to gain a competitive advantage. Little effort should be put into developing them further. Their strategic relevance is therefore low (Sommerlatte & Deschamps 1986, pp.50–52).

Key Technologies

Key technologies have a major impact on the competitiveness of a firm and thus are of high strategic value. Competitors do not yet master them, which is why they represent a great unique sales proposition (for a limited time). They directly influence critical performance parameters and cost structure of its products. Evaluating the impact of a technology on competitive dynamics can reveal key technologies (Sommerlatte & Deschamps 1986, pp.50–52).

Pacing Technologies

Pacing technologies are still being developed and typically are in an early maturity state. They have a good chance of becoming the key technologies of the future, giving them also a high strategic relevance. A close monitoring is advisable (Sommerlatte & Deschamps 1986, pp.50–52).

These strategic relevance categories of technologies change over time such that some pacing technologies become key technologies and some key technologies become base technologies. It is important to re-evaluate the strategic relevance of a BU's technologies at regular intervals to avoid developing those technologies further which have lost their strategic relevance (Sommerlatte & Deschamps 1986, pp.50–52).

What is considered the strategic relevance in the S&D approach is really an industry-specific technology maturity which can be evaluated with the S&D model: e.g. at a given point in time, the technology of highly integrated circuits gained and lost its strategic relevance for the computer industry much earlier than it did for the automotive industry or the consumer goods industry. The maturity it had for an industry at a given point in time directly influenced its strategic relevance for that industry. The reason for this is, that the industry-specific technology maturity advanced quicker for the computer industry than it did for the automotive industry. The strategic relevance can therefore be assessed exactly like the technology maturity, only that it needs to focus on a particular industry. An analyst who is not aware of an industry in which a technology is applied may therefore draw wrong conclusions about its strategic relevance. This is why determining a technology's strategic relevance should not be left to technology experts alone. According to the S&D approach, the management should be involved closely (Sommerlatte & Deschamps 1986, p.52).

2.1.2.3 Estimating Maturity State of Technologies

The maturity of a technology subsumes the current and hypothetical performance of a technology. The performance is determined by technology-specific performance parameters, which over the course of a technology's maturity typically develop along an s-shaped curve from a very low level towards the hypothetical performance maximum (Foster 1986). However, not only do performance parameters change with the maturing of a technology. Other factors influence or are influenced by it, too. SOMMERLATTE & DESCHAMPS provide a set of factors along with a description of how they change over the course of maturity in table 2.5 in section 2.2.3.2. They distinguish between four states of maturity, namely emergence, growth, maturity, and age. This book will deviate from this nomenclature to avoid confusion, because the term "maturity" does not only stand for the third maturity state in the model, but also for the general concept of maturity. In this approach the corresponding maturity state will therefore be called "saturation", in accordance with several other technology maturity models presented in section 2.2.3.1. For the same reason, the last maturity state will be called the "decline" rather than the "age" state.

Determining this maturity can happen at a given point in time, but also continuously e.g. in the form of a monitoring (Porter et al. 2011; Porter et al. 1991). A monitoring implies the observation of a technology over an extended period. The scope of the observation (i.e. which technologies are relevant) has to be set in advance. A focused search for information relevant within the context of that scope follows. In this structured approach, changes are observed reliably and quickly. These changes then have to be interpreted (Pillkahn 2008, p.98). A monitoring is useful in order to identify changes in the maturity and the strategic relevance of technologies. However, it is unable to identify strategically important technologies outside of the monitored set. This is why a firm should regularly perform a scanning to identify relevant technologies such as described in step 1 in figure 2.4. All technologies which are identified as relevant in that step should then be monitored.

The strategic relevance of a technology depends on the exhaustion of its competitive potential in a certain industry. This means that the strategic relevance of a technology for a certain industry is loosely connected to its general maturity judged with the S&D model independent of an industry branch (see figure 2.5).

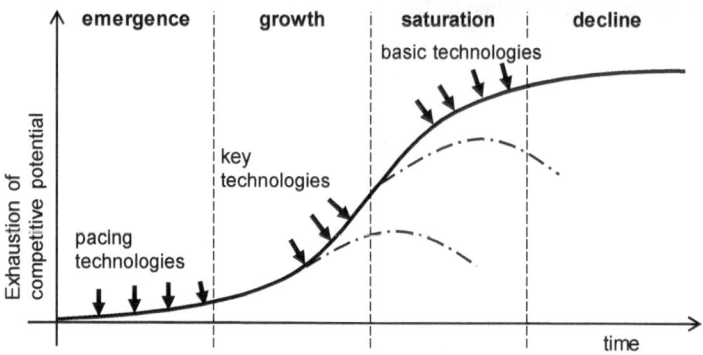

Fig. 2.5 Typical coincidence between maturity state and strategic relevance of a technology according to SOMMERLATTE & DESCHAMPS (1986)

The S&D model also presents hypotheses for alternative sequences, where a technology does not reach its full potential (e.g. because performance parameters of a substitute technology increase more quickly). Such a technology is abandoned and loses its strategic relevance when entering a state of decline early.

2.1.2.4 Determining the Technological Position of Business Units

The (relative) technological position of a business unit is its capability to exploit a technology in comparison to competitors. An excellent technological position is necessary to perform well in an industry. On the other hand, the technological resources necessary for this are limited. According to the resource-based view, a firm-wide deliberate distribution of these technological resources is necessary for success of the whole firm (Kraaijenbrink et al. 2010). The technological position of a business unit depends on its technological resources which are divided into the readily available **internal resources** concerning key and pacing technologies on the one hand, and corresponding **external resources** which need to be acquired / accessed before they can be put to use on the other hand (Sommerlatte & Deschamps 1986, pp.56–60). Technological resources can thus be separated into external and internal resources (see figure **2.6**). The availability of these resources for a certain technology in comparison with competing businesses determines a business unit's relative technological position for that technology (Sommerlatte & Deschamps 1986, pp.56–60).

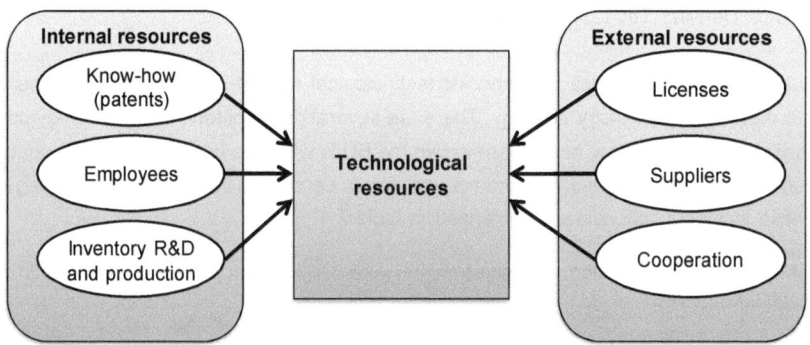

Fig 2.6 Internal and external technological resources connected to the relative technological position of a business unit according to the interpretation of the resource-based view of SOMMERLATTE & DESCHAMPS

SOMMERLATTE & DESCHAMPS remain vague about the actual assessment of technological resources – are they considered by their numbers, or by their monetary or some other value? A point of critique which arises from this conceptualization of a firm's competitive advantage in the resource-based view and its application in the S&D model cannot be readily dismissed (Kraaijenbrink et al. 2010): it is not the value of an individual resource that matters but rather the synergistic combination or bundle of resources created by the firm, as postulated by more recent views such as the dynamic capabilities approach. A SWOT analysis according to PAUL & WOLLNY (Paul & Wollny 2011) with a focus on the internal and external technological resources and the technological position may prove useful in determining the strategic fit of alternative strategies derived in the next section 2.1.2.5.

It is important to note that the technological position is subject to change. Internal as well as external technological resources may change, for example if certain employees leave the firm or if a competitor gains knowledge. In order to hold or enhance the strategic position, it may become necessary to change the supply of technological resources connected to a certain technology, e.g. because the strategic relevance of this technology changed. Acquiring, losing, or realigning technological resources takes time. The quicker a firm can react to a new situation / opportunity, the better for its technological position. This speed is determined by the so-called dynamic capabilities (Eisenhardt & Martin 2000). These dynamic capabilities are especially valuable in industries with quickly changing strategic relevance such as currently the case, for example in the telecommunication industry.

2.1.2.5 Deriving Technology Strategies per Business Unit

Business units can exploit their specific technological strengths by incorporating them into a suitable technology strategy. There are several different technology strategy options depending on how active or re-active the BU is willing to become and what spectrum of the technologies which are relevant for its conduct is involved in that strategy. These strategic options are summarized in table 2.1.

Table 2.1 Alternative technology strategies by activity and technology spectrum of the BU adapted from SOMMERLATTE & DESCHAMPS (1986)

		Technology leadership	Technological niche strategy
Technology behavior	active		
	re-ac-tive	Technological presence	Technological rationalization
		full	selected

Spectrum of technologies in an industry

These technology strategies lead to the following behavior (Sommerlatte & Deschamps 1986, p.62):

- **technology leadership strategy** means the establishment of a leading technological position throughout all technologies relevant for an industry.
- **technology presence strategy** means the ability to harness all technologies relevant in an industry, at least one of them from a leading technological position, when possible.
- **niche technology strategy** means the concentration on a limited number of critical technologies in an industry where a strong technological position is feasible.
- **technology rationalization strategy** means the short-term increase of profitability of a business unit by maintaining only its critical technologies at the cost of R&D firms which do not have a direct impact on market position or cost.

Strategic options of a business unit depend on its competitive and technological position and technological (and industrial) maturity. According to the S&D approach a business has the following means to exploit its technological resources (Sommerlatte & Deschamps 1986, pp.61–62):

- **sell** its **technological know-how**, e.g. in the form of licenses, thereby creating economies of scale across firms and relieving the own R&D budget. This should be done with caution if licenser and licensee are competitors.
- **buy technological know-how** from an external source, e.g. in the form of licenses or acquisitions. This leads to an increase of proprietary know-how and should be done if a firm is conducting its own technology development is too laborious or time-consuming, or if it will not lead to a significant competitive advantage.
- conduct **technology development with a partner**, effectively creating economies of scale across firms. Again, this has to be done with caution if the cooperating partners are competitors. It is useful e.g. between OEMs and their suppliers.
- **conduct** its **own technology development**, effectively creating its own technological know-how. This strategy can be sub-divided in four variants (Sommerlatte & Deschamps 1986, p.62), juxtaposed in table 2.1.

The more mature a technology becomes, the less room there is for technological advances. In early states of maturity, little is known about a technology. There is much room for technological breakthroughs and there are many opportunities to improve a technology's performance. At the same time, substitute technologies may prove more successful and render a technology obsolete (Pillkahn 2008, pp.187–188).

Technologies play a major role in the strategic mix and may have a strong impact on the competitive position of a business unit. Even disadvantageous developments can be corrected (Sommerlatte & Deschamps 1986, p.64). This is why during early states of maturity, there is much room for strategic decisions.

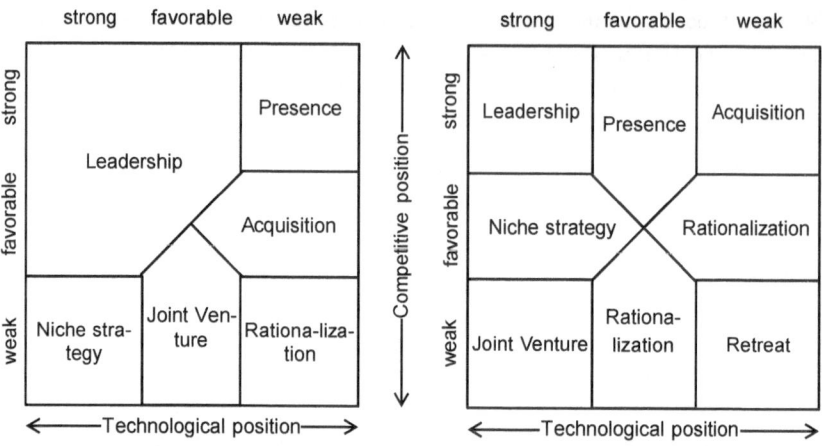

Fig. 2.7 Technology strategies in emergence to early growth (left) and late growth to early maturity (right) as a subject to technological and competitive position of a firm according to SOMMERLATTE & DESCHAMPS (1986). Along with increasing maturity of a technology, the competitive and technological position requirements for more comprehensive technology strategies also increase

With increasing maturity of a technology, major technological advances become less probable and are replaced by much smaller incremental advances. Technology leadership is only open to business units which already have a relatively strong competitive and technological position. Figure 2.7 displays natural development options for early (left diagram) and more advanced (right diagram) maturity states as interpreted by the S&D approach. Along with increasing maturity of a technology, the competitive and technological position requirements for more comprehensive technology strategies also increase. This means that the leadership area has gotten smaller, at the same time the rationalization area has increased and there is now a retreat area for business units with a weak technological and competitive position. The rationalization and retreat areas can be expected to grow even bigger when the technology in question matures more, but the S&D approach does not provide advice concerning strategic options in late saturation and then to ultimate decline. SOMMERLATTE & DESCHAMPS probably do not consider such a technology attractive, because it presumably is being replaced by a follow-up substitute technology in such a case, and major earnings can not be expected from exploiting it any longer. On the other hand, a technology which has been in its decline state for a long time may still leave room for an attractive niche strategy, such as the long-in-decline perforated tape data storage technology is used to create a paper trail for electronic voting machines to impede voter fraud (Holzman

& Jamison 2007; Petersen & Jaecks 2005; Riera & Brown 2003). On the other hand, it is conceivable that late entrants with a notable reputation in a particular sector of an industry outside of the one in question may gain – as an act of cross-industry-innovation – a considerable competitive position through the use of a technological position which proves to be less industry specific than expected (Khan & Möhrle 2012; Enkel & Gassmann 2010). Unfortunately, the S&D model does not provide empirical evidence for its figures, which is probably why they are kept relatively vague.

In figure 2.8 strategically solid options depending on the competitive position during the maturity process are displayed. Choosing a strategy outside of this selection is possible but according to the S&D model implies an increased risk of failure (Sommerlatte & Deschamps 1986, p.60).

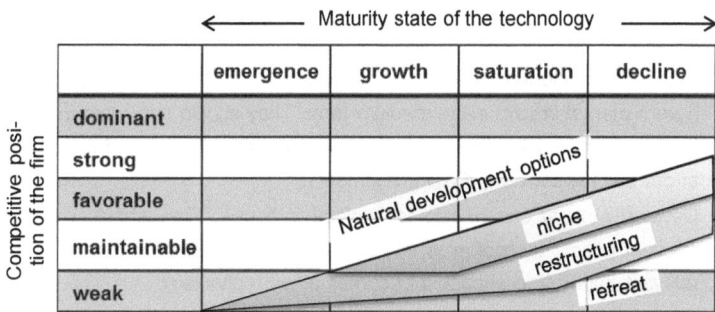

Fig. 2.8 Technology strategy options as a subject to competitive position of a firm and technology maturity state according to SOMMERLATTE & DESCHAMPS (1986)

In the end, the technology strategy has to be derived by each business unit in cooperation with the firm's management. Obviously factors which are not mentioned within the S&D model, such as technology development speed (Kurzweil 2005, pp.44–69) or influence on a political level (Oliver & Holzinger 2008), should also play a role in decision making. The framework provided, although it may be a striking and plausible one, can therefore only be considered an outline for this step of technology strategy building and must be exploited deliberately.

2.1.2.6 Prioritizing Technology Strategies for Investments and R&D Programs

Two factors have to be considered to prioritize between the technology strategies described in the past section 2.1.2.5, and resolve the behavior when it comes to actual technology appropriation decisions:

- What are the costs connected to a technology investment and can they be afforded?
- If it becomes necessary to focus on certain areas of the technology, what will they be?

The strategic relevance of a technology is of essential significance during selection of the technological focus. SOMMERLATTE & DESCHAMPS propose a set of basic behavior suggestions for business units which depend on this strategic relevance (Sommerlatte & Deschamps 1986, p.66). They propose business units should:

- Monitor technologies which may become relevant for the industry but will not have a market impact in the medium term. They should not invest in them, however, unless they belong to an extraordinarily strong group of firms which can afford such speculative R&D investments.
- Develop at least one pacing technology in-house. They should monitor other relevant pacing technologies in a way that enables them to quickly acquire the relevant knowledge in case it becomes a key technology.
- Try to control all key technologies of their industry. This means they should conduct their own R&D or at least take part in cooperative technology development.
- Reduce technology development to a minimum once they become basic technologies of the industry.

Once the technology strategies and investment priorities have been settled, specific instruments of technology development have to be considered. These can be roughly characterized as so-called make-or-buy decisions. The distinction of make-or-buy decisions dates back to COASE (Coase 1937). Buy decisions may include know-how (patents[1], licenses), ready-made parts, knowledgeable experts, entire departments or firms, whereas make decisions refer to knowledge generated from resources present in the firm. Recently also plural sourcing (make AND buy) strategies are being discussed (Puranam et al. 2013; Veugelers & Cassiman 2013). The chosen direction depends on the strategic relevance of a technology as well as on the speed at which

---

[1] Throughout this work, the term "patents" refers to patents for invention.

technology maturation takes place. According to different authors such as GASSMANN & BADER, AMARA et al., or HOWELLS et al. (Gassmann & Bader 2010, pp.33–66; Amara et al. 2008, p.1532; Howells et al. 2003, p.52) the instruments open for technology sourcing and appropriation are

- Legal instruments: Patents, copyrights, trademarks
- Secrecy: trade secrets; confidentiality agreements; work contracts
- Publicity: Defensive publications / disclosure
- Technology-specific: lead-time advantage, complexity of design

The faster technologies in an industry mature and the faster they are thus replaced by new ones, then the less valuable are heavily codified instruments. This is often the case for young industries. Codified instruments become more valuable for technologies developing at a slower pace.

2.1.2.7 Determining Firm-Wide Technologies and Defining Technology Strategies

Certain threats and opportunities can not be recognized at the level of a single business unit. These are often connected to the impact of technology decisions on other business units in the same firm. There are six groups of tasks connected to such cross-links which the management board of a firm is responsible for (Sommerlatte & Deschamps 1986, pp.68–73). These encompass six aspects (all bullets represent translated citations from the book by SOMMERLATTE & DESCHAMPS):

- Making sure synergies are exploited between technologies and technology development of the separate business units. This includes the consideration of advantages connected to firm wide standardization on the one hand and product differentiation on the other.
- Monitoring, developing, or appropriating new technologies which are not yet of major strategic relevance for any business unit. Access to new technologies may happen through licenses, hiring of technology experts, joint ventures, acquisitions, or contract research.
- Allocating technical and financial resources to technology development of business units.
- Ensuring cooperation between technology-related and other corporate functions. A technology strategy can only be implemented effectively when it is in line with the business strategy and its functional elements like the marketing and production strategy. Experts from relevant departments have to be included in the strategy building.

- Monitoring technological development outside the firm and recognizing threats and opportunities. It is a task of every business unit to monitor the technology development of competitors and of substitute technologies. The firm's management should also consider
  - o **market factors** such as supply gaps or new demands
  - o **economic factors**, i.e. changed factor costs, cost shifts in other industries or buyer's cost constraints
  - o **regulations or laws**, which limit or support the use of certain products
- Balance risks of the firm's technology portfolio. Refer to the next section 2.1.2.8 for a detailed description.

2.1.2.8 Aligning Technological Risk Portfolio

Every technology strategy is connected to a risk of failure, i.e. if the technology invested in turns out to stay short of performance expectations, whether entirely or in part. According to SOMMERLATTE & DESCHAMPS, the technological risk of a technology strategy in this sense depends on two factors (Sommerlatte & Deschamps 1986, p.73):

- The uncertainty of success of technology strategies, that is, the probability that technological goals can be met within planned investment and time limits, and
- The extent to which the business depends on a certain technology, and hereby the stakes are put at risk.

In combination, these factors determine the technology risk (see figure 2.9)

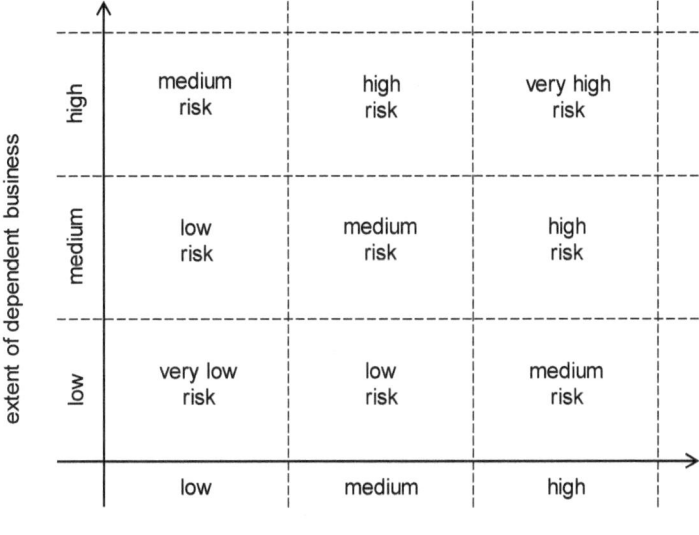

insecurity of technology strategy

Fig. 2.9 Technology risk matrix depending on the extent of dependent business and insecurity of technology strategy according to SOMMERLATTE & DESCHAMPS

The uncertainty of a technology strategy again depends on several aspects, summarized by SOMMERLATTE & DESCHAMPS (Sommerlatte & Deschamps 1986, p.73) to be the

- maturity state of a technology,
- technological position of the firm,
- reliability of technological assumptions,
- type of chosen technology strategy and strategic relevance of technology in the industry,
- dependence of technology on other technologies in that industry, and the
- reliability of R&D department's plans henceforth.

Although this may be a comprehensive collection of the relevant dimensions, neither of them is operationalized and no precise statement about the actual risk can be deduced from the framework in figure 2.9. More recent research on the subject of corporate risk, such as SARTOR & BOURAUEL integrate technological risk into a bigger framework and also succeed in operationalizing its dimensions, either monetarily (see figure 2.10) or by other means (Sartor & Bourauel 2012, pp.37–88). Many of the approaches presented in the book can be used for a more solid operationalized approach to managing risk in strategic technology management.

Financial risks	Operational risks	Business risks
Market risks i.e. stock- and commodity prices, currency and interest rates	**External risks** i.e. natural disasters, terrorism, technological risks, political-juridical risks	**Performance risks** i.e. procurement, production, sales
Solvency and credit risks i.e. default risk, change of creditworthiness	**Internal risks** i.e. misappropriation, IT-problems, human failure	**Interaction risks** i.e. provider, customer, bank

Fig. 2.10 Risk categories adapted from SARTOR & BOURAUEL (2012)

The technology-related risks can be managed or distributed with a set of investment tools including deferral, staging, exploration, scale alternation, outsourcing, abandonment, leasing, compound, or strategic growth options (Benaroch 2002). Further detailed technology portfolio considerations regarding value maximization, risk balance, and firm strategy integration can be found e.g. in DICKINSON et al. (Dickinson et al. 2001).

2.1.3 Newly Enabled Capabilities to Assess Technology Maturity Automatically as a Functional Option to Improve the S&D Approach in General and the S&D Model in Particular

It becomes clear in section 2.1.2 that many decisions connected to the technology strategy finding process include the knowledge of a technology's current maturity.

Whether it be assessed directly by the relevant business units, the staff of the firm's management itself, a designated department, or an external firm, there are several desirable qualities of this maturity assessment. This section therefore enumerates and specifies certain desirable conditions of this maturity information for all of its potential recipients. It furthermore assesses the S&D technology maturity model concerning these conditions.

According to STEINKE or PIPINO et al., whose research influenced these thoughts, a model for assessing technological maturity should meet the following four properties (Steinke 2004; Pipino et al. 2002):

- It should be **valid** to make sure that it measures what it is supposed to measure. Validity is a complex concept and its elements can be evaluated separately, if they apply (Messick 1992). Since the S&D model is not operationalized, any validity types which need measurements (such as test, criterion, construct, internal, or external validity) do not apply. Instead, for the model to be valid, the adoption of it must be well-founded and correspond accurately to the real world. Validity of the S&D model is based on the extensive experience of the authors and its face validity is high. For the same reasons, the content validity, which makes a statement regarding whether the model covers a representative sample of the behavior domain to be measured, is also relatively high (Foxcroft et al. 2004, p.49). The discriminant validity, on the other hand, is tested with an expert-based approach in section 4.2 and is relatively low.

- It should be **reliable** to meet the demands of a solid strategy building process which will form existential decisions for the firm, and to foster the management's confidence in the values. A robust model allows precise information of the management despite incomplete information or abnormal behavior of a technology or its maturity indicators. This is especially important, because the technology maturity model will not be used to assess a single technology, but to compare several technologies, possibly from different industries, developing at different speeds, and evolving from different technology drivers (technology push vs. market pull). Reliability of the S&D model values depends on the experts who generate them because it is subjective. This makes the S&D model vulnerable to personnel fluctuation. One would think that the robustness of the S&D model was high because it uses several different data sources as a basis for its indicators. Since interpretation and weighing of model factors is made by technology experts, however, the reliability of the S&D model also depends on its consistent application.

- A model should therefore also be **objective** to enable comparison of different technologies by the management, not just of direct substitute technologies, but also of technologies evaluated in previous monitorings and of potential development alternatives during technology strategy finding. An objective model ideally is also transparent and reproducible to allow verification of maturity results and to possibly modify maturity metrics ex post, when modifications are deemed necessary. An expert-based approach is hard to make objective and the relatively vague S&D model can hardly be considered objective because it lacks a transparent algorithm or reproducible results as far as the technology maturity is concerned. For example, it does not weigh its metrics in a definite way.

- And it should be **useful** which means that it provides an added value beyond existing approaches. Usefulness can be split up into several subcategories, most importantly:

  o It should be **quick**, to provide the relevant information to the management as soon as possible, thus allowing the management to react quickly, giving all subsequent processes additional time and therefore fostering the dynamic capabilities of the firm. The S&D model does not provide detailed information on how the technology maturity is assessed exactly. This book assumes they propose a manual, expert-based approach.

  o It should be **scalable** and **inexpensive** to allow a continuous and dense monitoring of all relevant technologies including substitute technologies and candidate-pacing technologies. An expert-based approach is relatively expensive, especially during a calibration phase where the assessment interval is defined. This limits scalability. Another scalability restriction is the fact that technology experts need to be identified within the firm for all technologies relevant now and in the future.

The S&D model has major shortcomings concerning these requirements. Despite its timeliness concerning the functional set-up within the S&D approach, the implementation lacks several proper tools which have only become available after the original publication. In the following section, changes will be proposed to improve the S&D model and fit it to current possibilities and requirements. Above all, harnessing recent achievements in IT is a major point of possible improvement. An example of successful harnessing recent achievements in IT is industrial production. Standardization and subsequent automation has led to steep performance and efficiency improvements, which would not have been possible without the help of IT (Glohr et al. 2014, pp.101–109; Akerberg et al. 2011). The process relies on involving data, in the particular case of industrial production, large amounts of sensor data. The equivalent to this sensor data for technology maturity assessment is technology maturity relevant information. Since this is not readily available for technology maturity, especially not in a machine readable form, an identification and operationalization of the relevant information is essential. The changes to the S&D model are therefore ordered in three consecutive steps:

1. Standardization
2. Operationalization
3. Automation

The first step to improve technology strategy building is by **standardizing** the technology maturity assessment. Most technology driven firms currently rely on some kind of toolset to support their purposes. Different departments, sometimes even different persons in the same firm may have different approaches of assessing the maturity of a technology, be it consciously or unconsciously, explicitly or implicitly (Porter & Cunningham 2005, pp.3–15). It may be based on the same technology maturity model, but often it seems to be a highly specific modification of it to best suit the user's needs. And even though it may be elaborate, well-proven, reliable, and featuring a well-established system of handling instructions – it is different for different applications, and therefore incompatible between applications. A strict standardization would speed up the information exchange on top of enabling a quicker evaluation process. It would also make the assessment more transparent, reproducible, and reliable. Standardization also brings speed advantages during results evaluation if the responsible manager is accustomed to the format of the report and knows where to look for the necessary information. Standardization in this context refers to two concepts. First of all, it is the rudimentary standardization of indicators and sequence of the process. And secondly it is the access of all business units to the same information. Or as PORTER puts it (Porter 2005):

"*Having standard information dramatically enhances managerial receptivity.*

- *Standard information becomes familiar information.*
- *Familiar information becomes credible information.*
- *Credible information gets put to use in decision-making.*
- *Information that is used gets requested "next time."*
- *Information that is requested repeatedly merits automation of its generation.*"

The next step after a strict standardization is the **operationalization** of technology maturity. Without this step, no measurable information is available, making it a very subjective concept which relies largely on human judgment and interaction. Currently, some technology maturity models, among them the S&D model, feature a set of factors which influence or are influenced by technology maturity. This is a good start for operationalization of technology maturity, but it currently requires experts to invest much time into the evaluation. When operationalized, this work can be done on a large scale by non-experts in less time, validly, reliably, and objectively. Furthermore, the operationalization renders **automation** possible. An automated process can profit from steadily increasing speed and decreasing prices of information technology equipment. It requires little human interaction during the process, leaving experts with more time for other tasks. Human mistakes during the evaluation process can be minimized. Consequent automation makes the process much faster than sole operationalization, is less expensive, and in consequence highly scalable.

2.1.4 Technology Management Office as a Structural Option to Improve the S&D approach

The S&D approach is structured in a way that it involves all relevant parties in technology strategy finding and implementation. However, it fails to name explicit responsibilities, especially when a technology strategy is confronted with new technological findings. The approach depends on sensible decisions made by its employees regarding how potentially important information is spread without providing standardized procedures. When certain information is required, the management has to request it from the appropriate site. This may result in delayed or impeded information transfer. To ensure proper information coordination, a firm that heavily relies on technologies may consider implementing a technology management office (TMO) analogous to a project management office (Crawford 2010). A TMO can be integrated structurally as a cross-sectional business unit at the position of the technology management box in figure 2.3, but it can also be outsourced, as proposed by PORTER & CUNNINGHAM (Porter & Cunningham 2005, pp.299–302). A decentralized implementation *"tends to be perceived as an extra burden, not core to the individual's job descriptions"* (Porter & Cunningham 2005, p.300). The centralized approach of a unit inside the firm, favored by PORTER & CUNNINGHAM, aids in keeping track of and critically evaluating all relevant technologies with an equal set of methods and a fixed sequence of institutionalized transparent processes (Porter & Cunningham 2005, p.300). When the technology maturity assessment approach presented in this book is used as a tool by the TMO, it is able to handle the analysis of a large number of well-defined technologies. This would make it a predestined tool for monitoring purposes. Once implemented, a monitoring is a routine task. It can therefore be performed transparently by a TMO, which independently reports strategic relevance changes to the appropriate departments immediately. This process step is especially suitable for support by a TMO, which could take over the task of assessing technology maturity altogether. This helps build routine, and thus improves speed and reliability of the maturity information. A TMO can aid the firm and its business units in making solid technology strategy decisions by transparently providing all relevant information. This helps speed up strategy building and base business decisions on robust information, making the technology strategy more objective. A technology management office can support the firm's management by collecting and providing all necessary information from each business unit, thus enabling a quicker, more robust and objective decision on transparent and reliable data. All of these risks, considerations, and alternative tools can be collected and condensed for the management by the firm's TMO, creating a single responsible department for technology strategy related questions and making all processes and the decision base more reliable and objective. A more elaborated concept of a TMO cannot be covered within the scope of this book and must therefore remain subject to future research.

2.2   Defining Basic Terms and Mechanisms of Technology Maturity and Developing a Characterization and Operationalization Framework for Theoretical Technology Maturity Models

The last section 2.1 describes the motivation for using technology maturity models and presented the S&D model as part of the S&D approach for creating technology strategies (Sommerlatte & Deschamps 1986). This approach introduces a set of steps necessary to understand and honor the importance of a technology for a business unit as well as for an entire firm. As mentioned in the previous section, the S&D model is embedded in the S&D approach for generating a technology strategy. Both were described in the mid-1980s. There are diverse technology maturity models more or less similar to the one used in the S&D model which have been described since then. The findings described in them may add to the S&D model. The goal of this section is to give an overview of research on technology maturity models thus far, pointing out crosslinks to improve the S&D model and illuminating research gaps. It starts out by delineating important concepts connected to technology maturity measurement (section 0). Then it describes a characterization framework for a multitude of existing and future maturity models (section 2.2.2). And finally it presents a synopsis of technology maturity models with the S&D model and criticizes a general lack of operationalization (section 2.2.3).

2.2.1 Delineating Technologies as the Objects of Maturity Measurement

Before measuring technology maturity can be explained, it is necessary to define the basic elements of this task: **technology, maturity,** and **technology maturity.** Many have tried and come up with different definitions, some complementary, some contradictory, some inconsistent. It will not be the focus of this book to come up with a generally accepted, new, better, and more universal definition. Much rather this section will provide working definitions which leave the subject matter unambiguous in the presented context.

A general definition of a *technology* is given by BURGELMAN et al: *Technology refers to the theoretical [...] knowledge, skills, and artifacts that can be used to develop products and services as well as their production and delivery systems.* (Burgelman et al. 2009). This definition is able to consider a broad variety of concepts as a technology. However, it is restricted to technologies which are made explicit (as opposed to tacit or implicit knowledge). In this way, a technology maturity measuring approach which relies on textual information is able to work. This is what makes this technology definition especially suitable for the approach in this book.

On top of a direct definition of what a technology is, certain distinctions have to be made. This especially includes a differentiation of a technology, its applications, as well as industries based on it. This also requires establishment of a hierarchical order of technology interrelation. An interrelation of a technology, its applications, and dedicated industries was observed and elaborated by ANSOFF et al. (Ansoff & McDonnell 1990; Ansoff 1980). Certain generic technologies can be applied as different products or processes to serve different markets and therefore different applications. An example is a carburetor, a device for vaporizing a liquid and mixing it with a gas. When this technology is applied in the paint industry, it may become an automatic paint sprayer, in the aerospace industry a jet backpack (Burgelman et al. 2009, p.63). Obviously, the application of a technology, or the industry branch in which it is used, may make a difference in respect to technology maturity. It is therefore necessary to explicitly consider and further sub-divide the application(s) of a technology during its definition.

There are several systematic approaches which consider the interrelation of technologies by presuming a hierarchical structure, such as the differentiation of component technologies and system technologies (Christensen 2013; Henderson & Clark 1990). The approach in this book will rely on a generic approach to defining and differentiating technologies further published by TAYLOR & TAYLOR, who postulate the taxonomic differentiation of technologies into applications, paradigms, and generations (Taylor & Taylor 2012): the **application** of a technology is described by the purpose for which it is used. A **paradigm** represents a particular technological approach that is used to achieve a target application. It is characterized by being based on *"scientific principles that are distinctly different to those of existing technologies"*. A **generation** represents a particular form or variation of a technological solution, but shares the underlying scientific principles of all other generations within the same paradigm. Table 2.2 shows a classification of technological developments for music storage. The table displays a taxonomic order of technologies. These serve to identify technologies which are interdependent, thus framing a relevant technology and establishing explicit boundaries where ambiguities would otherwise be very likely. The entire concept can be understood strictly hierarchically: a paradigm represents the collective of its generations, and the application represents the collective of its paradigms. Also, the superordinate concepts inherit an increasing maturity of their subordinates, a more mature set of generations thus leading to a more mature paradigm.

Table 2.2 Application, paradigms, and generations of music storage according to TAYLOR & TAYLOR (2012)

Applica-tion	Technology for storing music							
Paradigm	Analog-phono-graphic		Analog-magnetic			Digital		
Genera-tion	Cylin-der	Rec-ord	Reel-to-reel	8-track cartridge	Compact cassette	Compact Disc	MP3

←Granularity

Time→

It can be criticized that the concept rather arbitrarily denominates three hierarchical levels whereas further granularity is certainly available (see section 4.1 for examples). Nevertheless the concept of hierarchical differentiation and connection is very helpful for technology delineation.

After the term technology has been defined, the term maturity is delineated next. **Maturity** originally is a biological term. During maturation, certain phases are passed in a so-called "life cycle". These phases are characterized by certain relatively stable conditions which change slowly in comparison to the time which has elapsed during the life cycle thus far. Each different phase is introduced by a clearly defined event (conception) or relatively short transition phases (puberty), during which conditions change much more quickly. This concept is exemplarily displayed for the maturing of mammals in figure 2.11. It is a linear phase model with exactly one individual as object of interest (rather than an entire population experiencing the phases simultaneously). Each phase is connected to a distinct behavior which may be very different for separate phases. E.g. in the terms of dependence / required behavior: mammals initially require comprehensive parental assistance but slowly lose dependence on their parents until a phase when they become self-sufficient.

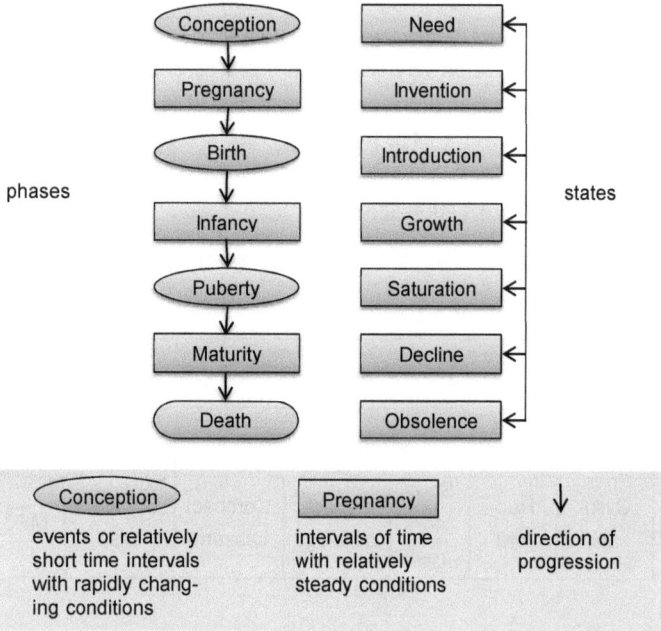

Fig. 2.11 The difference between phases and states illustrated on the basis of the life of mammals and technologies. Boxes represent intervals of time with relatively steady conditions whereas ovals represent events or relatively short time intervals with rapidly changing conditions. Source: own figure, compare e.g. TANNER (1990)

Many characteristics of technologies suggest they also pass through such a process. Often it is referred to as a life cycle. The term "life cycle" implies a recurring pattern in the development of a concept similar to that of biological processes (Specht et al. 2002, p.64). The conceptual foundation of the model is the orderliness of the innovation process, which is why it is often referred to as the "linear model". Just like the phases described for mammals above, several states can be differentiated for technologies as well. Technologies are born, grow in importance as they spread, attain a dynamic maturity and then enter their declining years as they lose importance (Patton 1959). The hypothetical foundations of the linear model can be found as early as 1920 by MEES (Mees 1920), who hypothesizes that a typical sequence of the introduction of products based on a certain technology might be

- Theoretical proposal
- Scientific activity
- Laboratory feasibility
- Operating prototype
- Commercial introduction

Current models such as the one described in IRANI & LOVE still possess a similar sequence and set of states (Irani & Love 2010). Analogously, WATTS & PORTER state: "*In the "clean" case, one would expect to see the topic first rise, then decline, in fundamental research; with a similar but lagged pattern in a more applied research database; followed in turn by evidence of development, application, and possibly impact.*" (Watts & Porter 1997, p.29). The concept is interpreted schematically by MARTINO in figure 2.12.

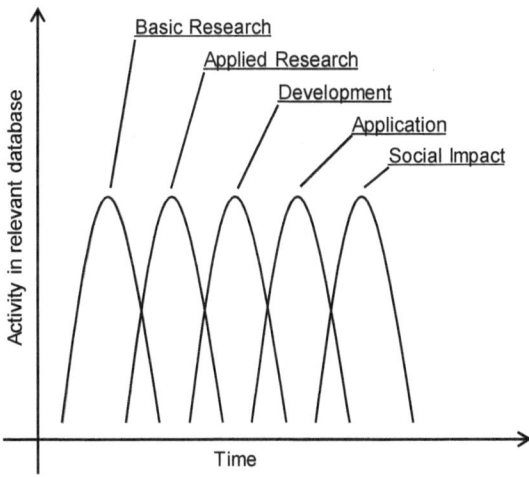

Fig. 2.12 Linear model by WATTS & PORTER (1990) as interpreted by MARTINO (2003)

Despite its name, the linear model may also subsume a number of alternative linear development paths. An intuitive source of discrimination is the main driver of technology development, which can be either science-based or demand-based (classically, technology push vs. market pull). Most linear models neither consider different drivers of technology nor change in the sequence like a second growth state after a state of maturity was reached or a sudden obsolescence right after the emergence of a technology. An advanced form of the "linear model" as described in BALCONI et al. (Balconi et al. 2010) does consider such behavior which deviates from one single string of events. Such a model is less suitable for forecasting, but much closer to the actual behavior of technologies during maturation. This makes it useful for assessing the current technology maturity situation and react accordingly.

Despite well documented similarities between biological and technology maturity processes, obviously there are some key differences between these which have to be considered when using this metaphor:

- Technologies are no "individuals" and can only be observed indirectly in the manifestation of e.g. products or processes. Instead, development of the same technology in different institutions may cause it to be in different states of maturity at once and even experience parallel developments.
- At the time of birth, mammals have an average life expectancy, whereas that of different technologies varies considerably even for technologies of the same kind, i.e. which serve the same purpose (short-lived HD-DVDs vs. long-lived book printing; both data storage).
- Along these lines and unlike for mammals, the different states of a technology does not have an expected duration.
- For a technology, the state changes do not become obvious by clearly observable events or transition phases and can even co-exist in different manifestations (e.g. the laser technology for use in car headlights, for writing information onto a data storage device, or as part of military weapon systems). Rather, transitions between the states happen in a creeping fashion with possibly several active states at once.
- Phases of the life cycle for almost all animals are strictly linear - invariable and irreversible[2]. For technologies, this is not necessarily true. A mature or declining technology may experience a second state of growth such as the electric-powered vehicle, which has recently picked up in development speed after having

---

[2] Certain lower animals such as hydras, naididae, or starfish are able to "rejuvenate" under certain conditions.

reached a state of decline at the beginning of the 1900s (Christensen 2013, p.236). Herein lies the reason why the intervals are called states rather than phases in this book.

- The time of death for mammals is usually intrinsic; most importantly it is not related to the life cycle phase of a younger generation. There is however a direct relationship between the decline of a current technology and the emergence of a new substitute technology with a dominant design (Kaplan & Tripsas 2008).

The findings in this section show that technology maturity works differently than biological maturity in many respects. The so-called technology life cycle is actually a collection of states which appear in a roughly anticipated sequence but may deviate from it, even rejuvenate or exist in multiple maturity states while performing creeping transitions. In this book it is therefore referred to as "technology maturity" with different, possibly parallel "states". A relevant display of technology maturity states which takes these peculiarities into consideration is attempted in section 4.8.

2.2.2 Developing a Framework for Maturity Model Characterization

The S&D technology maturity model is one of many. It is necessary to understand how it is different from other models before certain aspects of these other models can be used for improvement of the S&D model. Depending on why and how technology maturity models are used, various aspects differ between models. This section develops and presents a framework for maturity model characterization. It starts out by presenting a standard nomenclature in section 2.2.2.1. The next section 2.2.2.2 differentiates models by their purpose and focused object. In the section following, a model's characteristics connected to the different maturity states are elucidated in section 2.2.2.3. Characteristics which are used for evaluation of the technology maturity in a model are discussed in section 2.2.2.4. As a conclusion, a summary of the framework is presented in section 2.2.2.5.

2.2.2.1 Maturity Models: Nomenclature

This section establishes a nomenclature for model parameter identification to make a precise discussion possible. A resemblance to structural equation model nomenclature is intended (Backhaus et al. 2003, pp.333–352). Since the goal of the approach in this book is to operationalize the theoretically driven S&D model, this nomenclature will highlight the boundary points between theoretical and operationalized models. An operationalized technology maturity model consists of manifest variables which can be measured, and latent variables which are hypothetical constructs and therefore cannot be measured directly. They are represented by rectangles (manifest) and circles (latent) in exemplary figure 2.13. The single latent endogenous variable of this model is the construct "technology maturity", which it regards as central and intends to describe. The measuring model of this latent endogenous variable is the technology maturity value, a manifest nominal variable which takes on the form of different maturity states. Technology maturity is influenced by a set of factors which represent latent exogenous variables. These factors can be approximated by certain indicators which collectively represent the measuring model of latent exogenous variables. The creation of this measuring model is the actual operationalization. All variables will be called the "model parameters". Each manifest variable also possesses a residual value. It represents influencing factors not captured in the model which explain a deviation from the ideal value. Correlations between indicators or between factors are not considered in this example model. In addition, it makes no claim to be complete in regard to indicators and factors.

With the concept in figure 2.13 in mind it is possible to typify maturity models in respect to their usability for machine-based approaches. The following typology is proposed:

- **Theoretical maturity models** do not specify indicators and just resort to latent exogenous variables instead.
- **Semi-theoretical maturity models** possess indicators only for some of the latent exogenous variables to describe the context of technology maturity.
- **Semi-operationalized maturity models** assign at least one indicator to each of the latent exogenous variables but lack a precise algorithm to estimate the technology maturity from indicator values.
- **Operationalized technology maturity models** provide a full measuring model of latent exogenous variables and are thus able to estimate a technology's maturity algorithmically. It is the purpose of this book to present such a model.

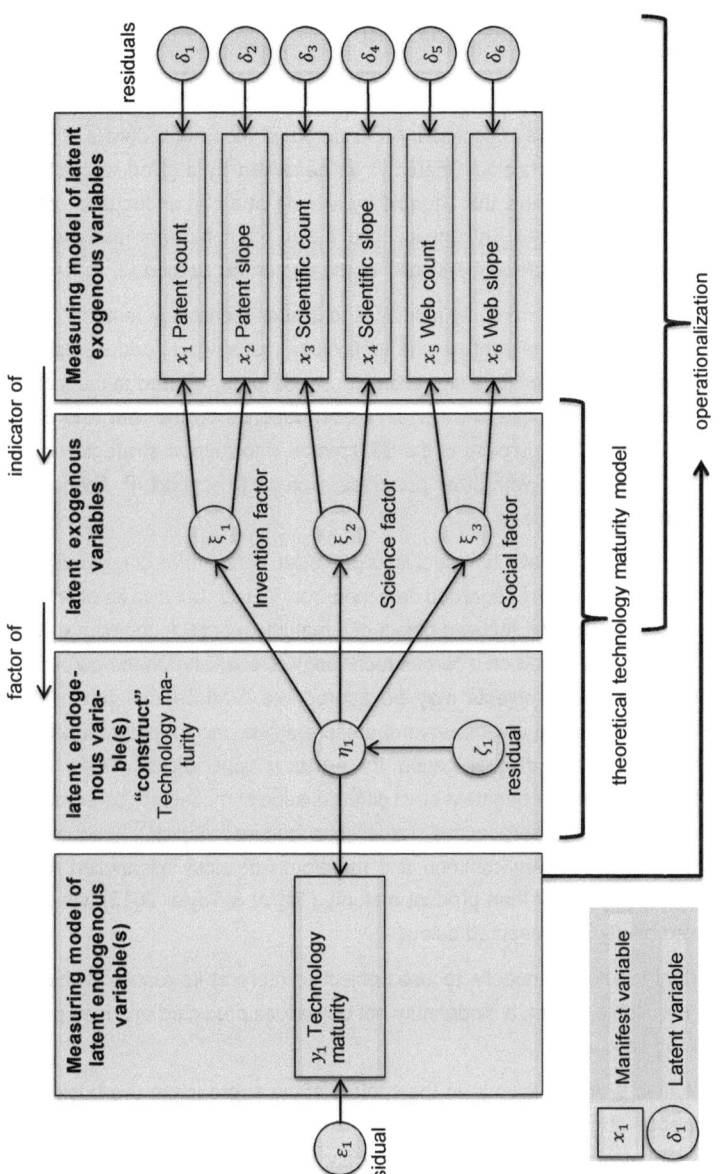

Fig. 2.13 Elements of theoretical technology maturity models and their operationalization

2.2.2.2 Model Purpose and Focused Object

This section will present and delineate the related characteristics of a model's purpose and its focused object. This is necessary to understand theoretical details of the latent endogenous variable (technology maturity) as perceived by a given technology maturity model, which considers this variable by looking at a certain focused object and to support a certain purpose. In consequence it also offers more or less explicit handling instructions, which will be mentioned at the end of this section.

The purpose of technology maturity models is to assess technology maturity. The general purpose of knowing the approximate technology maturity is to deduce appropriate and advantageous behavior for a firm and its business units, tailored to the technology maturity. The special purpose of a certain model depends on the user and can span diverse applications. The purpose of the S&D model is to support strategic technology management, but models with other purposes such as to support IP, finance, or HR may also find its results useful.

The focused object of a maturity model is its particular perspective of regarding a technology. A technology can be regarded detached from its use, but also its different manifestations may become the focused object of a maturity model. A common example is the focus on products based on a certain technology. Depending on the purpose of the model, different focused objects may be appropriate. Various existing models are vague about their focused object. Several authors argue, this inevitably leads to confusion, imprecision, and disqualification for practical applications (Taylor & Taylor 2012; Höft 1992). They propagate a strict differentiation of models for different focused objects (which they call "perspective" rather than "focused object"). Product maturity models, especially, are very common and therefore frequently misapplied to assess technology maturity rather than product maturity (Taylor & Taylor 2012), which is why they will also briefly be presented below.

It is important to know a model's focused object to interpret its results. If the focus is put on an unsuitable object, a model may not behave as predicted and may potentially lead to wrong conclusions.

A differentiation is advantageous in the context of the approach in this book because a query must be structured according to the model purpose: in an analysis concerning the maturity of electric mobility (a generic technology) it may be reasonable to search for brand-specific terms such as E-up, Volt, or F-Cell (all specific products based on the above technology). This may, however, produce a picture of this technology which is biased towards the maturity of the particular products. Results will lead to very different interpretations because the models used as the foundation of the interpretation are designed to focus on a specific object.

Technology maturity models typically sketch directly technology-related information over time, detached from products or markets based on these technologies. This may be information such as technology performance or technology prevalence. Technologies in this sense can not be observed directly, making them less intuitive than products. Technology maturity models often start with the first idea and development of the technology and end with its rejection due to a successor technology with better performance.

Product [technology] maturity models typically sketch product-related information over time such as sales volume, turnover, or profits. They often start the observation with the launch of a product and its introduction into the market, and end when the product disappears from the market. Products incorporate and thus represent a certain technology (i.e. a certain model diesel motor car). However, the technology is not necessarily represented by just a single product (i.e. diesel cars from another producer; diesel engines onboard ships). Therefore, when sales for one product decline, it does not automatically mean that the entire technology (i.e. diesel motorization) declines too. On the other hand, a product most often incorporates more than just one technology (diesel motors feature many metallurgical technologies, for example). Obviously, the same product can not be used to assess the maturity of all technologies it is based on. Still, if used with cautious consideration of these limitations, product maturity models may help the management to better understand a technology's maturity.

There are **other maturity model types**, which will not be analyzed in-depth in this book. Examples are

- industry maturity (Bos 2013; Livesey 2012; Höft 1992, pp.103–113)
- service maturity (Shareef et al. 2011; Inaganti & Aravamudan 2007; Potts 1989, pp.100–104)
- project maturity (Brookes & Butler 2014; Link 1985, pp.17–20)
- long economic cycles (Duijn 2013; Devezas & Korotayev 2011; Kondratieff 1979)

These may add to the model presented in this book, but their link to technology maturity is less accentuated than it is for product maturity. Their inclusion will therefore remain subject to future research.

Interpretation of results usually is done by the recipient of a maturity assessment and strongly depends on a models purpose and focused object. The more specifically the user and his or her interest is known, the more specific the handling instructions can be. For the approach in this book, specific handling instructions of a certain model are helpful if the model purpose and focused object coincide with those of the model in this book. Otherwise, only general handling instructions are of interest. The specificity can range from explicit process sequences which describe how to proceed in detail e.g. by means of examples, to vague descriptions of the situation which do not include concrete handling instructions at all, just to name the extremes.

In conclusion, the important dimensions of a maturity model are the

- Model purpose
- Model focused object
- Handling instruction specificity

2.2.2.3 Model States

This section discusses the range and segmentation of the maturity process covered in different technology maturity models. These model parameters are key to understanding the precision a model can offer for fine adjustments of management behavior advice and handling instructions. All models considered here designate a number of different names and attributes to maturity states they intend to differentiate. Also, most models see maturing as continuous and to a certain extent linear process which can, despite its continuous nature, be represented in a state diagram. States are artificial periods assigned to the process for different reasons so different states of technology maturity will often require appropriate action, e.g. a newly introduced technology may need to be aggressively advertised if few people know about it; and if a technology declines, no longer needed know-how can be sold. These states all last for a certain duration. It is therefore sufficient to group periods of time which require similar action. These groups represent the states of the state diagram. Necessary action is proposed in the form of handling instructions. Models most notably vary in their count of states and span which together determine their granularity.

The count of states is the amount of states which are differentiated in a model. This number depends on either the amount of different strategic implications deemed necessary by the author, or it depends on the amount of behavior changes of the observed variable during the entire maturity process. The more states a model has, the more different actions can be suggested. However, a model can only have as many states as the variables show behavior changes. Typically, the models have between three to five states (Höft 1992), but they can have many more. An example is the technology/strategic readiness level model which originally consisted of 6-7 states (Mankins 2009; Sadin et al. 1989) and since 1995 until now has typically had 9 (Mankins 1995).

The span of a model marks the start and end points of observation which are considered in that model. The span is selected depending on the period which is deemed relevant during a technology's life time. A larger span covers a longer period in the maturity process of a specific focused object. Larger spans allow for more states without increasing the granularity. Models with a larger span usually have more states, but not a higher granularity. A typical span is between any combination of two of the following:

- invention (first idea);
- innovation (marketization);
- maturity (no further growth);
- decline (no further use or sales).

In summary, important information on a model's states is its

- State count
- Model span

The granularity is also important information and can be derived from these two.

2.2.2.4 Model Factors

Maturity assessment and maturity state estimation in (semi-)theoretical technology maturity models takes place under consideration of the model's factors. The factors differ in certain dimensions which will be shown in this section. It is important to know that factors of such a technology maturity model are suggested information sources for field experts who then interpret the information to deduce a technology maturity state. Each model offers factor behavior description for the different states, sometimes of just one factor per state, sometimes many in combination. The following section will look at dimensions of factors which influence validity, reliability, objectivity and utility of the underlying model.

Some factors are more easily operationalized than others, meaning they suggest a measure such as would *patent activity* as opposed to *social acceptance, for example*, which is much harder to put into numbers. This property of factors will be called "measurability potential". The higher the measurability potential of a factor, then the more probable a correlation exists between the factor and its indicator. For exclusively theoretical models, a higher measurability leads to a higher objectivity because statements can be falsified more directly. Effectively this will serve as the rationale for picking certain factors and omitting others so that a coarse differentiation is sufficient. The approach in this book will therefore differentiate between low and high measurability potential only.

For any factor there may be a lag between the origin of a signal and the time it can be measured, which we will call "signal delay". A low signal delay is beneficial for a precise reaction to new circumstances. For example, we can compare the signal delay of indicators based on microblogs such as Twitter to those based on patent filings. Signals from microblogs are available (approximately) instantaneously, so this can be considered a "low" signal delay. Due to a common lag of 18 months between the filing and the publication of a patent, the signal delay would be "high" for indicators based on this medium. Since the purpose of the resulting model will be technology maturity assessment, and the maturity of technologies typically proceeds at a relatively slow pace, a signal delay of less than a month can be considered low.

The factor count is the number of different factors described in the maturity model. It is sufficient to assess the causality relations of a construct to determine whether it is formative or reflective (Weiber & Mühlhaus 2009, p.36; Hermann et al. 2006, p.47). This in turn dictates whether it is necessary to consider all the factors of a model or whether it is sufficient to look at a few selected ones (See figure 2.14):

- **Reflective construct**: a reflective construct influences its factors. If the construct changes, all factors change along with it. This means a rich information basis because any additional factor considered transports the same signal in a different way. The correlation among the indicators is high. Accordingly, it may be sufficient to just consider a single factor and its indicator.
- **Formative construct**: if, on the other hand, the different factors influence the construct, it is called a formative construct. When more factors influence the outcome of a concept, each single factor accounts for less of the outcome. Factors may even show conflictive results if observed separately, if the impact of one factor outweighs that of a second one. Typically a low correlation between the indicators will be observed. For this type of setup all factors should be considered by taking all separate indicators into account.

formative construct   **reflective construct**

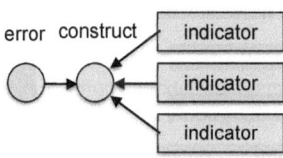

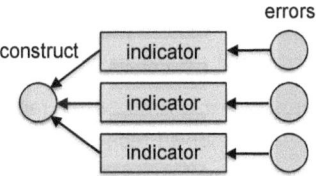

Fig. 2.14 Reflective and formative constructs and their main components, construct, indicators and error terms in comparison

"Whereas reflective indicators are essentially interchangeable (and therefore removal of an item does not change the essential nature of the underlying construct), with form- ative indicators omitting an indicator is omitting a part of the construct." (Diamantopoulos & Winklhofer 2001)

Arguably, technology maturity is best designed as a formative construct: increased R&D activity will influence a technology's maturity, and so will an increased debate among the general public. This would favor models which regard many factors over those with few. Since the approach in this book will not make use of a structural equa- tion model, further thoughts on this design are not necessary. In either case, consid- ering additional factors may enhance the results and will not impair them.

Theoretical models are designed to be interpreted by field experts, who rely on diverse information sources suggested by the factors. Examples for typical information sources of experts are

- Personal and professional experience
- Anecdotal evidence
- Interpretation of fellow experts (e.g. single expert opinions, workshops, surveys)
- Dedicated scientific studies (roadmaps, ...)
- Text media (scientific journals, patents, standards, press and online media, etc.)
- Other media (TV, Radio...)
- Conferences and conventions
- Mixed source

Experts typically don't rely on just one of these sources. For example, if they only relied on press and online media, they would not get detailed technical information on most technologies. If, on the other hand, they exclusively relied on dedicated scientific stud- ies or patents, they would not know about the public perception of their technology field. This is because all media address a certain aspect of a subject (such as a technology) in detail and filter out the rest. In consequence, the more diverse and representative the information sources suggested by the factors, the more valid, reliable, objective and useful the results will be.

A standardized variable is one which remains the same, independent of the subject of observation (i.e. observed technology). Some models consider non-standardized factors. For example, the famous s-curve concept is based on technology-specific performance parameters (Foster 1986). Although analog and digital photography serve the same fundamental purpose, when evaluated with the s-curve model, digital photography has different performance parameters than analog photography, such as sensor resolution, battery life, or shutter lag. This makes it hard to compare technologies which are not directly related and do not possess the same specific parameters. This dimension will be referred to as "variable standardization". If a model encompasses standardized variables, it can be applied more universally and its result can be compared more easily.

To summarize this section, the following relevant dimensions of model factors were identified:

- Variable measurability potential
- Signal delay
- Factor count
- Information source(s)
- Variable standardization

2.2.2.5 Summary of Framework Dimensions

As a result of the sections 2.2.2.1 to 2.2.2.4, several clearly distinguishable characteristics of technology maturity models were identified. These will serve as a characterization framework for existing models in this book. Its dimensions are:

- Model purpose
- Model focused object
- Handling instructions specificity
- State count
- Span
- Variable measurability potential
- Signal delay
- Factor count

- Information source(s)
- Variable standardization

2.2.3 Profiles of Selected Popular Models

Now that important characteristics of maturity models have been defined, this section will give an overview of important linear models as defined in section 0. Mostly it serves to illustrate the multitude of different models and to display when model principles emerged and how they developed, overlap, and focus on different functions in section 2.2.3.1. It depicts how the different models assign maturity states, how they interpret them, and how they deduce handling instructions. It will not give a complete overview as this has been done by other authors such as TAYLOR & TAYLOR, GODIN, HÖFT, or COX (Taylor & Taylor 2012; Godin 2006; Höft 1992; Cox 1967). Rather, it will look at the S&D model in greater detail to present its latent variables and evaluate its operationalization potential in section 2.2.3.2. It will close with a section criticizing the presented model in the light of standardization, operationalization, and automation. Thus a transition to the following section 2.3 is established, where maturity models presented in this section will be taken up again to support and improve operationalization of the S&D model.

2.2.3.1 Overview of Influential Technology Maturity Models Between 1920 and 2013

The goal of this section is to give an overview of the emergence and development of the linear technology maturity model until today. This serves to better understand the surroundings and improvement potential of the S&D model. Two aspects are therefore highlighted in these models: the operationalization approach and deduction of strategic technology management advice. Table 2.3 provides a chronological overview of different linear models from the years 1920-2013, compiled mostly from different extensive reviews (Taylor & Taylor 2012; Godin 2006; Höft 1992; Cox 1967). The models all describe the behavior of indicators over time, are very influential among such models, and/or connect model states to strategic technology management handling instructions. The table provides for each model

- the disseminating work,
- if deemed necessary, a short description pointing out what the model does differently than other models before it, hinting towards purpose and focused object of the model,
- the phases or states the model differentiates, revealing state count and span of the model,
- a note on whether or not the model relies on quantitative measures to assess the technology maturity, which shows the variable standardization.

Table 2.3 Chronological overview of influential technology maturity models

Authors	Short description	Phases / States	Quantitative measure(s)
(Mees 1920)	One of the first to describe technology maturity as a linear process (Balconi et al. 2010)	(1)pure science (2)development (3)manufacturing	none
(Schumpeter 1939)	Elaborates his excursion on business cycles in his famous research on economic development (Schumpeter 1911).	(1)invention (2)innovation (3)imitation	none
(Stevens 1941)	This Arthur D. Little associate describes an extensive model of technology maturity.	(1)fundamental research (2)applied research (3)test-tube or bench research (4)pilot plant (5)production (6)improvement (7)trouble shooting (8)technical control of process and quality	none
(Bichowsky 1942)		(1)research (2)engineering / development) (3)factory / production	none
(Furnas 1948)	The first approach to draw a schematic of the sequence in the linear model, and also provides alternative sources for technologies	(1)exploratory and fundamental research (2)applied research (3)development (4)production	none

(Mees & Leermakers 1950)		(1)research (2)development ((2.1)establishment of small-scale use (2.2)pilot plant and models (2.3)adoption in manufacturing)	none
(Brozen 1951a)		(1)invention (2)innovation (3)imitation	none
(Brozen 1951b)		(1)research (2)engineering development (3)production (4)service	none
(Maclaurin 1953)		(1)pure science (2)invention (3)innovation (4)finance (5)acceptance	none
(Ruttan 1959)		(1)invention (2)innovation (3)technological change	none
(Ames 1961)		(1)research (2)invention (3)development (4)innovation	none
(Rogers 1962)	Identifies the theoretical social factors and mechanisms behind innovation diffusion. No direct advice for technology management, but creates awareness for mechanisms and possible developments	(1)innovators (2)early adopters (3)early majority (4)late majority (5)laggards	Percentage of people having adapted technology
(Scherer 1965)		(1)invention (2)entrepreneurship (3)investment (4)development	none
(Schmookler 1966)		(1)research (2)development (3)invention	none
(Mansfield 1968)		(1)invention (2)diffusion (3)innovation	none

(Myers & Marquis 1969)		(1)problem solving (2)solution (3)utilization (4)diffusion	none
(Utterback 1974)	Meta-study on where and how in a firm innovation is created.	(1)generation of an idea (2)problem-solving or development (3)implementation (4)diffusion	none
(Utterback & Abernathy 1975)	Introduces dominant design concept and puts it in the maturity perspective. Laborious empirical tests of the model by DROR showed that operationalization was in fact possible (Dror 1989).	(1)fluid (2)transient (3)specific	count of product and process innovations
(Ford & Ryan 1981)	Promote appropriation strategy which includes technology sales (e.g. in the form of licenses) on top of product sales to fully exploit a firm's know-how portfolio. Gives strategic handling advice for each maturity state of the model. Establishes awareness for the value of a technology which does not fit into a firm's product portfolio.	(1)technology development (2)technology application (3)application launch (4)application growth (5)technology maturity (6)technology degradation	market penetration of technology
(Sommerlatte & Deschamps 1986)	Presents a semi-theoretical framework for strategic technology management. Main focus is on strategic advice for combinations of technology maturity, a firm's relative technological know-how and its competitive position.	(1)emergence (2)growth (3)maturity (4)age	several indicators from diverse sources

(Foster 1986)	Maps the performance of a technology in technology-specific parameters compared to the money spent on its development. No states are named, but the s-curve pattern is described, which is the basis for many subsequent models. Also, the model describes the replacement of an old technology by a new, "disruptive" one and why it happens despite the initially lower performance parameters of the new technology.	-	technology specific performance parameters
(Anderson & Tushman 1990)	Based on (Abernathy & Utterback 1978). Separates maturity process of a new technology into two major phases: a state of ferment after a discontinuity during which no dominant design has been found and a state during which the now-discovered dominant design is improved incrementally.	(1)discontinuity (2)ferment (3)dominant design (4)incremental evolution	technology specific performance parameters
(Ansoff & McDonnell 1990)	Connects markets, technologies/paradigms, and products and predicts different development patterns. Differentiates between stable, fertile, and turbulent technology development	-	demand for technology
(Popper & Buskirk 1992)	Mixed focused object, but mostly product life cycle focused. It propagates differentiated marketing strategies for products based on technologies of different maturity.	(1)cutting edge (2)state-of-the art (3)advanced (4)mainstream (5)mature (6)decline	several indicators from product-related sources

(Mankins 1995)	Technology readiness levels are a systematic system for evaluating the maturity of a particular technology during development. Still used at national agencies such as NASA and ESA (Mankins 2009) for project progress measurement and comparison, typically of flight systems. Phase count varies depending on implementation of the model.	TRL 1-7 (1-9)	implementation of characteristics described in phase descriptions
(Watts & Porter 1997)	Strongly data-driven model which links technology maturity states to publication behavior in certain repositories. No general rule set for strategic management behavior is provided, focus is more on additional information which can be derived from the metadata of the data in the repositories. Several subsequent publications failed to prove the concept.	(1)fundamental research (2)applied research (3)development (4)application (5)societal impacts	publication activity
(Fenn 1999)	The so-called hype cycle describes the expectations of the general public towards the performance of a new technology over time. It serves to establish awareness for the development of the expectations to prevent unfavorable investment decisions. It differs from most other models in that it describes a very particular curve progression. (Fenn & Raskino 2008)	(1)technology trigger, (2)peak of inflated expectations (3)trough of disillusionment (4)slope of enlightenment (5)plateau of productivity	Technology performance vs expectations; technology visibility

(Roberts & Liu 2001)	Strong focus on the decision to form strategic alliances or acquire other firms instead. Describes what the priorities/strategy of a firm should be in each maturity state of a technology, depending on that firm's possibilities. Based on the model by (Anderson & Tushman 1990).	(1)fluid (2)transitional (3)mature (4)discontinuities	firm's propensity to ally or acquire
(Kim 2003)	System dynamics simulation approach to analyze mechanisms/factors of technology transitions. Groups technologies hierarchically into paradigms and generations. In principle based on (Foster 1986).	(1)introduction (2)rapid growth (3)maturing (4)decline	technology's utility, switching cost, performance uncertainty
(Haupt et al. 2007)	Summarizes and juxtaposes most important patent-based maturity indicators. Empirical analysis of statistical significance of each indicator but not of the interplay of indicators. Builds on (Sommerlatte & Deschamps 1986).	(1)introduction (2)growth (3)maturity	several established patent indicators
(Bevilacqua et al. 2007)	Indicator-based product maturity model that shows a concept to incorporate economic and environmental considerations into a sustainable development process. Indicators are technology-specific.	(1)conception (2)design & manufacture (3)service (4)disposal	product specific performance and environmental indicators
(Irani & Love 2010)	Promotes a cost-benefit system which assigns benefits of IT-projects of a firm to strategic, tactical, and operational views to justify expenses for intangible and/or non-financial benefits.	(1)feasibility (2)justification (3)requirements definition/engineering (4)system design (5)details design (6)test & preoperation	none

	Serves to establish awareness for non-financial benefits in technology management.	(7)implementation (8)operation (9)maintenance & post-implementation (10)audit/evaluation	
(Foden & Berends 2010)	Presents an integrated framework for different established tools used in technology management. Main tool categories are identification and monitoring of technologies, selection and approval of technologies, capability development, and IP protection. The framework shows when and how to use and combine them in the course of a technology's proceeding maturity.	(1)Identification & monitoring (2)selection & approval (3)development research (4)acquisition & adaptation (5)exploitation & review (6)protection	tool specific
(Kim et al. 2012)	Show an operationalized model for discovering and monitoring emerging technologies which is based on Gartner's hype cycle approach (Fenn 1999). It applies a decision tree-based machine-learning approach.	(1) irruption (2) frenzy (3) turning point (4) synergy (5) maturity	Scientific literature and patent features
(Chang 2013)	Proposes a technology maturity model especially suitable for knowledge-based innovations in contrast to industrial innovations. It attributes the impact of radical knowledge economy innovations to network effects and coins a new term "super radical innovations". Based on ANDERSON, TUSHMAN (1990).	-	technology specific performance parameters

Not focused on strategic tech-nology management implica-tions.	

2.2.3.2 Latent Variables of the S&D Model and Need for Operationalization

Now that the development of technology maturity models, their theoretical foundations and current findings have been presented, this section will present in detail the S&D technology maturity model with the goal of better constituting the need for operationalization. The section starts out by explicitly placing the S&D model in the framework presented in section 2.2.2. It continues with a presentation of the latent variables of the S&D model and their hypothesized development during a technology's maturation. The section closes with a collection of criticism from the pertinent literature on the technology maturity models from the last section 2.2.3.1 in general and the S&D model in particular.

Table 2.4 Delineating the S&D technology maturity model

	S&D model
Model purpose	strategic technology management
Model focused object	technology maturity
Handling instructions specificity	medium
State count	4
Span	1st market potential – degeneration
Latent variable count	many
Information source(s)	technological, economical
Measurability potential	high
Signal delay	high
Variable standardization	yes

The model presented by SOMMERLATTE & DESCHAMPS in 1986 has the purpose of recommending a certain behavior towards strategic technology managers before the backdrop of technology maturity questions, as described in greater detail in section 2.1. The model differentiates between the general maturity of a technology and the strategic relevance of a technology in a certain industry branch. The main idea is to assign a strategic relevance to each technology in the technology portfolio of a given firm. This helps technology managers decide how to handle a certain technology. The model is designed as a technology maturity model with four states (emergence, growth, saturation, decline). It is a semi-theoretical model that relies on experts. Extensive technology expert inspection and valuation of information from mostly economic and technological sources is necessary to deduce handling instructions with sufficient precision. To help the experts consider and appraise the relevant information, the model provides the latent variable documentation in table 2.5.

Table 2.5 Latent variables of the S&D technology maturity model and their expected development during maturation adapted from SOMMERLATTE & DESCHAMPS (1986)

	emergence	growth	saturation	decline
A. Insecurity of technological performance	high	medium	low	very low
B. investments in technology development	low	maximal	low	negligible
C. Number of application areas	unknown	increasing	established, plenty	decreasing
D. Type of development requirements	scientific	application oriented		cost oriented
E. impact on cost/ performance rate of products	secondary	maximal	marginal	marginal
F. patent count	increasing	high	decreasing	decreasing
G. patent type	concept patents	product centric	process centric	process centric
H. Access requirements	scientific	personnel	licenses	know how
I. Availability	very restricted	restructuring	market oriented	high

The model is helpful in that it provides certain assumptions concerning the development of its latent variables over the course of a technology's maturity. On the other hand, the S&D model, along with the majority of the models in table 2.3, has many shortcomings, which have been documented by numerous critics. Many of them were recognized early on and most of them still have not been solved today. The criticism addresses different general facts (G) but much of it can be directly or indirectly linked to the lack of operationalization (O):

- G: No theoretical foundation (Höft 1992)
- G: No defined level of technology aggregation / taxonomy (Taylor & Taylor 2012; Tiefel 2008; Höft 1992; Dhalla & Yuspeh 1976, p.103)
- G: No power of prognosis / forecasting (Höft 1992)
- G: Unconsidered use of the models brings severe danger of misinterpretation when a certain signal is sent (Grantham 1997; Höft 1992; Dhalla & Yuspeh 1976)
- O: No or insufficient empirical validation (Tiefel 2008; Höft 1992; Dhalla & Yuspeh 1976)
- O: No objective empirical analysis possible because concepts cannot be measured (Tiefel 2008)
- O: No clearly defined course / pattern (Taylor & Taylor 2012; Grantham 1997, p.4; Höft 1992; Dhalla & Yuspeh 1976; Patton 1959)
- O: No clear delineation of states / unambiguous estimation of current state (Höft 1992; Dhalla & Yuspeh 1976, p.104)

Important criticism is connected to the fact that the S&D model is a (semi-) theoretical model lacking the opportunity to objectively measure technology maturity. Operationalization of maturity relevant attributes enables objective empirical studies and thus validation. This improves the probability of a correct prognosis. In summary, literature identifies an apparent need for operationalization.

2.3 Operationalizing Theoretical Technology Maturity Indicators

The S&D model gives detailed strategic technology management advice in connection to each state of maturity, as presented in section 2.1. It is among many other models describing theory regarding the behavior of technologies during their maturation. Section 2.2 provides a framework for these technology maturity models, gives an overview over the most important ones, and shows how the S&D technology maturity model fits in among the others. It concludes by summarizing shortcomings, many of which are connected to a lack of operationalization. (Semi-)Theoretical models offer rich handling instructions for each technology maturity state. They do not, however, offer an objective and unambiguous method for assessing the current maturity state. It is often a question of interpretation how these models are used for assessment. A consistent operationalization can make decisions much more objective and transparent. Moreover, it establishes the basis for automation.

Operationalization of theoretical technology maturity models is by no means easy. Technology maturity is a fuzzy concept that cannot be measured directly. As described in detail in section 2.2.2.1, operationalization is the process of making the factors of technology maturity precisely measurable in terms of empirical observations. Indicator assignment, however, is not an obvious process. Indicators can be assigned to latent exogenous variables based on assumptions made in theoretical models. Due to their nature, these theoretical models have not been evaluated empirically other than in some cases as opinions in the course of a survey. The following sections will therefore illustrate the steps necessary for identifying, surveying, and combining promising maturity indicators. This section picks up the S&D model's latent variables for technology maturity assessment as a basis for operationalization.

It is the goal of the following section to operationalize the S&D model while using useful bits from other popular models presented in section 2.2.3.1. It is structured as follows: Section 2.3.1 presents an indicator typology, and shows which type indicators the S&D model exploits. Next, section 2.3.2 explains how technology-related information spreads during maturation. The subsequent section 2.3.3 discusses how during this information spread, different media focus on different aspects of technology maturity depending on motivation of authors and readers. The following section 0, presents how information contained in these media can be tapped for operationalization. And the concluding section 2.3.5 shows how information from different sources can be integrated for reasons of robustness.

2.3.1 The Typology of GRUPP and Options for More Indicators

The past section 2.2.2 presents a maturity model characterization framework and shows its application in section 2.2.3. It does not include a comprehensive maturity indicator typology, however, which permits us to identify information gaps in a maturity model which are not yet covered by its indicators. This section will therefore provide a typology of different indicator types which are connected to the innovation process and analyze which of these are present in the S&D model. It will conclude by pointing out which type of indicators could help further increase the precision of the S&D model.

Table 2.6 Indicator typology based on GRUPP (1997)

1. Input	2. Output	3. Progress	4. Feedback
1.1 R&D staff	2.1 Scientific publications	3.1 Properties, Brands, Innovation Count	4.1 Social Networks, Chats, Emails
1.2 Internal R&D expenses	2.2 Patent applications	3.2 Sales, Revenue, Profits	4.2 Blogs, Boards, Search Engines
1.3 External R&D, technical consulting	2.3 Standards documents	3.3 Macroeconomic Effects on R&D Intensive Markets	4.3 Wikis (collaboratively created encyclopedias)
1.4 Effort for acquiring knowledge, fees, licenses		3.4 Production Growth, Employment, Foreign Trade	4.4 Newspapers, Periodicals
1.5 Investments in R&D intensive equipment, materials, components			4.5 Press Agencies

It is helpful to cluster possible indicators according to the information source they rely on. This will allow a structured search for new information sources and indicators which have not yet been covered in the S&D model and would potentially add to its precision. Such an indicator typology for parameters relevant during innovation was put forward by GRUPP (Grupp 1997, p.145). An enhanced version of this typology covers the following types of indicators (see table 2.6):

a first type are "innovation indicators" which rely on the **input** side **(1)** of a technology, namely such that are connected to the R&D staff (1.1), external R&D and technical consulting (1.2), the effort necessary to create general technical rules and specify standards (1.3), the effort for acquiring knowledge, fees, and licenses (1.4), the cost of standards specification (1.5), and the investments in R&D intensive equipment, materials, and components (1.6).

GRUPP's typology also covers those indicators on the **output** side **(2)** of such a technology, which can be sorted roughly along an axis with the extremes sciences on the one side and technology on the other. It contains the groups of scientific output (2.1) and development output (2.2). These two can be supplemented by the output of standards defined by groups of firms to facilitate technology use (2.3).

Thirdly, the typology by GRUPP names indicators based on the **progress (3)** of the technology in markets and society, in particular performance properties of the technology and products based upon it, brands, and the innovation count (3.1), sales, revenue, and profit generated through trade (3.2), macroeconomic effects on R&D intensive markets which can be linked to the technology (3.3), and production growth, employment, and foreign trade based on it (3.4).

The typology by GRUPP was enhanced to better suit the purposes of the approach in this book to furthermore encompass **feedback** indicators **(4)**, which can be ordered according to whether they represent facts or opinion. They are separated into the types of private conversation among few selected participants (4.1), statements by single or few people made public to a large audience (4.2), texts written collaboratively for a large audience which underlie some kind of peer review (4.3), fact-based texts which may include opinion (i.e. political) (4.4), and texts which represent facts.

Table 2.7 S&D model's latent variables according to the GRUPP typology. The bold letters represent the S&D model's latent variables of table 2.5, the numbers are GRUPP'S indicator types as defined in table 2.6 above

1. Input		2. Output		3. Progress		4. Feedback
	B		**I**			
1.1	**H**	2.1	**D**	3.1	**ACE**	4.1
1.2	**H**	2.2	**DFG**	3.2		4.2
1.3	**H**	2.3	**D**	3.3		4.3
1.4	**H**			3.4		4.4
1.5						4.5

Table 2.7 provides an overview of the indicator sources currently considered in the S&D model and serves to identify potential white spots. It refers to the letter notation for the S&D model's latent variables in table 2.5 and the number notation for the indicator typology in table 2.6. The S&D model's variables were assigned to the GRUPP subtype which best fit the description. If the description of the variables in the S&D

model was vague, it was assigned to the indicator type instead of a subtype. Obviously this makes it harder to operationalize because the link to a potential indicator is less clear.

In summary, not all of the GRUPP types are covered by the S&D model. This means that there is much room for hypotheses and for testing additional indicators to improve precision or ease of use of the S&D model and its operationalization.

A structured evaluation of the latent variables mentioned in the S&D model according to the GRUPP typology further clarifies table 2.7:

Input Indicators (1)

The two input indicators which can be found in the S&D model are its latent variables **B** and **H**.

Investments in the technology development (B) are input indicators. The description by SOMMERLATTE & DESCHAMPS (Sommerlatte & Deschamps 1986, p.53) is relatively short and imprecise as to which GRUPP subtype it might be, which makes it harder to operationalize.

Access requirements (H) are also in general type 1 indicators. They can however be much better assigned to the subtypes if they are divided into their components maturity state-wise. The S&D model asserts that during the emergence state, scientific abilities are the key to gain access to the technology. This means type 1.2 indicators are triggered during this state. During the growth state, personnel replaces the scientific abilities which belongs to 1.1 indicators. Licenses, which are the requirement for the saturation state, are best represented by type 1.4 indicators. And know-how during the decline state can be revealed by 1.3 indicators.

Output Indicators (2)

Four output indicators can be found in the S&D model: the latent variables **D**, **F**, **G**, and **I**.

Type of development requirements (D) can be interpreted as a combination of types 2 for the maturity states emergence (2.1), for growth and saturation (2.2 and 2.3) and type 3.1 for the decline state.

Patent count (F) is a relatively straightforward type 2.2 indicator. Since it claims that technological maturity can be estimated based on simple patent count, this may be the simplest indicator in the set of S&D indicators.

Patent type (G) is a straight-forward type 2.2 indicator.

Availability (I) is defined as "low or inexistent during the emergence state and high in the saturation state" (Sommerlatte & Deschamps 1986, p.53), which seems rather vague. It could be interpreted as availability of the technology for firms, which would make it type 2. Alternatively it could be interpreted as availability of products based on the technology, making it type 3.

Progress Indicators (3)

The S&D model provides the three progress indicators **A**, **C**, and **E**.

Insecurity of technological performance (A) parameters are type 3.1 indicators because they are determined by the technology's performance parameters.

Number of application areas (C) can be interpreted as progress indicators (3), SOMMERLATTE & DESCHAMPS probably intended it to be of type 3.1. The number of application areas is determined by the performance of a technology and the possible eventual limits of this performance in comparison to substitute technologies. This indicator is thus closely related to the insecurity about the technological performance (A) described above.

Impact on cost / performance rate (E) of products is a type 3.1 indicator. It is also closely linked to the technological performance (A), but focuses on another product parameter – cost.

Feedback Indicators (4)

None of the S&D model's latent variables is a feedback indicator.

Conclusions about the View of the S&D Model

The overview by GRUPP shows that many variables are influenced by technology maturity. The S&D model covers only part of these, without explicitly mentioning the others. In particular, feedback indicators seem to offer an opportunity to enhance the original S&D model. Other models which rely on the same maturity structure as the S&D model, offer theoretical insights into variables which were not included in the S&D model. It is possible to integrate them into the S&D model. This is especially useful to make the model more robust and possibly more precise than it is at the present stage.

2.3.2 Information Scattering in Different Text Media

The previous section 2.3.1 shows that the S&D model provides a selection of latent variables relevant for maturity assessment. When compared to the comprehensive indicator typology by GRUPP, however, it became clear that the S&D model lacks information from certain sources which is potentially relevant. Above all, feedback indicators based on information generated by the users of a technology are ignored. To make sure no important data source is overlooked, this section clarifies how information relevant for the different indicator types is generated and spread over the course of a technology's existence.

Table 2.8 Innovation and information diffusion core aspects juxtaposed (Sources: see table)

Innovation is an idea, practice, or object that is perceived as new by an individual or other unit of adoption (Rogers 1983, p.11)	**Information** is an objective (mind independent) entity. It can be generated or carried by messages (words, sentences) or by other products of cognizers (interpreters). Information can be encoded and transmitted, but the information would exist independently of its encoding or transmission. (Audi 1999)

Communication channel is the means by which messages get from one individual to another (Rogers 1983, p.17)

Rate of adoption is the relative speed with which an innovation is adopted by members of a social system. (Rogers 1983, pp.21, 23)	**Rate of spread** is the relative speed with which an *information* is *received* by *formerly uninformed* members of a social system.

Social system is a set of interrelated units that are engaged in joint problem solving to accomplish a common goal (Rogers 1983, p.24)

The spreading of information is referred to as information diffusion. Information diffusion is an analogy to ROGERS' diffusion of innovations (Rogers 1962). Some of the key concepts of innovation diffusion will therefore be modified to use them for information diffusion. Innovation diffusion seeks to explain how, why, and at what rate new ideas and technology spread through different groups of adopters. Accordingly; diffusion is an epidemiological process by which an innovation is communicated and adapted over time among the members of a social system. The four core aspects of the model are the innovation, communication channels, time, and social system (Rogers 1983, pp.10–37). Table 2.8 clarifies these core aspects and their counterparts in information diffusion.

Along these lines, information diffusion works as follows: when new technologies emerge, many people are involved. Scientists, inventors, developers, producers, marketers, and users interact with a technology in different ways. Often the interaction between these people and the technology is documented (i.e. people leave tracks in textual data). According to the linear model (see section 0), this documentation happens roughly as follows: scientists study a new technology and publish their findings (i.e. basic and applied research). Inventors develop these findings further and protect their inventions with patents (development). Products based on these technologies are advertised in press and web (application). Experts and consumers search the web for technology-related documents and consumers state their opinions and questions regarding this technology or product in blogs, on message boards and social networks (social impact). It can be assumed that the technology maturity relevant information is contained within the documents generated in this process. This is an important realization because the documents are explicit data, promoting further the identification and allocation of manifest variables to the latent variables of the theoretical S&D model necessary for operationalization.

The task is thus to tap the relevant information contained in these documents. It can be retrieved and evaluated with help of a discipline called "informetrics" (Nacke 1979). Informetrics is the study of quantitative aspects of the production, dissemination and use of information, regardless of its form or origin (Tague-Sutcliffe 1992). It employs well-documented methods from the disciplines mathematics, especially statistics. Typically it differentiates between analysis of content, structure, and usage. It encompasses several sub-disciplines, most prominently differentiated by the form the information is stored in: bibliometrics, scientometrics, and webometrics (Björneborn & Ingwersen 2004). This makes informetrics an ideal discipline for analysis of information diffusion based on information contained in certain documents as described above.

Relevant research in the context of applying informetrics to operationalize linear models has been conducted by different people: WATTS & PORTER hypothesized a pattern of publication activity which would reveal the current maturity state of a technology (Watts & Porter 1997). MARTINO interpreted the approach by Watts and Porter (Martino 2003). PORTER & CUNNINGHAM expanded on the approach by Watts and Porter (Porter & Cunningham 2005). JÄRVENPÄÄ et al. tested the hypotheses empirically in several publications (Järvenpää et al. 2011; Järvenpää 2009; Järvenpää & Mäkinen 2008b; Järvenpää & Tapaninen 2008). However, the majority of the research did not produce the expected results. Some came to sound conclusions but is effectively based on anecdotal evidence and cannot be inductively used for theory building (one technology; subjective interpretation); in neither case was a universal (mathematical) model the result. A recent approach from a model by GAO et al. generates promising results (Gao et al. 2013). They combine a total of 13 patent-based indicators with help of a k-nearest-neighbor machine-learning approach and also normalize the underlying data in their model. Still, several concerns arise regarding its robustness and universality, and, in addition, its precision remains vague.

The approach in this book relies on information source combination and data normalization procedures described in the following sections. Also, it intends to learn more from theoretical models not least because they offer rich handling instructions.

2.3.3 Identifying Text Media Suitable for Informetric Analyses

The question which is considered in this section is: what information is relevant for the latent variables and indicators described in the maturity models presented in section 2.2.3.1? The emphasis is on those models with a connection to the S&D model, as described in section 2.2.3.2. The information relevance depends on what information each separate maturity model calls for. As stated in section 2.3.2 on information diffusion, different aspects of human interaction with a maturing technology are recorded in different media. This section describes in detail selected text media which are deemed to be of high relevance for technology maturity assessment. The description offers detailed information on which aspects of human-technology interaction influence the respective media.

The section is structured as follows: first, an extensive overview of the essential aspects of human-technology interaction documentation is given in section 2.3.3.1. This provides a framework for characterizing text media in the context of informetric analyses. Next, patents and scientific literature as representatives of traditional text media are discussed and then characterized according to this framework in section 2.3.3.2. New text media are represented by web searches accordingly in section 2.3.3.3. Finally, the information contained in these text media is linked to the hypotheses concerning the behavior of the S&D model factors in section 2.3.3.4.

2.3.3.1 Framework for Characterizing Text Media in the Context of Informetric Analyses

This section provides a framework for characterizing text media regarding essential aspects of human-technology interaction. This framework is applied in the following sections 2.3.3.2 on traditional text media and 2.3.3.3 on new text media. In the approach in this book, the following three aspects are regarded as essential:

- **Author and recipient specific aspects**
- **Effort of creation specific aspects**
- **Analysis specific aspects**

Each aspect covers a number of characteristics described in detail below, along with a unified characterization scale to provide comparability across the text media. The characterization shall cover the majority of documents from a certain text media type, although individual documents can differ from the description. The following characteristics are evaluated:

Author and recipient specific aspects are such which characterize the author and the intended recipient of a certain document. This characterization is limited to the qualifications necessary to become an author or recipient of a certain document type. It is assumed that if a higher qualification of an author or recipient is necessary, that document is based on a higher level of expert knowledge with a background in the relevant technology.

- **Author qualification**: what are the requirements the author needs to fulfill for publishing the document?
    - o general interest [the person is interested in the technology and may understand the use of it]
    - o basic knowledge [the person is able to understand the basic principles of the technology]
    - o detailed knowledge [the person is able to understand the technology in its entirety]
    - o expert knowledge [the person is able to understand the technology in its entirety as well as additional knowledge about it]
    - o heterogeneous [several knowledge levels are present]
- **Recipient qualification**: what are the requirements the reader needs to fulfill for understanding / making use of the document? The scale is the same as for the author qualification above.

Effort of creation specific aspects are related to any effort necessary for creating and publishing a certain document. It is assumed that the greater the effort necessary to create a document, the higher the average quality of a document's contents and the higher the expectations connected to publication of that document.

- **Technology barriers**: difficulty of technology-based problems to be solved before the document can be published
  - o none [a general interest in the subject matter is sufficient to create content to be published]
  - o low [a general understanding of the impacts a technology may have is sufficient to create publishable content]
  - o moderate [the basic principles of the technology need to be understood to create publishable content]
  - o high [technology has to be understood entirely for publishing content]
  - o very high [technology has to be understood entirely and additional knowledge has to be created for publishing content]
- **Legal barriers**: barriers for the author before document can be published
  - o none [law does not apply for author of document]
  - o low [general law has to be considered]
  - o moderate [simple additions to general law have to be understood and taken into consideration]
  - o high [extensive specific laws have to be understood and taken into consideration. Aid from specialists is advisable]
  - o very high [law specialists have to check the document to guarantee conformance with the law]
- **Economic barriers**: expenses which are connected to publication of a single document
  - o none [document may be published without additional cost]
  - o low [small monetary expenses are connected to publication. Can typically be covered by author]
  - o moderate [Expenses that cannot typically be carried by a single person, but cannot be considered a large amount of money for an organization.]
  - o high [publication of such a document is connected to considerable expenses for an organization. Therefore typically there is a limit to the amount of this type of document]
  - o very high [even for large organizations or states, publishing this document is connected to costs that consume a considerable part of the budget. Typically only very few of this type of document are published]
- **Formal barriers**: any effort which prolongs the publication process and is not directly connected to the content of the document (e.g. Peer Review)
  - o none [the content can be published as it is and does not have to follow any formal procedures whatsoever]

- o low [a minimal effort has to be made to publish the document. Usually the publication process is automated and does not require other people to check the content before publication.]
- o moderate [a person may be involved in the publication process to check correct formal procedures.]
- o high [several people are involved in the publication process and have to check the content as well as the correct formal procedures of publication. The approximate format of the publication is given. Typically, a prior state of the art research has to be conducted.]
- o very high [numerous people are involved in the publication process and have to check the content as well as the correct formal procedures of publication. The format of the publication is specified in detail and compulsory. A comprehensive prior state of the art research has to be conducted.]

Analysis specific aspects correspond to effort and benefits during retrieval and analysis of a certain document. They offer information regarding the ease of use and immediacy of a certain data source.

- • **Retrieval barriers**: Any effort required for information retrieval including legal, economic, and formal barriers. This field gives some idea of the ease of use of the corresponding media for the data analyst.
  - o none [extensive databases are available and freely accessible]
  - o low [partial databases are available and freely accessible]
  - o moderate [(extensive or partial) databases are available for a subscription fee or at the cost of elaborate preparation/adjustment]
  - o high [no databases are available, but documents are freely accessible]
  - o very high [no databases are available and document access is expensive]
- • **Time from filing to publication**: the longer the time between filing and publication, the larger the lag between technology event and feedback. The division was chosen based on typical values.
  - o none (immediately up to some hours)
  - o short (one day up to one week)
  - o moderate (several weeks up to two months)
  - o long (several months up to a year)
  - o very long (more than a year)
- • **Document length**: longer documents potentially contain more information, but are also harder to process for the data analyst

- o very short (a maximum of a few words in the range of a full sentence)
- o short (several sentences up to half a page)
- o moderate (between one and ten pages max.)
- o long (usually 10 to 50 pages)
- o very long (more than 50 pages in general)
- **Document structuredness**: more structured documents allow for a quicker and more precise data analysis.
  - o none (continuous data [e.g. text] without structure)
  - o low (possibly separation of text body and heading, possibly meta data fields author, and date)
  - o moderate (defined length; table of contents; at least one, possibly several separate fields with different headings but without clearly defined content; Several meta data fields such as author, place, date etc.)
  - o high (Abstract; Table of contents; Separate fields with different headings and approximately outlined content; Several meta data fields such as author, place, date etc.)
  - o very high (Abstract. Tables of content, figures, tables; Numerous fields with separate given headings and clearly defined content. Extensive meta data fields. Content categorization systems)

The framework presented in this section can be used to characterize most textual media. It is useful in determining advantages and disadvantages of a medium for an analysis because it puts any medium in the context of other media without having to analyze these in greater detail.

2.3.3.2 Traditional Text Media

Traditional text media (henceforth "traditional media") cover formats which have been around for a long time and are well-defined. Originally these formats were mostly paper-based, but typically now they can be accessed in bulk in online databases. Typical examples which are promising in the context of technology maturity assessment are: patents, standards, scientific literature, and press. These can be subdivided further. For more similar sources see e.g. (Faulstich 2004). Of the traditional media, only patents and scientific literature are used in the approach in this book because they proved to contain valuable information in the past, which is why they are explicitly and exhaustively exploited in several maturity models presented in section 2.2.3.1, and because the information can easily be accessed. These two media are presented in detail in the following.

Patents

According to (World Intellectual Property Organization 2008) a patent is *"a set of exclusive rights granted by a state (national government) to an inventor or their assignee for a limited period of time in exchange for a public disclosure of an invention. A patent owner has the right to decide who may - or may not - use the patented invention for the period in which the invention is protected. The patent owner may give permission to, or license, other parties to use the invention on mutually agreed terms. The owner may also sell the right to the invention to someone else, who will then become the new owner of the patent. Once a patent expires, the protection ends, and an invention enters the public domain, that is, the owner no longer holds exclusive rights to the invention, which becomes available to commercial exploitation by others."*

An invention must, in general, fulfill the following four conditions to be protected by a patent (World Intellectual Property Organization 2008):

- It must be of practical use.
- It must show an element of novelty, that is, some new characteristic which is not known in the body of existing knowledge in its technical field. This body of existing knowledge is called "prior art".
- It must show an inventive step which could not be deduced by a person with average knowledge of the technical field.
- Its subject matter must be accepted as "patentable" under law. In many countries, scientific theories, mathematical methods, plant or animal varieties, discoveries of natural substances, commercial methods, or methods for medical treatment (as opposed to medical products) are generally not patentable.

People interested in the publication and reading of patents can be estimated comparatively precisely. Patent **authors** are inventors or technology driven firms. Inventors are the source of the IP, and firms want to secure and exploit their valuable IP against the competition. These two groups directly influence the quantity of patents being published. Patent protection costs money (e.g. filing, maintenance, and most importantly, litigation costs). A firm is only willing to pay for this, if it can expect some sort of corresponding countervalue. This does not mean that more money spent on a patent automatically makes this patent more valuable. Rather, it represents a speculative investment into the technology which can be seen as a firm's confidence in the success of a certain invention or technology. Patent **recipients** are other inventors. Patents provide not only protection for the owner but valuable information and inspiration for future generations of researchers and inventors (World Intellectual Property Organization 2014). Other patent recipients are technology driven firms and IP firms, recently also increasingly business intelligence firms. These deduct strategic information from patenting behavior of their competitors or clients.

In most countries, patents require 18 months from first filing to publication and it takes even longer for them to come into force. This does not include the time from the first idea for an invention until formal filing of the patent, which may also be considerable. This long time span produces a lag between invention / technological relevance and potential indicator values.

As displayed in figure 2.15, patents have shown a steady increase in application and publication activity for at least the past 30 years (World Intellectual Property Organization 2012).

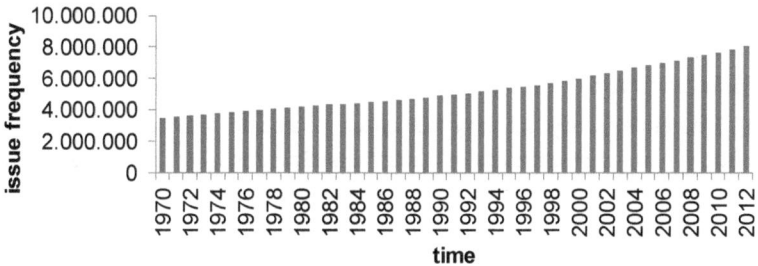

Fig. 2.15 Total granted US patents 1970-2012 by year of grant

Patents are created from a technology / financial perspective rather than a general public / end user / consumer perspective. They are able to show the industry interest in / importance of a technology.

Patent documents are published at no or low cost in the national language by national patent offices or at higher cost by special aggregation / added value firms. They are publicly available without special permit / status. Economic retrieval barriers exist in the form of subscription and / or preparation costs. Despite moderate additional cost, comprehensive retrieval is possible and usual.

The characteristics of patents as a text medium according to the framework of section 2.3.3.1 can be found in table 2.9.

Table 2.9 Characteristics of patents as a text medium

degree of author knowledge	expert knowledge
degree of recipient knowledge	expert knowledge
technology barriers	very high
legal barriers	very high
economic barriers	high
formal barriers	very high (Suhr 2000)
retrieval barriers	moderate
time from filing to publication	very long
word/page count	long
structuredness	very high

Scientific Literature

Scientific literature is any scholarly publication related to research discoveries. It serves to disseminate new findings of researchers. Scientific literature can be differentiated into journals, conference proceedings, monographs, theses, and working papers, to name important types (Schembri 2007; Kling & McKim 1999).

- It is the intention of **journal papers** to spread the knowledge about cutting-edge research results and participate in a scholarly debate about these results. Furthermore, authors of such articles often seek approval in the academic society. Highly recognized authors can achieve a better paid employment, which is the reason of the recent success of performance indices such as the *Hirsch-Index* (Hirsch 2005) or the *Impact Factor* (Garfield 2006).
- As in journal papers, it is the intention of **conference proceedings** to spread the knowledge about cutting-edge research results and participate in a scholarly debate about these results. Furthermore, authors of such articles often seek approval in academic society. Highly recognized authors can often achieve a better paid employment.
- **Theses** and **Dissertations** often are the result of final projects at universities. They represent a subgroup of **monographs**. All have in common that the author wants to collect and enhance all current knowledge on one single special subject. The drive may be purely academic or may have an economic part, when the author participates in the earnings from book sales.
- **Working papers** are often preliminary publications of scientists who want to discuss their findings, share references (and possibly discuss formal issues etc.) with the scientific community.

Any of the above can be differentiated further. It is beneficial to do this if it serves to differentiate important nuances and distinguish similar signals. What all scientific literature has in common however, is summarized below.

Scientific literature **authors** are researchers. The direction of their research is led by **funding institutions** within certain limits. These are typically universities or research institutions, which in turn are funded by national entities like states, regional entities like the European Union, industrial firms, or NGOs. All **recipients/readers** of scientific literature try to keep themselves informed in a certain research matter. They are typically technology experts themselves.

Scientific literature has a scientific perspective on technology, with a focus on very recent discoveries which may not have a commercial application (yet). Usually scientific literature is not written from an economic / general public standpoint. It can show single developments and in batch development speed of an entire technology. It is therefore an indicator of the importance of a maturing technology (over time). Identifying the main driver of a technology (prevailing funding institution type) could reveal what determines the direction of technology development.

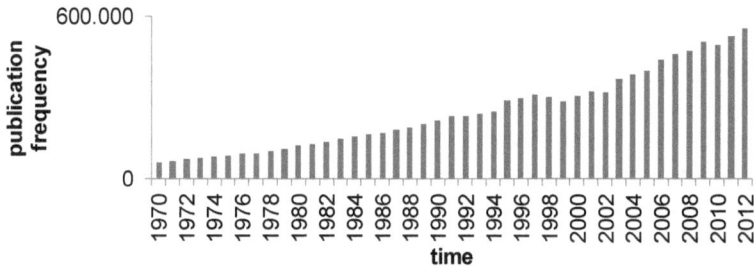

Fig. 2.16 Scientific literature published by ScienceDirect 1970-2012 by year of publication

The amount of scientific literature published has increased at a constant rate in the past years (see figure 2.16). Diverse data bases exist which provide collections of up-to-date scientific literature. Examples are INSPEC (Information Service for Physics, Electronics, and Computing), Web of Knowledge, Current Contents Connect, Conference Proceedings, and ScienceDirect. These data bases provide certain meta data at no or low cost and more detailed data as well as added value content at a considerably higher cost. The coverage of these data bases cannot be exact because it is not known how many publishers exist and no single accepted definition of scientific literature exists. A comprehensive retrieval as for patents is therefore impossible. Extensive retrieval is possible with data from just one of the above named source already.

The characteristics of scientific literature as a text medium according to the framework of section 2.3.3.1 can be found in table 2.10.

Table 2.10 Characteristics of scientific literature as a text medium

author knowledge	expert knowledge
recipient knowledge	detailed knowledge
technology barriers	very high
legal barriers	low
economic barriers	none - low
formal barriers	high - very high
retrieval barriers	moderate - high
time from filing to publication	moderate - high
word/page number	moderate - long
structuredness	moderate

2.3.3.3 New Text Media

New text media (henceforth "new media") differ from traditional media in many ways. Most important is the fact that anyone can become an author and so theoretically reach a large audience. Typically, there is no preliminary quality control and very low cost of dissemination, allowing quick publication and even audience feedback. Many different forms of new media exist. Most are not even remotely formally defined (yet) and there is a tendency for convergence (Jenkins 2006). Some examples are (micro-)blogs, message boards and forums, wikis, web search, rating sites, and social networks in general (Lister et al. 2008).

The approach in this book relies on web search to contrast patents and scientific literature. Web search was chosen over other new media for several reasons:

- Information in the new media is used for assessing the "social" state in the linear model of technology maturity. Information for this should be gathered from the broadest audience possible. Web search represents a large audience because most internet users also rely on the use of search engines. This is not true of most other new media which typically represent only a certain sub-group of internet users (Weber & Jaimes 2011; Spink et al. 2002; Morrell et al. 2000).

- Authors of web searches are people who are usually not even aware they produce content. This makes it easier to identify their interest for the subject matter as the driving force behind publication (Weber & Jaimes 2011).
- Web searches proved to be a valuable information source for other unlikely fields such as pandemic disease surveillance (Thompson et al. 2014; Nsoesie et al. 2013; Ginsberg et al. 2009)
- Unlike most other new media, web search data has been accessible freely (i.e. without cost or privacy restrictions) and comprehensively for the past few years instead of just the past few months. The reason for this is that it is collected centrally at large search engine providers such as Google.

Web Search Queries

Web search queries happen when search terms are entered into a search engine during an internet user's search of the world wide web. These search terms are collected in bulk at the search engines. Certain meta data are stored along with the search terms, such as the location where in the world the search was conducted. Google Trends can be used for web usage analysis of the Google search engine (Choi & Varian 2012).

There are very low barriers of participating in this form of data generation. An increasing number of people world-wide use the internet. Almost all people using the internet also use search engines. Many heterogeneous people participate. Whenever someone searches for a certain technology he/she is interested in, he/she the appears in the statistics. It differs from other social media in that it is generated without the conscious act of authoring a piece of text. It constitutes the analysis of the usage of a medium which is not or only to a limited extent possible for traditional media. Since it is an unconscious participation, most users (**authors**) do not follow a "publication intention". Many are not even aware that there are recipients/readers of their created patterns. Instead, they are interested in the search results which help them increase their knowledge about a certain subject such as a technology. On the other hand, many stakeholders are interested in the evaluation of this search behavior (**recipients**). First and foremost, firms want to understand how the general population receives their products. Where a high search volume may give a hint towards both, success or failure, low search volumes almost always mean a low awareness and / or visibility. Other recipients may encompass interest groups as diverse as policy makers, social scientists, or epidemiologists.

The web searches are suitable for analysis of general public interest and awareness connected to a technology or products based on it. It reflects technology interaction with the general public. Laymen rather than technology experts create this data. This may lead to imprecisions regarding the technology definition. The technology may be perceived as the form it comes in, e.g. as a product. Also, online searches may originate from opinion or attitude. This leads to higher search volumes than expected for ideologically marked technologies, politically pushed technologies, or such technologies which polarize opinions.

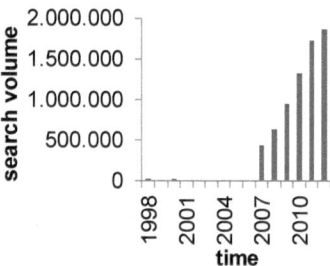

Fig. 2.17 Web search queries in millions in Google Trends 1998-2012 based on data from the website Statistic Brain, which were collected from different sources (Statistic Brain 2013). The count of web search queries increased at a high rate throughout the entire period covered by the data. Absolute search query volume for the years 2001-2006 is unfortunately not available. The 4 million queries in the year 1998 and the 22,000 million queries in 2000 are too low to be displayed

Only some search engines provide the data they collect. The most important search engine of Europe and Northern America (Google) does this at no cost. The web search queries at Google have increased strongly since the service went online in 1998 (see figure 2.17). Analyzing Google Trends data therefore allows for conclusions about these regions only. Some major drawbacks of Google Trends data are the following:

- It comes heavily normalized without documentation, effectively as a "black box".
- Retrieval is restricted to simple search strategies without advanced / complex features such as wild cards, truncation, nested search or even conjunctions (i.e. the connection of several search terms).
- There is no feedback on the correctness of a search strategy, i.e. it cannot be known whether the author actually meant what he was searching for.
- The service is not guaranteed and may be discontinued without notice

On the other hand, there are major benefits of the Google Trends data:

- It is available freely
- It is made available immediately when a search is performed.

- It is based on a rich, versatile, and representative source
- It is very structured, effectively making data cleaning unnecessary
- It is possible to combine it with other data provided by Google, e.g. search term prices (Google AdWords) for gauging industry interest in a technology.

The characteristics of web search queries as a text medium according to the framework of section 2.3.3.1 can be found in table 2.11.

Table 2.11 Characteristics of web search queries as a text medium

author knowledge	heterogeneous
recipient knowledge	heterogeneous
technology barriers	none
legal barriers	none
economic barriers	none
formal barriers	none
retrieval barriers	low
time from filing to publication	none
document length	very short
structuredness	very high

2.3.3.4 Linking Information Contained in Text Media with Hypotheses of the S&D model

The past sections 2.3.3.2 on traditional media and 2.3.3.3 on new media presented diverse text media and associated information. To put this information to use, it is necessary to understand why and how it may be related to a technology's maturity. This link is established with help of the S&D model's hypotheses. This section will describe the value for S&D model-based maturity assessment of the information contained in each text medium described above.

Some of the characteristics of the S&D model factors are hard to operationalize with a single indicator. It is easier to split up these factors into a number of new factors which are easier to operationalize, as done in table 2.12.

The following paragraph hypothesizes which media contain relevant information for the factors named in table 2.12, named by their letter, one by one. All statements are hypotheses which aim at relating the media to the factors. This section does not respond to the problem of extracting the relevant information from the media. This is done in subsequent sections.

Table 2.12 Latent variables of the S&D technology maturity model split up into new factors which can be operationalized and their expected development during maturation

	emergence	growth	saturation	decline
A. Insecurity of technological performance	high	medium	low	very low
B. Investments in technology development	low	maximal	low	negligible
C. Number of application areas	unknown	increasing	established, plenty	decreasing
D1. Scientific development requirements	high			
D2. Application oriented development requirements			high	
D3. Cost oriented development requirements				high
E. impact on cost/ performance rate of products	secondary	maximal	marginal	marginal
F. patent count	increasing	high	decreasing	decreasing
G1. Concept patents	high			
G2. Product patents		high		
G3. Process patents				high
H1. Scientific access requirements	high			
H2. Personnel access requirements		high		
H3. Licenses access requirements			high	
H4. Know how access requirements				high
I. Availability	very restricted	Restructuring	market oriented	high

A. Information on the insecurity of technological performance is contained in scientific literature. As pointed out in section 2.3.3.2 on scientific literature, it contains recent findings. Many articles feature a paragraph about the research gap which cannot be closed by the article at hand. This points to future research. Relevant information is also contained in web search data: section 2.3.3.3 states that some searches are triggered by a lack of detailed knowledge about a technology. The insecurity about the performance of a certain technology is such a case and may lead to a search query.

B. Investments in technology development in the sense of GRUPP's input indicator (see section 2.3.1) can best be measured based on statistics on R&D spending. When these are not available (e.g. for small firms), however, such spending leads to accumulated know-how in a firm in the sense of an output indicator. Depending on its technology strategy (see section 0), it may either file patent applications or publish defensive publications to protect its new knowledge. Public investment in certain technology fields may also lead to an increased research interest and publication volume. Therefore these two media may contain relevant information. Even the application or publication volumes are already a signal, as stated in section 2.3.3.2 on the motivation of patenting and publishing scientific literature.

C. The higher the number of application areas the more firms from different industries may find a technology interesting. If one presumes that a firm name can be linked to a certain industry or set of industries, then patents can help to identify which firms (and thus industries) are associated with a certain industry. Additionally, if an industry becomes involved with a new technology, some of its customers may want to investigate this, leading to an increasing volume of web searches related to the technology.

D1. The height of scientific development requirements of a technology can be deduced from the contents of the scientific literature published on it at that time. Higher scientific development requirements may lead to an increased volume of scientific publications. However, since not every increase must be rooted in the rise of scientific development requirements, it takes an analysis of the scientific literature's contents to reveal such an increase. **D2.** Application-oriented development requirements result from the necessity of firms to set themselves apart from a number of competitors all offering the same product. This may lead to patent applications protecting useful USP features of products. **D3.** Cost-oriented development is necessary when products based on a certain technology cannot be differentiated in any other way than by its price because a dominant design has already been established. This makes the market more transparent for the customers because products can easily be compared based on the price. Price searches can be conducted as web searches. When price differentiation becomes important, the amount of web-based price searches can be expected to rise.

E. The impact of a technology on the cost / performance rate of products increases the affordability of these products. This produces a larger market for them, including a larger audience. This audience may want to make an informed decision on whether or not to buy such a product. A way of getting relevant information is a web search. If the products can be directly linked to the technology, web search activity for the products can be gauged to retrieve information on this factor.

F. The patent count is a factor that can be operationalized rather easily as it is evidently linked to patenting activity.

G1. Concept patents are a certain type of patents which cannot be identified directly through the meta data of patents, but rather by analyzing each patent's content. Nevertheless, patents are needed for extracting this kind of information. The same holds true for **G2.** product patents and **G3.** process patents.

H1. Scientific access requirements to a certain technology, just like scientific development requirements are contained within scientific literature. This may lead to an increased output of scientific literature, but the height of the access requirements may as well have to be deduced from the content of this literature. **H2.** Is relatively vague about what personnel access requirements are, such as whether they are more related to quantity or certain qualities of the personnel. In any case, relevant information may be contained in patents, if this personnel regularly files patent applications. The sole number of persons connected to a certain technology can be deduced from the inventor field of a patent or the author field in scientific literature, whereas qualitative conclusions can be drawn from further analysis of patents or scientific literature published by the same persons. **H3.** Generally a license is the permission to do something, but it is especially the case in an industrial context – it can be assumed – that licenses access requirements are related to intellectual property rights. In this case, the holder of an intellectual property right, such as a patent, may grant a license to a second party which may then exploit the invention described in that patent. This type of information is contained in extended patent related data, but may not be publicly accessible. **H4.** Know-how access requirements are again not very well elaborated in the S&D model. They can be interpreted as implicit knowledge-related requirements, i.e. knowledge which is not present in a written form. This interpretation makes it hard to determine this factor based on any textual information.

I. Availability of a technology triggers its use and therefore complications with it on the consumer side. This again leads to web search activity related to these problems.

Table 2.13 Different text media help with the analysis for different factors of the S&D model hypotheses

	Text Media
A. Insecurity of technological performance	scientific literature, web search
B. Investments in technology development	patents, scientific literature
C. Number of application areas	patents, web search
D1. Scientific development requirements	scientific literature
D2. Application oriented development requirements	patents
D3. Cost oriented development requirements	web search
E. impact on cost/ performance rate of products	web search
F. patent count	patents
G1. Concept patents	patents
G2. Product patents	patents
G3. Process patents	patents
H1. Scientific access requirements	scientific literature
H2. Personnel access requirements	patents, scientific literature
H3. Licenses access requirements	(patents)
H4. Know how access requirements	-
I. Availability	web search

It became clear in the paragraph above that relevant information on most of the factors described in the S&D model can be deduced from the media described in section 2.3.3. See table 2.13 for an overview of media which contain relevant information for the factors of the S&D model.

2.3.4 Deriving Relevant Indicator Values

Traditional and new media that contain useful information for technology maturity indicators are identified and discussed in the past section 2.3.3. It also becomes clear that tapping the relevant information contained in these media is possible in different ways. Some of these are more straight-forward than others because the information is readily available. At the same time, operationalization of certain factors may require a more sophisticated approach. The latter unfortunately impedes easy tapping of additional information sources, if it becomes necessary.

This section presents a generic operationalization mechanism suitable for the operationalization of many factors of the S&D model and similar models. It is constructed as follows: the first section 2.3.4.1 presents a text data focused indicator typology. It gives insights into how different operationalization mechanisms are constructed. Furthermore, an operationalization of the S&D model's latent variables is attempted. The second section 2.3.4.2 presents a generic operationalization mechanism suitable for operationalizing many factors of the S&D model and similar models by harnessing a parameter which all text media sources have in common: publication activity.

2.3.4.1 Text Data Focused Indicator Typology

This section presents a classification for indicators based on the information they rely on. Ordered by increasing comlpexity, these are **activity indicators, meta data indicators**, and **full text indicators**. Each type is characterized in three paragraphs:

- A short general definition of the indicator type for delineation in later sections, including prominent subgroups where regarded as helpful.
- Example indicators with a short explanation and an explanatory figure

Each type can be sub-divided further, but this is not deemed necessary in the present context.

Activity Indicators are indicators based on the publication activity or other activity related to the technology in question in a certain period of time (see e.g. figure 2.18). Sometimes referred to as "basic indicators" (Tseng et al. 2011). A prominent subgroup of activity indicators are usage indicators. These allow conclusions concerning the user interaction with media. They are based on information that is generated after publication of the actual documents, the usage of documents. This information can therefore not be found on the actual documents and is often subject to constant change over the course of time. They are often used to determine the price of advertisement in a medium, but are also useful for assessing the knowledge of / interest in a subject matter.

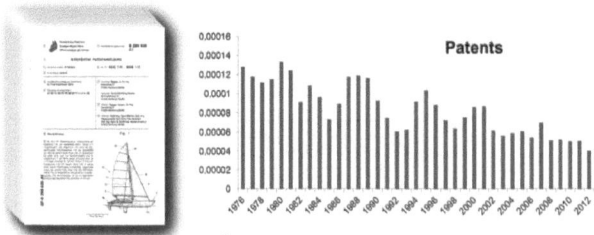

Fig. 2.18 Activity indicator - publication activity over time

Typical examples are *document count* per time slice; *document count growth* over time. Typical usage indicators are *download / view / click indicators*, which count the interactions with a document electronically; *reach indicators*, which approximate the viewership of a medium if the necessary data is not surveyed electronically (Tseng et al. 2011).

Meta Data Indicators are based purely on data that is provided with the documents outside of the full text. Typical meta data indicators are counts of list items like authors or forward- and backward citations. Other examples are time-related indicators, e.g. based on the publication date or the document age. A prominent sub-group of meta data indicators are network indicators for which documents are not considered in isolation, such as displayed in figure 2.20. Rather, the connections between documents are collected and meta data from different documents is considered. Through this, new information is generated. They are also known as structure indicators.

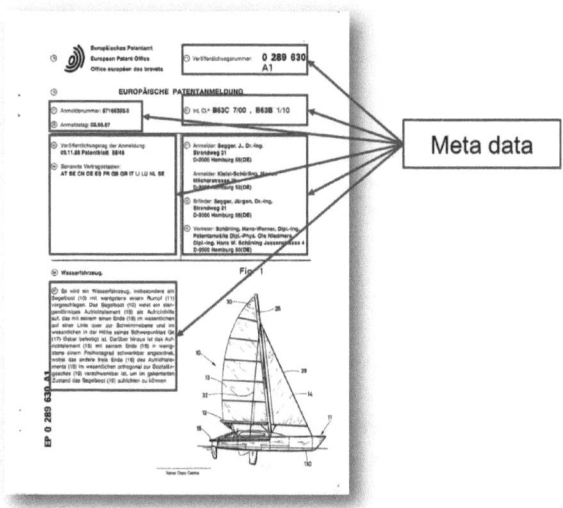

Fig. 2.19 Meta data of a document may serve as information basis for meta data indicators

Typical meta data indicator examples include *classification indicators*, which further cluster the relevant documents and allow for specialized activity indicators connected to subgroups; *summation indicators*, which summarize certain parameters on a document like the citation count or the author count; *difference parameters* which compare two values in the meta data of a single document like the duration between filing and publication of a document.

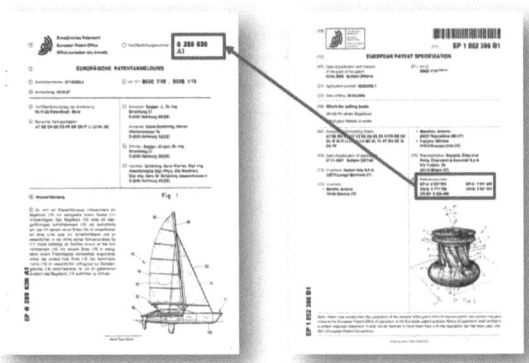

Fig. 2.20 A document pointing to another relevant document by citing it may be the information basis of a network indicator

Typical network indicator examples include *immediacy indicators*, which analyze a time difference between source and destination documents; *citation network indicators*, which analyze the position of a document within a network, e.g. based on social network analysis; *cross-media indicators*, which focus on the inter-medial connection of documents.

Full Text Indicators are based on the full text of a document, as depicted in figure 2.21. These indicators attempt to grasp attributes in the text which are not included in the meta data. These may include but not limited to the text relevance, originality, quality, and tonality.

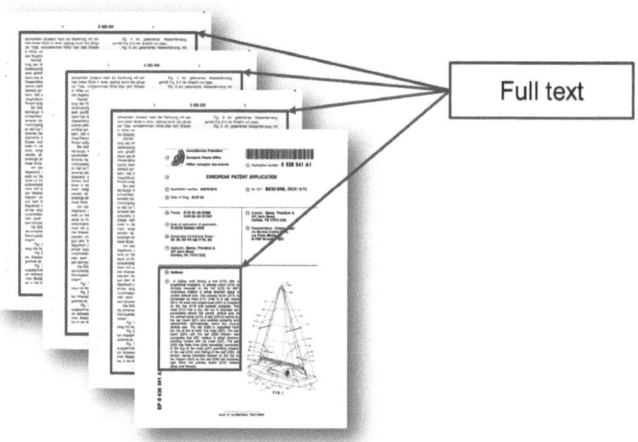

Fig. 2.21 Full text analyses may encompass substantial additional data evaluation

Typical examples include *key word indicators* based on certain words or word combinations like n-grams, collocation; *structure indicators* like SAO-analyses (subject-action-object) (Gerken & Moehrle 2012; Moehrle & Gerken 2012).

S&D Model Indicator Types

As stated at the beginning of this section, operationalization of the factors of the S&D model requires different approaches. Since it is the goal of this book to present a generic operationalization approach, and since section 2.3.2 showed how a lot of different perspectives on the same technology can be found by looking at different text media, it is reasonable to present an operationalization mechanism which works for all media types. This requires for a suitable mechanism to rely on data that is available for all text media.

As described in section 2.3.3, text media may be as different as **patents** on the one hand, which contain rich meta data including application, publication, and grant date, the applicant, assignee, classification codes, citation information, and several text fields for the title, abstract, claims, or description and also have strict rules and standards for publication. And **microblogs** (such as Twitter) on the other hand, which contain only a limited number of characters in text, an author alias, and a time of publication, but almost no formal publication restrictions. Of course, all text media contain textual data and also some kind of meta data, but that does not mean that they all use the same language or, even if they do, the same words for the same concepts. Actually, especially in the case of online media and particularly microblogs, misspellings are rather common (Han & Baldwin 2011; Choi et al. 2014; Zhao et al. 2011). Furthermore, few text media feature identical meta data such as an unambiguous author's name, affiliation, or citation information. What they all do have in common, however, is a time of publication (even the time of publication of a search request can be considered a time of publication), which can be used for activity indicators. The approach in this book therefore relies on activity indicators to be able to use the broadest possible set of media types without having to redefine new operationalization mechanisms with each new operationalization. This approach allows taking advantage of the linear model as described in section 2.3.2 on information diffusion.

Table 2.14 Different factors of the S&D model hypotheses require different indicator types to evaluate the text media

S&D model factors	Text Media	Type
A. Insecurity of technological performance	scientific literature, web search	full, activity
B. Investments in technology development	patents, scientific literature	activity
C. Number of application areas	patents, web search	meta, activity
D1. Scientific development requirements	scientific literature	full
D2. Application oriented development requirements	patents	full
D3. Cost oriented development requirements	web search	activity
E. impact on cost / performance rate of products	web search	activity
F. patent count	patents	activity
G1. Concept patents	patents	full
G2. Product patents	patents	full
G3. Process patents	patents	full
H1. Scientific access requirements	scientific literature	full
H2. Personnel access requirements	patents, scientific literature	meta
H3. Licenses access requirements	(patents)	(meta)
H4. Know how access requirements	-	-
I. Availability	web search	activity

Obviously not all theoretical model factors can be operationalized with this approach. But several of them can, and the mechanism can even be used as an exploratory approach to finding new indicators which may be especially suitable for estimating a technology's maturity.

Table 2.14 relies on the typology constructed in this section to typify the S&D model factors as described in section 2.3.3.4. All those model factors which can be operationalized based on the activity type are taken into account for operationalization in the subsequent sections. It is always possible to produce more complex approaches if the considered model factors do not allow for a sufficiently precise characterization of a technology's current maturity state.

2.3.4.2 Activity Indicators

The S&D approach features only a (semi-)theoretical technology maturity model. Section 2.2.3.2 points out where the S&D model lacks latent variables with explanatory value for technology maturity. Then, section 2.3.3 presents text media which could be used as information sources for operationalizing latent variables of the model and such ones yet lacking in it. Finally, section 2.3.4.1, specifically table 2.14, summarizes the type of indicator necessary to tap the information contained in these text media relevant for the factors of the S&D model. It also justifies the exclusive use of activity indicators in the scope of the approach in this book. Even though activity indicators can be created for different media types with the same operationalization mechanism, it still takes careful consideration to make them valid, reliable, objective, and useful. This section aims to clarify this further and eventually present operationalization mechanisms which are likely to fulfill these requirements.

In order to design a useful operationalization mechanism for these factors, it is necessary to define certain desirable indicator properties which are deemed useful in maturity assessment. This section names such desirable indicator properties, and uses these to design generic operationalization mechanisms suitable for harnessing a multitude of different text media sources.

Four especially desirable indicator properties are identified in this book. An indicator that fulfills these, should:

1. be based on suitable media sources
   a. rich in technology maturity relevant information
   b. accessible for the public
2. be based on detailed existing theoretical maturity models
   a. to achieve sound recommendations for the current strategic situation

      b. to fit into established frameworks and simplify implementation
3. make technology maturity assessment possible with incomplete data and an ongoing maturing process
      a. not all data from emergence necessary
      b. not all data until decline necessary
4. provide similar signals in the same states of maturity for different technologies
      a. occur within a known interval
      b. exhaust this interval or at least exploit it in large part

These desirable indicator properties are discussed one by one in the following.

Desirable **indicator property 1** calls for an operationalization mechanism that is generic, because with such a mechanism a multitude of text media can be tapped as information sources. Among such text media would certainly be ones that are rich in maturity relevant information and at the same time accessible for the public. For an operationalization mechanism to be generic, it should be possible to use it on any text medium without having to adjust the calculation formula. It allows the expansion of an operationalized technology maturity model by additional indicators based on other text media which serve as new information sources, should new ones become available or old ones have to be replaced. As explained in the past section 2.3.4.1, the approach in this book will implement an operationalization mechanism which produces activity indicators for different text media. Activity indicators are based on the sole existence of documents, so they can be measured for any text medium. Meta data indicators and full text indicators both require information which may not be present in all text media.

Desirable **indicator property 2** is fulfilled by the approach in this book, because it intends to exemplarily operationalize a detailed existing theoretical maturity model, namely the S&D model. The S&D approach, in which it is embedded, offers the relevant strategic technology management advice demanded by indicator property 2.

Desirable **indicator properties 3 and 4**, to make technology maturity assessment possible with incomplete data and an ongoing maturing process and to provide similar signals in the same maturity states for different technologies, demand precise fine-tuning of existing operationalization mechanisms, which to date succeed in neither property 3 nor 4. Characteristics which influence these indicator properties will therefore be discussed in detail below.

According to hypotheses in certain semi-theoretical and semi-operationalized models such as the ones described in DUBARIĆ, LINDEN & FENN, MARTINO, and WATTS & PORTER (Dubarić et al. 2011; Linden & Fenn 2003; Martino 2003; Watts & Porter 1997), the absolute document count over time generates a typical pattern (see figure 2.22) which can be used for technology maturity assessment and even publication volume prediction. They belong to the group of activity indicators. In the easiest case they theoretically fulfill desirable indicator properties 1 and 2. In empirical studies, however, they did not succeed in fulfilling indicator properties 3 and 4.

Activity indicators (document count over time) were tested and caused doubt on several occasions. They were tested visually (Gao et al. 2013; Järvenpää et al. 2011; Järvenpää 2009; Järvenpää & Mäkinen 2008a; Järvenpää & Mäkinen 2008b; Järvenpää & Tapaninen 2008; Lee & Nakicenovic 1988) or tried to fit curve models (Rai 1999; Bewley & Fiebig 1988; Norton & Bass 1987; Fisher & Pry 1971; Bass 1969; Gompertz 1825) to predict future publication volumes (Sood et al. 2012; Höök et al. 2011; Ryu & Byeon 2011; Chen et al. 2010; Kapur & Chanda 2010; Lou et al. 2009; Kucharavy & Guio 2008; Kucharavy & Guio 2007; Meade & Islam 2006; Sharif & Islam 1980). The approaches mentioned above all were aiming to predict future behavior. In this respect they differ from the intention of this approach where only the current state of maturity is to be estimated. All approaches came to the conclusion that prediction was possible, but if at all, then only for a very limited period of time. This has implications for estimating the current state of maturity as well, because the imperfect curve fit that leads to problems with the prediction may be due to the lack of precision of current maturity assessment. It is therefore necessary to understand why the approaches named above struggled with imprecisions in the data.

The reason for this is that all approaches assume that the indicators develop in a typical pattern as a function of technology maturity (see figure 2.22). This may be a simple bell curve as in the case of MARTINO (Martino 2003), the cumulative view on the bell curve famously known as the s-curve (Foster 1986) as interpreted for document publication count by ERNST (Ernst 1997), or a more complex function shape as for the hype cycle (Linden & Fenn 2003).

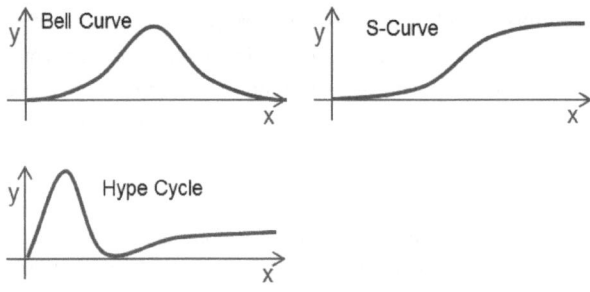

Fig. 2.22 Different ideal indicator development shapes

In the simple case of a known bell curve, all it takes to estimate a technology's maturity is the current position on the function. This position is determined unambiguously by only two parameters: the height and the slope of the function. Still, all studies named above failed at this seemingly easy task. Why is it apparently so difficult to determine the current position? Even though the function is essentially a bell curve, it may differ in certain parameters which influence its actual shape. These parameters are summarized in the morphology of assumed curve functions. Parameters that cause this can be ordered in three groups (Stasinopoulos & Rigby 2007):

- location parameters
- scale parameters
- shape parameters

The morphology is explained based on the bell curve but is also true for other curve functions, as exploited for example in GAMLSS (Generalized Additive Models for Location, Scale, and Shape) models (Rigby & Stasinopoulos 2005). What is important to note is that all parameters become evident only during maturity development and are not known at the beginning of the development. The morphology is the reason of misinterpretation of single values so it is important to understand how they may cause the actual function to differ from the ideal pattern. All descriptions below are interpreted by their impact on maturity assessment if the typical bell curve function is assumed.

Location parameters shift the function along the x-axis as displayed in figure 2.23. If the location parameters change, the start and end of all states are shifted by the same amount.

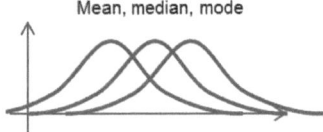

Mean, median, mode

Fig. 2.23 Location parameters of a function

Scale parameters stretch or shrink a function while the location parameters remain the same, as displayed in figure 2.24.

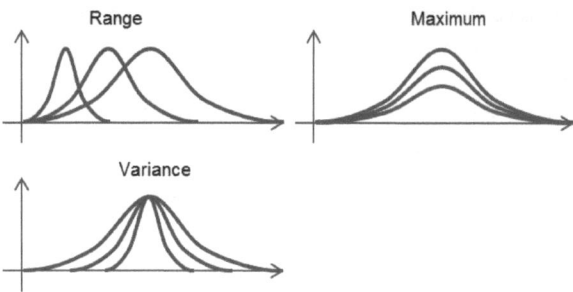

Fig. 2.24 Scale parameters of a function

These parameters have an effect on the slope or the height of the function and can therefore lead to misinterpretations. If the *range* changes, all states should become shorter or longer by the same factor. The slope of the function locally is lower (for an extended range) or higher (for a reduced range) than the typical function. The *variance* has a similar effect on the function as the range, but the fixed location is the maximum of the function rather than its origin. For a changed *maximum*, the slope of the function is changed by the same fraction for the entire function. All states should remain the same.

Shape parameters affect the shape of a function rather than simply shifting it or stretching/shrinking it, as displayed in figure 2.25.

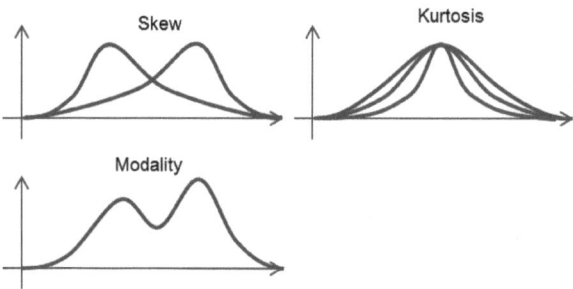

Fig. 2.25 Shape parameters of a function

They can be estimated in terms of higher moments using method of moments (Hansen 1982). Skewness is the 3rd moment. A different skewness means differing slopes for the increasing and decreasing side of the function. This results in a change of the maturity state length ratio (shorter for states in fat tail, longer in slim tail). Kurtosis is the 4th moment and has an influence on the ratio of states in the center of the function to that on the edges. The larger the kurtosis, the shorter the center states. *Modality* causes multiple local maxima. This may result in two possible interpretations:

- Interpretation "*separate technologies*": The search strategy was formed wrong and contains multiple technologies which should not be part of the same interpretation and results. This means that the search has to be re-written to exclude documents which do not belong. See figure 2.26, left.

- Interpretation "*technology rejuvenation*": New findings uncovered new technology potentials and lead to a resumed technology development after a later state was already reached. This is the case, for example, when a technology already has reached a state of maturity, but later returns to a second growth state. See figure 2.26, right.

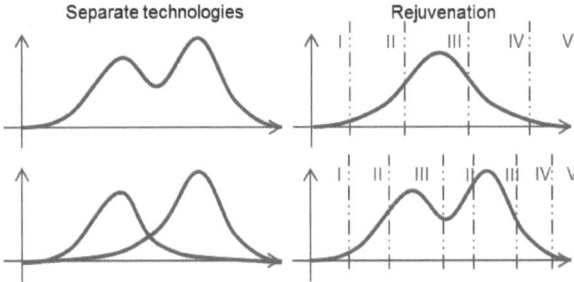

Fig. 2.26 Alternative interpretations for multimodal indicator development

In the approach in this book, correct information retrieval is assumed, so a modality larger than 1 will be interpreted as rejuvenation of the technology in focus.

All scale and shape parameters lead to an unexpected relation of height and slope when compared to the ideal curve function. The ideal indicator has to be robust against these effects in order to be able to fulfill desirable indicator property 4.

Even if they did produce typical patterns, the absolute publication counts for a certain technology during a given time span were not suitable for assessing technology maturity because they differ too much for different technologies. For example, a technology with a broad definition will produce a function with different scale parameters than one which is defined narrowly. If not all data is available from emergence to decline (desirable indicator property 3), desirable indicator property 4 is not fulfilled. This makes the indicator only suitable for ex-post analysis, disqualifying it for maturity evaluation of currently active technologies.

Again it has to be noted that it is sufficient for the purpose of the approach in this book to estimate a technology's current maturity state rather than to predict its future development. A curve fit, as it was required by the studies mentioned at the beginning of this section, would be desirable to enable forecasting, but it is not necessary. However, an operationalization mechanism needs to take into account the potential changes to the indicator development due to the function morphology mentioned above in order to be able to satisfy the desirable indicator properties and especially understand whether a certain indicator value is high or low. Two operationalization mechanisms are described below, that in combination may meet these requirements.

Operationalization Mechanism: Fraction of Relevant Documents per Year

Different text media types show different publication trends. As can be seen in figures 2.15, 2.16, and 2.17 in sections 2.3.3.2 and 2.3.3.3, for most media this took on the form of a relatively strong increase over the past 40 years. The absolute in- or decrease of the total publication volume y_{total} has to be considered when analyzing publication volumes connected to a certain technology. If the in- or decrease of publications connected to a technology $y_{specific}$ exactly corresponds to the total publication development, the relative importance of that technology does not change. A simple trend analysis, as typically done in linear model approaches such as by JÄRVENPÄÄ, MARTINO, or WATTS & PORTER, may show increasing trends even though the relative importance of a technology decreases (Järvenpää 2009; Martino 2003; Watts & Porter 1997). As explained above, this results from the exclusive view on $y_{specific}$, while omitting y_{total}. There may be different reasons behind the increase of the total publication volume of most media in the past 40 years. Publication behavior may change, but especially for databases which collect and integrate data from different sources, the coverage of the used database may simply have been extended over time. The definition of a technology may not be clear and may be subject to constant change, especially in the new media. If the search terms necessary to identify a technology change, this may lead to a decrease of hits. Also if coverage changes for one or another reason outside of technological developments (e.g. political motivation), this can have a big influence on the indicator value development $y_{specific}$. It primarily affects scale and shape parameters and through this distorts maturity state attribution.

Better suited for comparative studies are relative values. This means that indicator values are rescaled to a known interval such as [0,1]. This is called normalization and comprises adjusting values measured on different scales to a notionally common scale. Normalization fixes distortion of indicator development concerning scale and

shape parameters. A normalized indicator fulfills 4a of the desirable indicator properties. But how can a normalization be undertaken, which leads to desirable properties
of the resulting function? Rather ran plotting the raw activity $y_{specific}$, the indicator
should display the development of a technology's importance concerning its problem-
solving ability for the "application" it serves. This challenge can be taken on by observ-
ing a technology's surrounding environment. To really understand the situation of a
technology, substitute technologies have to be well-known, too. An approach for identifying relevant technologies is given in TAYLOR & TAYLOR (2012), as interpreted in section 2.1.1 (Taylor & Taylor 2012): As a first step, the application a technology serves
has to be well-defined. Then the current paradigm of that application has to be identified. Bordering paradigms have to be identified as well. All generations, also parallel
ones, need to be identified and portrayed. Their interrelation has to be described: successor, predecessor, competitor. Next, search strategies for the generation in question
(i.e. the technology) and its direct neighbors have to be generated. Rather than count-
ing absolute numbers of documents, the relative share of a single generation $y_{specific}$
in comparison to the absolute count for the selected application y_{total} are calculated
according to formula (2.1).

$$y_{specific,normalized} = \frac{y_{specific}}{y_{total}}$$

This puts the focus on the relative importance of the technology in the application pe-
riphery and represents a new indicator. It effectively implements the theoretical approach by TAYLOR & TAYLOR (Taylor & Taylor 2012). This indicator may represent different latent variables depending on the media which it is used on. For example, if it is
applied to patents, it can be used to represent variable F: patent activity of the S&D
model. If it is instead applied to scientific literature, if can be used to gauge the first
maturity state of variable H: access requirements, which is hallmarked by scientific
ability. If on the other hand it is applied to web search, variable I: availability of the
technology can be indicated, especially during the mature state of a technology, which
is distinguished by its market orientation, which in turn can be hypothesized to trigger
an increased web search volume. Each of these interpretations is much closer to the
original intention of what should be measured by the theoretical maturity models
named above than the absolute document count. Even though documents are filed
continuously throughout the year, to make use of standard time series analysis methods, discretization is necessary. To determine meaningful indicator values, it is therefore necessary to sum up all publications within a certain period of time. Examples are
all publications within a day, a week, a month, or within a year. To avoid potential

seasonal effects (Lei et al. 2009), the approach in this book suggests the calendar year as discretization basis, unless indicated otherwise.

This indicator does not require downloading of any data, which makes it very cost effective and grants access to a multitude of different media sources where a regular subscription would be too cost intensive. This permits the analysis of information diffusion as described in section 2.3.2. The indicator requires a very low calculation effort which does not change for additional records. This makes it suitable for very large data sets. It is suitable for automation. The same holds true for the indicators described below, which are based on the same data and thus do not require an additional retrieval process.

The drawback of this indicator is, again, that it will not cause the same values for two technologies in the same maturity state, unless these two technologies had a similar relative importance during their maturation. This indicator does therefore not fulfill desirable indicator property 4b, especially related to the scale parameter "maximum". This can be somewhat compensated by only comparing technologies on the same hierarchical level of the classification model by TAYLOR & TAYLOR (Taylor & Taylor 2012). Nevertheless, the indicator fulfills all desirable indicator properties as absolute document count does, plus 4a. It is therefore a better indicator than the absolute document count. The different applications of the indicator assume different indicator developments. As mentioned at the beginning of this section, for the simplest form of a bell curve as the one in figure 2.22 it is necessary to know the height and slope of the function to determine the current position. For the same reason as for absolute numbers, the relative publication fraction in a given time span alone is therefore not suitable as a maturity indicator. What is still missing, is the slope of the indicator value at that time.

Operationalization Mechanism: Slope of Relevant Documents per Year

In order to determine the position on a curve assuming a bell curve shape, the height in not enough. It is necessary to also know the activity slope of the corresponding medium, or more precisely, the first derivate of the normalized publication slope. The values for this are restricted to the interval (-1,1), which is convenient, as it makes further normalization unnecessary. Moreover, it can be assumed that this interval is exploited to a large part, if theoretical models are somewhat accurate.

Since the publication behavior is not a continuous but a discrete function, it cannot be differentiated, however. A simple approach for approximating the slope of the publication behavior locally based on limited data is a linear regression. This causes several problems, which have to be considered during evaluation. The indicator value lags behind the actual slope, especially for long time slices. On the other hand, the longer the time slices, the smoother the result, which is especially important for locally unsteady development paths, e.g. through seasonal effects or microtrends. A good fit needs to be found. Different data sources may require different time slice widths.

For approximating the slope for successive years, one can make use of a well-established method from financial mathematics, and apply a rolling linear regression (Zivot & Wang 2006, pp.313–360). Since values for this indicator have to be found for each year, the regression window (i.e. the years in consideration) has to be shifted by one year for each new year. This is called a rolling regression, and since it is a linear regression, a rolling linear regression. If the slope for the current year shall be calculated, the last available value is the publication height of the current year, particularly not after. The slope for the current year thus has to be calculated based on past years rather than future years.

Two resulting factors from such an analysis are slope β_t and intercept α_t at time t. The intercept is not of interest in this context, because future values will not be predicted, and will therefore be omitted. Only the slope β_t will be used in subsequent analyses.

A simple approach suitable for this task is one presented by ZIVOT & WANG (Zivot & Wang 2006, pp.328–329) based on the work of FAMA & MACBETH (Fama & MacBeth 1973): For a window of width n where $n < T$, with T being the total count of years of data available, the rolling linear regression model is displayed in formula (2.2).

$$y_{t^*}(n) = X_{t^*}(n)\beta_{t^*}(n) + \varepsilon_{t^*}(n); \ t^* = n, \dots, T$$

Where t^* is the currently observed point in time, $y_{t^*}(n)$ is an $(n \times 1)$ vector of normalized publication activity, $X_{t^*}(n)$ is a $(n \times 1)$ matrix of the points in time contained in the window, $\beta_{t^*}(n)$ is the slope, and $\varepsilon_{t^*}(n)$ is an $(n \times 1)$ vector of error terms. The observations in $y_t(n)$ and $X_t(n)$ are the n most recent values from times $t - n + 1$ to t. The rolling least squares estimates are computed for sliding windows of width n and increment m.

Note that, because the rolling regression uses n data points, the first time t for which a regression model can be formed is at $t = n$. Although the new observation at a certain time t^* is univariate, the entire vector $y_{t^*}(n)$ of observations from $t^* - n + 1$ to t^* is used to estimate $\beta_{t^*}(n)$.

Obviously, the model parameters in this setup for consecutive t, overlap. Therefore, the vectors $y_{t^*}(n)$ and $y_{t^*+1}(n)$ will be correlated, just like any two $y_{t'}(n)$ and $y_{t''}(n)$ which are less than n periods apart. This is a statistical problem, because despite this correlation, the rolling regression method still assumes each regression model has independent error terms. Formally, formula (2.3) must be assumed.

$$Prob(Y_{t^*} = y_{t^*}|B_{t^*}) = Prob(Y_{t^*} = y_{t^*})$$

where

$$B_{t^*} = \{Y_t \, t = 1, ..., t^* - 1\}$$

(Leeds 2012, p.5)

Exponential smoothing is another simple approach which could be used instead of rolling simple linear regression, but it does not solve the problem of overlapping time slices. The approach was chosen for its simplicity over more elaborate approaches such as using Kalman filters for linear systems, or others presented by HAMILTON (Hamilton 1994).

Other Possible Operationalization Mechanisms Derived from the Same Data, Not Applied in the Approach in this Book

Another possible indicator is the second time-derivative of the normalized publication slope. It is calculated by the easy formula (2.4).

$$\beta_t(n) - \beta_{t-1}(n)$$

It is able to indicator the direction in which the slope changes. This is especially interesting for more complex curve functions. Since the approach in this book presumes a simple bell curve function, as stated above, height and slope are sufficient.

Furthermore, the error variable ε_t of the simple regression adds noise to the linear relationship and is high for windows in which a sudden trend change happens. This is an indicator by itself, because it can differentiate between states of linearity and states of change. It will however not be part of the model presented here either.

2.3.5 Employing and Combining Indicators

Two operationalization mechanisms were described in the previous section 2.3.4.2, one for the height and one for the slope of a publication pattern. They can be applied to a number of different text media to produce indicators. According to the S&D model hypotheses, many of these indicators are suited to estimate a technology's current maturity state s. It would be most convenient, if there was a single indicator which performed best for all s. Section 2.3.5.1 discusses under which conditions this can be achieved and what can be done if these conditions are not met. It assumes that all technology maturity indicators are hypothesized to display certain patterns over the course of a technology's lifetime and discusses the usefulness of such patterns for maturity assessment under certain conditions. Section 2.3.5.2 presents a number of approaches which use indicators in combination rather than independently. The section systematically juxtaposes the relevant hypotheses. Section 2.3.5.3 concludes with the finding that indicator combination is useful and necessary, and it therefore presents ways for combination of indicators.

2.3.5.1 Hypothesizing Indicator Behavior

This section will hypothesize how indicators may develop over time and under which circumstances they are suitable for differentiating certain maturity states. This is necessary to understand that it is improbable for a single indicator to be able to distinguish between a lot of subsequent maturity states. An expected activity of the model factors during each maturity state must be known for operationalization of the S&D model with the indicator mechanic described in section 2.3.4.1. S&D model factors suitable for this purpose can be found in table 2.14, whereas their expected behavior is described in table 2.12. An overview of the resulting activity indicators and their expected behavior can be found in table 2.15.

Table 2.15 Overview of expected behavior of S&D model factors which can be operationalized with help of activity indicators

	emergence	growth	saturation	decline
A. Insecurity of technological performance (web search)	high	medium	low	very low
B. Investments in technology development (patents, scientific literature)	low	maximal	low	negligible
C. Number of application areas (web search)	unknown	increasing	established, plenty	decreasing
D3. Cost oriented development requirements (web search)			high	
E. impact on cost/performance rate of products (web search)	secondary	maximal	marginal	marginal
F. patent count (patents)	increasing	high	decreasing	decreasing
I. Availability (web search)	very restricted	Restructuring	market oriented	high

But which of these should be used for the actual maturity assessment? Is one indicator enough? A proposal comes from a paper by HAUPT et al. (Haupt et al. 2007). In their research they identified common patent-based indicators and they rely on the maturity states of the S&D model (see section 4.7.1 for an in-depth description of the indicators). Rather than approximating absolute values for each state, they look at the transitions t from one state to another. They chose a technology (cardiac pacemakers) which did not yet reach its decline state and thus are restricted to the three states s_1 emergence, s_2 growth, and s_3 maturity. This leaves them with the two transitions t_1 emergence-growth and t_2 growth-maturity. Since the indicators take on values on an open scale, the absolute values have no meaning. Only comparatively they can signal a maturity state transition, i.e. when the values of one state deviate significantly from those of a second state. The precise magnitude of this deviation is of no interest so long as it is statistically significant. This means, maturity state changes can cause only three indicator reactions d: They can either fall (-), rise (+), or not change significantly (0) during each transition. If they stay the same, the indicator is not suitable for indicating a maturity state change. Figure 2.27 is an example of an indicator which does not change significantly between states $(t_1; t_2) = (0; 0)$. It should therefore not be considered an indicator. Figure 2.28 can not identify the transition t_1, whereas t_2 can be recognized well $((t_1; t_2) = (0; +))$. Obviously, variations of this pattern with a similar informative value exist: $(0; -), (+; 0), (-; 0)$.

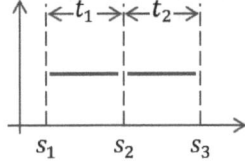

Fig. 2.27 Example of function behavior which is unfit as an indicator

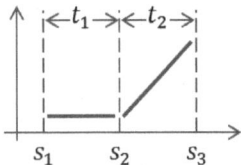

Fig. 2.28 Example of indicator behavior which allows for recognition of the latter out of two transitions between states

If they rise or fall for two consecutive transitions $(-; -), (+; +)$ (see figure 2.29), these cannot be told apart, since the absolute indicator value to be expected in s_2 and s_3 is unknown. Such a behavior is therefore only suitable to indicate that the technology is currently not in s_1, however not to understand whether it is currently in s_2 or in s_3.

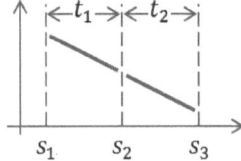

Fig. 2.29 Example of indicator behavior which allows for recognition of the former out of two transitions between states

Only if the indicator development is opposed for both transitions $(+; -), (-; +)$, the indicator is suited for differentiation of two consecutive transitions (or differentiation of three maturity states). Figure 2.30 shows an example of a change in activity.

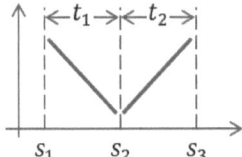

Fig. 2.30 Example of indicator behavior which allows for recognition of two consecutive transitions between states

The count of maturity states $|s|$ determines the transition count $|t| = |s| - 1$. A count of three states or two transitions (emergence-growth; growth-maturity) leads to a total of $|d|^{|t|} = 3^2 = 9$ possible indicator behavior combinations. Table 2.16 shows a comprehensive overview of the behavioral patterns described above. In conclusion, only some indicator behavior patterns allow for actual state differentiations and represent useful indicator behavior. Only the two progressions $(+; -), (-; +)$ can be used for identifying both transitions.

If an additional maturity state and therefor an additional transition t_3 (maturity-decline) is introduced, the count of potential combinations goes up to $|d|^{|t|} = 3^3 = 27$. All these combinations are displayed in table 2.17.

Table 2.16 Possible indicator behavior for two consecutive maturity state transitions. A "+" means the indicator rises significantly from two former to the latter, a "-" means the indicator decreases, and a "0" means it remains at a similar level before and after the transition

t_1	t_2
0	0
+	0
-	0
0	+
+	+
-	+
0	-
+	-
-	-

Table 2.17 Possible indicator behavior for three consecutive maturity state transitions

t_1	t_2	t_3
0	0	0
+	0	0
-	0	0
0	+	0
+	+	0
-	+	0
0	-	0
+	-	0
-	-	0
0	0	+
+	0	+
-	0	+
0	+	+
+	+	+
-	+	+
0	-	+
+	-	+
-	-	+

0	0	-
+	0	-
-	0	-
0	+	-
+	+	-
-	+	-
0	-	-
+	-	-
-	-	-

Still, the indicator has to show an alternating behavior to be useful for identifying all three transitions. This is again only true for two of the combinations $(+; -; +), (-; +; -)$. In fact, it remains true for any number of additional states, making it less and less probable for an indicator to correctly differentiate between states the more states there are.

In summary, for absolute (non-normalized) values, where the actual value during a maturity state is unknown, only an indicator which significantly alternates between low and high values is suitable for differentiation of all states. This is true for any technology maturity indicator, not just those presented in this section. Increasingly complex indicator behavior is necessary for state assessment in a model with increased granularity based on a single indicator. A maturity assessment based on a single indicator with known indicator value change direction for each maturity state transition, as described in tables 2.16 and 2.17 is therefore only suitable for models with a low granularity. For maturity models with a number of different maturity states, indicator combination may be a viable solution, if the indicators to be combined are not correlated.

2.3.5.2 Adding Robustness by Using Indicators for Tasks Where They are Strong

Section 2.3.5.1 concludes that single indicators are only useful for maturity models with relatively few states and that a combination of indicators is sensible for more complex models. This section discusses additional reasons for and approaches to indicator combination. Single indicators may be able to discriminate between a progression of maturity states. If the indicators only have maturity information available for a part of the lifetime of a technology, maturity state estimation may not be possible. Also, a single indicator is prone to error. For example if an indicator shows an uncommon behavior and the signal is interpreted wrongly, a wrong reaction may be triggered.

Moreover, most indicators work well for the discrimination of some states, but not so well for others. For either of such cases it is much more sensible to consider a combination of indicators. If an indicator is strong in discriminating certain states but weak for others, it can be used where it is strong and omitted where it is weak. If several indicators are strong in identifying a certain pair of states, they can be used for redundant information to strengthen the reliability further. Alternatively the information source which can be accessed more conveniently or the indicator which can be calculated more easily can be used exclusively, and the other one as a backup.

Fig. 2.31 Linear model as interpreted by Martino (2003)

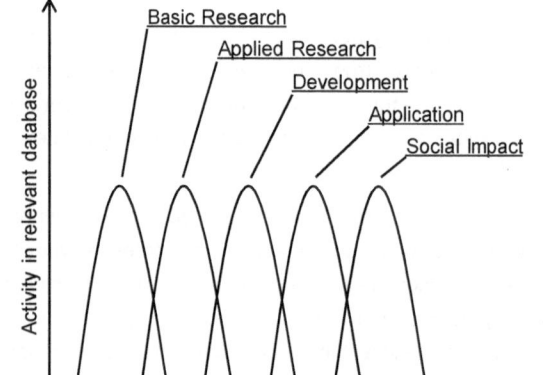

This has been recognized in technology maturity research just as for other disciplines, and it is reflected e.g. in information diffusion models like the one by WATTS & PORTER (Watts & Porter 1997), as interpreted by MARTINO (Martino 2003) in figure 2.31 and JÄRVENPÄÄ (Järvenpää 2009). They state that certain activity is triggered by a certain maturity state, thus being able to indicate this state very exactly, but no other state at all. They can be considered "locally precise". Their development hypotheses refer to a curve point sequence as displayed in figure 2.32. An overview of assumptions made by different authors concerning this particular model is given in table 2.18. All fixed values are marked by 0 or 1, 0 standing for impossible combinations (first end of publication activity of text medium A, then start of publication activity of text medium A is obviously false), 1 for tautological combinations (first start A, then end A). All other fields are a collection of hypotheses from different research.

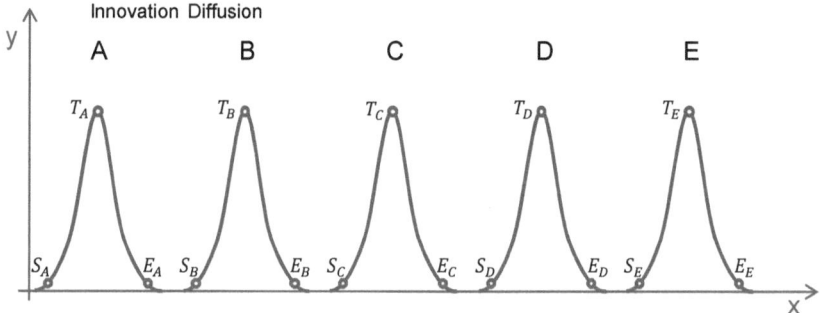

Fig. 2.32 Indicator development throughout the information diffusion process with the publication activity functions of the text media A, B, C, D, and E

JÄRVENPÄÄ only interprets the order of the start points of the curves S_i with $i \in \{A, B, C, D, E\}$ and the following sequence: A $\rightarrow$ B $\rightarrow$ C $\rightarrow$ D $\rightarrow$ E. Transitivity implicates that A $\rightarrow$ C and analogously for the other curves. The Hypotheses by JÄRVENPÄÄ are represented by a **J** in table 2.18. WATTS & PORTER created the disseminating article and explicitly stated that the preceding curve decline before the next one starts. This implies the same order as JÄRVENPÄÄ, but also adds hypotheses for the top points of the curves, which are displayed as a **P** in table 2.18. No statement about curve ends is made. MARTINO takes all assumptions from above and adds in his sketch graphic also end points (see figure 2.31). This may not be meant as a realistic hypothesis, but it will be included in this table represented by an **M**. Certainly table 2.18 is too simplistic to honor the complexity of reality and real-life empirical data does not show similarly accentuated curves (Järvenpää et al. 2011; Järvenpää 2009). However, considering the height and slope of the curves as indicators is a promising approach to form first hypotheses. All hypotheses are tested in section 4.7.5. JÄRVENPÄÄ finds the model to work well for technologies that originate in science (Järvenpää et al. 2011), as suggested earlier by BALCONI et al. (Balconi et al. 2010).

In summary, the start, top and end points of publication activity curves in different media are useful reference points for theoretical indicator combination. More complex indicator behavior, which would allow for a more fine-grained differentiation of maturity states based on a single indicator, may not be fully exploited on this basis. Nevertheless, in combination, simple indicators may match or exceed the granularity of such a complex indicator. At the same time, a combination of indicators is less susceptible to noise and error and therefore more robust. The higher the granularity of a model, the more important is an elaborate approach for indicator combination.

Table 2.18 Indicator curve point progression hypothesized in different approaches: **J** (Järvenpää 2009), **P** (Watts & Porter 1997), **M** (Martino 2003)

The following table is read as "first" (rows) → "then" (columns):

first \ then	S_A	S_B	S_C	S_D	S_E	T_A	T_B	T_C	T_D	T_E	E_A	E_B	E_C	E_D	E_E
S_A	0	J	J	J	J	1	P	P	P	P	1	M	M	M	M
S_B		0	J	J	J		1	P	P	P	M	1	M	M	M
S_C			0	J	J			1	P	P		M	1	M	M
S_D				0	J				1	P			M	1	M
S_E					0					1				M	1
T_A	0	P	P	P	P	0	P	P	P	P	1	M	M	M	M
T_B		0	P	P	P		0	P	P	P		1	M	M	M
T_C			0	P	P			0	P	P			1	M	M
T_D				0	P				0	P				1	M
T_E					0					0					1
E_A	0	M	M	M		0	M	M	M	M	0	M	M	M	M
E_B		0	M	M			0	M	M	M		0	M	M	M
E_C			0	M				0	M	M			0	M	M
E_D				0					0	M				0	M
E_E					0					0					0

2.3.5.3 Selecting a Suitable Approach for Estimating the Technology Maturity State from Indicator Data

What is still missing is a rule base for how indicators behave with technology maturity and how technology maturity can be assessed quantitatively and interpreted by a machine (i.e. a computer). This is what all indicator-based approaches for technology maturity assessment mentioned above have been lacking.

Theoretical technology maturity models provide hypotheses concerning indicator behavior. The existence of these behavior patterns has to be verified in empirical analyses before they can be exploited. There is a large set of approaches from the field of machine-learning fit for this purpose. Machine-learning approaches are able to process large amounts of data, discover patterns in data, and construct so-called classifiers for a desired task. Machine-learning approaches can be divided in unsupervised and supervised learning approaches (Huang et al. 2006, p.2). Unsupervised learning approaches are designed to discover structure in the data (e.g. through a cluster analysis) and are therefore not suited for the task at hand. Supervised learning approaches, on the other hand, are trained on labelled examples, i.e., they work with input data where the desired output is known and generalize the underlying classification rules. In the case of the approach in this book, the label indicators the maturity state. Each maturity state is considered a "group". The supervised learning approach attempts to generalize a function or mapping from inputs to outputs which can then be used to speculatively generate an output for previously unseen inputs the help of the classifier. The approach in this book makes use of supervised learning to enable the connection with existing theoretical maturity models. Figure 2.33 shows a schematic flow chart of such an approach according to BIRD et al. (Bird et al. 2009).

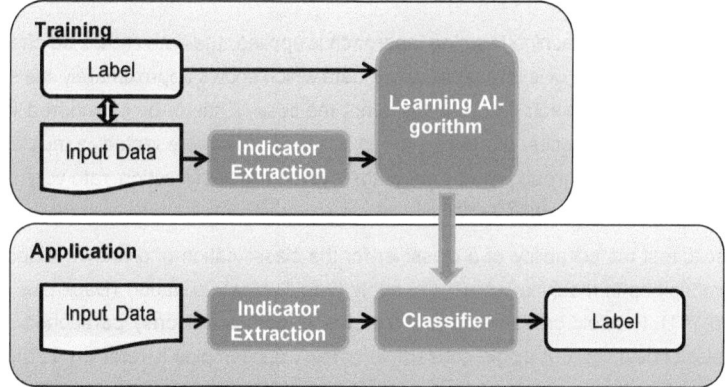

Fig. 2.33 Schematic flow chart of a supervised learning approach

A supervised learning approach is divided in two phases, the training phase and the application or test phase (Hastie et al. 2009, pp.1–8). During the training phase, the approach uses input data or its indicator values and an associated label (of a maturity state) to train a classifier. This classifier is used in the application phase to label previously unseen data. If instead of unseen data, test data with a known label is used, the second phase is also referred to as test phase. During the test phase, the correct label and the label which was assigned by the classifier can be compared. This allows an evaluation of the classifier's performance. The performance of the classifier in large parts depends on the actual learning approach, which thus has to be selected carefully (Hastie et al. 2009, pp.1–8).

The purpose of the machine-learning approach is to combine indicators in a way that they best divide between degrees of maturity. In this respect, general usefulness of indicator sets should be estimated and sets of indicators should be compared. It should be noted, that the indicators are numerical values whereas the dependent variable is a categorical variable. In summary, the learning approach should enable a simple and straight-forward technology maturity assessment.

Parametric machine-learning approaches name certain desirable prerequisites of the data. These often include:

- Independence: the indicator observations are randomly sampled
- Multivariate normality: Each indicator shows a normal distribution for each group
- Homoscedasticity: variance of an indicator are the same for each group (i.e. maturity state)

Before a parametric machine-learning approach is applied, the data should be checked for these. Furthermore, it is advisable to use data which shows approximately the same count of elements for each group. If this is not the case, it has to be considered in the interpretation of the results. If e.g. one group is heavily overrepresented, a misclassification in favor of this group will not affect the overall misclassification rate very much (Backhaus et al. 2003, pp.179–181).

In order to test the suitability of a classifier for the classification of unknown objects, it is commonplace in machine-learning to apply (v-fold) cross validation (Backhaus et al. 2003, p.181). In v-fold cross-validation, the original data is randomly partitioned into v equal size subsamples. A single subsample of the v subsamples is retained as the test data for testing the model, and the remaining $v - 1$ subsamples are used as training set. The cross-validation process is then repeated v times (the *folds*), with each of the v subsamples used exactly once as the test data (see figure 2.34).

data partitioned into 5 subsamples

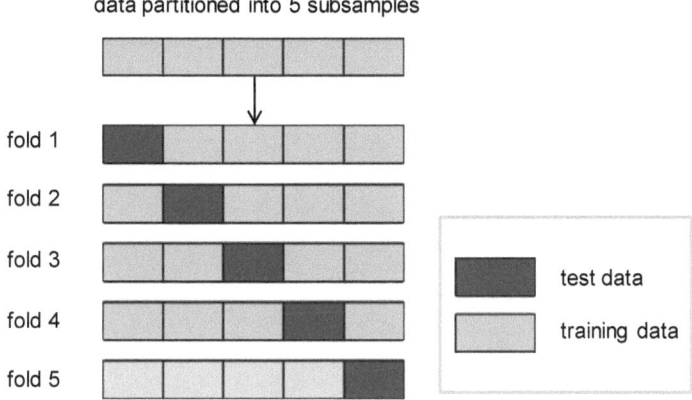

Fig. 2.34 An example of 5-fold cross validation

This setup allows building a classifier as described above from part of the training set and using the remaining data as test data in prediction v times, each time with independent training and test sets while still using the entire data for training and testing. The label results of the prediction process are then compared to the original label. A standard method for doing this is a confusion matrix, also called contingency table. Each column of the matrix represents the instances in a predicted group, while each row represents the instances in an actual group. The advantage of this is, that the maturity states are on an ordinal scale. A confusion matrix allows to intuitively differentiate neighboring states, which represent only a "small error", from groups which lie further away. For an even more compact form, (Backhaus et al. 2003, pp.179–181) propose calculation of the misclassification rate $Err^*(y)$ according to formula (2.5).

$$Err^*(y) = \frac{Number\ of\ incorrect\ classifications}{Total\ number\ of\ classifications}$$

The drawback of this is, that the information about the intensity of a misclassification is lost: It does not make a difference whether a technology in the emergence state is classified as one that is in the growth state or in the decline state anymore, although the former is a much less grave mistake than the latter.

This paragraph concludes the theoretical considerations of the approach in this book. The following sections describe an empirical analysis which is designed and performed based on these considerations.

3 Designing an Empirical Analysis

In the past section 2, theoretical foundations of strategic technology management were summarized and the need for technology maturity assessment was justified. The S&D model was presented as an example of a (semi)theoretical technology maturity model. It was compared to many other such models, and it was prepared for operationalization. For this operationalization, an operationalization mechanism was presented with which several factors of the S&D model and similar models can be operationalized based on the publication activity in text media databases. A number of such text media have also been presented. Now an empirical analysis becomes necessary to evaluate the operationalized model.

This section presents the empirical part of the approach in this book. It shows the design of an empirical analysis suited to estimate technology maturity empirically based on the S&D model. This section consecutively defines the goals of this analysis, produces an appropriate empirical design which especially comprises the selection of suitable technologies as cases as well as the necessary data collection and statistical analyses, and specifies performance measures suited to test its results. The analysis is structured loosely along the lines of the nine-step data analysis approach by PORTER & CUNNINGHAM as listed in table 3.1.

Table 3.1 The nine-step data analysis process by (Porter & Cunningham 2005, p.323) serves to structure the data-driven analysis

Nine-step data analysis process
1. Issue identification
2. Selection of information sources
3. Search refinement and data retrieval
4. Data cleaning
5. Basic analyses
6. Advanced analyses
7. Representation
8. Interpretation
9. Utilization

A flow chart of the analysis is depicted in figure 3.1.

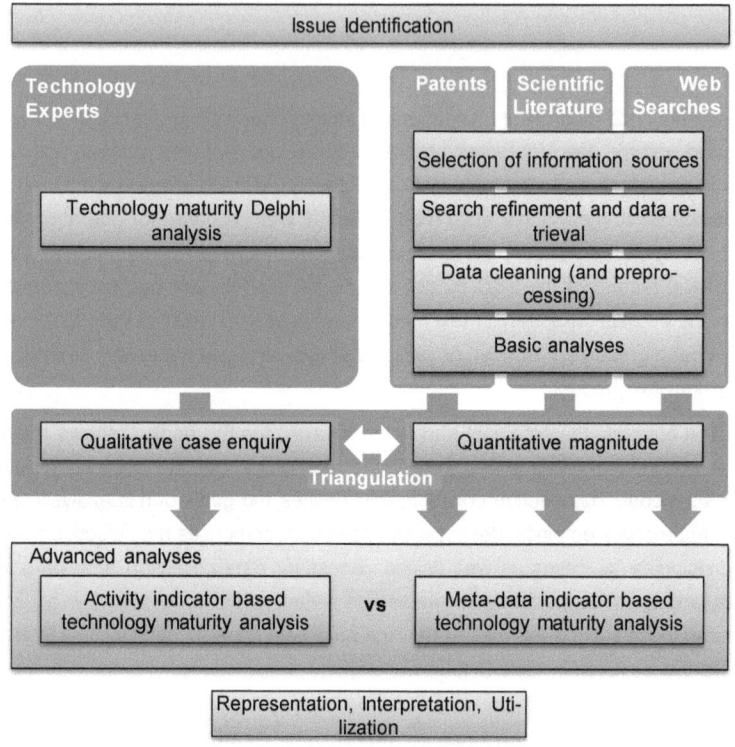

Fig. 3.1 Analysis design flow chart

It is designed as follows: during an early **issue identification** step a number of technologies for maturity assessment are selected and defined. For the analysis, cases (i.e. technologies) are selected in the light of the research question "**How should an approach be constructed with which existing theoretical maturity models can be operationalized to allow for valid, reliable, objective and useful statements regarding the maturity of a technology?**".

Since the cases serve to illuminate technology maturity, a longitudinal analysis design seems appropriate. According to Yɪɴ, a single case is a common and suitable design for longitudinal case studies (Yin 2013, pp.49, 52). This single case will consist of a technology application with a number of its generations from different paradigms as defined by TAYLOR & TAYLOR (Taylor & Taylor 2012) and in section 0. Despite being designed as a single case, this thus represents an approach according to the "diverse" method as described in SEAWRIGHT & GERRING: the selected cases are likely to represent the full variation of maturity development in the population (Seawright & Gerring 2008, pp.297–301). This leads to a maximum variance along the relevant dimensions, i.e. the assumed technology maturity indicators. To identify fitting technologies for the diverse method, the technologies all represent different paradigms and generations of the same technology application. On top of realizing the diverse method, this approach has several practical advantages over one where the technologies are not related:

- It only takes one set of technology experts to evaluate technology maturity for all technologies, effectively eliminating coordination/communication effort between experts from different fields.
- It resorts to only one technology application, i.e. one normalization basis, and therefore does not require formal definition of additional applications and corresponding data retrieval and cleaning. This also prevents an otherwise very likely inappropriately sized normalization basis for the comparison between different technology applications.
- It also sheds light on whether maturity indicators remain valid over long periods of time.

There is unfortunately also a severe disadvantage connected to this approach: It cannot be verified whether the resulting operationalized technology maturity model can be used for technology applications outside of the case in consideration. However, although it may not be universally valid, it may be assumed that other technologies which originate from the same driver, i.e. science, follow a similar pattern and work relatively well with the resulting classifier (Balconi et al. 2010). Testing this may be subject of subsequent research.

Following issue identification, a technology expert-based and an indicator-based approach serve to assess technology maturity of the sample technologies, effectively representing two of six sources of evidence according to YIN (Yin 2013, pp.101–109): archival records and interviews. To date, no definitive approved approach for expert-based technology maturity assessment exists. Therefore the **Delphi method** such as described in GARSON (2013) was conducted and provides the maturity information for all technologies during each year of the analysis (Garson 2013). The indicator-based approach depends on different text media types, namely patents, scientific literature, and web search. The first step of this approach serves to **identify suitable infor-**

mation sources, which is actual databases rather than just media types. Subsequently, the alternating functions of **search refinement and data retrieval** are handled. They follow the purpose of providing a sound information basis for the subsequent steps by developing a suitable search strategy per technology and information source. **Data cleaning and preprocessing** is covered in the same section, as the search strategy is expected to produce sufficiently clean data. Due to the chosen approach, redundancy and unnecessary variations are not a problem in the data. The **basic analyses** include descriptive statistics of the information sources in general and the technology application and generations in detail.

To prevent criticism that the approach in this book only intends to reproduce expert opinion, an additional step outside of the PORTER & CUNNINGHAM data analysis approach is included to increase its validity. It describes the **methodological triangulation** of the expert-based and the indicator-based approach. This step intends to solve the question to what extent expert and indicator-based approach results coincide if considered separately.

Table 3.2 The advanced analyses comprise several analyses to check whether the data fulfills the necessary properties for the machine-learning based analysis to work properly, other analyses to prepare the data for the machine-learning approach as well as to actually conduct it

Step	Method	Result
i. Calculate and compile data sets		One data set per year and technology
ii. Define maturity states	Delphi method	Data sets with group label
iii. Indicator selection	Wilcoxon-Mann-Whitney, Kruskal-Wallis, Random forest	Indicator ranking and best indicator combination
iv. Assess approach assumptions	Box's M, Shapiro-Wilk, Levene's Test, boxplots	Statement: which analyses is the data suitable for?
v. Use data sets to train classifier in R	Linear discriminant analysis (LDA)	Classification functions (classifier)
vi. Test discriminative value of classifier	Repeated V-fold cross validation	Misclassification rate of classifier

The more elaborate **advanced analyses** comprise the actual indicator-based supervised machine-learning based maturity assessment. It consists of several steps as shown in figure 2.33 (Schematic flow chart of a supervised machine learning approach) and table 3.2. The goal of these analyses is to generate an ubiquitous operationalized model for technology maturity assessment.

In *step i.*, all indicator values are calculated and compiled in a set for each year and each technology. In *step ii.* these indicator data sets are labeled with the results from the Delphi method which is also available for each year and each technology. Since the discriminative value of each indicator is unknown, *step iii.* applies a pair-wise Wilcoxon-Mann-Whitney test for each sensible maturity state transition and a reverse feature elimination step based on random forests. The outcome is a preliminary idea of how valuable each indicator is by itself and in combination for assessing technology maturity. This provides the chance to exclude less valuable or redundant indicators, thus streamlining the analysis. During *step iv.*, the assumptions of subsequent analyses are tested. This includes especially the assumptions of normality and homoscedasticity of most parametric analyses which can be used as a machine-learning approach. In *step v.* the labeled indicator data sets from step ii. are used as input data for a linear discriminant analysis to determine a technology maturity classifier. In *step vi.* finally, the accuracy of the classifier from step v. is evaluated. Obviously, the same data can not be used to train the learning approach and to test it. A repeated cross validation is performed to obtain suitable test data. To benchmark the quality of the activity maturity indicators developed in section 2.3.5.1, the results of steps v. and vi. are contrasted to those of a set of well-established and tested patent meta data maturity indicators described in HAUPT et al. (Haupt et al. 2007).

Finally, the usefulness of the results is illuminated during the steps of **representation, interpretation, and utilization**, which put the results to use by applying the S&D model as described in section 2.1.

4 Execution and Results of the Empirical Analysis

The analysis design has been clarified and justified in section 0. Section 0 describes in detail how each step of the analysis was carried out and what its results were.

The tools used in this analysis include the open source statistical software R in its release x64 3.1.1 (2014-07-10). R was used for implementing the different statistical analyses and handling larger data volumes. Eclipse Kepler Edition was used as a debugging environment of the R code. Excel 2010 was used for quick data collection and exploration, transformation, and processing of smaller data volumes.

In section 4.1, issues are identified. This means that a number of technologies for maturity assessment are selected and defined. Section 4.2 describes the expert-based approach to technology maturity assessment. It consists of the Delphi method which serves to estimate maturity states for each technology in each year based on expert evaluation. The following section 4.3 identifies suitable information sources, which are actual databases rather than just media types. In section 4.4 the alternating steps of search refinement and data retrieval are dealt with. Data cleaning is covered in the same section. The basic analyses described in section 4.5 include descriptive statistics of the information sources in general and the technology application and generations in detail. Section 4.6 describes the methodological triangulation of the expert-based approach and the indicator-based approach. In section 4.7 the advanced analyses are described, essentially presenting an operationalized S&D model. In section 4.8, finally, the usefulness of the results of the approach presented in this book is explained during the steps of representation, interpretation, and utilization.

4.1 Issue Identification

The first step of the analysis design sketched in figure 3.1 is the issue identification. This step lays the foundation for the data collection as it outlines working definitions of the technology application and several technology generations as defined by TAYLOR & TAYLOR (Taylor & Taylor 2012) and in section 0, to generate the data necessary for a longitudinal case study according to YIN (Yin 2013, pp.49, 52). These definitions must serve as an unambiguous technology delineation for the expert-based approach in section 4.2 as well as for the generation of search strategies in section 4.4 to ensure that both refer to the same subject matter.

In this analysis, the technology application was selected to be non-volatile, machine-readable data storage because it fulfills certain properties which are advantageous for an analysis (compare CHRISTENSEN on fruit flies and disc drives (Christensen, 2013, chapter one)):

- It has spawned many different clearly distinguishable paradigms and generations. Technology experts thus have a relatively clear and consistent idea of how mature separate generations are.
- Many of its generations have passed through all maturity states in the time period under consideration. This provides a rich information basis for an analysis.
- It is the basis for a number of mass consumer products. This generates rich feedback in the social media because it is of interest also for technology laymen.

Non-volatile memory does not lose stored information when its power is turned off. Machine-readable media are able to store data in a format optimized to be read by machines (in contrast to a printed book, for example, which is specifically designed to be read by a human). The actual technologies which were subject to the research can be found in table 4.1.

Defining explicit technology generations is easier than defining a generic technology application, because technology generations usually are connected to certain media with a definitive name. A technology application constitutes a superordinate concept for its every single technology generation. Instead of carefully delineating all technology traits, a historical sequence of the technology generations will therefore suffice to tell them apart. In the beginning, machine readable information was stored mechanically in the forms of pins and holes on paper *punched cards* or *perforated tape*. A first paradigm change took place when punched cards were replaced by *magnetic tape* and *floppy discs* as well as *hard discs* which stored the information magnetically rather than mechanically. Later, after a transition phase of the magneto-optical *MiniDisc*, optical memory became available in the form of *Compact Discs* (CDs), later *Digital Versatile Discs* (DVDs), *Blu-rays*, and *High Definition Digital Versatile Discs* (HD-DVDs). In the past few years, non-volatile semiconductor memory has increasingly penetrated the market in the form of USB sticks and memory cards. Both are forms of so-called *Non-Volatile Random-Access Memory* (NVRAM). *Resistive random-access memory* (ReRAM or RRAM) has been speculated to eventually replace NVRAM as the next generation data storage technology in the past years (Stammers & Robinson 2014; Halfacree 2013; Hruska 2013) and are therefore also included in the analysis.

Table 4.1 Generations and corresponding paradigms of the analyzed data storage technologies

Generation	Paradigm
punched card	mechanic
perforated tape	mechanic
magnetic tape	magnetic
floppy disc	magnetic
hard disc	magnetic
MiniDisc	magneto-optic
Compact Disc	optic
Digital Versatile Disc	optic
Blu-ray	optic
HD-DVD	optic
NVRAM	electronic
ReRAM	electronic

As stated by TAYLOR & TAYLOR, it is important to understand a technology's environment to know what certain development patterns mean (Taylor & Taylor 2012). The selected technologies offer a copious overview of data storage technologies. This includes most technology's past, current, and future competing paradigms and generations. What becomes obvious is that the TAYLOR & TAYLOR differentiation of paradigm and generation is rather random because the granularity of it is arbitrary. The application can be formulated to encompass only the former generation (storing data on a magnetic tape), and the entire point of view is shifted as can be seen in this example:

- data storage (application)
- magnetic (paradigm)
- magnetic tape (generation)
- compact cassette
- Type II (chromium oxide)
- TDK SA
- C90 (45 minutes per side)

This is also a problem in the approach presented in this book, because the selected technologies may not be on the same level (e.g. the very narrowly defined compact disc and the very broad hard disc). Still, the hierarchical differentiation helps very much in delineating and clustering different approaches to a certain application. If necessary, the current system could be extended by a fourth level such as "manifestation". This is subject to future research.

4.2 Using the Delphi Method for Letting Experts Typify Technology Maturity

Each sample technology application was typified according to its maturity over the course of time. The goal is to pinpoint maturity changes based on the S&D model. The main challenge is that the S&D model is subject to the interpretation of experts. Each expert may interpret the model and the weight of its latent variables differently. And so this needs to be synchronized. To avoid a dominant personality among the experts influencing the overall outcome of the interpretation, intensive talk among experts had to be prevented. This can be accomplished with the Delphi method. The method furthermore eliminates certain weaknesses of conventional interviews such as response bias, inaccuracies due to poor recall, and reflexivity (Yin 2013, p.102).

The Delphi method was originally intended as a forecasting tool (Dalkey & Helmer 1963). In its original purpose it is used to test whether among diverse experts consensus can be achieved regarding the probability of a certain future development. In this analysis its consensus finding rather than its consensus testing properties will be applied for consensus finding in a group of experts regarding the maturity state of the selected technology applications over the past years. The approach includes a series of questionnaires interspersed with a controlled opinion feedback. The advantage of the Delphi method in this case is that experts are expected to be willing to deviate more from their original response if they are less familiar with it. This eventually leads to the "correct" response.

The Delphi method is constructed of the steps shown in figure 4.1 (Hsueh 2013): after the problem has been defined, a panel of experts is composed. They are provided with a questionnaire which surveys the relevant information. Once the experts gave their replies, the responses are analyzed. If no satisfactory consensus has been reached, the responses are pooled along with all additional information which was deemed relevant by the experts. Both are then spread out to the experts again, along with a new questionnaire, in another round of the Delphi method. Once a consensus has been reached, the results are evaluated.

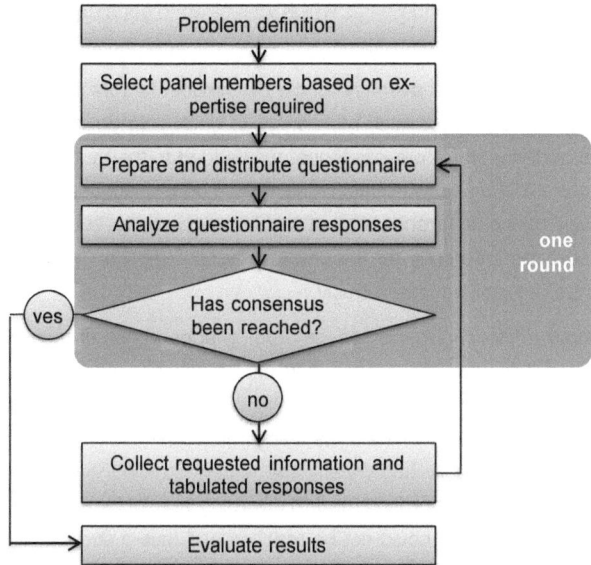

Fig. 4.1 Steps of the Delphi Method as described e.g. by HSUEH (2013)

As required in section 2.3.5.3 on training and test sets for supervised learning, each technology was assigned maturity states for each year from 1976 onwards. The approach in this work relies on independent expert valuation to assign these values.

A number of experts were selected especially for having worked with a distributed share of the different technologies. This was achieved by consulting experts who had worked intensively on and with data storage technologies during different time periods. The experts did not work on each technology with the same intensity, and all had a professional focus on a different technology, but all experts had dealt to some extent with all of the selected technologies at some point. Where necessary, they were willing to research the technologies further. This setup provided for the entire span of expertise to be covered extensively. This is also well reflected in the age of the experts. In total, a number of four experts were deemed sufficient to cover the relevant time period with significant overlap of the use of the different technologies to ensure diverse opinions. The oldest of them was born in 1940, one in 1970, one in 1980, the youngest in 1990. The oldest retired in 2005, all others currently still actively work professionally on and with data storage technology.

The original questionnaire and information basis which was given to each expert in the first round is provided in the Annex.

The experts were provided with a short overview of the S&D model factors in table 2.5 and asked to assign maturity states for each technology to each year between 1976 until now. An additional maturity state "pre-existence" was added to the model to also cover the time span before a technology existed. The S&D model describes different factors and their behavior during different states of technology maturity. It turned out that the factors behaved quite differently for the different technologies and that state limits could not always be determined unanimously.

In detail, all questionnaires differed in respect to the order of appearance of technologies to avoid any bias resulting from the order. Each expert was provided with data which according to the S&D model may be relevant for maturity typification (namely: patent and literature publication volumes as well as web search query volumes). Internet usage was explicitly suggested to accompany the expert knowledge of the respondents. In summary, the first Delphi round lead to diverging results by as much as 10 years for single states. Consensus could not be reached and thus a second round was conducted.

In the second round the experts relied more on their professional and personal experience to complement and integrate better the individual indicators given by the S&D model. Also, two kinds of information were given to the experts between the rounds: available data requested by any of the experts, and factors and considerations suggested as potentially relevant by any of them, especially websites. During their internet searches, the experts mainly looked up press releases on political or business decisions which marked important dates in the maturity of a technology (e.g. the decision by Toshiba to discontinue its HD-DVD related development as described in http://moviemet.com/news/breaking-news-toshiba-announces). This mode of controlled interaction serves to avoid the disadvantages of more direct interaction between experts. This was the original intention of the Delphi method (Dalkey & Helmer 1963). This round produced much more homogeneous results than the first round. The resulting maturity values were largely identical and maturity state changes differed by three years at most.

The arithmetic average of the years during which a maturity state change took place served to estimate each maturity state change. No "rejuvenation" in maturity was identified by any of the experts. Table 4.2 shows the years which were estimated by the experts as the first during which a technology entered a new state of maturity. The table covers changes during the years 1976-2012. For the years between 1976 and the first year mentioned for a technology, the state before that is valid. The table states, for example, that the punched card technology entered the decline state in 1978. This means that during the years 1976 until 1977 it was still in the saturation state. The table does not make statements regarding technology maturity states before the year 1976. The pre-existence state is not explicitly mentioned in the table because it does not have a predecessor and simply is assigned to all years before the first year of emergence.

Table 4.2 Overview of data storage technologies and expert assigned maturity states in the time period between 1976 and 2012. The progression of maturity states is pre-existence → emergence → growth → saturation → decline. The years in the table mark the first year during which a technology changes from the antecedent technology state to the one in the observed column

	emergence	growth	saturation	decline
PunchedCard				1978
PerforatedTape				1977
MagneticTape				2005
FloppyDisc		1980	1987	2000
MiniDisc	1988	1993	1995	2000
HardDisc		1983	1994	2010
CompactDisc		1985	1999	2003
DVD	1996	2000	2003	2007
Blu-ray	2002	2007	2011	
HD-DVD	2003	2007		2008
NVRAM	1993	1999	2011	
ReRAM	2010			

During each year, each technology is in a certain maturity state, that is to say, the floppy disc technology has remained in the emergence state for four years, in the growth state for seven years, in the saturation state for three years, and in the decline state for 13 years. The number of years in which all technologies spend in a certain maturity state can be summed up. When this is done for all maturity states, a distribution of maturity states is displayed where some states are represented more often than others.

The distribution of the maturity states during the years 1976-2012 displayed in table 4.3 shows a slight bias towards the states pre-existence and decline, whereas the remaining states have a similar distribution. The reason for this is probably the long time span, which allows for technologies to pass all maturity states. Technologies remain in the pre-existence state until they are invented and they typically remain in the decline state once they have entered it. The states at the beginning and the end of a technology's relevance are therefore slightly overrepresented.

Table 4.3 Distribution of maturity states for all technologies during the years 1976 - 2012

pre-existence	emergence	growth	saturation	decline
31%	11%	13%	17%	28%

For the short time span during which web search volumes have been available, only the six technologies which change maturity states in this time are analyzed in section 4.7 which relies on the results of the Delphi method performed in this section. This was done to avoid a bias towards the later states in the data. The states are distributed rather equally for the technologies which change maturity state between 2004 and 2012[3], as can be seen in table 4.4.

Table 4.4 Distribution of maturity states for technologies which change maturity state during the years 2004 - 2012

pre-existence	emergence	growth	saturation	decline
10.4%	14.6%	22.9%	22.9%	29.2%

In summary, the sample technologies are distributed in a balanced manner across all maturity states. The selected sample technologies were relevant throughout the entire time span which has been taken into consideration – thus the low pre-existence and decline state shares. The emergence state is generally short in comparison to the growth and saturation states. It is important to note that when a currently existing technology is assessed, the additional pre-existence state is an improbable outcome. This may make it seem like a superfluous maturity state to collect data on because nobody can know about a technology before it actually exists. Therefore we could consider dropping any data collected during years in which a technology was estimated in this section to be in the pre-existence state. The data on a pre-existing technology will be sparse at most since technologies which do not exist can, of course, neither be patented nor described in scientific publications. However, when a learning approach is able to have this state as its outcome, it can be used for monitoring a technology over

---

[3] A time period after the year 2004 was selected, because web search data is available starting in that year.

a period of time and possibly identify the transition from pre-existence to emergence, which is obviously very important. The pre-existence state will therefore remain part of the maturity model presented here.

As a side result of the Delphi method, the shortcomings of the S&D model's factors were discussed. It seems that the descriptions of the factors during each maturity state are too general/vague. Its results are in large part subjective and depend on which factor of the model is deemed most important for maturity assessment. They thus can be altered within a wide frame of personal opinion. This leads to a low convergence validity and thus construct validity. One could argue the approach in this book only tries to reproduce expert opinion, and since expert opinion is subjective, it is an imperfect rule base for a machine-learning approach. This is a sound plea. However, the approach in this book is also trying to set a new standard of objectivity which is based on the fuzzy theoretical rule base of the S&D model. Expert opinion is subjective, but homogenized expert interpretation of theoretical model rules enhances the (outer) criterion validity. The resulting machine-learning approach is therefore actually based on solid expert opinion derived with the Delphi method.

4.3 Selection of Data Sources

Text media types were described in the sections 2.3.3.2 and 2.3.3.3 and assigned to indicators in table 2.13 of section 2.3.3.4. Text media databases provide collections of documents of such media types. These databases serve as data sources from which the desired information can subsequently be deduced. The present section will present how the data sources were selected.

Data sources were selected in a fashion that the information contained in them allows for a view of the technology push and the market pull side. Therefore patents and scientific literature were contrasted by online search trends. Important properties along the lines of PORTER & CUNNINGHAM are discussed for each source below (Porter & Cunningham 2005, pp.69–94):

- The data sources should be based on a sufficiently large fraction of the population to produce reliable results with the lowest possible bias.
- The data should be current and frequently updated.
- It should be accessible via an advanced search functionality allowing for nested searches, negation, wild cards, proximity searches, and similar features to enable a good fit between precision and recall.

o Precision checks should be conducted easily. When, for example, title and abstract can be easily accessed, the relevance of an article quickly becomes obvious.

o Recall checks are harder to conduct. Even though the overall precision of the results may be high, important keywords or document classes (especially IPC for patents) may have been missed. Relying exclusively on such document classes should be avoided to prevent a poor recall because documents may not be classified completely at time of submission; there may be classification errors, and there may be classes which are hard to recognize as being potentially relevant (e.g. IPC class 0). There are recall evaluation scores available for collections in which documents possess a fractional relevance and must be put in the right order (Magdy & Jones 2010). However, in this application a Boolean relevance is required, which makes this type of approach unfeasible. Instead, a reasonable total of relevant documents in a database can be estimated based on assumptions made with knowledge about a technology generation. This is supported further by knowing the approximate total of relevant documents of one or several other technology generations serving the same application.

- Finally, the data should be accessible at a reasonable effort. If data collection and preparation requires substantial time and effort, it may be expedient to research and rely on alternative data sources.

Out of the rich variety of text media, different research describes different approaches to track information diffusion. WATTS & PORTER describe the use of explicit databases which are supposed to represent life cycle stages. They propose the activity in the science citation index, engineering index, US patents, newspaper abstracts daily, and business and popular press databases should be used to represent each one of five states in their technology maturity model (Watts & Porter 1997). JÄRVENPÄÄ et al. tested this approach empirically with a selection or all of the named sources and eventually were able to present visual evidence which hints towards meaningful patterns, at least for technologies which originated in science (Järvenpää et al. 2011; Järvenpää 2009; Järvenpää & Mäkinen 2008b). Precisely delimited expert databases allow for a relatively exact placement in the defined maturity states. Instead of deriving the current state of maturity directly from the activity in a particular database, the approach in this book intends to assess the current maturity based on the information in a number of different databases. Unfortunately the data sources described above were not available for the approach in this book, but since a direct link between the activity in a single database and a maturity state is not being made, less specialized databases in combination may deliver sufficiently precise information. More specialized databases may be desirable for future research if the precision of the results from the approach in this book proves to be insufficient. With this in mind, the following sources were selected:

US Patent Data (USPTO) and International Patent Data (DWPI Thomson Innovation)

Patents are in the center of attention for various reasons best described in section 2.3.3.2. But which patent database is best suited for the purpose of a large scale technology analysis? Currently the most influential patent system is located in the United States. The relevant USPTO data can be directly downloaded from the USPTO website free of charge. This may be a major reason for the popularity of this data. Many chose only US patents for reasons of accessibility, availability, ease of use, low cost, and relatively good representation of the technological developments throughout the world. This approach naturally generates a bias towards the US situation. The robustness of the results can thus far only be assumed. Therefore, data from an international patent database will be juxtaposed to the US patent data in this empirical analysis.

The approach in this book relies on international patent data provided by Thomson Scientific. Thomson provides patents from 48 different patent-issuing authorities worldwide. These authorities normally publish patents in their national language. This makes it hard to retrieve the relevant documents with a keyword-based search strategy. The firm Derwent provides translations of the patent data within the Thomson Scientific platform to a certain extent at additional cost. To avoid having to translate every single patent, Derwent forms patent families (i.e. patents which protect the same invention in different countries) and translates just one patent to represent the entire family. Even patents written in English are "translated", which ensures a homogeneous language throughout all patents. Two types of patents become part of such a DWPI patent family: Those referring to the same priority. And those which are more than twelve months older than the priority, and therefore cannot refer to it, but disclose the same subject matter as the original record and belong to the same applicant (Intellogist 2013).

Despite patent families being formed, a search in the Thomson Scientific data typically produces more results than a simple USPTO search. Depending on the calculation basis, this international approach requires much more calculation time. It may not be worth the effort, if the USPTO data provides the same signals. It will be one of the tasks of the following empirical analysis to determine whether US and international patent data provides complementary maturity information or can be seen as redundant.

Both databases allow complex and nested searches with logical combination, wildcard, and proximity operators. Keyword-based and IPC- or CPC-based searches are possible. The USPTO patent full text is accessible free of charge which enables precision checks of a search.

Scientific Literature (Science Direct)

Literature, as defined in section 2.3.3.2, is taken from the internationally renowned Dutch publisher Elsevier via its ScienceDirect service. ScienceDirect is one of the biggest scientific literature databases, others being, for example, Thomson Reuters' Web of Knowledge or Springer's SpringerLink. A combination of all of these databases would be ideal because none is exhaustive. Combination of retrieved data is complex, however, because duplicates need to be eliminated, which requires comprehensive downloads and an elaborate data cleaning process step. This is the reason why a single data base is regarded as sufficient for the purpose at hand.

ScienceDirect provides about 11 million articles from 2,500 international journals and 6,000 e-books, reference works, book series and handbooks (March 2013). The articles are recruited from four main fields:

- Physical Sciences and Engineering
- Life Sciences
- Health Sciences
- Social Sciences and Humanities

The search mask allows complex and nested searches with logical combination, wildcard, and proximity operators. Advanced search functionality provides useful metadata filters such as limit by year etc.

For most documents on the website, abstracts are freely available; the full text of individual documents can be purchased. This makes precision checks possible.

Web Search Queries (Google Trends)

At the time this research was conducted, Google Trends was the only source of web search data openly available. The choice is therefore made easy, even though some drawbacks have to be taken into consideration. It has been shown in different research that the data delivers an added value for the so-called "nowcasting", that is, drawing a picture of current events based on data (Carrière-Swallow & Labbé 2013; Kauffman et al. 2013; Choi & Varian 2012; Carneiro & Mylonakis 2009).

Whenever someone runs a web search query in Google, every single search query is recorded. This data can be accessed, but it comes heavily normalized: when a technology relevant search term is entered into Google Trends, it is juxtaposed with all searches in a given timeframe (a day). The highest fraction of relevant searches of all time is set to 100%. All other searches are scaled accordingly. This quota can be downloaded and will be used in this analysis. It shows the change in relative relevance of a subject.

Unfortunately, the exact normalization happens as a black box and no absolute numbers are provided. Workarounds do exist but are rather rough and it is unknown how well they perform in practice (Bauckhage 2011a; Bauckhage 2011b). In-tool-comparisons of multiple technologies should be avoided because they are then used by Google for an additional in-timespan normalization. Instead, each technology should be analyzed separately. This requires the analyst to download all relevant data for each single technology trend one at a time. It can then be compared with the approaches described in section 2.3.5.

As stated before in section 2.3.3.3, the Google Trends service offers a powerful web usage analysis tool. It is known to produce a bias towards countries where the service is mostly used, and omits other important countries such as China or Brazil. However, it is still widely used and gives a good general idea of current consumer situation. It thus represents the market pull side of a technology.

Relevance checks are hard to perform because it would be necessary to know what each user actually was looking for. Instead a regular Google search can serve to understand what was retrieved. Certain phenomena like homonyms can be identified in this manner. For example, a search for "pacemaker" returns results for cardiac pacemaker technology as well as the band "Gerry and the pacemakers". In such a case, the search strategy should be updated in order to restrict the search to "cardiac pacemaker" instead. This new search strategy will possibly exclude some relevant searches from the results, but since only relative data is made available, precision is more important in this case. Google offers categories which help categorize the searches more, but these will not be used as they represent another "black box".

It is important to note that Google Trends data is available from 2004 onwards. This means that no data is available for the years 1976 – 2003.

4.4 Search Refinement, Data Retrieval, and Data Cleaning

A mixed search with document classifications (where available) and keywords was conducted to identify relevant documents and is displayed in table 4.5. This table shows search strategies for technology paradigms and generations. The complexity[4] of the search strategies is relatively low. The technology generation rows are listed below the corresponding technology paradigm rows. Defining a search strategy for the corresponding technology paradigm on top of the search strategies for the technology generations defines an upper boundary for potentially relevant documents and therefore is able to give a rough idea of the recall. This mechanism is applied in the subsequent section 4.5.

Table 4.5 Technology search strategies for the USPTO data is based on a mixed strategy of classifications and keywords. It looks similar for the other databases

Paradigm	Generation	US Patent Search Strategy
mechanic		ICL/G06K001/02 OR ICL/G06K001/04 OR ICL/G06K001/05 OR ICL/G06K001/06 OR ICL/G06K001/08 OR ICL/G06K001/10 OR ICL/G06K001/16 OR ICL/G06K001/18 OR ICL/G06K013/$ OR ICL/G06K021/$
	punched card	TTL/("punch card" OR "punched card" OR "punchcard") OR ABST/("punch card" OR "punched card" OR "punchcard") OR ICL/G06K013/02 OR ICL/G06K013/04 OR ICL/G06K013/06$ OR ICL/G06K013/07$ OR ICL/G06K013/08 OR ICL/G06K013/16 OR ICL/G06K001/08 OR ICL/G06K001/16 OR ICL/G06K021/$
	perforated tape	TTL/("punch tape" OR "punched tape" OR "perforated tape" OR "perforation tape") OR ABST/("punch tape" OR "punched tape" OR "perforated tape" OR "perforation tape") OR ICL/G06K013/18 OR ICL/G06K013/20 OR ICL/G06K013/24 OR ICL/G06K013/26 OR ICL/G06K001/10

---

[4] The complexity of a search strategy is the minimum amount of information required to represent it (Kurzweil 2005, p.43).

magnetic		ICL/G11B005$ OR ICL/G11C011/0$ OR ICL/G11C011/10 OR ICL/G11C011/12 OR ICL/G11C011/14 OR ICL/G11C011/15$ OR ICL/G11C011/16 OR ICL/G11C015/02
	magnetic tape	TTL/("magnetic tape" OR "magnetized tape" OR "magnet tape") OR ABST/("magnetic tape" OR "magnetized tape" OR "magnet tape") OR ICL/G11B005/008 OR ICL/G11B005/584 OR ICL/G11B005/588 OR ICL/G11B005/592 OR ICL/G11B005/627 OR ICL/G11B005/78 OR ICL/G11B007/24009 OR ICL/G11B027/024 OR ICL/G11B027/032 OR ICL/G11B025/06
	floppy disc	TTL/("floppy disc" OR "floppy disk" OR diskette OR "ZIPdisc" OR "ZIPdisk" OR "flexible magnetic disc") OR ABST/("floppy disc" OR "floppy disk" OR diskette OR "ZIPdisc" OR "ZIPdisk" OR "flexible magnetic disc" OR "flexible magnetic disk") OR ICL/G11B023/033
	hard disc	TTL/("hard disk" OR "hard disc" OR "harddisk" OR "harddisc" OR HDD) OR ABST/("hard disk" OR "hard disc" OR "harddisk" OR "harddisc" OR HDD)
magneto-optic		ICL/G11B013/04 OR ICL/G11C013/06
	MiniDisc	TTL/(minidisk OR minidisc OR "mini disc" OR "mini disk" OR "magneto optical disk" OR "magneto optical disc") OR ABST/(minidisk OR minidisc OR "mini disc" OR "mini disk" OR "magneto optical disk" OR "magneto optical disc") OR ICL/G11B013/04 OR ICL/G11C013/06
optic		ICL/G11B007$
	Compact Disc	TTL/((CD AND (record$ OR music OR data OR information OR storage OR disk OR disc)) OR CD-R$ OR "compact disc" OR "compact disk") OR ABST/((CD AND (record$ OR music OR data OR information OR storage OR disk OR disc)) OR CD-R$ OR "compact disc" OR "compact disk")
	Digital Versatile Disc	TTL/((DVD AND (record$ OR music OR data OR information OR storage OR disk OR disc)) OR DVD-R$ OR "digital versatile disc" OR "digital versatile disk" OR "digital

		video disc" OR "digital video disk") OR ABST/((DVD AND (record$ OR music OR data OR information OR storage OR disk OR disc)) OR DVD-R$ OR "digital versatile disc" OR "digital versatile disk" OR "digital video disc" OR "digital video disk")
	Blu-ray	TTL/(Bluray OR blueray OR "blue ray" OR "blu ray") OR ABST/(Bluray OR blueray OR "blue ray" OR "blu ray")
	HD-DVD	TTL/("HD DVD" OR "high definition DVD" OR "high density DVD" OR "high definition digital versatile" OR "high density digital versatile") OR ABST/("HD DVD" OR "high definition DVD" OR "high density DVD" OR "high definition digital versatile" OR "high density digital versatile")
electronic		ICL/G11C011/21 OR ICL/G11C011/22 OR ICL/G11C011/23 OR ICL/G11C011/24 OR ICL/G11C011/26 OR ICL/G11C011/28 OR ICL/G11C011/3$ OR ICL/G11C011/40$ OR ICL/G11C011/41$ OR ICL/G11C011/42$ OR ICL/G11C011/44$ OR ICL/G11C015/04
	NVRAM	TTL/("non volatile random access" OR NVRAM OR "flash drive" OR "thumb drive" OR "key drive" OR "flash memory" OR "compact flash" OR "smartmedia" OR "multimedia-card") OR TTL/("MMC" OR "secure digital" OR "SD card" OR "memory stick" OR "xd picture card" OR "rs mmc" OR "minisd" OR "microsd" OR "intelligent stick" OR "nvSRAM" OR "FeRAM" OR "MRAM" OR "PRAM") OR ABST/("non volatile random access" OR NVRAM OR "flash drive" OR "thumb drive" OR "key drive" OR "flash memory" OR "compact flash" OR "smartmedia" OR "multimediacard") OR ABST/("MMC" OR "secure digital" OR "SD card" OR "memory stick" OR "xd picture card" OR "rs mmc" OR "minisd" OR "microsd" OR "intelligent stick" OR "nvSRAM" OR "FeRAM" OR "MRAM" OR "PRAM")
	ReRAM	TTL/("resistive random access memory" OR RRAM OR ReRAM) OR ABST/("resistive random access memory" OR RRAM OR ReRAM)

For each level of the technology: application, paradigm, and generation, and for each of the different media sources, USPTO and international patents, scientific literature, and web search queries, search strategies were defined in the following fashion:

1.) Search strategies were defined / refined.

2.) Documents were retrieved and cross-read for false positives and new search term candidates. During this step, especially systematic errors were identified.

Steps 1.) and 2.) were repeated iteratively until satisfactory results were produced, that is, where at least 90 out of 100 random results were well-fitting.

This approach ensures a relatively high precision while being suitable fast and giving a general idea of the recall. The final search strategies represent a mix of search terms and patent classes for patents, complex search terms for the "topic" field for scientific literature, and simple search terms for the web search queries. The strategies used for retrieval of the USPTO data can be looked up in table 4.5. The other data was retrieved analogously and search strategies can be found in .

Data cleaning and consolidation were not necessary. The iterative retrieval process described above produces relatively clean results. Due to the evaluation approach, redundancy and unnecessary variations are not an issue here.

4.5 Basic Analyses

This section presents descriptive statistics for the selected data in the period under consideration. It is divided in three parts: US and international patents, since it is source for both meta data and activity indicators; scientific publication activity in the ScienceDirect database; and Google Trends web search queries. The goal is to convey a general understanding of the data and the publication behavior in the different media types.

4.5.1 Absolute Invention Count per Year

A total of 29,644 USPTO patent issues with issue dates between 1976 and 2012 were evaluated. For the same timespan, judging by application date of their eldest member, 217,434 relevant international patent families were identified from the Thomson Scientific database. See figure 4.2 for the time series of the international patent family priorities and figure 4.3 for the time series of US patent issues. Both are based on the combination of the search terms for all technology paradigms presented in table 4.5.

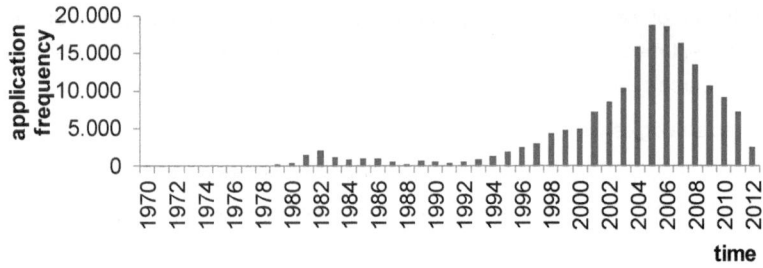

Fig. 4.2 International patent family applications connected to data storage technology (search strategies for technology paradigms from table 4.5 combined) as covered by Thomson Innovation in the years 1970 – 2012, assigned to years by application date

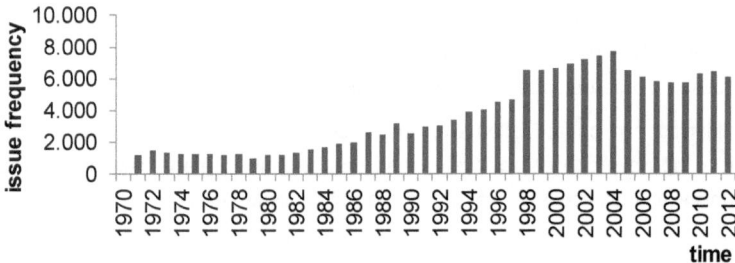

Fig. 4.3 US issued patents connected to data storage technology (search strategies for technology paradigms from table 4.5 combined) as covered by the USPTO in the years 1970 – 2012, assigned to years by issue date

Obviously the patent activity has increased continuously throughout the years from comparatively low numbers in the early 70s to a peak around the mid 2000s. This is true internationally as well as for the US.

This is important to know for the early years with low patenting volumes. During this period, single patents make up for a relevant percentage of the overall count. Especially for generation comparisons with an even lower count of relevant patents this should be kept in mind when interpreted. It makes an appropriate handling of outliers necessary.

There has been a notable decrease since the mid-2000s which may result from various causes. This decrease is more distinct for the international data for a simple reason: this data relies on the application date of the patent family which only becomes visible once the patent has been published 18 months after the application. Since the data was retrieved in early 2013, not all patent families are visible for 2012 or 2011. Still, this cannot be the only reason for the decrease because the publication lag is not present for the international data while the decrease is still clearly visible. Two other causes could be ruled out:

- Wrong keywords or wrong document classes: a combined strategy of keywords and document classes (IPC codes) eliminates this possibility. Although keywords can go out of fashion and ipc codes can be abandoned and go obsolete, both has been checked and is not true for the underlying data.
- Regional specific phenomenon: the phenomenon could be observed alike for US patents alone and for international patent families combined. It is thus not an effect from national laws or local business activity

The decrease may have several other explanations:

- Patents that improve the technology are not identified reliably
  - o Shift from hardware to software/information logistics patents, e.g. in the form of cloud storage, which are classified in other categories.
  - o Shift from concrete data storage patents to complex patents which only incorporate a data storage part not explicitly classified (Patent data can be broadly categorized as complex or discrete technologies. *"Complex technologies are usually defined as those for which the resulting products or processes consist of numerous separately patentable elements and for which patent ownership is typically widespread. Discrete technologies, in turn, describe products or processes that consist of a single or relatively few patentable elements and for which patent ownership is more concentrated. For example, smartphones fall into the category of complex technologies, whereas pharmaceuticals are considered a discrete technology."* Annex A of World Intellectual Property Indicators, 2011 edition, available at (World Intellectual Property Organization 2011, p.181))
- Shift from patentable to less patentable technology.
- Shift from patenting inventions to keeping them secret.
- Industry maturity has reached saturation or decline state, additional sales or profit too low to justify further development.
- Increasing market concentration makes additional development unnecessary.
- Physical limits prohibit continued improvements to the technologies.

Whatever the reasons for the observed decrease, the indicators described in section 2.3.4.2 are not affected by this behavior because they rely on relative values.

4.5.2 Absolute Scientific Publication Activity

A total of 150,516 scientific documents relevant for data storage were identified in the time from 1970 until 2012 in Elsevier's ScienceDirect database. See figure 4.4 for the corresponding time series.

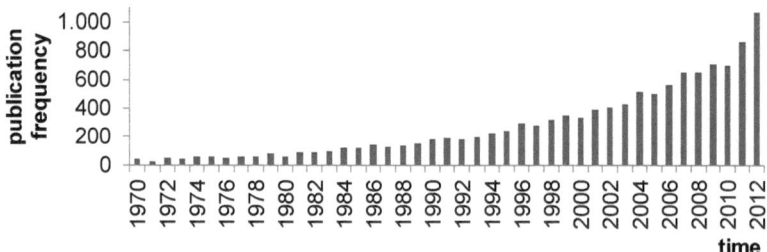

Fig. 4.4 Absolute scientific journal publication count connected to data storage technology during the years 1970-2012, assigned to years by publication date

Apart from some minor exceptions, a progressive increase of publication activity can be witnessed every year. Of course the chart in figure 2.16 of section 2.3.3.2 shows increasing absolute publication volumes while the absolute database coverage displayed in figure 4.4 also increases at a high rate. The importance of the technology application can therefore not be deduced from this graph. However, the pattern is very pronounced and an increase of the importance of data storage technologies seems probable. Again, the indicators described in section 2.3.4.2 rely on relative values and are therefore not affected by the publication trend.

4.5.3 Absolute Web Search Queries in Google Trends

The sections on patents and scientific literature shows bar charts of the absolute document volumes over time. In Google Trends, web search data is not provided in the form of absolute numbers. Furthermore, the Google Trends platform only allows simple search strategies consisting of one search term. A combination of the search strategies for different technologies is consequently not possible and the retrieved data can not be combined ex post either. A simple search for the term "data storage" shows a steady decline in the interest for this subject, as can be seen in figure 4.5.

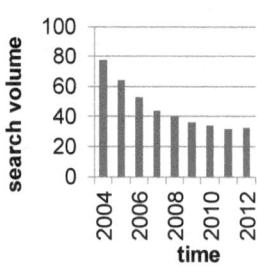

Fig. 4.5 Relative web search query volume for the term "data storage" in Google Trends between 2004 and 2012

This search may not be representative of the actual interest in the technology application, however. Searches for actual data storage technologies are not covered in it and may constitute the main share of searches. Yet, the observed pattern is in agreement with the results from the patent analysis which showed a decrease starting in the mid-2000s.

4.5.4 Juxtaposition of Absolute Document Frequencies for Technology Application, Paradigms, and Generations for Recall Estimations

Section 4.4 presented the search strategies which were used in this analysis and proposed the combination of all paradigm related documents as an upper boundary for recall estimations. This section therefore presents these upper boundaries in table 4.6. The relevant document frequencies were determined with the search strategies from table 4.5 for the USPTO data and with the corresponding search strategies of other media types in the Annex, each for a time period from 1970 until 2012.

To determine the overall technology application document frequency for the patents, the search strategies for all technology paradigms are combined into a single search strategy to avoid double counts. It is important to note that the search strategies for these paradigms consist exclusively of IPC-based search terms and unlike the search strategies for the generations do not contain any keyword-based search. This was done to keep the search strategy as comprehensive as possible while it stays independent of the technology generations and can therefore be used to determine a document frequency which can be used as an upper boundary to estimate the recall.

A different approach was chosen for the scientific publications because no IPC analogous classification system exists which could provide a technology generation-independent document count for the technology paradigms. Here, the technology paradigm document counts were determined based on a combined search strategy of all corresponding technology generation search strategies. Because of this approach, the technology paradigm document frequency can not be considered independent of the related technology generations and cannot serve as an upper boundary to estimate the recall. The technology application count was therefore determined with a separate and independent, more general search strategy, as displayed in the Annex. This frequency can then be used to estimate the recall.

Table 4.6 Absolute document counts for technology application and paradigms as an upper boundary for recall estimations of technology generation searches

	International patents	US patents	Scientific publications
all	**217,434**	**29,644**	**11,801**
mechanic	**6,373**	**552**	**96**
PunchedCard	83	270	47
PerforatedTape	13	98	52
magnetic	**74,335**	**24,243**	**2,027**
MagneticTape	10,217	6,090	549
FloppyDisc	2,002	1,468	514
HardDisc	26,219	5,188	997
magneto-optic	**5,853**	**394**	**72**
MiniDisc	3,450	976	72
optic	**79,607**	**10,409**	**3,452**
CompactDisc	22,695	4,296	2,875
DVD	30,821	1,839	570
Blu-ray	8,428	85	46
HD-DVD	2,349	39	20
electronic	**57,289**	**5,694**	**4,695**
NVRAM	17,330	8,613	4,576
ReRAM	1,229	136	128

Table 4.6 shows the document frequency for the technology application at the top row and the document frequencies for the paradigms (bold font) each followed by related generations (normal font) in the rows below. Most paradigms generate a document frequency at roughly the same order of magnitude as the application. And most generations for their part generate a document frequency at roughly the same order of magnitude as the corresponding paradigm. Three special cases have to be pointed

out because they deviate from the expectations: 1.) The US patent frequency for the magneto-optical paradigm is smaller than that of the minidisc technology generation. This happens due to the construction of the search strategy: the minidisc search strategy consists of IPC terms and keywords while that of the magneto-optical paradigm uses only IPC terms which all appear in the minidisc technology search strategy. 2.) A similar observation can be made for the NVRAM technology and the electronic paradigm for the US patents. Here the NVRAM does not use all of the IPC codes of the electronic paradigm, but the keywords it uses produce such a high document frequency that it still exceeds the expected upper boundary of recall. And 3.) the magneto-optical paradigm and the minidisc technology produce the exact same document frequency for scientific publications. This is because the search strategies are identical, as described at the beginning of this section.

In summary, it can be assumed that the recall for the technology generation search strategies is appropriately high.

4.6 Methodological Triangulation

Even though the S&D model is considered a semi-theoretical maturity model in this book, it still provides certain latent variables with a high measurability potential which enable non-experts to assess a technology's maturity. However, the latent variables may produce opposing signals regarding this maturity.

Experts, on the other hand, typically have relevant additional information which enables them to judge how mature or immature a technology is. The results of the Delphi method in section 4.2 provide another view on the same technologies. Still, expert opinion is subjective and not without fault.

Both approaches allow a different but limited view of the same technology. Combined in a suitable way, the disadvantages of either can be compensated by the strengths of the other (Guion et al. 2011; Östlund et al. 2011; Erzberger & Kelle 2003).

To check whether the results of the expert-based Delphi method and an interpretation of the S&D model produce converging results, the results of the Delphi method will be compared to the activity in certain media representing the S&D model factors associated with certain maturity states for three selected technologies: magnetic tape, compact discs, and Blu-ray. These technologies all cover different maturity states comprehensively and each corresponding search strategy produced a considerable data basis consisting of activity data for scientific literature, patents, and web search. The activity indicator development hypotheses in table 4.7 as derived from the S&D model in sections 2.3.3.4 and 0 will be assumed.

Table 4.7 Selection of maturity state indicators derived from the S&D model based on different media types as described in sections 2.3.3.4 and 0 (operationalization)

indicators	emergence	growth	saturation	decline
B. Investments in technology development (scientific literature activity)	low	maximal	low	negligible
C. Number of application areas (web search activity)	unknown	increasing	established, plenty	decreasing
F. patent count (patent activity)	increasing	high	decreasing	decreasing

The S&D model is constructed to assess technology maturity based on a set of factors which work as a whole. In this triangulation section, instead of combining all factors, they are interpreted separately with means similar to those used in chart reading known from technical analysis of stocks (Achelis 2013). These means especially include support and resistance levels, which represent resistance to change in activity. Support levels represent the highest values which the activity does not fall below for an extended period of time (Achelis 2013, p.13). Support levels are usually identified by a previous activity low (Murphy 1986, p.59). Analog to support levels, the activity does not surpass resistance levels for an extended period of time (Achelis 2013, p.13). These are usually identified by a previous peak (Murphy 1986, p.59). The means of technical analysis of stocks also encompasses trends, which, opposed to support and resistance levels, represent constant change in activity (Achelis 2013, pp.23–25). Trends can be positive or negative and they have a lower and an upper boundary forming a trend channel. Analog to support and resistance levels, in the approach in this book the upper boundary of a trend is identified by a peak while its lower boundary is identified by a low. The changes between the maturity states are marked by transitions between periods of consistent and trending activity, depending on the patterns described in table 4.7. As the state definitions of the S&D model are relatively vague, only a relatively imprecise interval for the maturity states can be derived.

The experts, on the other hand, provide exact statements regarding the boundaries of the maturity state intervals.

The triangulation of these state definitions reveals whether both approaches produce converging or diverging results. This will be done for the expert-based approach and the indicator-based approach. For this purpose, the S&D model indicator-based state approximations are projected onto the actual activity data and the expert-based state boundaries are then juxtaposed. Overlaps between the two approaches will be interpreted as converging outcomes.

The activity is measured as the fraction of technology generation per technology application specific publications, which will be regarded as a measure of importance (the more activity connected to a certain generation which helps solve a problem defined in the underlying application, the more important that generation is). The absolute activity values will not be compared across technologies. Only the activity slope will be regarded as of interest for maturity assessment.

4.6.1 Magnetic Tape as a Case Where Data is Available for the Later Maturity States Only

According to the experts, the magnetic tape technology changed from growth into saturation state in 1982, then from saturation into the decline state in 1996.

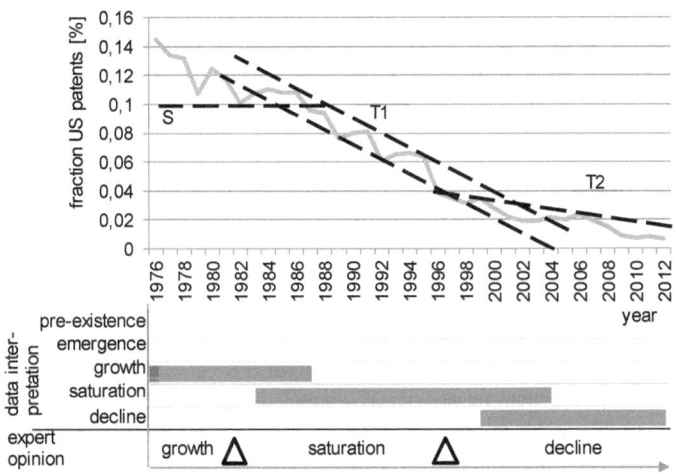

Fig. 4.6 6090 US patent grants connected to the magnetic tape data storage technology as a fraction of all data storage technologies between 1976 and 2012.

Figure **4.6** relies on a total of 6,090 patents. The fraction of US patent grants related to the magnetic tape technology compared to the total data storage US patent grants in a given year serve as an indicator (see section 2.3.5.1 for a detailed explanation of this operationalization mechanism). During the first years of this chart, a support level S is marked at 0.1%, which represents a relatively high level and can thus be attributed to the growth state. It lasts until 1987 before it falls below this level. The activity enters a falling activity trend T1 in 1983. This long time trend lasts until when in 2004 the activity grows beyond the upper boundary of T1. Since this decrease is rather uniform, it can be attributed to the saturation state. A peak in activity in 1999 defines the upper boundary of a new trend T2, which lasts until the end of the chart and marks the decline state. The overlap between the expert and S&D model based maturity states is considerable.

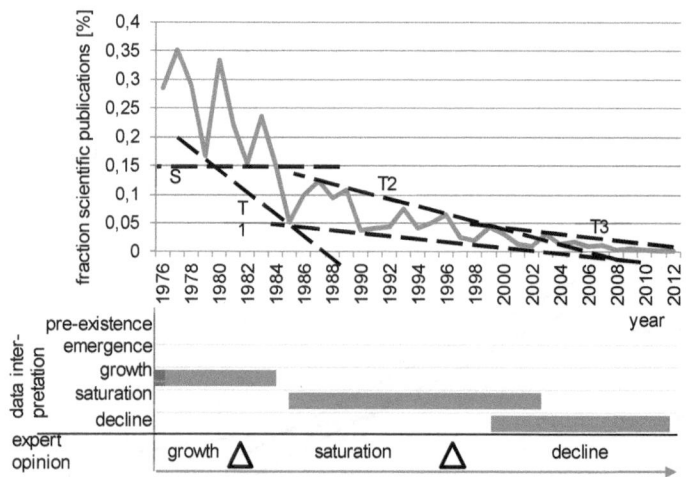

Fig. 4.7 398 scientific publications connected to the magnetic tape data storage technology as a fraction of all data storage technologies between 1976 and 2012.

Figure **4.7** shows the publication activity indicator based on 398 scientific publications. The fraction of scientific publications related to the magnetic tape technology compared to the total data storage scientific publications in a given year serves as an indicator. A support line S can be drawn at the 0.15%-level at the beginning of the chart. The activity falls below this line for the first time in 1984. It remains below S after this date and this can be interpreted as the end of the growth state. The lower boundary of an extreme downwards trend T1 intersects the lower boundary of a less extreme trend T2 in 1985, from when on the value can be considered low, marking the start of the saturation state. The funneling long time trend T2 starting in 1985 is broken in 2003, when for the first time the curve exceeds this trend canal. This happens due to a very low activity level, which cannot fall much further and can be considered the end of the saturation state. The curve falls below the upper boundary of this less steep trend T3 in 1999. After this date, the activity can be considered negligible and it thus marks the beginning of the decline state. Both experts and S&D model interpretation come to largely identical state intervals.

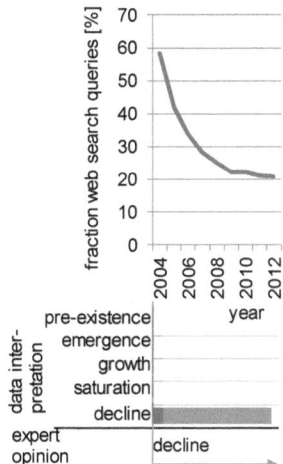

Fig. 4.8 Web search queries connected to the magnetic tape data storage technology between 2004 and 2012.

Figure 4.8 shows the web search activity for the magnetic tape technology, which declines since the first available year, 2004. According to the corresponding S&D model factor, this means that the technology is in its decline state. This is congruent with expert assessment.

In conclusion, expert and indicator-based assessment of magnetic tape technology do not contradict each other and can be interpreted as coming to very similar maturity intervals.

4.6.2 Compact Disc as a Case Where Data is Available for All Maturity States

The compact disc technology was judged by the experts to move into the emergence state in 1979, the growth state in 1987, the saturation state in 1996, and the decline state beginning in 2001.

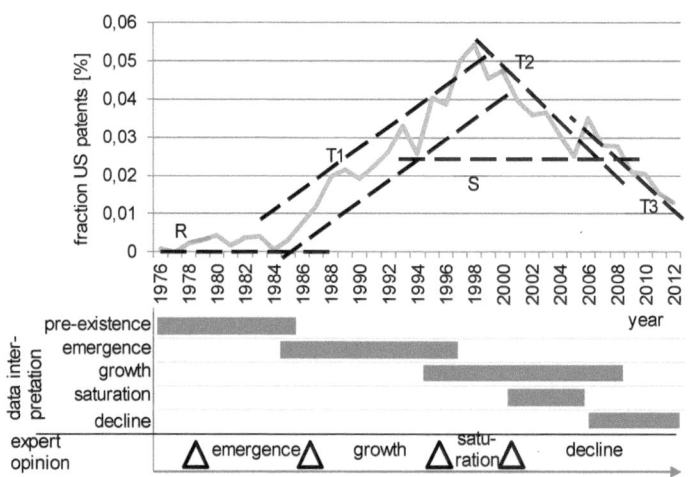

Fig. 4.9 US patent grants connected to the compact disc technology as a fraction of all data storage technologies between 1976 and 2012.

Figure **4.9** is based on 4,296 patents. According to the interpretation of the data, an initial resistance level R cannot be overcome until 1985. Before this date, the patent activity cannot be regarded as increasing and has therefore been attributed to the pre-existence state. In 1984 the lower boundary of a trend channel for trend T1 is defined, which lasts until 1996, where upper boundary of T1 is superseded. This period marks the emergence state. In 1994 a low marks the start of support level S, which lasts until the activity drops below it in 2009. This is a time period with a high activity and thus represents the growth state. The saturation state is estimated by the upper boundary of trend T2, which starts in 1998 and ends when the activity supersedes this border in 2005. It is followed by another falling trend T3. The activity first surpasses the lower boundary of T3 in 2006 and does not fall below it until the end. The indicator-based assessment lags behind for all states with this data. Only the decline state coincides with the expert opinion in part.

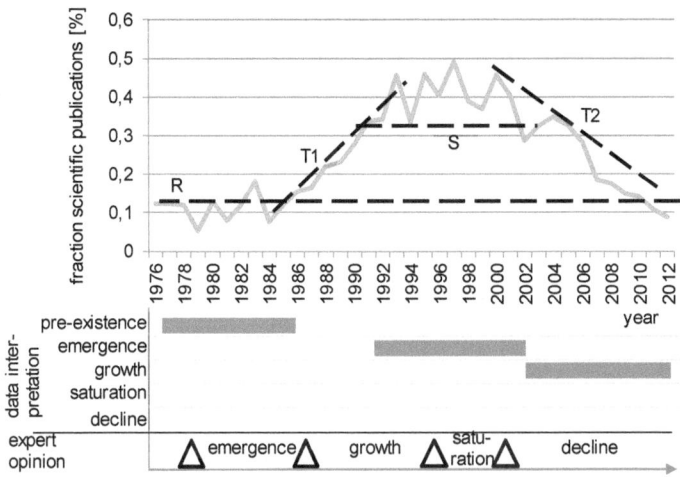

Fig. 4.10 Scientific publications connected to the compact disc technology as a fraction of all data storage technologies between 1976 and 2012.

Figure **4.10** relies on 2,839 scientific publications. A resistance level which lasts until 1985 when it is eventually superseded can be interpreted as a low activity, thus representing the emergence state. Then an increasing activity can be identified which cannot be attributed to any particular maturity state however, because the growth state calls for maximal activity. This is reached when a high support level is reached in 1991, and it lasts until the year 2002. A decline represented by the upper boundary of the trend T2 begins in 2000, which initiates the transition from the growth to the saturation state. This lasts at least until the year 2010 when the resistance level R, which marked the low activity of the emergence state, is undercut. The emergence state spans a very similar time interval for both approaches, but the S&D model-based growth definition takes a long time to arrive in comparison to the expert-based approach. The S&D model-based saturation state lags behind even more, and the negligible activity marked by the decline state cannot yet be recognized.

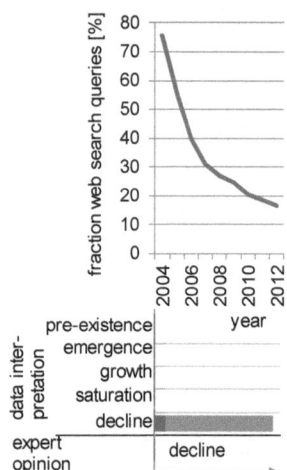

Fig. 4.11 Web search queries connected to the compact disc technology between 2004 and 2012.

Figure **4.11** displays the web search data as interpreted by the S&D model, which is congruent with the expert-based findings and estimates the CD technology to be in its decline state.

In conclusion, the S&D model-based media evaluation tends to lag behind the expert-based judgment for the compact disc technology, especially for the S&D model factors which are based on patents and scientific literature.

4.6.3 Blu-ray as a Case Where Data is Available for the Earlier Maturity States Only

According to the experts, the emergence state of the Blu-ray technology started in 2002. The technology is currently in its growth state, which started in 2007.

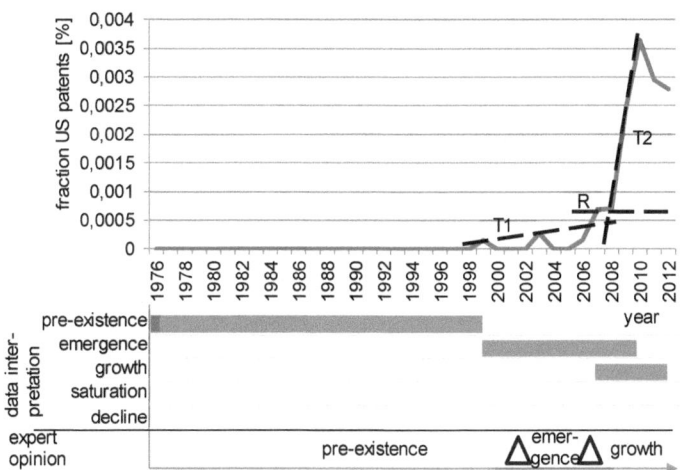

Fig. 4.12 US patent grants connected to the Blu-ray technology as a fraction of all data storage technologies between 1976 and 2012.

Figure **4.12** is based on 85 patents. A first sign of activity can be determined for the year 1999. This marks the end of the pre-existence state for the Blu-ray technology and the beginning of an increasing activity trend T1. The upper boundary of T1 is exceeded in 2006, but the growth does not stop at this point. Instead it rises as a new increasing trend T2 until the year 2010, when the lower boundary is crossed. The emergence state which is marked by increasing activity can thus be interpreted to last until the year 2010. A resistance value R marks the level of high activity which is characteristic of the growth state. It is first matched in the year 2007 and the activity does not fall significantly after this year until the end of the period under observation. Expert and S&D model-based analysis results overlap to a large extent.

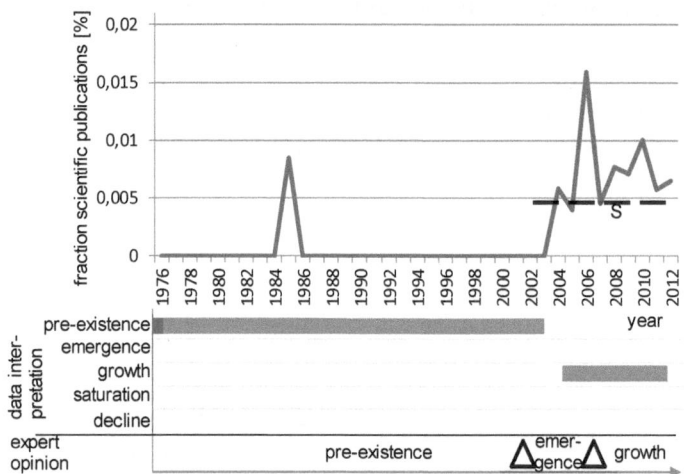

Fig. 4.13 Scientific publications connected to the Blu-ray technology as a fraction of all data storage technologies between 1976 and 2012.

Only 47 scientific publications are used as a data basis for the S&D model analysis as displayed in figure **4.13**. This is not much and should therefore be interpreted with great caution. The activity is at a very low level at all times in comparison to the other two technologies of sections 4.6.1 and 0. Little data can be expected to produce imprecise results. A single publication produces a peak in the year 1985. This can be considered an outlier and therefore be ignored in this evaluation. If this is done, the emergence state becomes very short and is hard to locate. A support level S is enduringly superseded post 2005. This year can be considered the beginning of the growth state. In summary, the S&D model-based growth state is placed a little ahead of that of the experts, but nevertheless the overlap is considerable.

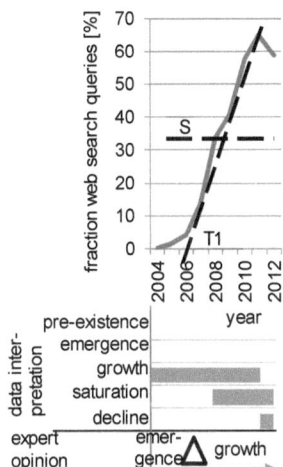

Fig. 4.14 Web search queries connected to the Blu-ray technology between 2004 and 2012.

Figure **4.14** shows the web search query activity connected to the Blu-ray technology. It starts out at a relatively low value. The S&D model states that the web search activity volume is "unknown" for the emergence state, making it effectively unable to recognize this particular state. Experts judge the year 2006 as the beginning of the growth state, while the web search activity has increased all the time since 2004. The lower boundary of this growth trend T1 persists until the year 2011, which marks the end of the growth state. The saturation is marked by "plenty" web search activity, which can be recognized by a support level which in this case was placed at a level of 35%. According to this, the saturation state begins in 2008 and has not yet ended. The S&D model allows us to interpret the decline of the indicator value since 2011 as a beginning decline state. Experts do not recognize this just yet. In this case, the expert judgment lags somewhat behind the indicator-based results.

Conclusion: for magnetic tape, results are very similar. For compact disc, some of the maturity states of the S&D model lag behind, whereas for Blu-ray, some of the maturity states of the expert-based assessment lag behind a little. In short, although only a fraction of the S&D model indicators was implemented, the approaches lead to slightly different but converging results. The triangulation in this section speaks in favor of the validity of the two approaches.

4.7 Advanced Analyses

The goal of the advanced analyses is to generate a ubiquitous model for technology maturity assessment following the analysis steps as described in the analysis design section 0 in figure 3.1 as well as to test the hypotheses regarding S&D model factor behavior presented in section 2.2.3.2 and the hypotheses regarding the sequence of media activity presented in section 2.3.5.2. Before either of these tasks can be performed, the indicators which are going to be used must be known. Each indicator relies on certain data. This data comes from different sources and in different quality and may need preprocessing before the information it contains can be extracted and exploited. Only when this has been done can the steps i.) through vi.) of the analysis as displayed in table 3.2 be approached. The statistical software R with the MASS package is used as a resource to calculate the advanced analyses in the approach in this book. The corresponding code can be found in the Annex.

This section consists of seven parts: In section 4.7.1 two contestant sets of technology maturity indicators are described in detail to determine which data sources to tap and which information to gather: a set of new activity indicators and as a benchmark a set of well-established meta data indicators. Section 4.7.2 takes into account biases resulting from the way the different indicators are constructed. Section 4.7.3 shows how the indicator values are calculated for each point of observation by example of the Minidisc technology and section 4.7.4 shows how these points of observations are assigned to their corresponding state of maturity for all technologies. In section 4.7.5 the S&D model factor behavior, ideal maturity indicator behavior, and curve point sequence hypotheses mentioned above are tested with help of the new activity indicators. In section 4.7.6 the data assumptions of the analyses used to evaluate the discriminative power of the indicators are checked, and then the performance of the activity indicators is determined, each separately and all in combination. As a benchmark, in section 0 the discriminative power of the established meta data indicators is determined, again each separately and all in combination. In a concluding remark, the misclassification rates of the indicator sets are compared.

4.7.1 Overview of Contestant Indicator Sets and Their Data Requirements

Section 0 describes the design of this analysis. One of the tasks of its design is to test the added value of an operationalized S&D model as presented in section 2.3.4.2. This test requires a calibration step which enables a benchmarking of the new approach. Useful as a benchmark is a set of indicators which is known to work well or is established for the purpose of maturity indication. This section will therefore present not only the activity indicators and their data requirements, but also a set of well-researched and established meta data indicators based on patent evaluation, which are known to differentiate relatively well between states of maturity. This setup will allow us to contrast these against the indicators which are hypothesized to allow easy access to valuable information contained in a number of different media sources as described in section 2.3.3.4. Properties of both indicator sets are explained and formulas necessary for their calculation are given in the subsequent sections 4.7.1.1 until 4.7.1.4 for the separate activity indicators and sections 4.7.1.5 until 4.7.1.10 for the separate meta data indicators.

The two contestant indicator sets in figure 4.15 define the data requirements of the approach in this book.

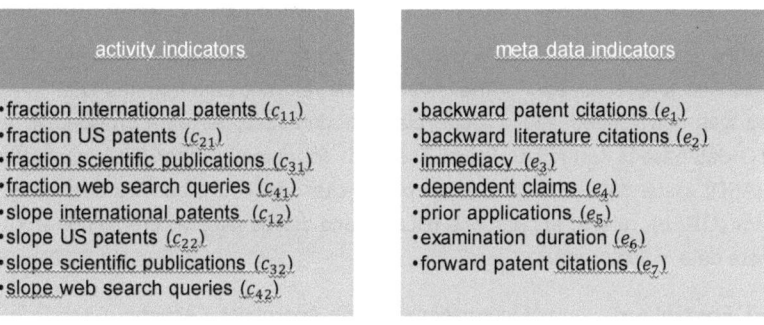

activity indicators	meta data indicators
•fraction international patents (c_{11}) •fraction US patents (c_{21}) •fraction scientific publications (c_{31}) •fraction web search queries (c_{41}) •slope international patents (c_{12}) •slope US patents (c_{22}) •slope scientific publications (c_{32}) •slope web search queries (c_{42})	•backward patent citations (e_1) •backward literature citations (e_2) •immediacy (e_3) •dependent claims (e_4) •prior applications (e_5) •examination duration (e_6) •forward patent citations (e_7)

Fig. 4.15 Overview of Haupt et al.'s meta data Indicators (Haupt et al. 2007) and activity indicators presented in section 2.3.4.2 (compare JÄRVENPÄÄ et al. (2011), MARTINO (2003), and WATTS & PORTER (1997)), which will be used to assess technology maturity in this analysis

The activity indicators were already described in detail in the past sections. They do not require a separate preprocessing step. This is different for the meta data indicators. These meta data indicators were all collected from a work by HAUPT et al., which in turn collected US patent-based indicators from multiple literature sources. In the work by HAUPT et al., each indicator was tested individually for its suitability to discriminate the S&D model maturity states emergence, growth, and saturation, excluding the decline state. They were found to discriminate relatively well (Haupt et al. 2007). However, HAUPT et al. did not base their findings on more than one technology and thus did not derive rules regarding which values their indicators might take on during the separate maturity states for untested technologies. They do not provide definitive rules regarding the combination of their indicators to estimate a technology's maturity. This will be elaborated in section 0, for each indicator separately and for all in combination.

To make the activity and meta data-based approaches comparable, both indicator sets will be combined in the same way, that is, with the help of a suitable machine-learning approach.

All meta data indicators are based on US patent meta data, but it is possible to "translate" most of the presented indicators into other media types than US patents, as they provide a similar document structure. Obviously other national or international patent data is suitable for such analyses, but also scientific literature is often similarly structured and thus allows for construction of analogous indicators. This is noted where applicable. It was not implemented, however, because the connection to technology maturity was only verified for US patents. The indicators were chosen as benchmark indicators for the operationalized S&D model rather than to extend the range of maturity indicators even further. A validity check is subject to future research.

Before the meta data indicators could be calculated, the necessary data had to be retrieved and preprocessed. For this purpose, the relevant data from the USPTO database was downloaded into a local relational database. All data provided in the USPTO database is sorted into fields. The fields for patent number (PN), application date (APD), issue date (ISD), backward patent citations (REF), backward non-patent citations (OREF), related applications (RLAP), and claims (ACLM) are all relevant for the meta data indicator set.

4.7.1.1 Fraction and Slope of International Patent Applications Activity

As explained in detail in sections 2.3.3.4 in overview in table 2.12 which provides the assumed indicator development and in table 2.14 of section 2.3.4.1, which links this development to a certain text medium, these two indicators can be used to represent factors **B.** (Investments in technology development) and **F.** (patent count) of the S&D model.

Like for all activity indicators, the data necessary is only the document count per year and there is no additional calculation effort for additional documents. To determine which S&D model factor outweighs any others empirically, the maturity state means of the indicator will be compared.

It is important to define which date to use in determining the patent count. Three dates are sensible choices for this task:

- The application date is the date on which the patent is filed. The application date is closer to the actual time of invention of a technology than the other dates described in this section below. Problematically, a patent and its application date becomes visible only after publication which takes place 18 months after the time of application at the earliest. Judging by the application date, the data from last year and the year before will therefore not include all the inventions filed in those years. The priority date is the date on which the first application was filed of all patents in a patent family. Subsequent patents of the same family may be filed within 12 months of the priority so the priority of a patent family may be a much earlier date than the application date of another patent in that family.

- The publication date is the date on which it is disclosed to the public. The publication date is the date on which the patent becomes visible to the public. The publication date is therefore the earliest date which can ensure that all patents for a past year are covered. Patents are usually still pending, i.e. not in force, by the time they are published. There is no guarantee that a published patent will actually be granted.

- The issue date is the date on which it is granted and legally comes into force. It represents the patents with the most definitive patent protection of the data available.

The application date is used to determine the patent count for the international patents. This means the data for more recent years is incomplete (see explanation "application date" above), which must be considered in the interpretation.

4.7.1.2 Fraction and Slope of US Patent Grants Activity

As described in section 4.7.1.1, these indicators are hypothesized to be able to respond to the same factors of the S&D model as the international patent indicators (that is, B. and F.). They use the same data as all indicators from the meta data set.

The USPTO reliably provides all issued patents from 1976 until today rather than for patent applications, which are only provided after 2001. Therefore the count of issued US patents will be used to determine the patent count. To assign each patent to a year, the issue date rather than the application date is used. This means that the US patent-based indicators lag behind the actual technology inventions. As described in section 4.7.1.9, this seemingly leads to an unnecessary distortion of the temporal assignment of a patent in comparison to the actual time of invention. Over the course of a technology's maturity, the time between application and issue date varies considerably. Since two types of patent information are included in the approach in this book, however, rather than providing redundant information, this approach implicitly includes an indicator similar to the examination duration as described in section 4.7.1.9 while still relying exclusively on activity indicators and without having to define a dedicated indicator.

It is important to note that in the case where only one source of a media type is used, withholding information longer than necessary should be avoided, i.e. the earliest available date should preferably be used. In the case of patents this is the application date or the priority date.

4.7.1.3 Fraction and Slope of Scientific Publications Activity

This pair of indicators based on scientific publications can be used to gauge factor **B.** (investments in technology development) of the S&D model. This speaks in favor of a peak during the growth state of this indicator. It is also useful for getting a first impression of the factors **D1.** (scientific development requirements) and **H1.** (scientific access requirements). This makes the indicator already peak during the emergence state. The latter two factor representations require additional elaboration of the indicator to tap the full potential of the information contained in scientific literature.

4.7.1.4 Fraction and Slope of Web Search Queries Activity

This indicator pair is the most versatile concerning the representation of the S&D model factors: The fraction of relevant web search queries is suited to indicate **A.** (insecurity of technological performance), which is hypothesized to peak in the emergence state. **C.** (number of application areas) is supposed to be at its maximum during the saturation state. **D3.** (cost-oriented development requirements) is hypothesized to be at its maximum during the decline state. **E.** (impact on cost / performance rate of products) reaches the highest value during the growth state. **I.** (availability) can be indicated, especially during the saturation state of a technology, which is distinguished by its market orientation and which in turn can be hypothesized to trigger an increased web search volume.

This is a set of in part contradictory hypotheses, covering predictions of peak values for every single maturity state almost equally. An interaction of the different model factors is probable as they can all influence the indicators to a certain extent. It seems reasonable to refine search strategies for these indicators to focus on one of the model factors at a time. In the scope of this book, however, this was not done. It is expected that one of the factors outweighs the others and lead to results of sufficient precision for maturity state attribution.

4.7.1.5 Backward Patent Citations and Backward Literature Citations

Patent applications cite both scientific publications (literature citations; e.g. MEYER (Meyer 2000)) and other patents (patent citations; e.g. NARIN et al. (Narin et al. 1987, p.148)). Citations document the connection between the invention, and preceding patent as well as non-patent literature (Knight 2012, p.53; Harrison & Rivette 1998, p.123; R S Campbell 1983, p.63), as displayed in figure 4.16. HAUPT et al. show that literature citations increase at the transition from emergence to growth, and remain at a similar level throughout growth and saturation (Haupt et al. 2007). They attribute this to the fact that at early states of a technology maturity there is still much fundamental (radical) new knowledge to cite which is published predominantly in scientific literature. They also show that patent citations increase for each of the transitions from emergence to growth to saturation. They ascribe this to the fact that incremental new results of applied research and product development that patents have to cite in later states are documented mainly in other patents. Strategic citation to increase the citation count of their own preceding work is not included in their reasoning.

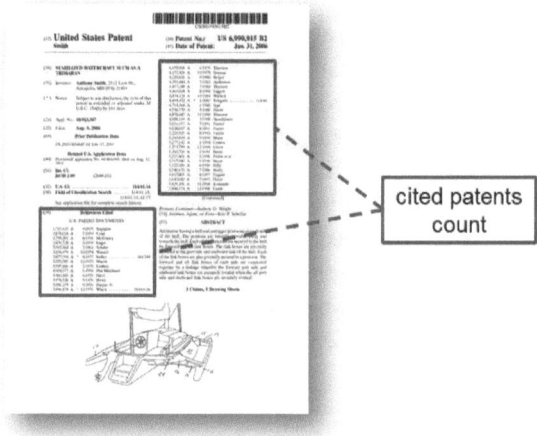

cited patents count

Fig. 4.16 Data collection for backward patent citations indicator

Following the same argumentation, a similar indicator can be constructed for scientific literature: citation of literature on basic or applied research takes on the role of backward literature citations, and citation of literature on development takes on that of backward patent citations.

The calculation effort for this indicator is low and increases linearly for additional records.

Backward Patent Citations: the (REF)-field contains the patent number of each cited patent. If more than one patent is cited, then the different patent numbers are listed in separate lines. The number of lines in this field were counted to retrieve the count of backward patent citations. This only takes US citations into consideration, but it should be a good approximation.

Backward Literature Citations: the (OREF)-field contains bibliographic information of each cited non-patent source. This is mostly scientific literature. If more than one source is cited, the different sources are listed in separate lines. The number of lines in this field were counted to retrieve the count of backward literature citations.

The original hypothesis implicitly suggests dividing backward patent citations by backward literature citations. This was implemented in this analysis. Additionally, the separate consideration of the two indicators was carried out.

4.7.1.6 Immediacy of Citations

The immediacy of a citation describes the period of time between the grant of the citing patent and the grant of the cited one (Ashton et al. 1983, pp.5–7; R S Campbell 1983, p.62), as displayed in figure 4.17. HAUPT et al. show evidence for a high immediacy for the emergence state. They consider this an artifact of their technology choice (pacemaker technologies). For both states, growth and saturation, they show a continued decrease of the immediacy, which means that the average time between citing and cited patents increases (Richard S Campbell 1983, p.139). They reason that the dynamics of development and thus the leeway to gain competitive advantages by patenting decrease; therefore there is no necessity anymore to react to others' or one's own innovations as quickly as possible (Haupt et al. 2007).

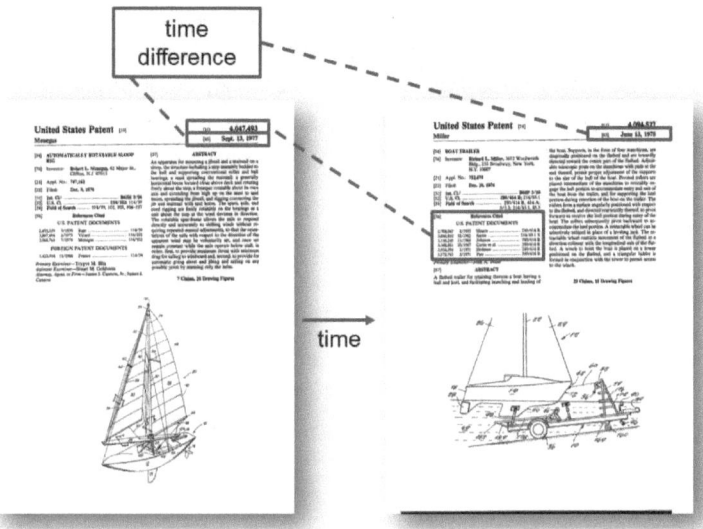

Fig. 4.17 Data collection for immediacy of citations indicator

An analogous indicator could be generated for different types of scientific literature, using the period of time between publication of the citing and the cited documents rather than grant dates.

The calculation effort for this indicator is slightly increased because grant dates for all cited patents have to be retrieved for each citing patent. Calculation and averaging of the time differences is a second step. The effort increases linearly for additional records.

Immediacy: for the (backward) immediacy, all patent numbers in the (REF)-field were collected. The (APD) of the corresponding patents were collected and the arithmetic average of the spans between (APD) of the citing and the cited patents were calculated.

4.7.1.7 Dependent Claims

Dependent claims describe in detail a corresponding independent claim (figure 4.18), while at the same time offering fallback options (Schickedanz 2000, p.68; Valle 1996, p.73). Normally, they contain just one single feature that gives further details concerning the main claim (Valle 1996, p.73). HAUPT et al. show that the number of dependent claims rises significantly in later maturity states. They attribute this to two assumptions: first, more substantiations can be made due to the differentiation of the technology. Second, in the face of an increasingly cumulative technology development (causing a stronger mutual dependency of the applicants) it is more important to have fallback options (Haupt et al. 2007).

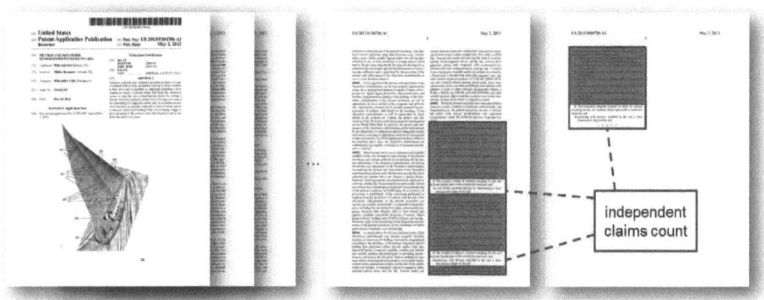

Fig. 4.18 Determining the dependent claims count is possible by first identifying independent claims and deducing their count from the total claims count

Claims are a property inherent to patents, which makes it difficult to transfer this indicator to other media types.

The calculation effort for this indicator is relatively low. It may become necessary to perform simple text-mining operations to separate independent and dependent claims if their count is not present in the meta data. The calculation effort increases linearly.

Dependent claims: the dependent claims count data collection is a three-step procedure.

1.) count lines in the (ACLM)-field to determine the total claims count
2.) count independent claims in the ACLM-field. These are not specially marked in the data provided by the USPTO. As an approximation, all lines containing keywords typically used as transitional phrases such as "comprising" which hint towards independent claims, are considered independent claims (United States Patent and Trademark Office & United States Department of Commerce 2014).
3.) Subtract number of independent claims from total claims count to derive dependent claims count.

4.7.1.8 Prior Application Count

A prior application is an earlier patent application of one's own work which can be referred to in a subsequent application within a 12-month-period, without having to differ from the first application regarding the novelty and the inventive step (Suhr 2000, p.23; Blankenstein 1988, p.7), see figure 4.19. HAUPT et al. show that a patent will refer to more prior applications for the transition from growth to saturation state (Haupt et al. 2007). They attribute this to the high development speed during the emergence and growth states on the one hand, which enables single firms to form differentiations of the technology before competitors are able to follow them, and on the other hand, allows the complexity of development during the saturation state which makes it difficult for competitors to gain a long-term lead in R&D (Haupt et al. 2007).

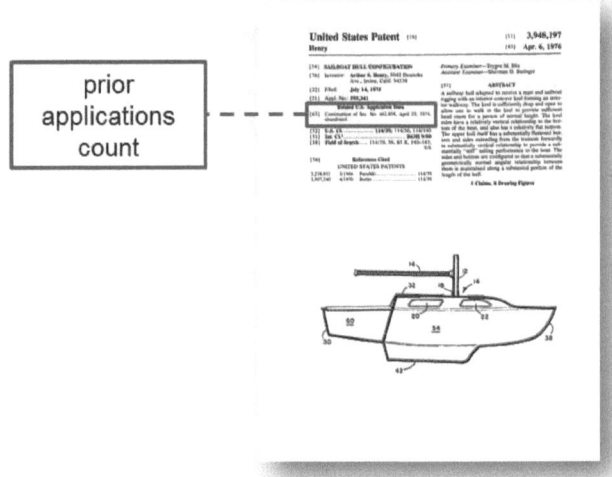

Fig. 4.19 Data collection for prior applications count indicator

Refinement and sophistication of one's own work can also be tracked in scientific literature in the form of self-citations. The motivation of authors of patents and scientific literature is considerably different, but it can be expected that both want to profit maximally off their research before anyone else can.

The calculation effort for this indicator is low, as it is usually present directly in the meta data. It increases linearly for additional records.

Prior applications: the (RLAP)-field contains the patent number of each prior application. The number of lines in this field were counted to retrieve the prior application count.

4.7.1.9 Examination Duration

The examination duration is the time difference between application and issue date of a patent, as displayed in figure 4.20. HAUPT et al. show that the examination process takes significantly longer during the emergence and saturation states than during the growth state. They attribute this to the fact that at the beginning of a technological development the applicants tend to formulate a broad claim in order to limit the chances for following applicants. This causes a long duration of the examination process. Independent of this strategic interest of the applicants, a basic invention is characterized by a broader claim range than subsequent inventions. The examination also lasts longer because the examiners still lack the specific experience concerning the new technology. After shorter examination processes in the growth state, a longer average duration for the saturation state follows because then the applications have to be compared to a higher technological standard (Haupt et al. 2007).

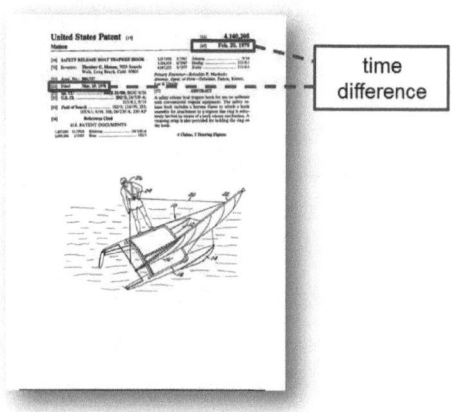

Fig. 4.20 Data collection for examination duration indicator

The examination duration also exists for scientific literature where a date of filing of an article and a date of acceptance (the review time) is also sometimes stored and made available. Just like for patents, when the technological standard has only been set, the reviewers may have to get the necessary knowledge and experience before they can comment. With an advancing technological standard, an increasing amount of prior art has to be considered. This leads to a longer review duration during the emergence and saturation states than during the growth state.

The indicator requires the retrieval of filing and grant dates and calculation of the time difference for each relevant patent separately. The calculation effort for this indicator is low and increases linearly for additional records.

Examination duration: the time span in days between (APD) and (ISD) is calculated to determine the duration of the examination process.

4.7.1.10   Forward Patent Citations

A reference to a firm's own patent received from another patent that is filed later is called a forward citation (Jaffe 2000; Carpenter et al. 1981). The index of forward citations counts the accumulated number of citations a patent received since it was granted, as displayed in figure 4.21. Young patents therefore show lower values of forward citations than older patents because they had less time to receive any. This time effect prevents forward citations to inform us about the maturity development in the recent past (Haupt et al. 2007).

HAUPT et al. assume an additional effect pointing in the same direction: patents that are granted in the emergence state have to be cited in the majority of all the following applications just because they constitute the basis of the new technology. In contrast to that, patents granted in the growth state document developments on specific branches of the technology. Thus, only applications on the same branch have to cite them (Ihnen 2000, p.556; Welte 1991, p.140). Therefore, forward citations decrease significantly from introduction to growth (Haupt et al. 2007).

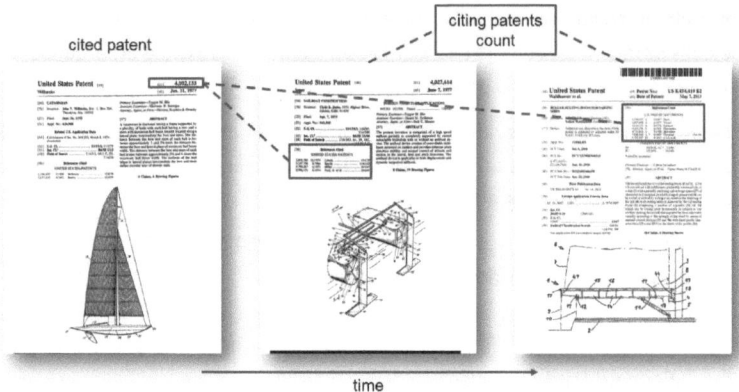

Fig. 4.21 Data collection for forward patent citations indicator

This same indicator can be calculated for any media type with the possibility of citation such as scientific literature. A similar behavior is probable, following the same argumentation as above: younger articles have less time to get cited and research on more mature technologies tends to be focused on more specific topics (branches) and thus gets cited less often than more general research.

All citing patents have to be retrieved for each cited patent. This requires a full search of the database for each cited patent. Summation and averaging of the citing patents is done in a second step. The calculation effort is low, but the retrieval effort coming along with each patent is slightly increased, rising linearly for additional patents.

Forward patent citations: to determine the count of forward patent citations, the corresponding patent number is searched in the (REF)-field of all other patents. The result count corresponds to the count of forward patent citations.

4.7.2 Considering Indicator Biases

All Indicators are evaluated based on their discriminant properties, separately and in combination. For each of these evaluations, a misclassification rate $Err^*(y)$ is given. Many machine-learning approaches are sensitive to a diverging number of observations (i.e. indicator values) per group (i.e. maturity state), which is why this number of observations has to be considered. The activity and meta data indicators are generated based on the same US patent data. But due to the different approaches how indicators are calculated, a different count of values is available in the training set for the machine-learning approach. The activity indicators generate the same amount of values each year (one value for each indicator per year and technology), but the meta data indicators generate an increasing amount of values when more patents exist in a given year for a given technology. The reason for this is that every patent document generates one separate value. This results in a much higher count of indicator values for the later years (see figure 4.3 in section 4.5.1 for the steadily increasing absolute US patent count) and thus a bias towards the technology maturity states predominant in that period.

A bias towards one of the maturity states should result in a decreasing misclassification rate (Backhaus et al. 2003, pp.179–181): for identical probabilities of each of the (five) maturity states, the misclassification rate of a random classification would be four in five, or 80%. If the probabilities are known and one of the maturity states is more probable, always choosing this state would result in a misclassification rate of 1-(probability of that state). This means for a known distribution of the maturity states that a higher bias will lead to a lower expected misclassification rate Err^*. This is equivalent with higher requirements that have to be met because an operationalized technology maturity model only is considered to work well when it is significantly better than a classification which is correct by coincidence. Therefore Err^* is used as a quality criterion for the approach in this book.

4.7.3 Compiling Activity Indicator Values for a Technology by Example of the MiniDisc Technology

Thus far, two contestant sets of technology maturity indicators were described: a set of new activity indicators and, as a benchmark, a set of well-established meta data indicators. Biases resulting from the way the different indicator sets are constructed were then investigated. This section shows how the new activity indicators differ from the absolute document count, which has been used in many similar analyses. There is one indicator value for each year, giving way for a time series analysis. Each technology generates indicator values for all six (or eight for the time period between 2004 and 2012) indicators every year. On top of that, the absolute document counts for US and international patents as well as for scientific publications can all be surveyed. To explain the indicator behavior, the trajectories of each indicator is displayed for the MiniDisc technology as an example in figures 4.22 to 4.32. A regression window size of three years for the slope indicators was selected and is used henceforth[5]. Notice the

---

[5] The selection process which led to this decision is described in detail in section 0.

difference between the absolute document counts and the corresponding fraction indicators which typically prepones the peak value.

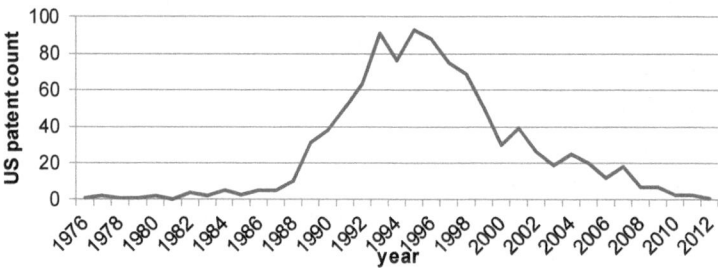

Fig. 4.22 Absolute US patents count relevant for the minidisc technology by issue date in the years 1976-2012

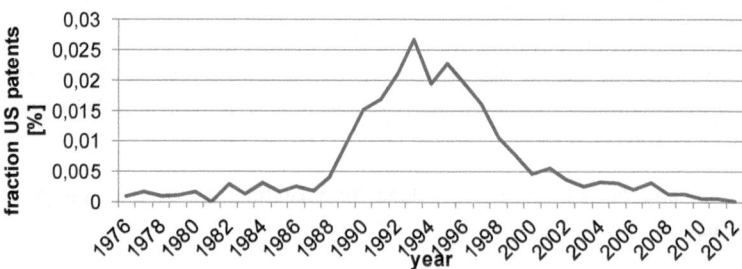

Fig. 4.23 Fraction of US patents relevant for the minidisc technology of all data storage technology US patents by issue date in the years 1976-2012

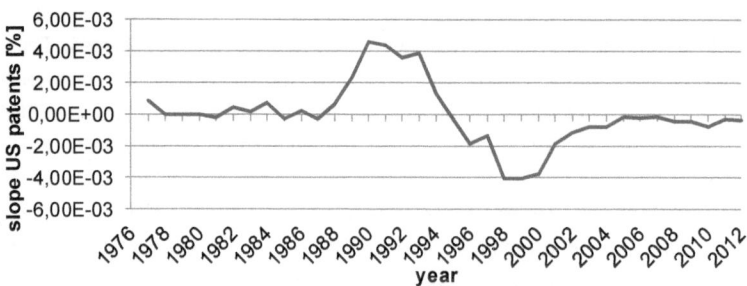

Fig. 4.24 Slope of data storage US patents relevant for the minidisc technology by issue date in the years 1976-2012

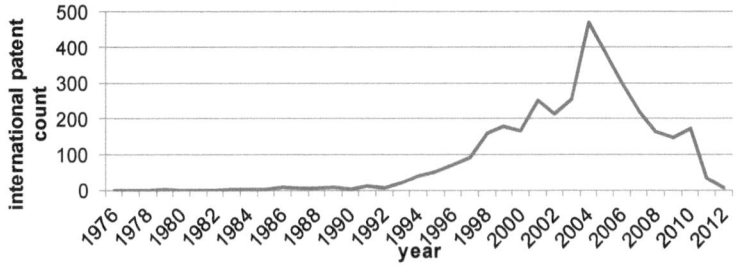

Fig. 4.25 Absolute international patents count relevant for the minidisc technology by application date in the years 1976-2012

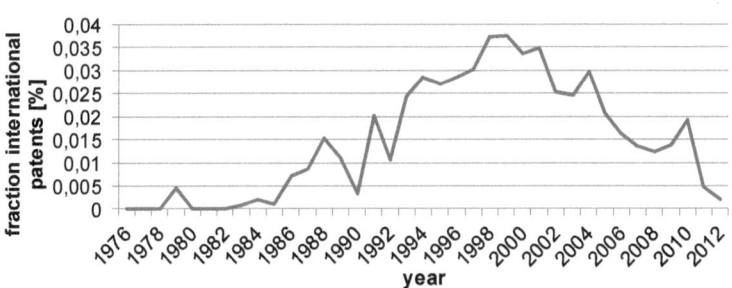

Fig. 4.26 Fraction of data storage international patents relevant for the minidisc technology of all data storage technology international patents by application date in the years 1976-2012

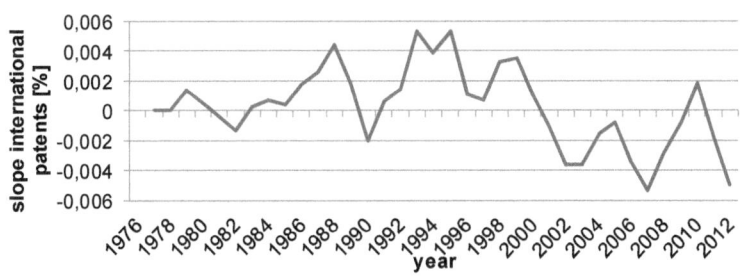

Fig. 4.27 Slope of data storage international patents relevant for the minidisc technology by publication date in the years 1976-2012

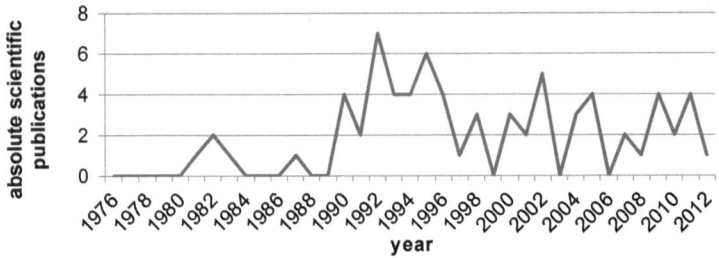

Fig. 4.28 Absolute scientific publications count relevant for the minidisc technology by publication date in the years 1976-2012

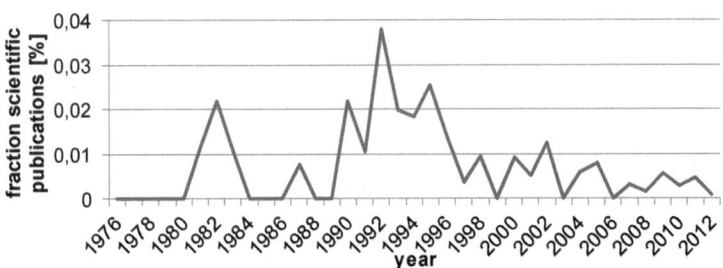

Fig. 4.29 Fraction of data storage scientific publications relevant for the minidisc technology of all data storage technology scientific publications by publication date in the years 1976-2012

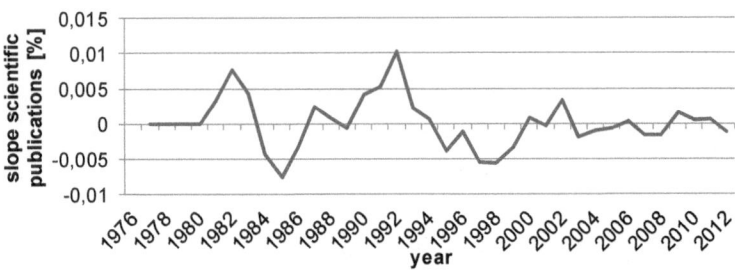

Fig. 4.30 Slope of data storage scientific publications relevant for the minidisc technology by publication date in the years 1976-2012

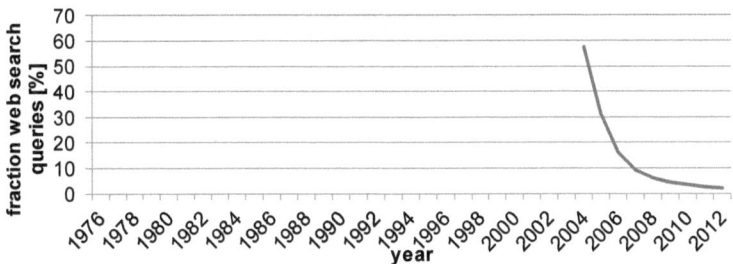

Fig. 4.31 Fraction of data storage web search queries relevant for the minidisc technology by query date in the years 1976-2012. The 100% value is determined by the relatively highest weekly value as provided by Google; the yearly values are the arithmetic middle of all weekly values in the corresponding year

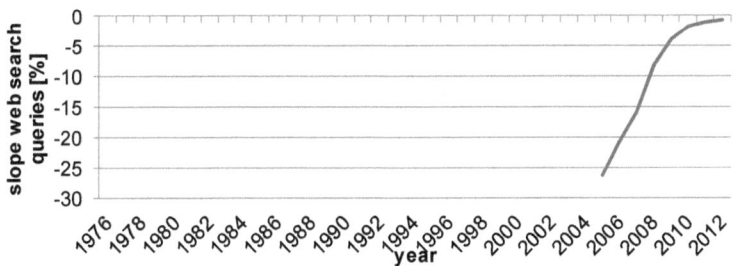

Fig. 4.32 Slope of data storage web search queries relevant for the minidisc technology by query date in the years 1976-2012

4.7.4 Assigning Activity Indicator Observations to States of Maturity and Determining the Distribution of Observations Across These States

In the last section 4.7.3, a set of indicator values was calculated for the minidisc technology for each year. All indicator values provide potentially relevant information about the minidisc technology maturity. It is yet unknown which indicators in the set are especially useful for estimating certain states of a technology's maturity. This cannot be deduced from the minidisc technology based indicator values alone. Rather, it depends on which indicator values or indicator value combinations show similar patterns during certain states of maturity for all technologies alike. When these are known, even as yet unknown technologies can be assigned to a maturity state based on their indicator values. To determine these typical patterns, the approach in this book therefore links indicator value combinations of all technologies to maturity states assigned by technology experts in the Delphi method in table 4.2 of section 4.2. Each set of indicator observations for each technology and during each year can be assigned a maturity state in this way. When all indicator observations have been assigned to a maturity state, the observations are aggregated by maturity state. This process is depicted in figure 4.33. The result is a number of observations which represent typical indicator value combinations for a maturity state. These can then be used as the input data for a Machine-learning approach such as the one depicted in figure 2.33 in section 2.3.5.3 where the indicator set observations serve as extracted features and the maturity information serves as the label. Such a machine-learning approach can then be used to derive the stipulated technology maturity specific patterns from the input data.

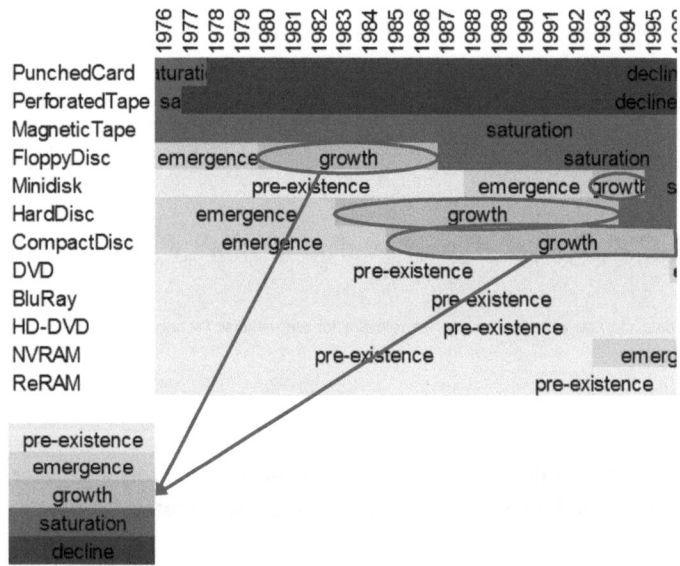

Fig. 4.33 Transformation of all indicator value sets from technology-and-year-based to a maturity-based assignment. Still, each indicator value set consists of six or eight indicator values: the fraction and slope of international and US patents, scientific publications, and, if applicable, web search queries

All the values for all six (eight including the web search query data) activity indicators are calculated with help of the R software and grouped in sets of observations by technology and year, as done for the minidisc technology in section 4.7.3. The activity indicators provide one set of values for twelve technologies over the course of 36 years, which results in a total of $12 \cdot 36 = 432$ indicator set observations without the web search data, where each set consists of six indicator values (namely: the fraction and slope of us patents, international patents, and scientific publications). According to the Delphi method in section 4.2, only 6 of the 12 technologies change their maturity state during the eight years for which web search data is available. All technologies which do not change state of maturity during the observed time period are excluded from the evaluation because they bias the error rate in favor of the short time span. Therefore, during this period of time the indicators provide $6 \cdot 8 = 48$ observations for each indicator set consisting of eight indicator values, namely the fraction and slope of US patents, international patents, scientific publications, and web search queries, each with an assigned maturity state label. These two indicator sets serve as the input data of the following activity indicator-based analyses. To estimate an effect of potential biases of this input data as described in section 4.7.2, the distribution of maturity states must be known. The distributions of maturity labels are equal to those of the Delphi method in tables 4.3 and 4.4 of section 4.2. The number of observations per maturity state and the median values of all technologies per indicator during each state of maturity are provided in tables 4.8 and 4.9 to enhance the comprehension of all subsequent analyses.

Table 4.8 Observation count and median values of activity indicator values for all technologies by maturity state between 2004 and 2012

Maturity state	0	1	2	3	4
Observation count ($\Sigma = 48$)	5	7	11	11	14
fraction international patents	0.0070	0.0320	0.1050	0.1774	0.1225
fraction US patents	0.0013	0.0007	0.0841	0.0583	0.0212
fraction scientific publications	0.0139	0.0159	0.3164	0.0814	0.0517
fraction web search queries	0	10	38.92	64.75	23
slope international patents	0.0011	0.0117	0.0126	0.0063	-0.0141
slope US patents	0.0003	0.0002	0.0028	0.0003	-0.0005
slope scientific publications	0.0023	0.0050	-0.0002	-0.0072	-0.0035
slope web search queries	0	4	-4	-4	-5

Table 4.9 Observation count and median values of activity indicator values for all technologies by maturity state between 1976 and 2012

Maturity state	0	1	2	3	4
Observation count ($\Sigma = 432$)	130	44	54	75	129
fraction international patents	0	0.0164	0.0623	0.1160	0.0017
fraction US patents	0	0.0026	0.0202	0.0342	0.0019
fraction scientific publications	0	0.0357	0.1583	0.0949	0.0028
slope international patents	0	0.0048	0.0067	0.0000	-0.0001
slope US patents	0	0.0007	0.0035	-0.0010	-0.0003
slope scientific publications	0	0.0013	0.0035	-0.0016	-0.0001

To understand how useful indicators or operationalized technology maturity models are in assessing technology maturity, it is necessary to first know with what precision technology maturity can be estimated without them. This general problem is described in section 4.7.2. Assuming an equal distribution of all maturity states, when a state is selected at random, then there is a one in five or 20% chance that the correct state is selected. This leads to a misclassification rate of

$$p(Err^*) = 1 - p(\text{selected state}) = 1 - 0{,}20 = \mathbf{80\%}$$

Only an indicator or a classificator which performs better than $p(Err^*)$ is of actual value.

Not all states exist for the same duration, however, so the maturity state distribution is not equal. When the distribution share of a maturity state is known, this a-priori probability can also be taken into consideration (Backhaus et al. 2003, pp.179–181). A strategy to estimate the current state of maturity would then be to randomly select states of maturity according to the distribution, which would serve the same results as the strategy to always select the state with the largest share of the distribution. This strategy will henceforth be referred to as the "trivial strategy". Its misclassification rate will serve as the benchmark in the following analyses. It is necessary to determine the maturity state distribution to derive the trivial strategy. The maturity state distribution shares are calculated according to formula 4.1 by dividing the count of observations of a certain state of maturity by the absolute count of observations in the given time span, as proposed in BACKHAUS et al. (Backhaus et al. 2003, pp.189–190). The underlying data can be found in tables 4.8 (2004-2012) and 4.9 (1976-2012).

$$p(m) = obs(m) \Big/ \sum_{\forall i} obs(m_i)$$

with

$p(m)$: distribution share of maturity state m

$obs(m)$: count of observations of maturity state m

i: referencing index for maturity states

Table 4.10 Distribution of maturity states for technologies which change maturity states during the time period 2004-2012 based on activity data indicators

p(pre-existence)	p(emergence)	p(growth)	p(saturation)	p(decline)
10%	15%	23%	23%	29%

The distribution of maturity states as displayed in table 4.10 is relatively uniform. No rule of thumb exists for the situation in which unequal sample sizes make heterogeneity of variance a problem (Keppel 2004). Even if there are many observations in the larger groups, the smallest group alone determines the statistical power of an analysis (Keppel 2004). The misclassification rate of the trivial strategy to always choose the maturity state with the largest share (decline) is

$$p(Err^*(activity)) = 1 - \max_{\forall m}(p(m)) = 1 - 0,29 = \mathbf{71\%}.$$

The data from 1976-2012 includes all twelve technologies because they all change maturity states to some extent during that time span.

Table 4.11 Distribution of maturity states for technologies which change maturity states during the time period 1976-2012 based on activity data indicators

p(pre-existence)	p(emergence)	p(growth)	p(saturation)	p(decline)
30%	10%	13%	17%	30%

Since the time span is much longer than for 2004-2012, and technologies take only a limited time from the point where they are introduced to the time they reach their decline state, most technologies covered in that period spend a relatively long period of time either in the pre-existence or in the decline state. This can easily be recognized in the values presented in table 4.11, where the corresponding states are clearly overrepresented. The misclassification rate of the trivial strategy to always choose the most probable state (either pre-existence or decline) is

$$p(Err^*(activity)) = 1 - \max_{\forall m}(p(m)) = 1 - 0{,}3 = 70\%$$

At this point, indicator data is available, each labelled with the maturity information from the Delphi method, and the expected results from the trivial strategy are available as a benchmark.

4.7.5 Comparing Hypothetical to Actual Indicator Behavior

Section 2.2.3.2 describes hypotheses of the S&D model latent variable behavior, section 2.3.4.2 hypothesizes activity indicator behavior, and section 2.3.5.2 summarizes hypotheses concerning the activity in certain text media during different maturity states by means of a curve point sequence. Thus far these hypotheses could not be tested because they had not been operationalized or applied to empirical data. Section 4.7.4 provides the necessary indicator sets complemented by technology maturity state information. In this section the hypotheses are tested with the help of these new activity indicators. The S&D model's hypotheses are tested in section 4.7.5.1, the activity indicator behavior is tested in section 4.7.5.2, and the curve point sequence hypotheses in section 0.

4.7.5.1 Comparing Hypotheses of the S&D Model Factors to Actual Indicator Behavior

The S&D model features a number of model factors which all assume a certain behavior during a technology's maturation. Unfortunately thus far, no efforts were made to operationalize these model factors and thus it was not possible to test whether the hypotheses of the S&D model were indeed accurate. A connection to latent variables of the S&D model is established for each activity indicator in sections 2.3.3.4 and 0. In section 4.7.1, several of the S&D model factors are operationalized by activity indicators, section 4.7.3 describes how they are compiled for an example technology, and section 4.7.4 describes how maturity information is assigned to indicator observations. This allows us to test the anticipated behavior of the S&D model empirically. As a first step, the behavior of each single activity indicator is therefore compared to the hypotheses postulated by the corresponding S&D model factors. From the S&D model there is at least one hypothesis for each indicator concerning its development over the course of a technology's maturity (see table 4.7 of section 4.6). Since the hypotheses do not consider combinations of indicator values, they can be tested by simply comparing the means of each slope indicator during each maturity state. This is done separately for each technology in order to avoid wrong conclusions due to a misclassification by the experts or a technology with unusual behavior. As an example, table 4.12

shows the mean values of the fraction of international patents indicator for all technologies, grouped by maturity state. The pre-existence state is included in the comparison despite not being included in any of the S&D model hypotheses. All comments only refer to the latter maturity states between emergence and decline, unless otherwise stated. It must be noted that the web search request indicators cannot be analyzed with the same approach because they are based on relative data which was normalized with an unknown approach.

Table 4.12 Mean fraction international patents indicator values for each technology, grouped by maturity state.

fraction international patents	pre-existence	emergence	growth	saturation	decline	row max
Blu-ray	0.000	0.037	0.094	0.069		0.09
CompactDisc		0.003	0.057	0.123	0.134	0.13
DVD	0.000	0.082	0.170	0.247	0.152	0.25
FloppyDisc		0.033	0.044	0.019	0.009	0.04
HardDisc		0.003	0.027	0.141	0.165	0.17
HD-DVD	0.000	0.014	0.040		0.011	0.04
MagneticTape				0.157	0.031	0.16
MiniDisc	0.002	0.012	0.026	0.032	0.019	0.03
NVRAM	0.001	0.031	0.103	0.217		0.22
PerforatedTape				0.036	0.000	0.04
PunchedCard				0.018	0.001	0.02
ReRAM	0.002	0.027				0.03

The fraction of the international and US patents are hypothesized to represent the S&D model factors **B.** (investments in technology development) and **F.** (patent count) of table 2.12 in section 2.3.3.4. These both assume an indicator development which leads to low values in the emergence state, high values in the growth state, and ever-decreasing values in the saturation and decline states. In other words: these hypotheses assume a typical pattern, independent of a technology, which can now be tested by comparing the indicator means in table 4.12 separately for each technology. The S&D model as displayed in table 2.12 makes use of terms such as "high" and "low" to describe indicator values during maturity states. Since the indicators in table 4.12 are not normalized, it is impossible to determine whether a certain value is high or low without considering the mean values of all other maturity states of a technology. The mean values of each separate indicator c can be transformed to a scale from 0% to 100% for the separate maturity states m according to formula 4.2, to establish a better overview.

$$c_{mt\%} = \frac{c_{mt} - \min_{\forall m}(c_{mt})}{\max_{\forall m}(c_{mt}) - \min_{\forall m}(c_{mt})}$$

with

mt: *given maturity state m and technology t*

c_{mt} : *mean activity indicator value in maturity state m*

$c_{mt\%}$: *normalized activity indicator value in* $[0\%, 100\%]$

This results in the lowest mean indicator value being 0% whereas the highest being 100% for each technology. A known scale makes it easier to compare the values for all maturity states with each other. Unfortunately, even for the long time period between 1976 and 2012, most technologies do not have values for all of the maturity states. Normalization should only take into account technologies for which it can be reasonably assumed that the maturity state with the highest values is actually included in the analysis. Technologies which do not feature indicator values for any one of the states of emergence, growth, or saturation will therefore be excluded from this consideration. This holds true for the technologies of HD-DVD, magnetic tape, perforated tape, punched card, and ReRAM. The results of the normalization is displayed in table 4.13.

For the Blu-ray and possibly floppy disc technologies, the S&D hypotheses seem to hold (low – high – decreasing – decreasing). However, the majority of the technologies produce a pattern which could be described as low – rising – maximal – decreasing, which can be seen from the mean of the values in the last row. This could be caused by a time difference which is produced by considering the patents at the time of their application rather than at the time of grant or publication. The S&D model does not explicitly state which date should be used. Fortunately in this analysis for the fraction of US patents indicator, the grant date was used, so it can be tested whether the difference between hypothesis and data is due to the timing choice. This is rather improbable, however, for the following reason: using its grant date rather than the application date postpones an invention by at least 18 months. A lag should therefore be expected which would delay the peak of activity. Table 4.14 shows the normalized fraction of US patents indicator values.

Table 4.13 Mean fraction of international patents indicator values (collected at time of patent application) for all technologies with observations of the emergence, growth, and saturation maturity states during the time period between 1976 and 2012, grouped by maturity state, rescaled to values between 0% and 100%

normalized fraction international patents	*pre-existence*	*emergence*	*growth*	*saturation*	*decline*
Blu-ray	0%	40%	100%	74%	
Compact-Disc		0%	41%	91%	100%
DVD	0%	33%	69%	100%	61%
FloppyDisc		97%	100%	29%	0%
HardDisc		0%	15%	85%	100%
MiniDisc	0%	33%	81%	100%	57%
NVRAM	0%	14%	47%	100%	
mean	0%	31%	65%	83%	64%

Table 4.14 Mean fraction of US patents indicator values (collected at the time of patent grant) for all technologies with observations of the emergence, growth, and saturation maturity states during the time period between 1976 and 2012, grouped by maturity state, rescaled to values between 0% and 100%

normalized fraction US patents	*pre-existence*	*emergence*	*growth*	*saturation*	*decline*
Blu-ray	0%	3%	65%	100%	
Compact-Disc		0%	61%	100%	57%
DVD	0%	13%	77%	95%	100%
FloppyDisc		31%	100%	80%	0%
HardDisc		0%	9%	59%	100%
MiniDisc	0%	55%	100%	64%	3%
NVRAM	0%	14%	72%	100%	
mean	0%	17%	69%	86%	52%

Again, some of the technologies behave differently, but the majority shows the peak during the saturation state. This can be seen from the mean of the values in the last row, which shows the same development pattern as for the international patent indicator, differing only by a few per cent. Only the floppy disc and MiniDisc technologies behave according to the S&D hypothesis. There is no obvious difference between using a patent's application or grant date for the purpose of maturity state analysis. Curiously, this contradicts findings in CHEN et al (2012), which would expect the application count to decline and the grant count to increase in relation to each other for increasingly mature technologies (Chen et al. 2012). The reason for this may be that the time between the application and the grant of a patent is negligible in comparison to the time a technology spends in a certain maturity state and that the effect of CHEN et al. is too small to affect the observations in this analysis.

Table 4.15 Mean fraction of scientific publication indicator values for all technologies with observations of the emergence, growth, and saturation maturity states during the time period between 1976 and 2012, grouped by maturity state, rescaled to values between 0% and 100%

normalized fraction scientific publications	pre-existence	emergence	growth	saturation	decline
Blu-ray	0%	68%	100%	83%	
Compact-Disc		0%	75%	100%	38%
DVD	0%	25%	43%	83%	100%
FloppyDisc		42%	100%	85%	0%
HardDisc		20%	71%	100%	0%
MiniDisc	1%	66%	100%	40%	0%
NVRAM	48%	100%	27%	0%	
mean	12%	46%	74%	70%	28%

The fraction of scientific publications are expected to resemble the S&D model factors **B.** (investments in technology development: low – maximal – low – negligible), **C.** (number of application areas: unknown - increasing - established, plenty - decreasing), and **H1.** (scientific access requirements: high during emergence state) of table 2.12. All three S&D model factor hypotheses describe different behavior scenarios, but nevertheless, with the available data neither of the expected patterns can be reproduced. The patterns described by the different technologies are inhomogeneous. The majority of the technologies show moderate indicator values in the emergence state, then a peak in either the growth or the saturation state and relatively high values in the respective other and very low values in the decline state. This translates into the pattern (moderate – high – high – negligible), which is not useful for differentiating the growth and saturation states, but at least for differentiating the other states from these two.

Table 4.16 Mean slope of international patents indicator values (collected at the time of patent application) for all technologies with observations of the emergence, growth, and saturation maturity states during the time period between 1976 and 2012, grouped by maturity state, rescaled to values between 0% and 100%

normalized slope international patents	pre-existence	emergence	growth	saturation	decline
Blu-ray	0%	19%	84%	100%	
Compact-Disc		0%	58%	100%	96%
DVD	0%	18%	57%	100%	76%
FloppyDisc		100%	18%	1%	0%
HardDisc		2%	0%	100%	64%
MiniDisc	0%	34%	60%	100%	5%
NVRAM	0%	15%	59%	100%	
mean	0%	27%	48%	86%	48%

Table 4.17 Mean slope of US patents indicator values (collected at the time of patent grant) for all technologies with observations of the emergence, growth, and saturation maturity states during the time period between 1976 and 2012, grouped by maturity state, rescaled to values between 0% and 100%

normalized slope US patents	pre-existence	emergence	growth	saturation	decline
Blu-ray	0%	3%	34%	100%	
Compact-Disc		21%	59%	100%	0%
DVD	0%	3%	40%	83%	100%
FloppyDisc		61%	100%	56%	0%
HardDisc		0%	6%	70%	100%
MiniDisc	43%	62%	98%	100%	0%
NVRAM	0%	10%	78%	100%	
mean	11%	23%	59%	87%	40%

Table 4.18 Mean slope of scientific publications indicator values (collected at time of publication) for all technologies with observations of the emergence, growth, and saturation maturity states during the time period between 1976 and 2012, grouped by maturity state, rescaled to values between 0% and 100%

normalized slope scientific publications	pre-existence	emergence	growth	saturation	decline
Blu-ray	0%	20%	88%	100%	
Compact-Disc		15%	78%	100%	0%
DVD	0%	8%	29%	66%	100%
FloppyDisc		13%	100%	50%	0%
HardDisc		100%	44%	32%	0%
MiniDisc	87%	61%	100%	83%	0%
NVRAM	97%	100%	7%	0%	
mean	46%	45%	64%	61%	20%

Analogously to the activity fraction indicators, the activity slope indicators can be transformed to a scale from 0% to 100% according to formula 4.2.

For the patent-based slope indicators, the observable pattern is pronounced and similar to the one of the patent-based fraction indicators and could thus be described as low – rising – maximal – decreasing. Unless there are systematic small differences (e.g. due to the lag between application and grant dates), these indicators should be checked for correlation, which would make them redundant. For the scientific publications the pattern is much less pronounced. In fact, every maturity state features a maximal value for at least one of the technologies and apparently there are no typical patterns. This finding stands in contrast to its use as a technology maturity indicator, but this will be tested in subsequent sections of this book.

All in all, none of the S&D hypotheses concerning the behavior of certain variables could be confirmed empirically. This may be due to two reasons: either a) the hypotheses are wrong and do not apply or b) they were operationalized wrong. The indicators found in the process still mostly produce typical patterns over the course of a technology's maturity and thus are candidates for use in technology maturity assessment.

4.7.5.2 Comparing Hypotheses Concerning Ideal Indicator Properties to Actual Indicator Properties

Section 2.3.4.2 presents a list of desirable indicator properties and concludes that most of these properties are fulfilled by the activity indicators introduced in the same section. Desirable properties 1 and 2 on the list are ensured by the setup of the operationalized S&D model: the indicators are based on easy-to-access information and they are based on detailed existing theoretical maturity models. Desirable property 3 is ensured by the mathematical construction of the indicators, which makes technology maturity assessment possible with incomplete data and an ongoing process of maturing. Desirable property 4.b could not be assured by theoretical considerations, however. Even though the indicator values occur within a known interval (desirable property 4.a), they do not exhaust this interval by any means. This is problematic because it makes the comparisons of different technologies difficult. A value that is "high" for one technology could be "low" for another one. To test whether this is a problem for the approach in this book, the actual values are analyzed in this section.

Table 4.19 Comparison of smallest (minmax) and largest (maxmax) maximum values for different technologies by indicator and the ratio between smallest and largest value, based on data collected between 1976 and 2012

indicator	$minmax$	$maxmax$	$\dfrac{maxmax}{minmax}$
fraction international patents	0,0321	0,2473	7,7004
fraction US patents	0,0029	0,1171	40,7783
fraction scientific publications	0,0074	0,6107	82,7594
slope international patents	0,0021	0,0247	11,9792
slope US patents	0,0002	0,0068	36,8690
slope scientific publications	0,0007	0,0220	32,7685

Important concepts when transforming an indicator to a known scale are the maximal and minimal values of that indicator. When looking at the row maximum in table 4.12 it becomes evident that the indicators produce different maximal values for each technology. For example, the maximal value of the fraction of international patents in table 4.12 is 0.25 for the DVD technology, whereas that of the minidisc technology is a mere 0.03, both during the saturation state. This results in a ratio of 7.7:1, which seems to make this indicator alone unfit for classification. Table 4.19 displays the minimal and maximal maxima across all technologies and maturity states by indicator, as well as the ratio between the smallest and largest maximum. It must be noted that the web search request indicators cannot be analyzed with the same approach because they are based on relative data which was normalized with an unknown approach.

Table 4.19 shows that the ratios between smallest and largest maxima are relatively high. It may be hypothesized that this is due to the "definition size" of a technology:

Hypothesis: the definition of a technology determines how many documents exist related to it. There are technologies of small and large definition size. Technologies of large definition size in each year systematically generate relatively large amounts of documents throughout all media, whereas those with a small definition size generate only few. Those technologies of large definition size thus also generate larger maximal indicator values throughout all indicators than those of small definition size.

Table 4.20 Comparison of technology definition sizes: maximal indicator values of all maturity states for each technology by overall maximum indicator value

max by maxmax	fraction international patents	fraction US patents	fraction scientific publications	slope international patents	slope US patents	slope scientific publications
Blu-ray	38%	2%	1%	29%	3%	3%
CompactDisc	54%	36%	62%	26%	42%	91%
DVD	100%	19%	13%	70%	27%	27%
FloppyDisc	18%	19%	24%	100%	35%	80%
HardDisc	67%	55%	16%	32%	42%	41%
MiniDisc	13%	20%	3%	8%	22%	5%
NVRAM	88%	100%	100%	42%	100%	100%

If this hypothesis were true, it could help in designing an improved indicator which takes into consideration the definition size of a technology to make comparisons across technologies of different definition sizes feasible. To test this hypothesis, the maximum indicator value of each technology throughout all maturity states can be compared across the different indicators. If the hypothesis applies, the indicator maxima of a technology should be at a similar height for each indicator when compared with the other technologies. Table 4.20 displays the maximal indicator value of a technology for an indicator divided by the maximal maximum of that indicator.

Indeed, disregarding some exceptions, a technology seems to produce a characteristic maximal value or "definition size" in comparison to other technologies.

One conclusion to this finding could be to only analyze and compare technologies of roughly comparable definition size with this approach. On the other hand, the interplay of indicators may cancel out the definition size effect and remains to be tested.

4.7.5.3 Comparing Hypotheses of the Linear Model Curve Point Progression to Actual Indicator Behavior

Section 2.3.5.2 introduces several hypotheses connected to the order of indicator activity, as displayed in table 2.18. Some of the activity indicators stem from sources similar to the ones mentioned in that section. This fact allows the sources to be assigned to R&D states of the work by WATTS & PORTER (Watts & Porter 1997). All slope indicators describe the growth slope of the relative document frequency. They do not resemble any of the indicators described in works based on WATTS & PORTER (Watts & Porter 1997). Only the fraction indicators, not the slope indicators, are suited to determine the activity in a certain media source. Unfortunately the sources they are based on are not identical. A concordance table is displayed in table 4.21.

Table 4.21 R&D states defined by (Watts & Porter 1997) and typical sources which are hypothesized to rise during these states as well as activity indicators which are based on related sources

R&D state	Typical source	Activity indicator basis
I - Basic research	Science Citation Index	Scientific publications
II - Applied research	Engineering Index	(ScienceDirect)
III - Development	US Patents	US and PCT Patents
IV - Application	Newspaper Abstracts Daily	Web search queries
V - Social impacts	Business and Popular Press	(Google Trends)

The end point hypotheses can all be discarded immediately based on the data at hand because the search strategies for all technologies retrieved results until the last year of the analysis, 2012. This eliminates all hypotheses which were unique to the work by MARTINO (Martino 2003). A restriction has to be made concerning the web search data representing curve IV-V. This is only available beginning in 2004, which is why neither start nor top can precede this year. Both patent sources representing curve III provide data beginning in 1976, the literature data representing curve I-II starts in 1970. The indicator curve point progression hypotheses can therefore be tested for three curves with the hypotheses deduced from table 2.18 of section 2.3.5.2 summarized in table 4.22.

The first year for which a search strategy returns a result is used to determine the starting point of a curve. The top point is determined by the highest value of the corresponding relative frequency indicator for each media type. This is exemplarily done for the minidisc technology in figures 4.34 to 4.37. The figures correspond to the figures 4.22, 4.25, 4.28, and 4.31, but the starting and top points of each curve are marked by dashed and dotted lines to clarify this approach.

Table 4.22 Indicator curve point progression hypothesized in different works, transferred to media used in the approach in this book as displayed in table 2.18: J (Järvenpää 2009), P (Watts & Porter 1997), **1** always true, **0** always false

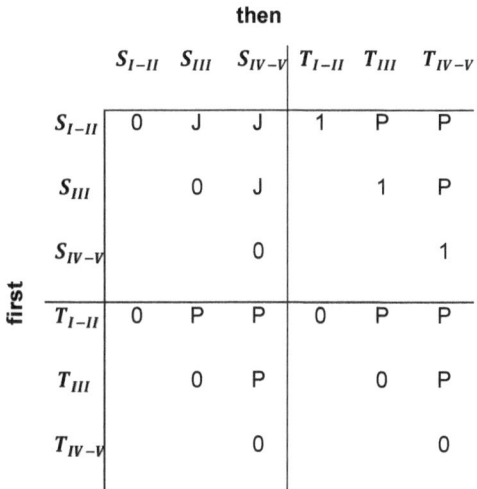

		then				
	S_{I-II}	S_{III}	S_{IV-V}	T_{I-II}	T_{III}	T_{IV-V}
S_{I-II}	0	J	J	1	P	P
S_{III}		0	J	1	P	
S_{IV-V}			0		1	
T_{I-II}	0	P	P	0	P	P
T_{III}		0	P		0	P
T_{IV-V}			0			0

(left label: **first**)

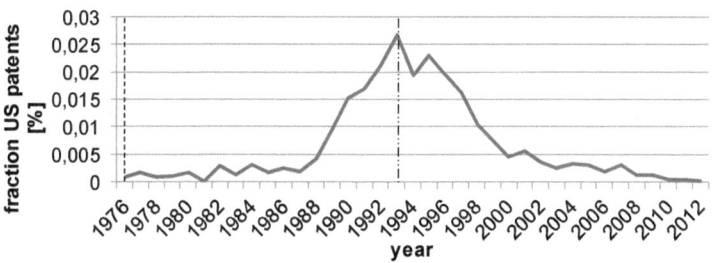

fraction US patents [%] — values 0,03 0,025 0,02 0,015 0,01 0,005 0 — years 1976 1978 1980 1982 1984 1986 1988 1990 1992 1994 1996 1998 2000 2002 2004 2006 2008 2010 2012

year

Fig. 4.34 Fraction of data storage US patents relevant for the minidisc technology with the starting point of the curve in the year 1976 marked with a dashed line and the top point of the curve in the year 1993 marked with a dashed and dotted line. It is important to note that the actual starting point of the curve may lie before the year 1976

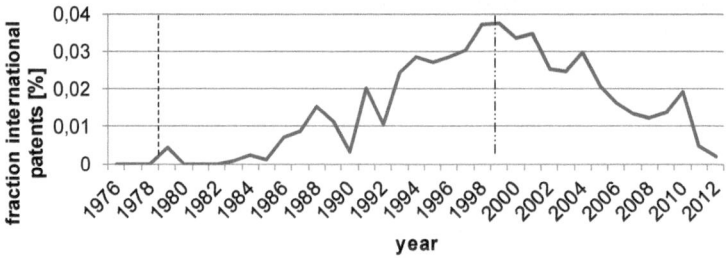

Fig. 4.35 Fraction of data storage international patents relevant for the minidisc technology with the starting point of the curve in the year 1979 marked with a dashed line and the top point of the curve in the year 1999 marked with a dashed and dotted line

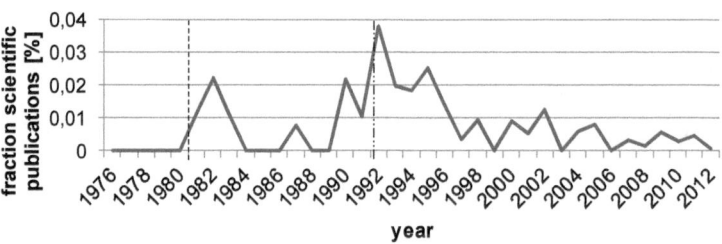

Fig. 4.36 Fraction of data storage scientific publications relevant for the minidisc technology with the starting point of the curve in the year 1981 marked with a dashed line and the top point of the curve in the year 1992 marked with a dashed and dotted line

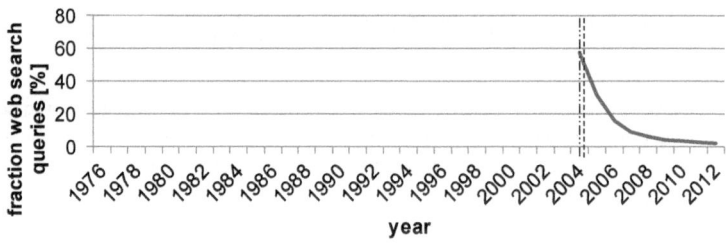

Fig. 4.37 Data storage web search requests relevant for the minidisc technology with the starting and top points of the curve in the year 2004

The results of this approach applied to each technology are shown in table 4.23.

None of the technologies is able to verify both the starting and top point hypotheses entirely. The same is true when looking at the starting point hypothesis separately. This is mostly due to the starting point of the web search data, which lies on the retrieval limit for all but ReRAM. The top point hypothesis is true for two technologies: Punched Cards and Blu-ray. In summary, several points appear in the anticipated order whereas most do not. The order of the curve points appears to be random considering the similarity of the technologies. The curve point hypotheses can be regarded as disproven. A similar analysis with non-normalized data was performed by JÄRVENPÄÄ et al. and confirms these conclusions (Järvenpää et al. 2011).

Table 4.23 Years of starting and top curve points for fraction indicators of different media. The order of the columns is arranged to fit the hypothesized order of media activity.

	Scientific Literature		US Patents		Worldwide Patents		Web Search	
	Start	Top	Start	Top	Start	Top	Start	Top
PunchedCard	1970	1970	1976	1979	1985	1994	2004	2005
PerforatedTape	1970	1973	1976	1977	1976	1976	2004	2012
MagneticTape	1970	1971	1976	1976	1976	1976	2004	2004
FloppyDisc	1976	1983	1976	1987	1976	1978	2004	2004
MiniDisc	1981	1992	1976	1993	1979	1999	2004	2004
HardDisc	1970	1978	1979	2009	1978	2010	2004	2004
CompactDisc	1970	1997	1976	1998	1980	2004	2004	2004
DVD	1996	2010	1997	2006	1995	2004	2004	2004
Blu-ray	2004	2006	2003	2010	2002	2009	2004	2011
HD-DVD	2005	2006	2001	2009	1997	2007	2004	2007
NVRAM	1976	1992	1976	2012	1989	2012	2004	2004
ReRAM	2003	2012	2002	2012	1998	2012	2010	2012

4.7.6 Using a Linear Discriminant Analysis to Gauge the Maturity Classification Performance of the Activity Indicators

A set of indicators was described in sections 4.7.1 until 4.7.4. Thus far, based on hypotheses from the literature, the characteristic values of these indicators are associated with states of maturity, and it is shown how actual indicators are calculated and then assigned to a state of maturity. Little is known about how well the indicators work for maturity assessment. This section will therefore gauge the performance of the indicators regarding this aspect. Section 0 presents a series of statistical tests on the available data to make way for analyses performed in the subsequent sections. Section 0 shows how a good value for the regression window of the slope indicators was determined. Section 4.7.6.3 presents thoughts on reducing the model by indicators which do not add to its classification performance. These are then tested with a random forest approach. And finally, section 4.7.6.4 performs a machine-learning approach to generate an operationalized technology maturity model based on the activity indicators and gauges its classification performance.

4.7.6.1 Assumptions of the Analyses Used

One purpose of the approach in this book is to present an operationalized technology maturity model which allows classification of technologies for which the current maturity state is unknown. The approach in this book will try to do this using a machine-learning approach. There are several suitable approaches for this task, such as the random forest approach presented in section 4.7.6.3. The advantage of this approach is that it is strictly non-parametric and thus does not require laborious assumption testing. However, the random forest approach has a drawback which makes it less suitable for the approach in this book: it is a stochastic approach and can only be reproduced when the entire random forest consisting of several hundreds or thousands decision trees is provided as a classifier. There is no simple and intuitive classifier as the result of the random forest approach. This is hardly satisfactory as the result of the approach in this book. Several parametric approaches such as a discriminant analysis provide intuitive classifiers which are easy to interpret, but they also make certain assumptions concerning the underlying data:

"The ability of discriminant analysis to derive discriminant functions that provide accurate classifications is enhanced when the assumptions of normality, linearity, and homogeneity of variance are satisfied." (Srivastava & Rego 2011, p.14.37)

Bearing this in mind, the data is carefully tested for homoscedasticity and normality according to the setup displayed in figure 4.38, which features a series of tests with decreasing sensitivity.

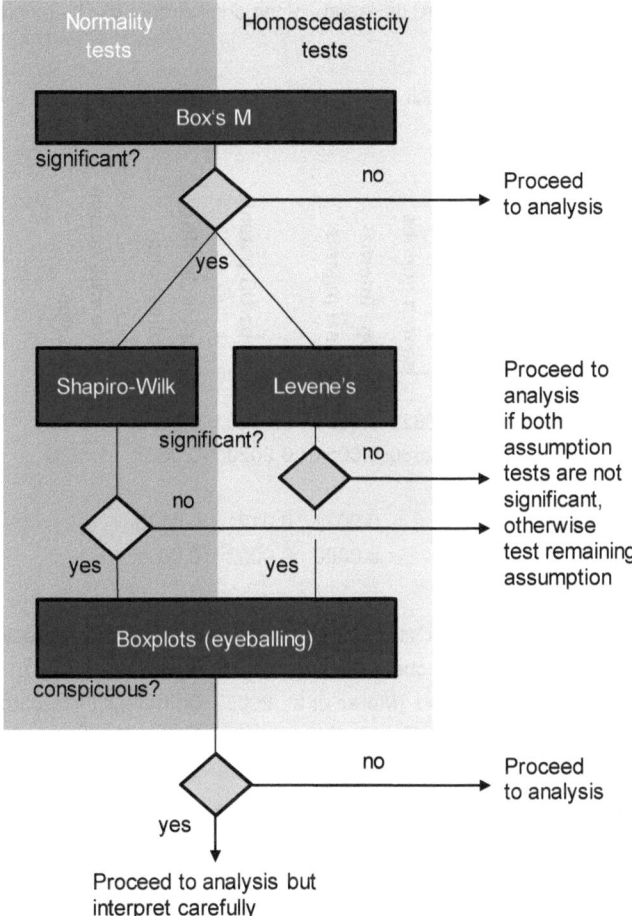

Fig. 4.38 Setup of statistical tests for normality (left side) and homoscedasticity (right side) which assures that data which does not comply with the assumptions of parametric analyses is treated with due caution. The tests are arranged with decreasing sensitivity

All tests were performed based on a regression window of three years for the slope indicators. Before data is tested, it can be pre-treated. In this case, it was standardized, which means that each indicator was first centered (subtracted mean from each value) and then divided by its standard deviation (Berrueta et al. 2007). To transform new data to this scale, the means and standard deviations of the original data can be found in table 4.24.

Table 4.24 Arithmetic mean and standard deviation (SD) of all indicator values in the time periods between 2004-2012 and 1976-2012

	fraction international patents	fraction US patents	fraction scientific publications	fraction web search queries	slope international patents	slope US patents	slope scientific publications	slope web search queries
2004-2012								
SD	0.0765	0.0409	0.1176	24.0623	0.0084	0.0026	0.0059	6.5404
Mean	0.1024	0.0327	0.0869	31.2580	0.0051	0.0020	-0.0003	-1.7980
1976-2012								
SD	0.0619	0.0269	0.1421		0.0021	0.0121	0.0128	
Mean	0.0397	0.0151	0.0817		0.0000	-0.0002	0.0001	

The data was also corrected for outliers. Outliers are observations that appear to break the pattern shown by the majority of the observations. Most multivariate analyses assume that they are dealt with beforehand (Møller et al. 2005). Considering the data from all available technologies, an indicator value is considered an outlier if for one maturity state it extends more than 1,5 interquartile ranges above the third quartile or below the first (compare e.g. BARNETT & LEWIS (Barnett & Lewis 1994)). Outliers are filtered in all subsequent analyses.

The significance of the results is indicated in the standard way as displayed in table 4.25.

The null hypothesis of Box's M is homogeneity of variance-covariance matrices, which is equivalent to both assumptions, normal deviation and homoscedasticity, being fulfilled in the data. This pretest was implemented in R at the 0.05 significance level. The corresponding code was taken from LIAW & MAITRA (Liaw & Maitra 2012). The time period from 1976 to 2012 provides a sufficiently large sample size for all maturity states (n>20) to apply a Chi-square approximation. The time period from 2004-2012, on the other hand, does not provide enough data, which is why it is calculated based on an F approximation instead. The results can be found in table 4.26.

Table 4.25 Significance level codes

Significance level codes
< 0.001 ***
< 0.01 **
< 0.05 *
< 0.1 .

Table 4.26 Results of Box's M homogeneity of variance-covariance matrices test for the activity indicators in the time periods of 2004-2012 and 1976-2012

Time slice	MBox	F	df1	df2	p-value
2004-2012	1751.5786	5.0511	144	1240	0.0000
1976-2012	4623.2442	4454.5915	84		0.0000

In both cases, the p-values show that the null hypothesis must be rejected. This means that the covariance matrices are significantly different for both observed time periods. The homoscedasticity and normality assumptions are therefore not fulfilled according to Box's M. Box's M is known to produce conservative results and to react especially sensitively to a lack of normality (Tabachnick & Fidell 2001). Other, less conservative approaches may lead to different results and are therefore tested.

To test normality, the Shapiro-Wilk test for normality was also implemented in R with help of the package shapiro.test(). The null hypothesis for this is that the values show normal deviation. For the normality assumption to be fulfilled, the test should be non-significant for all indicators. The results of the test can be found in table 4.27 for the period between 2004 and 2012 and in table 4.28 for the period between 1976 and 2012.

Table 4.27 Results of the Shapiro-Wilk normality test for the activity indicators in the time period of 2004-2012

Indicator	W	p-value	significance
fraction international patents	0.9272	0.005379	***
fraction US patents	0.7715	3.114e-07	***
fraction scientific publications	0.7084	1.87e-08	***
fraction web search queries	0.9183	0.002583	***
slope international patents	0.9235	0.00395	***
slope US patents	0.7667	2.481e-07	***
slope scientific publications	0.8916	0.0003402	***
slope web search queries	0.9431	0.02143	**

Table 4.28 Results of the Shapiro-Wilk normality test for the activity indicators in the time period of 1976-2012

Indicator	W	p-value	significance
fraction international patents	0.6943	< 2.2e-16	***
fraction US patents	0.6146	< 2.2e-16	***
fraction scientific publications	0.6405	< 2.2e-16	***
slope international patents	0.3926	< 2.2e-16	***
slope US patents	0.8346	< 2.2e-16	***
slope scientific publications	0.7661	< 2.2e-16	***

The test is highly significant for both time periods, which is why the null hypothesis has to be rejected according to this test. The indicators obviously all deviate from normality, which explains why the Box's M also showed highly significant values. At this point it can be assumed that at least the multivariate normality assumption has to be rejected and non-parametric analyses are best suited for subsequent data analysis. However, some parametric analyses allow a certain deviation from the assumptions, and thus the homoscedasticity assumption is tested as well. Instead of testing all variables at once, it is possible to apply a univariate Levene's test for homogeneity of variance (i.e. homoscedasticity) for each individual indicator, to relax the assumptions further. The null hypothesis of this test is the homoscedasticity of all groups which thus should be non-significant for all. The results of this test can be found in tables 4.29 and 4.30.

Table 4.29 Results of Levene's homoscedasticity test for each separate activity indicator for the time period of 2004-2012

Indicator	Df	F value	Pr(>F)	significance
fraction international patents	4	5.5355	0.001099	**
fraction US patents	4	7.7999	8.085e-05	***
fraction scientific publications	4	6.4768	0.000359	***
fraction web search queries	4	2.7592	0.03967	*
slope international patents	4	2.6995	0.04302	*
slope US patents	4	4.6795	0.003177	**
slope scientific publications	4	1.6873	0.1705	
slope web search queries	4	3.4355	0.01598	*

Table 4.30 Results of Levene's homoscedasticity test for each separate activity indicator for the time period of 1976-2012

Indicator	Df	F value	Pr(>F)	significance
fraction international patents	4	42.751	< 2.2e-16	***
fraction US patents	4	44.738	< 2.2e-16	***
fraction scientific publications	4	10.144	7.469e-08	***
slope international patents	4	16.823	8.101e-13	***
slope US patents	4	67.132	< 2.2e-16	***
slope scientific publications	4	7.2346	1.21e-05	***

And again, even though the assumptions of Levene's test are relatively low, the results are highly significant for most indicators. As a consequence, the null hypothesis has to be rejected for all indicators except for the slope of scientific publications in the shorter time period from 2004-2012. The homoscedasticity assumption must therefore be dismissed. As a last check to verify this,

"An easy eye-ball technique (for Discriminant Function Analysis as example) is to use the "split-data" function (compare groups) by the categorical dependent variable and then to create a scatterplot matrix for all the independent variables. Compare the scatterplots across the groups for the same independent variables. If no obvious differences, then the assumption has been met (variance-covariance matrices between/across groups are similar)." (Steyn 2013)

On top of applying these explicit tests, a visual test may deliver further insights regarding the data.

An increased misclassification rate can be recognized by performing a cross validation of the data. This is described in section 4.7.6.3.

Figures 4.39 and 4.40 show boxplots of the activity indicators presented in section 4.7.1 which give an impression of the distribution of the indicator values in the different maturity states. The box represents the second and third quartiles, separated by a black bar, the median value. The whiskers span the first and fourth quartiles. Outliers are marked by a circle. Figure 4.39 shows that the shorter time period between 2004 and 2012 produces indicator values which violate the homoscedasticity assumption throughout all indicators. Understandably, the pre-existence maturity state has a low variance in comparison to the other states. It is typically located around values of zero. The growth state, on the other hand, has a much higher variance most times than all or most other states. This is only different for the fraction and slope of international patents as well as the slope of scientific publications. Also, the normal distribution assumption is violated. Again, the growth state causes the most obvious violations for all indicators except for the fraction of international patents, the slope of scientific publications and the fraction of web search queries. Similar results can be observed in figure 4.40 for the period of time between 1976 and 2012, where indicators do not produce homoscedastic groups. Values for the indicators are roughly normally distributed except for the slope of scientific publications, which is biased towards 0 in all maturity states. In summary, the normality and homoscedasticity assumptions are violated. An important finding regarding the impact of such a situation on parametric analyses was published in 1972:

"The assumptions of most mathematical models are always false to a greater or lesser extent. The relevant question is not whether [...] assumptions are met exactly, but rather whether the plausible violations of the assumptions have serious consequences on the validity of probability statements based on the standard assumptions." (Glass et al. 1972, p.237)

In other words, homoscedasticity and normal distribution in an ideal situation are fulfilled. If they are not, however, the results of the analysis have to be interpreted carefully. Fortunately, many parametric analyses are not very sensitive to moderate deviations from normality (Lix et al. 1996; Harwell et al. 1992; Glass et al. 1972).

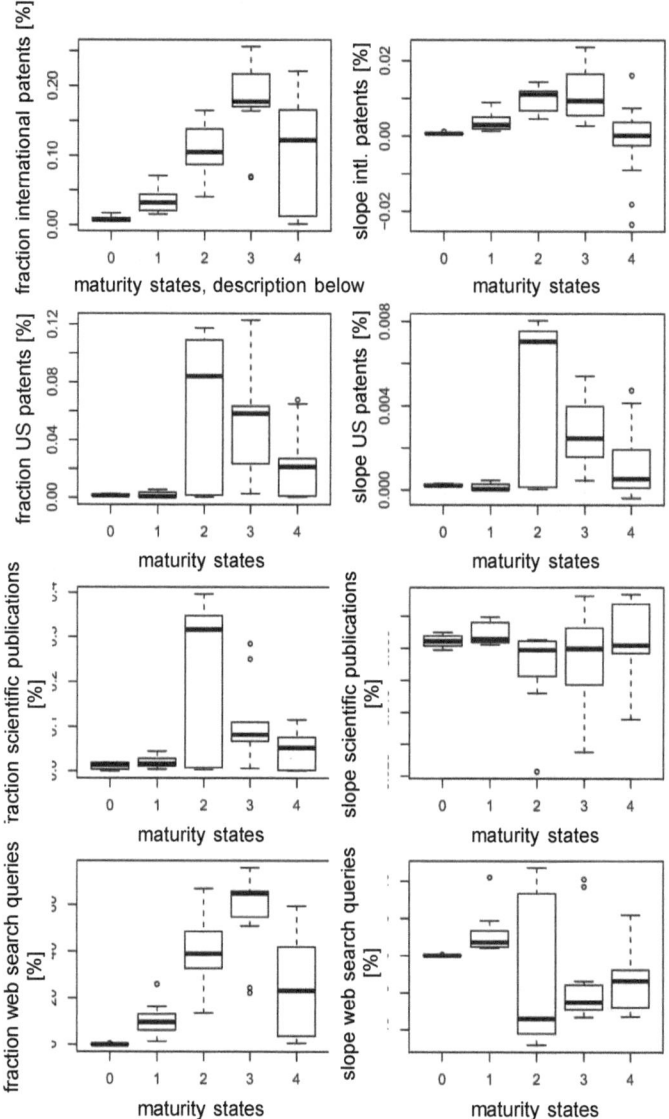

Fig. 4.39 Boxplots of all activity indicator values of all technologies by maturity state between 2004 and 2012 to display spread and distribution. The indicator values are grouped by maturity states to make visible the difference between the groups and get an idea about normality and homoscedasticity. The

group names are coded as follows: 0 – pre-existence, 1 – emergence, 2 – growth, 3 - saturation, 4 – decline

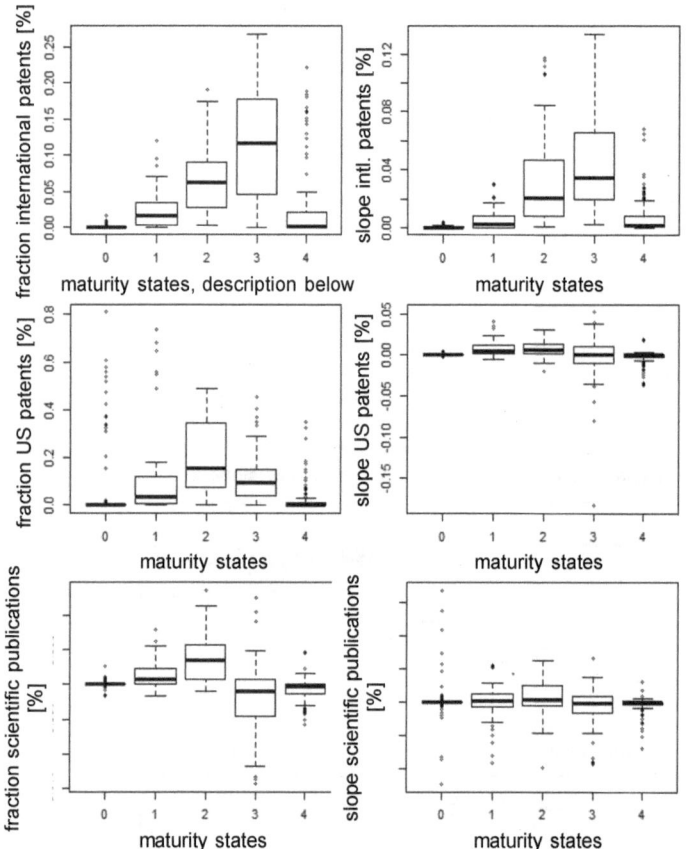

Fig. 4.40 Boxplots of all activity indicator values of all technologies by maturity state between 1976 and 2012 to display spread and distribution. The indicator values are grouped by maturity states to make the difference between the groups visible and give an idea about normality and homoscedasticity. The group names are coded as follows: 0 – pre-existence, 1 – emergence, 2 – growth, 3 - saturation, 4 – decline

4.7.6.2 Determining a Good Regression Window for the Activity Slope Indicators

The performance of a classifier depends in part on how well its indicators deduct the relevant information. One way of changing this mechanism is by defining a reasonable regression window size. This section focuses on tweaking the slope indicators by picking an adequate regression window size. Section 0 concluded that the results of parametric analyses performed on the data at hand should be interpreted with caution because neither the normality nor the homoscedasticity assumption is fulfilled. To select a reasonable regression window width for the slope indicators, the results of a parametric and a non-parametric analysis of variance (ANOVA) are assessed. The parametric ANOVA can be performed despite the non-normality and heteroscedasticity of the data determined in section 0, although the normality assumption violation may lead to false positives (Lix et al. 1996; Harwell et al. 1992; Glass et al. 1972) and the homoscedasticity assumption violation also may result in such type-I errors (Beuckelaer 1996). It does so equally for all regression window sizes since all analyses are based on the same data. Potential errors, therefore, may not influence the outcome of the analysis: so which regression window size best discriminates between the groups? Table 4.31 represents the significance level at which the different indicators show different values for each of the maturity state groups. Each column of the table shows the significance levels for each indicator for a certain regression window size between two and twelve years according to formula (2.2). The ANOVA determines whether the indicator values differ significantly between maturity states. A high level of significance is therefore beneficial for classification performance.

Table 4.31 An ANOVA for different regression window sizes for the activity slope indicators shows that different indicators work best with different regression windows

Regression window width [years]	2	3	4	5	6	7	8	9	10	11	12
2004-2012											
slope international patents	***	***	***	***	***	**	**				
slope US patents			.	.	.						
slope scientific publications											
slope web search queries	.	*	.								
1976-2012											
slope international patents	*	.									
slope US patents	**	**	**	**	**	**	**	**	**	**	**
slope scientific publications		*	*	**	**	**	**	**	**	*	*

The parametric ANOVA for the activity indicators with different regression window width shows that for different indicators, different widths are best (see table 4.31), e.g. for the slope of web search queries during the years 2004 until 2012, the best time slice width is 3 years, whereas for the slope of scientific publications during the years 1976 until 2012, the best width is 5 years or more. To keep it simple in the first approach, a single time slice width is selected for all indicators. This will be subject to further research. As stated in section 2.3.4.2, shorter time slices are preferred. The best overall results can be achieved for a width of three years for the data from 2004 to 2012 including web search data, and two, three, or five years for the data from 1976 to 2012, where three years represents the only variant with significance levels above the 0.1 level for all three slope indicators.

A similar, but non-parametric approach is to conduct a Kruskal-Wallis analysis for the different slope indicators and regression window sizes. Such a non-parametric analysis of variance technically performs a comparison of mean ranks rather than the actual means as for the parametric ANOVA. The result of this analysis can be found in table 4.32.

Table 4.32 A non-parametric Kruskal-Wallis test with different regression window sizes for the activity slope indicators shows that different indicators work best with different regression windows

Regression window width [years]	2	3	4	5	6
2004-2012					
slope international patents	***	***	***	***	***
slope US patents	***	***	***	***	***
slope scientific publications	**	***	***	***	**
slope web search queries	**	**	**	**	**
1976-2012					
slope international patents	***	***	***	***	***
slope US patents	***	***	***	***	***
slope scientific publications	***	***	***	***	***

The regression window size does not matter as much for the Kruskal-Wallis test was it does for the parametric ANOVA. Except for the slope of web search queries and the two year and six year windows for the slope of scientific publications, it leads to highly significant differences between the mean ranks of the separate maturity states at least at the 0.001 level for all indicators and window sizes.

As a result of these analyses of variance and the perception that shorter regression window sizes are beneficial for quicker reactions to new developments, analyses are from now on therefore based on regression windows of three years where applicable. This regression window size represents a relatively good fit, which is again confirmed in table 4.48 of section 4.7.6.4, which summarizes the performance of machine-learning-based analyses based on their misclassification rates for different regression window sizes.

4.7.6.3 Thoughts on Indicator Selection and Model Reduction

A number of indicators are readily available for analysis at this point of the analysis. An important thought must be made concerning the helpfulness of each single indicator for the resulting operationalized maturity model. Are all indicators really necessary? Linear discriminant analysis demands that the number of indicators do not exceed the number of observations (Berrueta et al. 2007). For the given data, the number of indicators do not exceed the number of observations for either the activity indicator data from between 2004 and 2012 (48 observations, vs. 8 indicators) or the data from between 1976 and 2012 (432 observations, vs. 6 indicators). Still, good practice (the principle of parsimony) demands models and procedures that contain all that is necessary for the modeling, but nothing more. When this is disregarded, and more terms than necessary are included in the model, this is called overfitting. Overfitting has several disadvantageous consequences and should therefore be avoided:

- *"Adding irrelevant [indicators] can make [classifications] worse because the co-efficients fitted to them add random variation to the subsequent classifications."* (Hawkins 2004)
- The resulting model contains indicators which do not add substantially to the classification success but have to be calculated each time. This increases the information retrieval effort (Hawkins 2004).

The former aspect must be considered the more important one in the context of the approach in this book. A rule of thumb by DEFERNEZ & KEMSLEY states that the onset of overfitting must be strongly suspected when (Defernez & Kemsley 1997):

$$\frac{n-g}{3} < i$$

where

n: number of observations
g: number of groups
i: number of indicators

According to formula 4.3, this results in

$\frac{48-5}{3} = 14,\overline{3} \not< 8$ (activity indicators, 2004 - 2012)

$\frac{432-5}{3} = 142,\overline{3} \not< 6$ (activity indicators, 1976 - 2012)

This means that for both data sets, overfitting does not have to be strongly suspected.

Still, at this point it is unknown whether all indicators are really necessary for modeling. There are a number of approaches for indicator selection and elimination. By increasing complexity, these include

a. determining zero and near-zero variance indicators because these actually do not qualify as indicators.
b. determining strongly correlated indicators and flagging them for elimination. It must be noted however, that even highly correlated indicators, as long as they are not perfectly correlated, may be complementary and therefore add to the classification results of a model. They should therefore not be considered to violate the principle of parsimony based just on this (Guyon & Elisseeff 2003). In fact, several sources even state that including de facto correlated indicators in a model does not hurt its classification performance (Hawkins 2004; Guyon & Elisseeff 2003).
c. determining each individual indicators' strength to discriminate between pairs of maturity states and flag weak or redundant ones for elimination. This approach does not take into account the adjuvant interaction of indicators, which may disqualify it as an elimination strategy. But it may prove helpful in understanding each indicator's contribution for the entire system's performance.

d. performing stepwise selection. This determines the classification performance of a model which was trained based on a subset of the available indicators. The subset is changed by recursively adding or eliminating single indicators form the training set and comparing the resulting model's performance to that of the former model. Whenever a certain increase in performance is noted, the new combination is accepted until no performance gains can be achieved (Guyon & Elisseeff 2003). However, stepwise selection has seen a lot of criticism, most importantly because of their failure to correctly identify the best indicator sets (as for correlated indicators, two indicators which perform poorly by themselves may provide a substantial performance increase in combination) and also because of their tendency to capitalize on sampling error, leading to results that are not replicable (Thompson 1995).

In summary, most indicator selection and elimination approaches have a number of shortcomings. Luckily, if the number of samples are small, overfitting concerns regarding the generalization ability of a classification model can reliably be allayed with a suitable repeated cross validation using multiple randomized partitionings of the available data, with model selection performed separately in each trial. This eliminates the need to select certain indicators and drop others (Cawley & Talbot 2010; Hawkins 2004). Nevertheless, the described approaches will be applied to the data to provide a general understanding of the data at hand.

During **approach a)** zero or near-zero variance indicators are identified. Tables 4.33 and 4.34 show indicators which show zero or near-zero variance in the relevant data. An indicator which has only one unique value is considered a zero variance indicator. Determining such an indicator is straight-forward. Determining a near-zero variance indicator was done with the help of the R package nearZeroVar from the caret library (version 6.0-24). To be flagged as having near zero variance, an indicator must fulfill two characteristics :

- The ratio $freqRatio$ of the frequency of the prevalent value to the frequency of the second most common value must be large. In this analysis $freqRatio$ must be above a threshold value $freqCut$.

- It must have few unique values relative to the number of observations. This means that the number of unique values $PercentUnique$ divided by the total number of samples (times 100), must be below a threshold value $uniqueCut$.

The $freqCut$ was selected to be 95/5, which is the default value in the package nearZeroVar and represents a strong tendency. And $uniqueCut$ was selected to be 10 for the same reason. The results of this analysis, based on a regression window of three years for the slope indicators, are displayed for the two time periods in tables 4.33 and 4.34.

Table 4.33 Zero and near zero variance indicator values in the data from between 2004 and 2012

2004-2012	freqRatio	Percent Unique	Zero variance	Near zero variance
fraction international patents	1.00	100.00	FALSE	FALSE
fraction US patents	2.00	97.92	FALSE	FALSE
fraction scientific publications	1.00	100.00	FALSE	FALSE
fraction web search queries	4.00	93.75	FALSE	FALSE
slope international patents	1.00	100.00	FALSE	FALSE
slope US patents	1.00	100.00	FALSE	FALSE
slope scientific publications	1.00	100.00	FALSE	FALSE
slope web search queries	2.00	97.92	FALSE	FALSE

Table 4.34 Zero and near zero variance indicator values in the data from between 1976 and 2012

1976-2012	freqRatio	Percent Unique	Zero variance	Near zero variance
fraction international patents	73.50	63.66	FALSE	FALSE
fraction US patents	40.33	68.06	FALSE	FALSE
fraction scientific publications	31.00	55.79	FALSE	FALSE
slope international patents	48.50	77.08	FALSE	FALSE
slope US patents	72.00	83.56	FALSE	FALSE
slope scientific publications	35.00	83.80	FALSE	FALSE

For the longer time period for the years between 1976 and 2012, the fraction of international patents shows a large $freqRatio$, but it is the only indicator in any of the two sets that lies beyond any of the threshold values. This analysis concludes that for neither time period does any of the indicators produce zero or near zero variance.

Approach b) aims to identify highly correlated indicators. To determine the correlation between indicators, Pearson's correlation coefficients for all pairs of indicators are calculated (based on a regression window of three years for the slope indicators). These are displayed for the two time periods in tables 4.35 and 4.36. As stated above, even highly correlated indicators, as long as they are not perfectly correlated, may be complementary. The threshold for a high correlation is therefore set to an absolute of .75, which is well below perfect correlation but at the same time high enough to produce only few matching indicator pairs.

Table 4.35 Correlations between indicators according to Pearson's correlation coefficient, using the data from the time between 2004 and 2012. High correlations > .75 are marked by a grey shading

2004-2012	fraction US patents	fraction scientific publications	fraction web search queries	slope international patents	slope US patents	slope scientific publications	slope web search queries
fraction international patents	0,63	0,47	0,67	0,46	0,56	-0,14	-0,58
fraction US patents		0,90	0,44	0,27	0,95	-0,61	-0,71
fraction scientific publications			0,31	0,25	0,91	-0,46	-0,71
fraction web search queries				0,33	0,47	-0,26	-0,20
slope international patents					0,31	-0,05	-0,01
slope US patents						-0,61	-0,68
slope scientific publications							0,20

For the longer time period between 1976 and 2012, only the fractions of US and international patents are highly correlated. For the time period between 2004 and 2012, three pairs of indicators have a relatively high correlation, namely fraction US patents – fraction scientific publications; fraction US patents – slope US patents; and fraction scientific publications – slope US patents. As stated above, this may be a clue that these indicators produce redundant information. From this analysis alone, however, the actual added value of each one of them can not be deduced.

Table 4.36 Correlations between indicators according to Pearson's correlation coefficient, using the data from the time between 1976 and 2012

1976-2012	fraction US patents	fraction scientific publications	slope international patents	slope US patents	slope scientific publications
fraction international patents	0,78	0,30	-0,03	0,05	-0,11
fraction US patents		0,43	-0,31	0,02	-0,20
fraction scientific publications			-0,02	0,27	0,41
slope international patents				0,63	0,00
slope US patents					0,16

During **approach c)** each individual indicator's strength to discriminate between pairs of maturity states is determined. Figures 4.39 and 4.40 on pages 197 ff. show boxplots of the indicator activity by maturity state. The main problem are groups like the growth state between the years 2004 and 2012, which cause a high intra-group variance for almost all indicators. They are likely to produce an overlap with other groups. Dedicated indicators which are suited to differentiate between these problematic and other groups may be able to solve this problem, however. Such indicators are therefore important for an operationalized technology maturity model because they will increase the chance of correct classification. To determine each individual indicator's strength to discriminate between pairs of maturity states, one would typically use paired t-tests. Since neither the normality nor the homoscedasticity assumptions are fulfilled, it is necessary to make use of non-parametric equivalents. A suitable analysis is the Mann-Whitney-Wilcoxon test which determines the mean differences between groups by building and comparing the rank sum of the available observations (Field 2009, pp.540–550). Unfortunately, when a lot of pairwise comparisons are made, the type-I error rate is known to inflate. A way of taking this into consideration is to use a Bonferroni correction, which uses the p-value multiplied by the number of comparisons made to determine the statistical significance level (Field 2009, p.565). This makes it important to ignore maturity state transitions which are improbable or not constructive in the context of the approach in this book. This is the case for the transitions from pre-existence to saturation or decline, because they only affect very small technologies with an extremely low life time. No harm is done in case a technology which is in fact in the saturation or decline state is mistaken for one which does not exist yet. All other transitions which skip maturity states such as pre-existence to growth or growth to decline are realistic scenarios and should be recognized by the final classifier. This leads to a number of 8 comparisons in total: pre-existence – emergence, pre-existence – growth, emergence – growth, emergence – saturation, emergence – decline, growth – saturation, growth – decline, and saturation – decline. For the time periods between the years 2004 and 2012 as well as 1976 and 2012 respectively, tables 4.37 and 4.38 show the results of these pairwise Mann-Whitney-Wilcoxon tests and tables 4.39 and 4.40 give an overview of the significance levels at which each indicator is able to discriminate between the given maturity states. Sample sizes and group medians for the different groups can be found in tables 4.8 and 4.9 of section 0.

Table 4.37 Pairwise Mann-Whitney-Wilcoxon tests between maturity states x and y (The states are coded as follows: 0 – pre-existence, 1 – emergence, 2 – growth, 3 - saturation, 4 – decline) for the time period between the years 2004 and 2012. Test results reported include the p-value, Bonferroni-corrected significance level (8 comparisons), W-score, effect size r, and z-score

indicator	maturity state x	maturity state y	p-value	Sign$_b$	W	r	z
fraction international patents	0	1	0,01.		2	-0,37	-2,57
fraction international patents	0	2	5E-04**		0	-0,51	-3,50
fraction international patents	1	2	3E-04**		2	-0,53	-3,66
fraction international patents	1	3	3E-04**		2	-0,53	-3,66
fraction international patents	1	4	0,224		32	-0,18	-1,21
fraction international patents	2	3	0,008.		21	-0,38	-2,64
fraction international patents	2	4	0,851		73	-0,03	-0,19
fraction international patents	3	4	0,021		119	-0,33	-2,31
fraction US patents	0	1	0,745		20	-0,05	-0,33
fraction US patents	0	2	0,221		16	-0,18	-1,22
fraction US patents	1	2	0,037		15	-0,30	-2,08
fraction US patents	1	3	0,002*		4	-0,44	-3,08
fraction US patents	1	4	0,015		16	-0,35	-2,43
fraction US patents	2	3	0,898		58	-0,02	-0,13
fraction US patents	2	4	0,317		96	-0,14	-1,00

fraction US patents	3	4	0,051	113	-0,28	-1,95
fraction scientific publications	0	1	0,343	11	-0,14	-0,95
fraction scientific publications	0	2	0,221	16	-0,18	-1,22
fraction scientific publications	1	2	0,479	30	-0,10	-0,71
fraction scientific publications	1	3	0,015	12	-0,35	-2,42
fraction scientific publications	1	4	0,287	34	-0,15	-1,06
fraction scientific publications	2	3	0,478	72	-0,10	-0,71
fraction scientific publications	2	4	0,095	108	-0,24	-1,67
fraction scientific publications	3	4	0,038	115	-0,30	-2,07
fraction web search queries	0	1	0,005*	0	-0,41	-2,81
fraction web search queries	0	2	0,002*	0	-0,44	-3,08
fraction web search queries	1	2	3E-04**	2	-0,53	-3,66
fraction web search queries	1	3	3E-04**	2	-0,53	-3,66
fraction web search queries	1	4	0,172	30	-0,20	-1,37
fraction web search queries	2	3	0,047	30	-0,29	-1,98
fraction web search queries	2	4	0,075	110	-0,26	-1,78
fraction web search queries	3	4	7E-04**	136	-0,49	-3,40
slope US patents	0	1	0,53	22	-0,09	-0,63
slope US patents	0	2	0,267	17	-0,16	-1,11
slope US patents	1	2	0,027	14	-0,32	-2,21
slope US patents	1	3	1E-04**	1	-0,55	-3,83
slope US patents	1	4	0,067	24	-0,26	-1,83
slope US patents	2	3	0,748	66	-0,05	-0,32
slope US patents	2	4	0,222	100	-0,18	-1,22
slope US patents	3	4	0,021	119	-0,33	-2,31
slope international patents	0	1	0,003*	0	-0,44	-3,02
slope international patents	0	2	5E-04**	0	-0,51	-3,50
slope international patents	1	2	0,003*	7	-0,43	-2,99
slope international patents	1	3	0,011.	11	-0,37	-2,53
slope international patents	1	4	0,11	71	-0,23	-1,60
slope international patents	2	3	1	60	0,00	0,00
slope international patents	2	4	3E-04**	139	-0,52	-3,62
slope international patents	3	4	7E-04**	136	-0,49	-3,40
slope scientific publications	0	1	0,268	10	-0,16	-1,11
slope scientific publications	0	2	0,145	41	-0,21	-1,46
slope scientific publications	1	2	0,015	65	-0,35	-2,42
slope scientific publications	1	3	0,211	53	-0,18	-1,25

slope scientific publications	1	4	0,488	59	-0,10	-0,69
slope scientific publications	2	3	0,699	54	-0,06	-0,39
slope scientific publications	2	4	0,434	62	-0,11	-0,78
slope scientific publications	3	4	0,501	64	-0,10	-0,67
slope web search queries	0	1	0,006*	0	-0,40	-2,77
slope web search queries	0	2	0,821	30	-0,03	-0,23
slope web search queries	1	2	0,479	47	-0,10	-0,71
slope web search queries	1	3	0,015	65	-0,35	-2,42
slope web search queries	1	4	5E-04**	92	-0,50	-3,47
slope web search queries	2	3	0,438	48	-0,11	-0,77
slope web search queries	2	4	0,687	69	-0,06	-0,40
slope web search queries	3	4	0,501	64	-0,10	-0,67

Table 4.38 Pairwise Mann-Whitney-Wilcoxon tests between maturity states x and y (The states are coded as follows: 0 – pre-existence, 1 – emergence, 2 – growth, 3 - saturation, 4 – decline) for the time period between the years 1976 and 2012.

indicator	maturity state x	maturity state y	p-value	Sign$_b$	W	r	N
fraction international pat.	0	1	9,14E-19***		621,5	-0,43	-8,85
fraction international pat.	0	2	9,06E-31***		43,5	-0,55	-11,53
fraction international pat.	1	2	3,80E-07***		476,5	-0,24	-5,08
fraction international pat.	1	3	1,35E-11***		421	-0,33	-6,76
fraction international pat.	1	4	4,25E-03*		3651,5	-0,14	-2,86
fraction international pat.	2	3	1,49E-04**		1230	-0,18	-3,79
fraction international pat.	2	4	3,81E-12***		5742	-0,33	-6,94
fraction international pat.	3	4	1,79E-19***		8493,5	-0,43	-9,03
fraction US patents	0	1	3,00E-11***		1144	-0,32	-6,65
fraction US patents	0	2	4,90E-27***		196	-0,52	-10,77
fraction US patents	1	2	2,70E-08***		409,5	-0,27	-5,56
fraction US patents	1	3	9,66E-16***		191	-0,39	-8,03
fraction US patents	1	4	7,53E-01		2747,5	-0,02	-0,31
fraction US patents	2	3	3,35E-03*		1410	-0,14	-2,93
fraction US patents	2	4	4,63E-11***		5633,5	-0,32	-6,58

fraction US patents	3	4	9,22E-24***	8922	-0,48	-10,05
fraction scientific publ.	0	1	5,21E-11***	1198,5	-0,32	-6,56
fraction scientific publ.	0	2	1,55E-19***	776,5	-0,44	-9,04
fraction scientific publ.	1	2	3,44E-04**	686,5	-0,17	-3,58
fraction scientific publ.	1	3	1,28E-02	1197,5	-0,12	-2,49
fraction scientific publ.	1	4	1,59E-06***	4193	-0,23	-4,80
fraction scientific publ.	2	3	2,34E-03*	2663	-0,15	-3,04
fraction scientific publ.	2	4	2,58E-19***	6395	-0,43	-8,99
fraction scientific publ.	3	4	9,01E-20***	8513,5	-0,44	-9,10
slope US patents	0	1	2,86E-12***	915	-0,34	-6,98
slope US patents	0	2	8,17E-26***	150	-0,51	-10,51
slope US patents	1	2	1,44E-07***	451	-0,25	-5,26
slope US patents	1	3	8,06E-01	1605	-0,01	-0,24
slope US patents	1	4	8,47E-12***	4798	-0,33	-6,83
slope US patents	2	3	3,28E-04**	2778	-0,17	-3,59
slope US patents	2	4	4,66E-20***	6481	-0,44	-9,17
slope US patents	3	4	2,24E-01	5332	-0,06	-1,22
slope international pat.	0	1	8,23E-18***	602	-0,41	-8,60
slope international pat.	0	2	1,96E-27***	178	-0,52	-10,85
slope international pat.	1	2	1,30E-06***	510	-0,23	-4,84
slope international pat.	1	3	2,67E-01	1852	-0,05	-1,11
slope international pat.	1	4	7,12E-09***	4499	-0,28	-5,79
slope international pat.	2	3	7,89E-03.	2582	-0,13	-2,66
slope international pat.	2	4	6,77E-15***	6029	-0,37	-7,79
slope international pat.	3	4	3,43E-01	5223,5	-0,05	-0,95
slope scientific publ.	0	1	1,62E-03*	1979	-0,15	-3,15
slope scientific publ.	0	2	1,94E-07***	1837	-0,25	-5,21
slope scientific publ.	1	2	5,60E-02	920	-0,09	-1,91
slope scientific publ.	1	3	1,16E-01	1936	-0,08	-1,57
slope scientific publ.	1	4	1,84E-09***	4563	-0,29	-6,01
slope scientific publ.	2	3	6,36E-04**	2741	-0,16	-3,42
slope scientific publ.	2	4	6,53E-11***	5618	-0,31	-6,53
slope scientific publ.	3	4	6,56E-02	5586,5	-0,09	-1,84

Table 4.39 Bonferroni-corrected significance levels of pairwise Mann-Whitney-Wilcoxon tests between maturity states (The states are coded as follows: 0 – pre-existence, 1 – emergence, 2 – growth, 3 - saturation, 4 – decline) for the time period between the years 2004 and 2012

2004-2012	0-1	0-2	1-2	1-3	1-4	2-3	2-4	3-4
fraction international patents	.	**	**	**		.		
fraction US patents				*				
fraction scientific publications								
fraction web search queries	*	*	**	**			**	
slope international patents	*	**	*	.			**	**
slope US patents				**				
slope scientific publications								
slope web search queries	*			**				

According to table 4.39, during the time period between 2004 and 2012 there is at least one indicator for any of the maturity state transitions which shows a significant difference in means. The two maturity states which are hardest to distinguish are growth and saturation. Only the fraction of international patents is somewhat suitable for this purpose. The transition from the emergence state to the decline state can be covered by the slope of web search queries alone and the transition from the growth state to the decline state can be estimated by the slope of international patents alone. Both indicators show the transition with a relatively high significance. All other transitions can be told apart by at least two distinct indicators. Remarkably, the fraction and slope of scientific publications show comparable low potential to discriminate between any maturity states.

Table 4.40 Bonferroni-corrected significance levels of pairwise Mann-Whitney-Wilcoxon tests between maturity states (The states are coded as follows: 0 – pre-existence, 1 – emergence, 2 – growth, 3 - saturation, 4 – decline) for the time period between the years 1976 and 2012

1976-2012	0-1	0-2	1-2	1-3	1-4	2-3	2-4	3-4
fraction international patents	***	***	***	***	*	**	***	***
fraction US patents	***	***	***	***		*	***	***
fraction scientific publications	***	***	**		***	*	***	***
slope international patents	***	***	***		***	.	***	
slope US patents	***	***	***		***	**	***	
slope scientific publications	*	***			***	**	***	

For the time period between 1976 and 2012, table 4.40 shows a high significance between maturity states for almost all transitions except for the one between growth and saturation, which was also hard to determine for the majority of the indicators in the time period between 2004 and 2012. All indicators are able to determine a number of transitions at a high significance level.

Table 4.41 Relevant results of Kruskal-Wallis tests on each indicator for discriminating between maturity states for the time period between the years 2004 and 2012

indicator	p-value	significance	df	chi-squared
fraction international patents	1,80E-04	***	4	22,23
fraction US patents	5,10E-03	**	4	14,82
fraction scientific publications	5,11E-02	.	4	9,43
fraction web search queries	7,22E-06	***	4	29,17
slope international patents	3,37E-05	***	4	25,87
slope US patents	5,34E-03	**	4	14,71
slope scientific publications	3,01E-01		4	4,87
slope web search queries	4,77E-02	*	4	9,60

In summary, the pairwise Mann-Whitney-Wilcoxon tests show that most indicators have a right to exist. Solely the fraction and slope of scientific publications show comparable low potential to discriminate between any maturity states during the time period between 2004 and 2012. To see whether this is increased when looking at the entire five maturity states, the non-parametrical equivalent to an ANOVA, a Kruskal-Wallis test can be performed. It is based on the rank order like the Mann-Whitney-Wilcoxon test, but it determines a single significance level for all groups in one value which does not have to be corrected like the separate Mann-Whitney-Wilcoxon tests. The results of this test can be found in tables 4.41 and 4.42 for the time periods starting in 2004 and 1976, respectively. The tables report the p-value, significance level, degrees of freedom, and chi-squared (which is equivalent to the H-statistic for the Kruskal-Wallis test) for each indicator. Again, observation counts and medians for the underlying data can be found in tables 4.8 and 4.9.

Indeed, table 4.41 shows that the indicators based on scientific publications distinguish between the maturity states at relatively low significance levels for the time period between 2004 and 2012.

Table 4.42 Relevant results of Kruskal-Wallis tests on each indicator for discriminating between maturity states for the time period between the years 1976 and 2012

indicator	p-value	significance	df	chi-squared
fraction international patents	3,85E-54	***	4	255,70
fraction US patents	5,51E-56	***	4	264,26
fraction scientific publications	2,59E-38	***	4	˙182,14
slope international patents	4,86E-23	***	4	110,82
slope US patents	2,71E-30	***	4	144,75
slope scientific publications	8,22E-20	***	4	95,67

Table 4.42 shows that the indicators all perform relatively well in discriminating between the maturity states for the time period between the years 1976 and 2012. This also holds true for the scientific publication-based indicators. Neither the Mann-Whitney-Wilcoxon tests nor the Kruskal-Wallis tests makes a statement regarding the performance of the indicators when they are combined with other indicators. These analyses alone are therefore not suited to eliminate the scientific publication-based indicators, albeit the two scientific publication-based indicators are identified as elimination candidates.

The last **approach d)** is to perform a stepwise selection of indicators. There are three variants of this which are often used (Berrueta et al. 2007; Steyerberg & Eijkemans 2000; Harrell et al. 1996): *forward stepwise variable selection*, which evaluates the addition of a new indicator while removing a previously entered one, *recursive feature elimination* evaluates the removal of a new indicator while adding a previously deleted one, and *forward entry and backward removal* only enters or removes variables, one at a time. Since at the beginning of this section it became clear that the models do not contain too many variables to be concerned about overfitting, recursive feature elimination should be an appropriate approach to variable selection.

There are many different approaches which implement recursive feature elimination. An increasingly used one is the random forest approach (Genuer et al. 2010). A random forest is able to classify data by averaging the classification results of a large number of binary decision trees. A convenient attribute of this approach is that those features which add least to a correct classification can be identified while creating the random forest. The only assumption it makes is that the observations must be independent (Rodriguez-Galiano & Ghimire 2012).

A very important aspect of the random forest approach is the data selection for each step in the approach. SVETNIK et al. and AMBROISE & MCLAHAN showed that improper use of resampling to measure performance results in overfitting (Svetnik et al. 2004; Ambroise & McLachlan 2002). An elaborate approach to generate a suitable data basis was therefore set up:

Just like in simulation, dummy indicators with normally deviated random values can be added to the initial model as a benchmark for the performance increase of all actual indicators (Segal 2004; Friedman 1991). This extends the input data of actual activity indicators by a number of normally distributed dummy random indicators against which the activity indicators can be tested. In this analysis, a number of 40 dummy indicator was deemed sufficient to minimize the risk that the actual indicators are picked by chance. Consequently each observation consists of m_{dim} indicators with m_{dim} being either $6 + 40$ or $8 + 40$, depending on the observed period of time.

To get performance estimates that incorporate the variation due to feature selection, Kuhn suggests encapsulating the actual indicator selection inside an outer layer of resampling (Kuhn 2014). In this approach the number of elements in the original data and the resampled data are equal. This is done 100 times. The resampled data is then used in a so-called "repeated random subsampling validation" with twelve repeats. Such a validation randomly splits the dataset into training and test data instead of partitioning it into equally sized folds like a v-fold cross validation. For each repeat the data is divided at random in ¾ of the observations as training set and ¼ as test set. The test set can be used for an out-of-bag error estimation in the form of a misclassification rate. To deal with the high variance of decision trees, each tree is generated from bagged data, as suggested by BREIMAN (Breiman 2001). Bagging means taking repeated samples from a single training set in order to generate a different bootstrapped training set for each tree. Each random forest consists of 500 decision trees in this approach. The resulting sample data configuration setup of this analysis for indicator selection is displayed in figure 4.41.

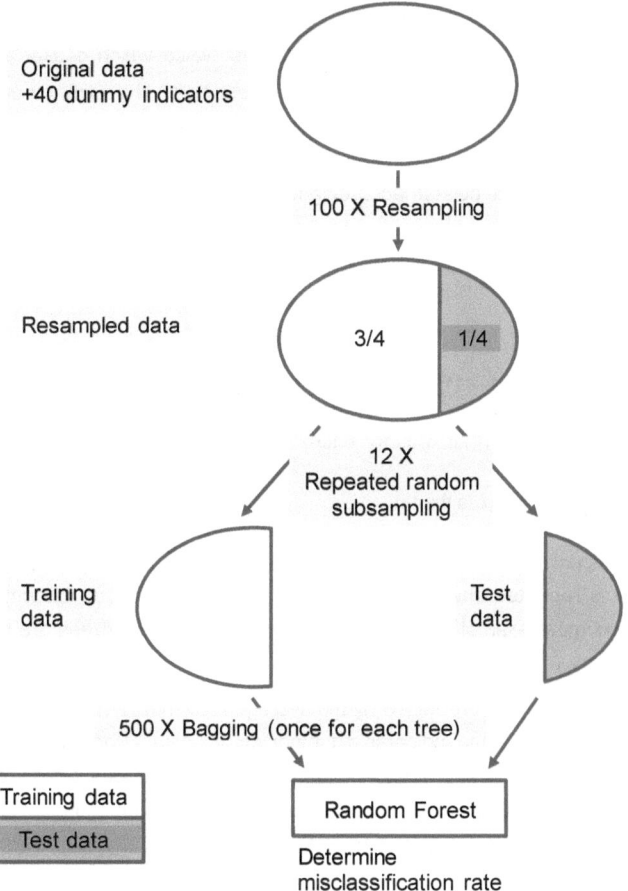

Fig. 4.41 Schematic sample data configuration for indicator selection based on the random forest approach

The package rfe from the caret library (version 6.0-24) was used to perform this analysis. The actual *recursive feature elimination* performed in the approach in this book is therefore structured according to the following description:

Each bootstrapped training data set is used to build a separate binary decision tree, binary meaning that each node has two branches. At each node a number of m_{try} of the m_{dim} indicators is selected at random, where m_{try} is approximately equal to

$\sqrt{m_{dim}}$, as proposed by BREIMAN (Breiman 2001). In this approach, m_{dim} is either 46 or 48, so $m_{try} \approx 7$. For each indicator in m_{try} the indicator value which causes the lowest Gini impurity is determined. This is called the best split. The Gini impurity measures how often a randomly chosen element from the set would be classified incorrectly if it were classified at random according to the distribution of groups in the subset (Deng et al. 2011). It is calculated according to formula 4.4.

$$I_G(f) = 1 - \sum_{i=1}^{m} f_i^2$$

with

$I_G(f)$: Gini impurity of the observed set

m: count of different groups i (i.e. maturity states)

f_i: fraction of items in group i in the set

The indicator with the smallest overall resulting Gini impurity is used exclusively to split the node. This step is repeated anew. A branch stops growing if a node becomes empty or there are no more examples to split in the current node. The trees are not pruned, as suggested by BREIMAN (Breiman 2001).

The importance of an indicator is determined by the average Gini impurity change generated through it. A large value then indicates an important indicator. For each of the 100 random forests a list of the best predictors is generated. This provides a probabilistic assessment of predictor importance rather than a ranking based on a single fixed data set. Even the randomly generated dummy indicators may rank high in some of the iterations, but if the activity indicators are better than random, they will prevail on average.

Since only a subset of indicators should be selected, a subset size should be reasonably set. The optimal combination and the resulting misclassification rate are determined for each subset size. Since the indicator sets in the approach in this book contain between six and eight indicators, a subset is reasonable to contain [3,10] for either set. This approach makes sure that even indicator subsets of well less than as well as of more than the full set of activity indicators are evaluated. The appropriate number of indicators is determined by the subset size which results in the lowest misclassification rate.

The results of the approach described above can be found in table 4.43 for the time periods between 2004 and 2012 as well as between 1976 and 2012 (each based on a regression window of three years for the slope indicators). Consecutively, figure 4.42 shows the performance profile for increasing numbers of indicators for the two time periods. The relevant R code can be found in the Annex.

Table 4.43 Misclassification rates for different indicator set sizes based on reverse indicator elimination with random forests for the data in the time periods between 2004 and 2012 as well as between 1976 and 2012 with the full set marked grey and the best set marked by a black frame. Set sizes larger than the full set result from inclusion of dummy indicators

Set size	Misclassification rate 2004 - 2012	Misclassification rate 1976 - 2012
3	0.33	0.19
4	0.29	0.16
5	0.24	0.14
6	0.22	0.13
7	0.22	0.14
8	0.23	0.15
9	0.26	0.16
10	0.28	0.17
⋮	⋮	⋮
48	0.37	0.24

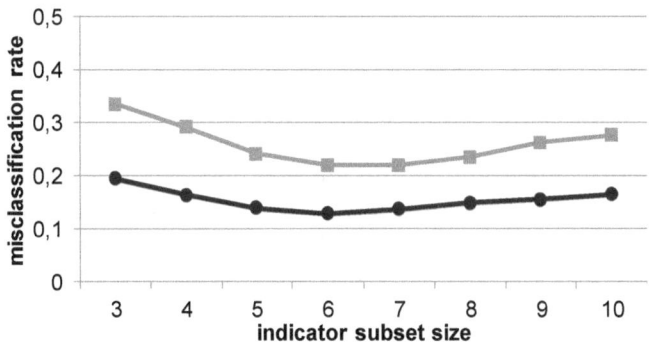

Fig. 4.42 Misclassification rates for different indicator set sizes based on reverse indicator elimination with random forests for the data in the time period between 2004 and 2012 (grey squares) and between 1976 and 2012 (black dots)

For the time period between 1976 and 2012 the full model leads to the best results. For the time period between 2004 and 2012, the fraction of US patents is the weakest indicator. This may be due to its strong correlation with the fraction of scientific publications and with the slope of US patents. Arguably the fraction of US patents could be dropped from the set. This is in contrast to the findings of the Mann-Whitney-Wilcoxon and Kruskal-Wallis tests performed earlier in this section, which determined the scientific publication-based indicators to be the weakest. In any case, the misclassification rate is almost at the same level for the full model and with a solid cross validation approach it can be expected that overfitting is not a problem.

In summary, all indicators presented here provide an added value, albeit not in all combinations. For both time periods the full model represents a relatively good choice of indicators and will therefore be used henceforth.

4.7.6.4 Performing a Linear Discriminant Analysis on the Activity Indicator Data

Thus far, indicators were selected, indicator data was collected, and maturity state labels were assigned to it. It was determined that typical assumptions of parametric analyses (normality and homoscedasticity) are not fulfilled, but that there are certain analyses which can compensate this. It was determined that indicators are useful to a different degree for discriminating between maturity states during state transitions. The purpose of this section is to combine the given information into a working operationalized maturity model. Next, misclassification rates of indicator combinations must be determined to understand whether the combination of indicators helps to differentiate between all maturity states.

Most machine-learning approaches, such as k-nearest neighbors, support vector machines, and neural networks are useful for classification based on indicator combination. However, these approaches provide no insights regarding the covariates that best contribute to the predictive structure. This is the advantage of a discriminant analysis (Archer & Kimes 2008). Unfortunately it is a parametric analysis which assumes normality and homoscedasticity. A discriminant analysis which does not have the strong assumptions of a linear discriminant analysis (LDA) is the more complex quadratic discriminant analysis. It does require a higher amount of observations in the training set (i.e. sample technologies), however, which is not available through the use of the indicators introduced in section 4.7.1 since these produce just one value per year and technology each. Fortunately, also an LDA, according to (Li et al. 2006) "frequently achieves good performances [...], even though the assumptions of common covariance matrix among groups and normality are often violated". The approach in this book will therefore apply the LDA nevertheless for the following reasons (Kotsiantis et al. 2007; Backhaus et al. 2003, pp.156–227):

- It is a simple machine-learning approach which finds the linear combination of features which best separate two or more groups (i.e. maturity states).
- It requires little effort to get a conservative idea of the usefulness of each indicator.
- Overfitting is not a big issue if the amount of degrees of maturity is low in comparison to the input data.
- It generates a simple and straight-forward canonical classification function without the need for an extensive training set.
- Its classification functions provide probabilities for all groups (maturity states) that an observation (a technology in a certain year) belongs to a group. This can be used to identify gradual changes over the course of a longer time period without the need to observe an actual change of maturity state. This is valuable in the context of technology monitoring.
- It relies on indicators which are relevant with a high probability (since they were derived from the S&D model). The dimensionality of the input space is relatively low, so dimensionality reduction is not necessary.
- It requires a relatively high number of observations for training compared to the count of individual indicators, but this is provided with the data basis of the approach in this book.

In this analysis, RAO's LDA (Rao 1948) is used for this purpose. It is a generalization of FISHER's LDA (Fisher 1936), which can handle more than just two groups. This is necessary because it will need to separate between the five different maturity states.

The LDA finds a linear combination of parameters (maturity indicators) which discriminates well between groups (maturity states). The algorithm weighs the indicators in such a way that the intra-group variance is minimized and the inter-group variance is maximized (Backhaus et al. 2003, pp.156–157). To achieve this, a number of projections of the data become necessary, where indicator observations from the same group are projected close to each other while the indicator observation means of the different groups are projected as far apart as possible. An LDA can handle up to $m - 1$ projections in this way, m being the number of groups (i.e. maturity states) in the data. The projections are called discriminant functions (Backhaus et al. 2003, pp.161–179). Once they are known, new technologies can be classified into a group. Three concepts for classification of new technologies can be differentiated (Backhaus et al. 2003, p.188):

- the distance concept
- the probability concept
- the classification functions

The distance concept will not be used for the approach in this book because it compli-
cates classification of new technologies for more than two groups (Backhaus et al.
2003, p.188). The probability concept will not be used because, despite it being the
most flexible, it is the hardest to comprehend for non-statisticians (Backhaus et al.
2003, p.188). Instead the classification functions will be used for the approach in this
book, because they are intuitive and provide function values which, when compared,
can be interpreted as probabilities that a technology belongs to a certain maturity state.
This enables the before-mentioned ability of the LDA to recognize gradual changes in
maturity.

The classification functions according to Fisher (Fisher 1936) for the approach in this
book are generated as described in LEGENDRE & LEGENDRE or BACKHAUS et al.
(Legendre & Legendre 2012, pp.673–682; Backhaus et al. 2003, pp.188–190;
Legendre & Legendre 1998, p.625) with help of code published on stackoverflow.com
(stackoverflow.com 2011). The entirety of the classification functions are called the
classifier. The decision to which group a certain technology pertains is made by this
classifier. The final classifier consists of a set of m classification functions the form of
equation 4.5.

$$\vec{y} = \vec{c} + (W \cdot \vec{x})$$

with

$\vec{y}$: vector of m classification scores (one for each group)

$\vec{c}$: vector of m constants (one for each group)

W: $m \times i$-matrix of weights for m groups and i indicators

$\vec{x}$: vector of the i indicator values

The classification scores in $\vec{y}$ can be interpreted as the probability that a technology
belongs to the corresponding group . The group is assigned to the input technology
based on which classification score in $\vec{y}$ is the highest. A final classifier consists of the
vector of constants $\vec{c}$ and the weighing matrix W. All it takes to perform a classification
of a new technology with such a classifier is solving the equation with the technology's
indicator vector $\vec{x}$ as an input and the classification scores $\vec{y}$ as an output.

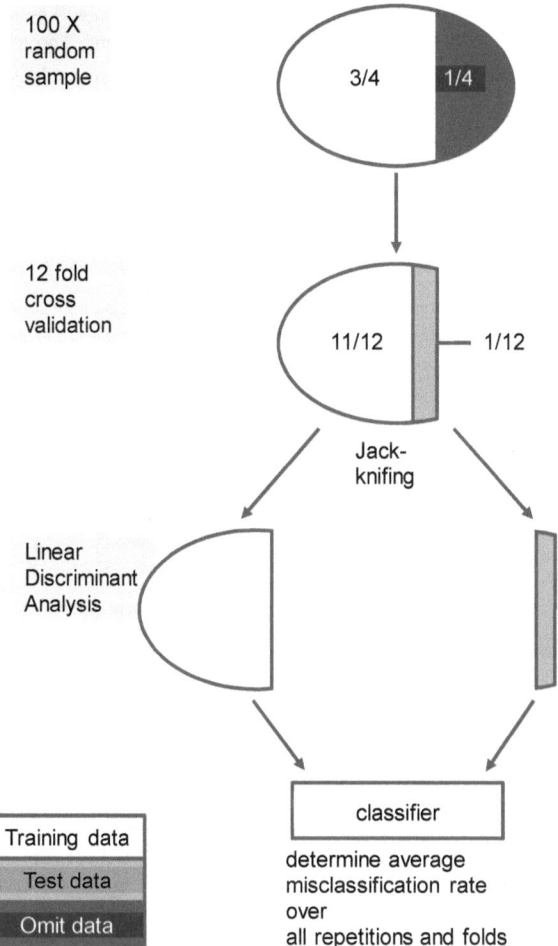

Fig. 4.43 Schematic sample data configuration for the linear discriminant analysis

The performance of a classifier is gauged with help of a cross validation, as described in section 2.3.5.3 and already performed within the scope of the random forest approach in section 4.7.6.3. The discriminative power of the classifier is determined by confusion matrix and misclassification rate. These are then used for comparison of the performance of meta data indicators and activity indicators. The cross validation approach in this LDA is similar to the one of the random forest approach in section 4.7.6.3.

It is depicted in figure 4.43. It makes use of the train() package from the caret library (version 6.0-24) to implement a 12-fold cross validation with 100 repetitions. The misclassification rate is averaged over all those approaches and an exemplary confusion matrix is deduced at random from one of the folds.

The final classifiers are described as the classification function parameters in table 4.44 for the years 2004 until 2012 and in table 4.45 for the years 1976 until 2012. See the description text of table 4.44 for an explanation how to interpret the tables.

Table 4.44 Classifier for five maturity state groups and activity indicators in the time span from 2004 to 2012. The values in the table represent indicator weights. The column sum of the indicator values times the corresponding weights represent the classification score of each maturity state. The column sum which produces the highest score determines the maturity state

	pre-existence	emergence	growth	saturation	decline
constant	-0.13	-3.00	-14.00	-12.00	-5.00
fraction international patents	5.00	16.00	22.00	38.00	27.00
fraction US patents	-0.60	-140.00	-341.00	-212.00	28.00
fraction scientific publications	3.00	59.00	149.00	72.00	-20.00
fraction web search queries	-0.02	0.06	0.25	0.31	0.09
slope international patents	15.00	188.00	337.00	189.00	-183.00
slope US patents	145.00	400.00	532.00	-261.00	-601.00
slope scientific publications	45.00	-44.00	-306.00	-332.00	-86.00
slope web search queries	0.09	0.49	0.80	0.12	-0.36

Table 4.45 Classifier for five maturity state groups and activity indicators in the time span from 1976 to 2012

	pre-existence	*emergence*	*growth*	*saturation*	*decline*
constant	-0.10	-0.72	-3.00	-4.00	-0.27
fraction international patents	0.02	10.00	13.00	39.00	14.00
fraction US patents	-6.00	-15.00	47.00	61.00	-10.00
fraction scientific publications	4.00	8.00	7.00	2.00	1.00
slope international patents	4.00	34.00	36.00	20.00	-17.00
slope US patents	-18.00	93.00	504.00	-488.00	-122.00
slope scientific publications	3.00	-5.00	28.00	-6.00	-16.00

Based on a regression window size of three years a misclassification rate $Err^*(activity_{short,\Delta=3})$ is produced of:

$$Err^*(activity_{short,\Delta=3}) = 0.1666667 < 71\% = p(Err^*(activity))$$

This misclassification rate is excellent in comparison to the trivial strategy.

The confusion matrix theoretically introduced in section 2.3.5.3 reveals more about the type and graveness of the misclassifications.

Table 4.46 Confusion matrix of the activity indicator based technology maturity model based on data from between 2004 and 2012

Predicted group

		pre-existence	emergence	growth	saturation	decline
Actual group	pre-existence	5	0	0	0	1
	emergence	0	6	1	0	1
	growth	0	1	10	3	0
	saturation	0	0	0	8	1
	decline	0	0	0	0	11

The confusion matrix in table 4.46 shows only few wrong classifications, which is in line with the misclassification rate. Furthermore, it reveals that if a state is classified wrong, it is almost always classified into a neighboring group. A misclassification of the pre-existence as the decline state or vice versa is plausible: assuming the bell curve described in figure 2.22 of section 2.3.5.1, the indicators can be expected to produce similar values at both ends of the curve. In this interpretation, the pre-existence state and the decline state can be considering neighboring states. This is also plausible regarding the strategic interpretation of the maturity states: technologies which do not exist yet or not anymore will trigger similar behavior (i.e. no reaction). If the pre-existence state and the decline state need to be differentiated nevertheless, a cumulative indicator which just adds up all consecutive values of an existing indicator could be applied. It should be noted that error rates differ for different time slice widths (see table 4.48), but most misclassifications still happen in neighboring groups.

For the longer time span between the years 1976 and 2012, a much worse performance can be observed. It still easily outperforms the trivial strategy:

$$Err^*\left(activity_{long,\Delta=3}\right) = 0.439814815 < 70\% = p\left(Err^*(activity)\right)$$

Table 4.47 Confusion matrix of the activity indicator based operationalized technology maturity model based on data from between 1976 and 2012

Predicted group

	pre-existence	emergence	growth	saturation	decline
pre-existence	121	23	13	3	67
emergence	5	5	2	0	0
growth	3	6	30	10	0
saturation	0	0	3	38	14
decline	1	10	6	24	48

Actual group

Table 4.48 Misclassification rates for different regression windows and indicator sets

Regression window width	With web search data	Without web search data
2	0.229	0.470
3	0.167	0.440
4	0.250	0.442
5	0.354	0.428
6	0.354	0.451
7	0.354	0.442
8	0.354	0.444

Table 4.47 shows that states from emergence through saturation are recognized correctly most of the time, or at least a neighboring group is estimated, which is plausible for technologies on the brink of entering a new state. Recognition of the pre-existence or decline states is unreliable and produces a broad scatter of states. This will produce "false positives" in the sense that emerging or growing technologies are typically more interesting than other ones. This may cause a strategic threat especially for technologies which are on the decline but are classified as being in emergence or growth state. However, it is relatively improbable that a technology is evaluated with this approach prior to its actual existence.

Table 4.48 shows the misclassification rates for different regression window sizes and indicator sets. It illuminates how the regression window size determines the misclassification rate. A maximum of eight years was chosen because this is well beyond the width that can reasonably be tolerated without putting too much weight on past developments.

For the data from between 2004 and 2012 with the web search data, by far the best window width is three years, producing a misclassification rate of merely 16.7%. For the data from between 1976 and 2012, the optimal regression window width is much less obvious. Even though five years seems to be optimal, the three years misclassification rate is almost as low while relying on a much shorter time span and thus putting more weight on current developments.

The short time span data including the web search data performs better because it can rely on more information. However, the web search data is not the main reason for this good performance. The combination of the indicators is important as can be seen by misclassification rates of the web search-based indicators alone.

Due to the long time span covered between the years 1976 and 2012, technology development speed may have changed. This makes the classifier based on the corresponding data comparatively imprecise because it intends to integrate indicator patterns generated by technologies with lower and higher development speeds. The technologies covered are more inhomogeneous. This may be a more realistic scenario for evaluating technologies outside of the given technology application "data storage" with the classifier.

The following remain as points of future research: interestingly, the misclassification rate of the random forest approach in section 4.7.6.3 provides much better results for the time period between the years 1976 and 2012. The reason for this may be that it is better suited to make use of the additional information from the longer time period through being non-parametric and non-linear. As a contrast to the LDA-based approach, the recent random forest approach was performed and showed potential for improvement regarding misclassification rate, as presented in section 4.7.6.3.

4.7.7 Using a Linear Discriminant Analysis to Gauge the Maturity Classification Performance of the Patent Meta Data Indicators

In their work, HAUPT et al. present a set of patent-based meta data indicators which significantly change with a technology's maturity state (Haupt et al. 2007). They determine the actual indicator values for the cardiac pacemaker technology. They do not assume that these values are identical for other technologies, but they hypothesize that the patterns they describe are similar. A generic rule base can therefore be established analogous to the activity indicator data, with help of a linear discriminant analysis. As in the corresponding section 4.7.6 on the performance of the activity-based indicators, in this section on the meta data indicators, a linear discriminant analysis (LDA) is performed. This section is also built up analogously except for the trailing section 0 on considerations concerning a good setup of the analysis. Section 4.7.7.2 describes how the LDA's assumptions are tested. The performance of a sensible combination of the meta data indicators is derived and the performance of this combination is determined in section 4.7.7.3.

4.7.7.1 Considering Possible Implications of the Different Indicator Evaluation to Avoid a Low Performance of the Indicators Due to Unfortunate Analysis Setup

This section sums up analysis design choices which may have decreased the performance of the meta data indicators in comparison to the activity indicators, and proposes viable solutions to avoid or compensate this performance loss.

Firstly, the patent indicators described by HAUPT et al. are intended for discrimination of a technology's maturity states. However, HAUPT et al. could not describe a precise approach of how to use the indicators for determining the current maturity of a technology without knowing data for each state of maturity. This is due to the fact that only one, namely the cardiac pacemaker technology, was analyzed in their research, and thus no generic pattern could have been deduced. A total of twelve technologies are analyzed in the approach in this book so generic patters can be deduced. It makes use of an LDA to do so. However, an LDA is only one approach of many to describe and exploit the patterns the indicators describe during different maturity states of a technology. The classification performance may be influenced by this choice, so as far as the activity indicators are concerned, future research should consider different approaches for enhanced performance.

Secondly, the decline state could not be tested for the cardiac pacemaker technology and the pre-existence state was not defined in the S&D model or in the work by HAUPT et al. This means that the maturity model in the setup was altered because at least an additional two maturity transitions have to be recognized by the indicators. This may have a large impact on the classification performance of the indicators, too. It could be ruled out by ignoring at least the pre-existence state altogether. HAUPT et al. even suggest that the introduction state of a technology could be identified by the absence of dominant competitors, i.e. effectively by an average technology observer or human intelligence instead of indicators. Relying on human intelligence is not an option for the approach in this book however, as it is intended to monitor a large number of technologies algorithmically. These additional two maturity states may therefore have a major impact on classification performance of the meta data indicators.

Thirdly, a lack of product-relatedness of a technology is mentioned in the work by HAUPT et al. as a potential source of problems for determining the current maturity state by example of the work by HALL et al. (Hall et al. 2001). The data storage technologies described in this book are as product-related as the cardiac pacemaker technology, so problems related to this choice are ruled out.

Fourthly, the indicators described by HAUPT et al. were tested on patent data from the two firms which are perceived as the main competitors in the industry by an average technology observer (Haupt et al. 2007). This is advantageous because not all patents identified by the search strategy have to be examined for their technological relevance. Due to the extended period of time from which the data was collected for the empirical analysis in this book however, the top firms may change (unlike for the cardiac pacemaker technology). This is why the entire dataset was considered. There are two effects which cause this data to be unevenly spread throughout a technology's existence and thus to produce less reliable indicator data for maturity states with less available data:

- There is less patent data for less mature technologies – this effect is exploited by the activity indicators and described in the corresponding section 2.3.4.2.
- There is also less patent data available for older technologies which originated in years where fewer patents were issued, as described at the beginning of this section 0.

Both effects of this uneven spread intensify each other. If the number of observations is not approximately equal, the class membership decision will be biased towards the class with the most representatives (Berrueta et al. 2007). There are two approaches which may help with this problem:

- Drawing same size samples for each maturity state to perform the LDA
- averaging the indicator values during a certain time interval, i.e. a year as for the activity indicators.

As a solution to these two and other potential problems related to the patent count, all tests and analyses are performed twice:

- with the full set of data
- with a random sample with equal observation size for each maturity state.

Averaging the values would change the actual indicators from the way they were described in HAUPT et al. (2007), so this approach was avoided (Haupt et al. 2007).

For the samples to be of the same size without bootstrapping additional values, the maximum size can be as large as the smallest maturity group size, which is the pre-existence state with 134 observations. Since some of the groups contain many more observations, all analyses are repeated 100 times and their results are averaged.

And fifthly and finally, the activity indicators of the previous section may be considered to have an unfair advantage over the meta data indicators in this section. The meta data indicators are based on the same data source for all indicators, i.e. patents, rather than a selection of different media types. This may cause that instead of performing differently well for different maturity states, indicators produce redundant information and work well only for indicating the same maturity states. Here, the indicators based on different media types may have an advantage, which is bought at the cost of a considerable additional search effort.

4.7.7.2 Assumptions of the Analyses Used

As for the activity indicators, the assumptions of the LDA must be tested. Due to the construction of the indicators, a total of 25,120 observations were made, which is many. At the same time, the data is highly skewed (see table 4.51), mostly for the obvious reason that few patents exist for the pre-existence and introduction states of technologies. The power of an analysis depends on the sample size in the group with the least samples. This means that despite the large amount of data available here, the actual statistical power can be expected to be relatively low. Eliminating the pre-existence state could be considered at this point again. However, the sampling approach described in section 0, where an equal size sample from each maturity state is drawn at random, produces a distribution without skew. In the following, all analyses are justified and described for the full set of data and the results of the analysis based on the equal size sampling approach are mentioned complementarily.

Table 4.49 Results of Box's M homogeneity of variance-covariance matrices test for the meta data indicators

MBox	chi-squared	df	P
15362.8524	15277.0207	112	0.0000

To test the homogeneity of the variance-covariance matrix, Box's M is conducted as a pretest, implemented in R at the 0.05 significance level. The test becomes more sensitive with a growing number of observations (International Business Machines (IBM) 2011). The results of this pretest can be found in table 4.49.

The Box's M is highly significant for the full set of data and therefore has to reject the null hypothesis of homogeneity of the variance-covariance matrix. For the equal size sampling approach, the Box's M test also shows highly significant results with a p-value < 2.2e-16.

For the full set of data a lack of normality cannot be checked with the Shapiro-Wilk test because it is intended to work with sample sizes between 3 and 5,000, which is exceeded by the n = 25,120 of the meta data indicators. It is not sensible to perform this test with such a high number of observations. The Shapiro-Wilk shows a highly significant result for the equal size sampling approach with a p-value < 2.2e-16 for all indicators and therefore rejects the null hypothesis of normally distributed values. It can therefore be assumed that the normal distribution assumption must be rejected also for the full data.

As a last pretest, the Levene's test for homogeneity of variance is applied to each individual dependent indicator instead of for all at once. The null hypothesis of this test is the homoscedasticity of all groups, which thus should be non-significant for all indicators. The results of this test for the full data can be found in table 4.50.

And again, even though the assumptions of Levene's test are relatively low, the results are significant for three of the seven indicators. As a consequence, the null hypothesis has to be rejected at least for the immediacy, prior applications, and forward patent citations indicators. Their homoscedasticity assumption must therefore be dismissed.

Table 4.50 Results of Levene's homoscedasticity test for each separate meta data indicator

	df	F value	Pr(>F)	significance
backward patent citations	4	1	0.2501	
backward literature citations	4	1.0201	0.3961	
immediacy	4	5	0.001007	**
dependent claims	4	0.9411	0.4395	
prior applications	4	3	0.01555	*
examination duration	4	15.842	2.15E-12	
forward patent citations	4	5.591	0.0001977	***

Despite the pretests, which in large parts reject the assumptions of the LDA, the boxplots in figure 4.44 show that the patent-based meta data indicators fulfill homoscedasticity and normality assumptions much better than the activity indicators do. Only the non-patent backward literature citations indicator does not show a proper normal distribution. The reason for this is that only few patents are based on non-patent literature and thus only few provide values above zero for this indicator. An interesting fact can be seen for the prior applications indicator. This produces a negligible amount of values for the pre-existence maturity state. This is plausible because technologies which do not exist yet obviously are not tracked in patent data either. Even though it is plausible, it is problematic for an LDA because it prevents reasonable statistical analyses for the pre-existence maturity state based on this indicator. Drawing a separate set of boxplots for the equal size sample approach is not sensible because the boxplots in figure 4.44 already show the underlying distribution.

The boxplots confirm the findings from the previous tests in this section. For most of the meta data indicators, the assumptions are not violated as gravely as for the activity indicators. At the same time, the between-group variance seems to be lower than for the activity indicators.

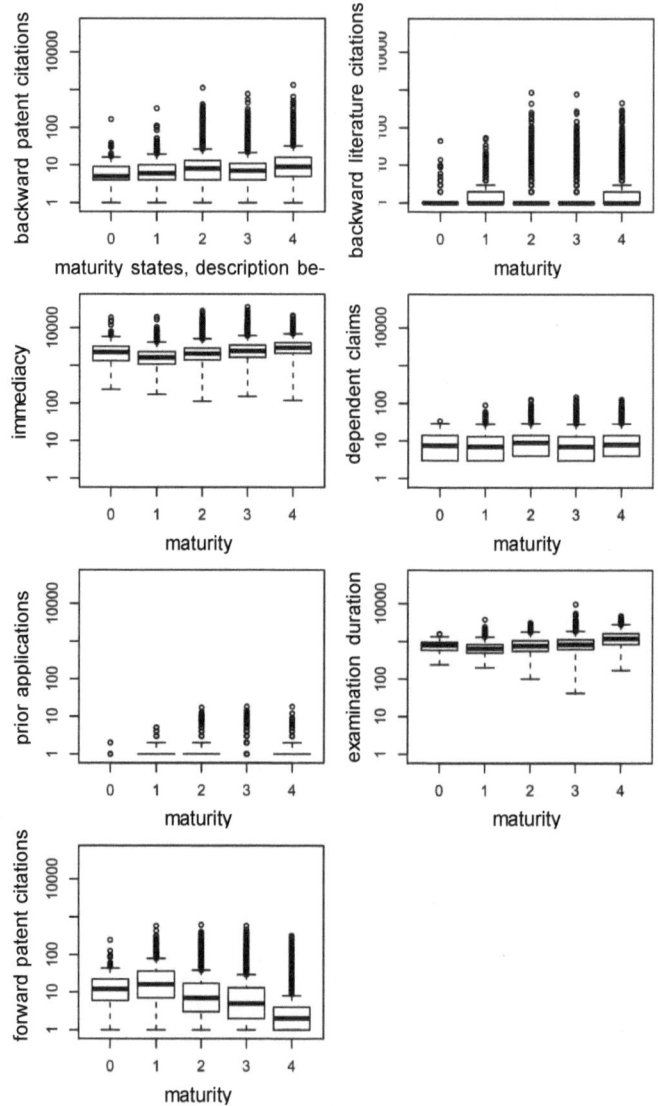

Fig. 4.44 Boxplots of all meta data indicator values between 1976 and 2012 by maturity state to display spread and distribution. The indicator values are grouped by maturity states to make visible the difference between the groups and get an idea about normality and homoscedasticity. The group names are coded as follows: 0 – pre-existence, 1 – emergence, 2 – growth, 3 - saturation, 4 – decline

4.7.7.3 Performing a Linear Discriminant Analysis on the Patent Meta Data Indicators

To establish the trivial strategy, the distribution of maturity states for the meta data indicators needs to be calculated according to formula 4.1. This time, indicator values are not aggregated by year but based on single documents. Each indicator value generated by a single patent can be allotted to one maturity state and counts as an observation. This is important to note because the frequency of patent publication has increased considerably since 1976. This causes a distribution bias towards maturity states which are predominant in years with a high patenting volume, i.e. the later years (see figures 4.2 and 4.3 in section 4.5).

As a result, the distribution of maturity states is less uniform for maturity states than for the activity indicators (see table 4.51).

Table 4.51 Distribution of maturity states for technologies which change maturity states during the time period 1976-2012 based on meta data indicators

p(pre-existence)	p(emergence)	p(growth)	p(saturation)	p(decline)
1%	3%	33%	46%	17%

As expected, the distribution of maturity state probability is biased towards later years when most technologies have taken on an advanced maturity state. The expected misclassification rate of the trivial strategy to always choose the saturation state is

$$p(Err^*(meta)) = 1 - \max_{\forall m}(p(m)) = 1 - 0.46 = 54\%$$

It is therefore much harder to succeed in outperforming the trivial strategy accuracy than for the antecedent indicator sets.

Table 4.52 Distribution of maturity states for the equal size sample approach

p(pre-existence)	p(emergence)	p(growth)	p(saturation)	p(decline)
20%	20%	20%	20%	20%

The equal size sample approach on the other hand produces a uniform distribution, as shown in table 4.52.

This leads to a misclassification rate of the trivial strategy of

$$p(Err^*(meta)) = 1 - \max_{\forall m}(p(m)) = 1 - 0.2 = 80\%$$

The classifier for the full data set based on the indicators as presented by HAUPT et al. is displayed in table 4.53 (Haupt et al. 2007).

Table 4.53 Classification function parameters for five maturity state groups in the time span from 1976 to 2012 as determined by an LDA. The rows represent factors for the patent meta data indicator values which were calculated according to HAUPT et al.(2007) and the columns represent the factors for maturity state equations. The sum of all indicator values each multiplied by the corresponding factors for an entire row add up to the corresponding maturity state score. The maturity state with the highest score is selected as the current maturity state of the analyzed technology

	pre-exist-ence	emer-gence	growth	saturation	decline
constant	-3.38	-2.90	-3.27	-3.58	-5.86
backward patent citations / backward literature citations	0.0263	0.0338	0.0522	0.0437	0.0521
immediacy	0.0009	0.0006	0.0006	0.0008	0.0008
dependent claims	0.0698	0.0708	0.0869	0.0712	0.0759
prior applications	0.0478	0.3300	0.3730	0.3160	0.4740
examination duration	0.0033	0.0031	0.0036	0.0040	0.0056
forward patent citations	0.0341	0.0491	0.0262	0.0225	0.0136

The result of the cross validation of the full data set for the entire operationalized technology maturity model is:

$$Err^*(meta_{combined}) = 0.5128583$$

$$Err^*(meta_{combined}) = 51\% < 54\% = p(Err^*(meta))$$

This is just below the expected result from the trivial strategy and classifies more than half maturity states wrong. By itself this is unacceptable as a foundation for strategic decisions. The confusion matrix in table 4.54 can be analyzed to understand the reasons for the wrong classifications.

The confusion matrix shows explicitly that the patent data volume for technologies increases with the maturity of a technology until the decline state. The correct group is determined more often than any incorrect group by itself except for the actual emergence state which is often misclassified as growth or saturation state. Most wrong classifications happen in neighboring states with what may be a normal distribution around the actual maturity state.

When an LDA is performed repeatedly 600 times with the equal size sample approach, it produces misclassification rates of an average of $p(Err^*(meta)) = 65\%$. Although this looks like a worse result than the 51% from the full data set, it means a significant increase when compared to the trivial strategy which in this case produces a misclassification rate of 80%.

Table 4.54 Confusion matrix of the patent indicator based operationalized technology maturity model with the backward citation indicators considered in combination based on data from between 1976 and 2012

Predicted group

		pre-existence	emergence	growth	saturation	decline
	pre-existence	0	0	0	0	0
	emergence	3	32	94	97	12
Actual group	growth	7	190	1196	769	148
	saturation	124	623	6561	9911	3092
	decline	0	8	387	768	1098

4.8 Representation, Interpretation, and Utilization of the Advanced Analysis Results

The purpose of the analysis was to understand whether it is possible to derive technology maturity from text media-based indicators. From the findings in sections 4.1 to 4.7 it can be safely said that this is indeed possible. These sections also gave insights into what indicators and indicator combinations work well and which do not, as well as how they perform against established patent indicators. Unfortunately, not all information resulting from the analysis is used as a result from the concentration and simplification of the available information.

The loss of information is an effect of the LDA. In the original LDA approach, only the highest value out of all equations in the system is relevant to estimate the current maturity state. This is a reasonable approach. An indicator combination which matches a certain group well scores high in that group. A score of zero in a certain group means that the data does not match that state at all. If at least one value is above zero, the algorithm successfully identifies a match. If instead the values for all maturity states are below zero, the algorithm could not find a matching pattern, but due to its original design, it still picks the highest score to determine the group. This allows for a very intuitive interpretation of the analysis, but it comes at the cost of potentially valuable information which is readily available. When in contrast all values are considered, more elaborate interpretations become possible. The approach in this book suggests that an unusual behavior has been identified in a case with all negative values – apparently it does not match the patterns identified in the training set. The relation of values offers another approach for interpretation. The following scenarios are conceivable:

- A single highest value. This leads to an obvious decision congruent with the classical LDA solution.
- Values of neighboring maturity states of almost the same height. This means the technology is in a transition from one maturity state to another.
- Values of the same height but not neighboring. This could mean different things: either a.) the data contains several different technologies in a differing maturity state; or b.) the technology is leaping from one maturity state to another, for example when a technology is abandoned after the emergence state and enters the decline state right away, compare (Albert et al. 2011).

It will be the goal of this final step of the empirical analysis presented in section 0 to show how this information can be put to use based on the S&D model. It will also become clear that more information is needed to put to use the knowledge of the maturity state of a technology. For this purpose, the actual technology maturity results will be discussed and it will be shown how they can be put to use in combination with the S&D model and which practical managerial implications can be deduced with their help. For this purpose, the results of the empirical analysis, or, to be more precise, the values of each of the classification functions will be compared. These values can be used to estimate to which maturity state a set of indicator values most likely belongs.

Figures 4.45 through 4.50 present the technologies analyzed based on the dataset including web search data. This data set covers the data of six technologies between the years 2004 and 2012: hard disc, NVRAM, ReRAM, DVD, Blu-ray, and HD-DVD. According to expert judgment, all of these technologies change their technology maturity state during this period of time at least once. Each classifier score for the maturity states is displayed as a bar. All indicators are calculated based on a regression window of 3 years. To understand the added value of analyzing the additional classifier scores, the six technologies will be analyzed during the years 2006 and 2012. This also allows for an analysis of the technological development speed. To understand the precision of this approach, the three optical disc technologies will be compared in detail by comparing the visualization of every year during that period.

4.8.1 Applying the S&D Model to Hard Disc Technology

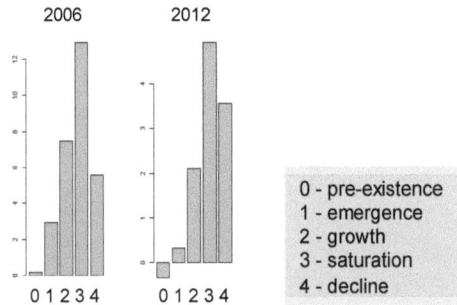

2006   2012

0 1 2 3 4   0 1 2 3 4

0 - pre-existence
1 - emergence
2 - growth
3 - saturation
4 - decline

Fig. 4.45 Hard disc maturity state classification values for the years 2006 and 2012 based on the activity indicator based technology maturity model including web search data

Hard discs were estimated by the experts to be in the saturation state during 2006 and in decline in 2012. As can be seen in figure 4.45, judging by the indicators, the hard disc technology does not change maturity state between years 2006 and 2012. The saturation state is still the most probable in 2012. However, a gradual maturing of the technology is obvious. The decline state bar rises from third to second highest while all states before the saturation state decrease. This is an obvious advantage of the additional classifier values approach: the speed of the development can be perceived much more finely when a tendency towards the other maturity state is known. While the decline state will take another couple of years to prevail, the hard drive technology has certainly been a basic technology for a long time, as displayed in table 4.55. The strategic value of HDDs for the industry is relatively low. Still, there is a large market for hard disc drives which is not yet in decline, as can be read in the media (Coughlin 2013; Gasior 2013), and even slightly back in growth again in 2014 (Coughlin 2014). A reason for this may be that mobile devices have little on-board storage and to a great deal rely on cloud storage, which in turn depends on HDDs. This means that other factors in the HDD industry determine the competitiveness of a firm.

Table 4.55 The hard disc technology is located in the saturation state at the brink of the decline state

Maturity state technology	pre-exist-ence	emergence	growth	saturation	decline
Hard disc				⟳→	

4.8.2 Applying the S&D Model to NVRAM Technology

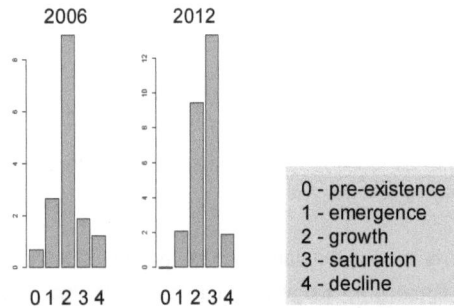

Fig. 4.46 NVRAM maturity state classification values for the years 2006 and 2012 based on the activity indicator based technology maturity model including web search data

The NVRAM technology moved from the growth to the saturation state between 2006 and 2012 according to expert judgment. In the visualization of the year 2012 in figure 4.46 the technology is still much closer to the growth state than to the decline. Actually, juxtaposed with the highest state score, the score for the decline state did not increase at all. It could be assumed that the maturity of this technology develops relatively slowly. This makes it a key technology on its way to becoming a basic technology, giving it a moderate strategic importance in the industry as displayed in table 4.56.

Table 4.56 NVRAM recently left the growth state and is now in the saturation state

Maturity state technology	pre-exist-ence	emergence	growth	saturation	decline
NVRAM				⟳→	

4.8.3 Applying the S&D Model to ReRAM Technology

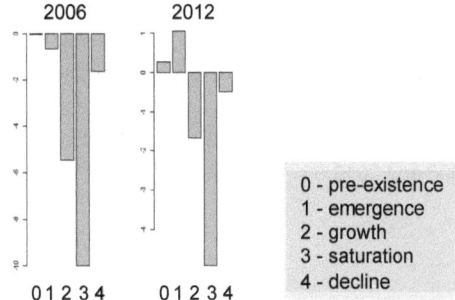

2006   2012

0 - pre-existence
1 - emergence
2 - growth
3 - saturation
4 - decline

0 1 2 3 4   0 1 2 3 4

Fig. 4.47 ReRAM maturity state classification values for the years 2006 and 2012 based on the activity indicator based technology maturity model including web search data

Experts assessed the ReRAM technology to have moved from pre-existence to emergence between 2006 and 2012. This is confirmed by the bar graph in figure 4.47, which shows that even in 2012 the technology still shows certain patterns of a technology in its pre-existence state. This makes ReRAM a pacing technology for the industry of non-volatile, machine-readable data storage (see figure 2.5 and table 4.57), giving it a high strategic relevance and making a close monitoring especially advisable.

Table 4.57 ReRAM was just recently introduced as a technology and is now in the emergence state

Maturity state technology	pre-exist-ence	emergence	growth	saturation	decline
ReRAM		↻⟩			

4.8.4 Checking the Reaction Time and Precision of Activity Indicators on Optical Disc Technologies: DVD, Blu-ray, and HD-DVD

Sections 4.8.1 to 4.8.3 show how it is possible to put the newly generated maturity information to use in the S&D approach. It is important to know the speed at which a technology advances through the maturity states, which is why e.g. the information technology advisory firm Gartner Inc. labels each technology they assess with one of a number of development speed labels, which describe after how much time a technology will have passed through its hype cycle (Fenn & Raskino 2008). Knowing this speed increases a firm's dynamic capabilities, especially because it enables timely responsiveness, as described in section 1. Estimating a technology's maturity development speed is possible with at least two observations. But it is yet unknown how precisely it can be estimated with the new technology maturity assessment approach. In order to estimate the precision of this approach, three optical disc technologies are assessed year after year between 2006 and 2012.

4.8.4.1 DVD

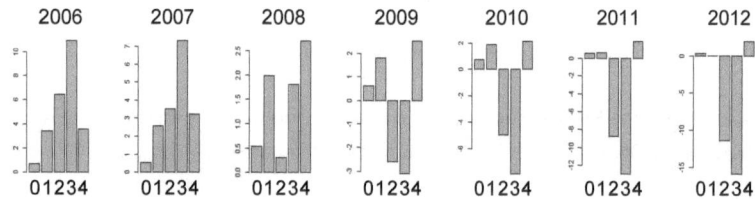

Fig. 4.48 DVD maturity state classification values for the years 2006 through 2012 based on the activity indicator based technology maturity model including web search data

The DVD technology was estimated by the experts to having gone from saturation state in 2006 to decline thereafter. This is in agreement with the indicator-based approach displayed in figure 4.48, although the latter assigns the DVD to the saturation maturity state a year longer. This puts the DVD beyond any strategic significance. It can be regarded as obsolete (see table 4.58) and any firm still active in it should consider an immediate retreat from developing it further.

Table 4.58 The DVD technology has moved to the decline state and can now be regarded as obsolete

Maturity state technology	pre-exist- ence	emergence	growth	saturation	decline
DVD					◯

4.8.4.2 Blu-ray

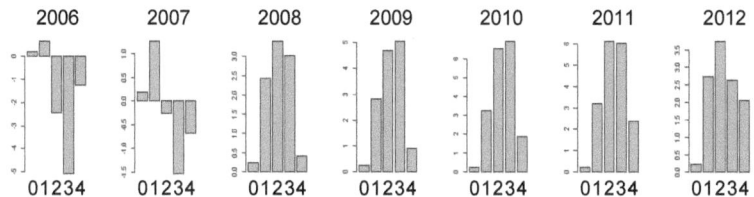

Fig. 4.49 Blu-ray maturity state classification values for the years 2006 through 2012 based on the activity indicator based technology maturity model including web search data

The experts assessed the Blu-ray technology to have moved from the emergence state in 2006 on to the growth state in 2007 until 2010 and the saturation state from there on after. The data draws another picture, however: Fig. 4.49 shows that the technology moves from emergence in 2006 and 2007 on to the growth state in 2008 and right on to the saturation state in 2009 until 2010, only to go back to the growth state in 2011 and even more clearly in 2012. This technology was "rejuvenated", as described in section 0 on the "technology life cycle". This rejuvenation in the data may have been caused by the interesting market environment during the early years of the Blu-ray technology. It was a direct competitor of the HD-DVD described below, which was eventually withdrawn in 2008 (Ricker 2008). The rejuvenation of the technology may be an artifact in the activity data due to the competition with the HD-DVD, which shows a very similar pattern to Blu-ray in 2006 and 2007. After a short break in the exhaustive technology race in 2009, more competitors started developing the now sole blue laser-based optical disc data storage technology, leading to a second state of growth (see table 4.59).

Table 4.59 The Blu-ray technology is shifting back and forth between the growth and saturation states

Maturity state technology	pre-existence	emergence	growth	saturation	decline
Blu-ray			⟲⟳		

4.8.4.3 HD-DVD

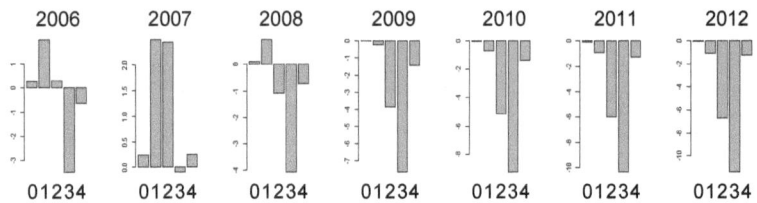

Fig. 4.50 HD-DVD maturity state classification values for the years 2006 through 2012 based on the activity indicator based technology maturity model including web search data

The experts estimated the HD-DVD technology to be in emergence state in 2006, growth state in 2007, and decline in 2008 and after. This is largely backed up by the indicator-based approach displayed in figure 4.50 which puts the technology in the emergence state in 2006, too, then in a transition between emergence and growth in 2007, moving back to the emergence state in 2008 and to pre-existence in 2009 and after. The classifier estimates the technology to be in pre-existence between 2009 and 2012 because it is designed to select the highest value. The highest value in this case is close to zero. However, all other groups score negative. This is a clear sign that the technology shows an uncommon behavior. The technology may have been considered a strong pacing technology in 2007, but caution was advisable at the latest when it showed the uncommon behavior starting in 2008. The data shows blatantly which technology won the race when comparing the HD-DVD and Blu-ray bar graph patterns for 2008 (see table 4.60).

Table 4.60 The HD-DVD technology has lost the battle against the Blu-ray technology and is now in the decline state

Maturity state technology	pre-exist-ence	emergence	growth	saturation	decline
HD-DVD					◯

5 Measuring Technology Maturity: Conclusions

To conclude this book, a summary of the findings will be shown, followed by the quality criteria and shortcomings. The main research question of this book is:

How should an approach be constructed with which existing theoretical maturity models can be operationalized to allow for valid, reliable, objective and useful statements regarding the maturity of a technology?

This book provides an approach which is able to respond to this question, albeit with some shortcomings. It delineates technologies based on an approach described by TAYLOR & TAYLOR (Taylor & Taylor 2012), which ensures that different technologies are defined at a similar level of aggregation. To make technologies comparable which originate from different drivers such as market pull or technology push which cause publication in different media types to peak in a differing sequence, the operationalization mechanism is designed in a way to make it compatible with most media types, thus also allowing for inclusion of additional media in the future, if deemed necessary. Instead of linking a high activity in one of these media to the presence of one maturity state, as proposed originally in WATTS & PORTER (Watts & Porter 1997), the interplay of indicators is considered with help of a linear discriminant analysis (LDA). This approach allows for the technology maturity to be determined according to a complex yet linear rule set which works for technologies that originate from different drivers.

The technology maturity model by SOMMERLATTE & DESCHAMPS ("S&D model") was operationalized with these indicators, which allows the resulting model to profit from the strategic advice in the original strategic technology management approach ("S&D approach") (Sommerlatte & Deschamps 1986, pp.37–76). The model was chosen mainly for two reasons: for its relatively well-defined maturity states and for its popularity. The well-defined maturity states made it well-suited for operationalization in the first place. And the popularity of the model led to much subsequent research providing relevant improvements until this day such as different works by ALBERT et al., GAO et al., HAUPT et al., HÖFT and ERICKSON et al. (Albert et al. 2015; Gao et al. 2013; Albert et al. 2011; Haupt et al. 2007; Haupt et al. 2004; Höft 1992; Erickson et al. 1990).

The S&D model has certain hypotheses concerning the behavior of its indicators during different maturity states of a technology (Sommerlatte & Deschamps 1986, p.53). Once the S&D model was operationalized, these hypotheses could be tested with an empirical analysis. This analysis required as input the maturity state of each tested technology at a given point in time. A two-round Delphi approach was chosen to gain this information with help of four technology experts. It resulted in technology maturity information for twelve different technologies and each year during the years 1976 until 2012. The development of each indicator was then compared to the according hypothesis. None of the S&D hypotheses concerning the behavior of certain variables could be confirmed empirically. This may be due to two reasons: either a) the hypotheses are wrong and do not apply, or b) the model factors were operationalized wrong. The indicators found in the process still mostly produce typical patterns over the course of a technology's maturity and thus are well-suited for use in technology maturity assessment.

Once it was clear that the indicators do produce maturity relevant information, they could be combined to determine the maturity state of yet unclassified technologies. To avoid using indicators which weaken the overall classification performance, several analyses for indicator selection were performed. These determined that none of the indicators shows zero or near-zero variance, only very few are strongly correlated; they determined each indicator's contribution for the entire model's performance and conducted a stepwise selection based on a random forest approach. The stepwise selection concluded that all indicators should be used for good classification results of the model.

A good combination of the indicators for maturity classification is determined with an LDA as the basis of a supervised machine-learning approach, which automatically determines indicator patterns during the different technology maturity states and weights each indicator during each state of maturity. The twelve technologies for which the experts determined the maturity during each year are used to train the LDA and generate a generic classifier which is able to determine the maturity of as yet unknown technologies. Misclassification rates as low as ~16% could be achieved with this approach. It can be said that the results of the classifier are generally not far from expert judgment. The classifier can improve the decision base for persons who are not experts in a technology or a maturity model, especially for technology monitoring purposes.

In comparison to previous approaches, the approach presented in this work profits mainly from two effects: on the one hand it is able to harness information contained in diverse media sources such as scientific literature and web search requests on top of patents. And on the other hand, differing from many approaches before it such as (Järvenpää et al. 2011), it can implement normalized activity indicators which provide information similar to that of a curve discussion. This book also provides examples of how the relevant maturity related information can be communicated to the management intuitively.

5.1 Quality Criteria and Limitations

It is generally agreed upon that validity, reliability, and objectivity are important quality criteria for research, not just for quantitative but also for qualitative research (Steinke 2004; Pipino et al. 2002). Since the approach in this book can also be applied in business, another quality criterion is its utility. In this section, advantages and limitations will therefore refer to these important four criteria. The first three criteria, validity, reliability, and objectivity are regarded as minimal requirements, whereas through the utility of the approach actual advantages for its application are created. Table 5.1 shows a list of concepts relevant for the quality of research based on STEINKE and PIPINO et al. which are deemed worth mentioning (Steinke 2004; Pipino et al. 2002).

Table 5.1 Important quality criteria for the approach presented in this book, compare STEINKE (2004) and PIPINO et al. (2002)

validity	reliability	objectivity	utility
internal validity	robustness	transparency	speed
external validity	definitiveness	reproducibility	intuitiveness
transferability			inexpensiveness
			scalability
			flexibility

Validity: The entire section 0, especially sections 4.6 about the methodological triangulation and section 4.7 on the performance of the operationalized technology maturity model aim to establish the *internal validity* of the approach. Also, the approach is built upon a machine-learning approach which aims to create a universal classifier for any additional technology. The cross validation performed in section 4.7 establishes *external validity* and thus in terms of utility shows the *transferability* of the classifier in table 4.44 or table 4.45 to yet untested technologies. At the same time, the approach as in the analysis design of figure 3.1 can be transferred to other technology maturity models. And the activity indicators described in formulas (2.1) and (2.2) of section 2.3.4.2 can be transferred to most text-based information sources.

Reliability: The indicators described in this work are based on a number of different information sources. Maturity assessment is possible with this approach even with partial information (e.g. missing information from one information source or missing data for one year), making it *robust* against uncommon behavior of a technology in one of these, e.g. the patent domain. This aids in establishing *reliability* of the approach and makes it superior to approaches which are exclusively built on a single information source. When new information sources become available and are deemed useful, new indicators need to be designed. Even if the exact curve progression of a new activity indicator is unknown, as long as it is relatively simple and shows a repetitive pattern such as in figure 2.22, the means presented in section 2.3.5.1 can be used to describe it. The performance of a new indicator can easily be gauged against existing indicators by applying the approaches described in section 4.7.6.3. Its effect on the overall performance of the approach can be gauged by a cross validation as described in sections 0 and 0. Even if a new indicator shows a more complex activity pattern, additional activity indicators can be derived from the existing ones relatively easily (such as equation (2.4) in section 2.3.5.1). This adds further to the robustness of the approach and therefore to its reliability. Furthermore, it enables relatively easily a *flexible* hand-tailoring of the approach to rely on sources which are available for a firm at no or low cost. This modularity makes the approach very cost-effective and *inexpensive*.

Objectivity: All indicators described in this work are based on publicly available data. This makes the approach *reproducible* for anyone interested, adding to its *objectivity*. Even more so, because the information the approach relies on can not be tempered with. Even though the results are generated by an algorithm, the interpretation is still done by people, e.g. managers. But these people rely on the actual information rather than hearing an interpretation from an expert or cascades of other people. This also adds to the objectivity of the approach.

Utility: The design of the indicators as activity indicators allows for a very *inexpensive* use of additional high-quality information sources (see sections 2.3.4.2 and 4.7.1). Often, specialized search engines provide a simple search count result at no cost, whereas meta data or full text data is only available for a high fee. The activity indicator design furthermore allows use of the data without elaborate data preprocessing, unlike for indicators which require information contained in the metadata or full text of a document. This means that once the search strategy was sufficiently checked for correctness, the data can be directly used in the model. This does not just enable a *speedier* evaluation. It is also a requirement for successful automation of the process, which in turn is a requirement for the process to be *scalable*, making possible a continuous monitoring of all relevant technologies. The approach presented in this work also provides an *intuitive* visualization of the results in the form of bar graphs such as figure 4.48 in section 4.8. This makes the analysis results accessible to managers without the need for additional explanations by methodological or technological experts. Furthermore, once a technology definition exists, the data necessary for maturity measurement can be re-used for other purposes, which make its collection the more appealing. One such a use would be the standardized or automated generation and allocation of relevant technology information as described in WILBERS et al. (Wilbers et al. 2010). It is also important to note that a data-based analysis is able to solve a form of the so-called "agency dilemma" (Eisenhardt 1989) of an expert-based analysis: the technology expert in the position of the agent and possessing more information concerning a technology's maturity, acts in his own interest (i.e. selecting the technology of the own expertise to be assigned a larger budget) rather than fulfilling activities useful for the principal, the manager in charge of budget allocation (i.e. selecting the most promising technology). This constellation is driven by asymmetric information and can be solved e.g. by providing the manager with the necessary information from an independent third source.

Limitations of using publication slope patterns as maturity indicators are connected to the mathematical approach described in section 2.3.4.2 on the one hand and to the quality of the technology definitions on the other.

Limitations connected to the *mathematical approach*: the approach can only serve to assess the maturity of technologies which were identified in advance. This helps e.g. in a monitoring, but it will fail to discover new technologies. Moreover, the activity and slope indicators defined in section 2.3.4.2 assume that technologies always produce similar patterns. Over an extended period of time, however, these patterns may change (e.g. when generations of technologies replace each other at an increasing speed, the equation (2.2) will produce more extreme values, which may or may not influence the classification performance). In addition to technology development speed, the indicators are also sensitive to technology definition size: when little data is available for a given technology, it will exhibit a higher variation between years than a technology for which considerable data is available. A solution to this has yet to be found. The system should therefore only be used for technologies of approximately the same definition size and only for a limited period of time before it has to be trained with new data, requiring an analysis to be performed as the one described in the analysis design of figure 3.1 anew. The slope indicators presented in section 2.3.4.2 may be seen as in conflict with the independence assumption of the LDA because they are based on a regression and thus incorporate values from other years, as noticed by (Leeds 2012, p.5). This also has an impact on the cross validation results of section 4.7.6.4 unless the cross validation is performed through leaving out an entire technology rather than just the observations from random years. Furthermore, the first and the last maturity states (pre-existence and decline) produce only little data. During these states, a signal can change quickly between years, and it will almost certainly exhibit a high variation. During these maturity states, the signal strength of the indicators is lower and therefore the patterns are not as distinctive for different technologies as for maturity states which produce a higher indicator signal strength. Finally, problems may occur because a parametric approach (the LDA) is used on data which clearly does not fulfill the assumptions it makes.

Limitations connected to the *technology definitions*: since no additional steps are taken for data cleaning, an elaborate search strategy is absolutely crucial for the approach to work. The definition of search strategies for the technology application on top of technology generations constitutes an additional step of data retrieval, which is laborious and time-intensive. Here it loses to the patent-based approach described in HAUPT et al (2007), which relies on knowledge of just the main competitors in a technology field and thus only requires the input of an average observer of the field (Haupt et al. 2007). The approach described in this work requires special knowledge in data retrieval and leads to a prolonged search strategy definition phase. The search strategy results have to be checked by experts in maturity model AND technology, or in collaboration. Also, the technologies which are selected for the empirical analysis in this work by design all need to be from the same technology application and thus are relatively closely related. This makes the universality of the resulting classifier questionable. Furthermore, the approach cannot differentiate between incremental and radical innovations which require different reactions by management (Christensen 2013). If done by laymen, the search results may be wrong and can subsequently lead to false conclusions. This cannot be recognized from the results alone. In the case of a continuous monitoring, every now and then it has to be checked whether the current technology definition still represents what is needed. This causes additional effort, but if it is neglected, wrong conclusions could be drawn.

As a concluding remark regarding the use of this approach, it is important to note that the maturity information alone is not sufficient to establish a technology strategy in a firm. It has to be backed up by additional information and it has to be put to use in a process such as the one described in section 2.1. Experts may be able to come by without the indicator-based approach, but on a strategic level, when many different technologies need to be compared, the indicator-based approach described in this work may prove to be a valuable input.

5.2 Directions for Future Research

The proposed technology maturity operationalization provides a conceptual approach in the much researched field of technology and innovation management. It is based on an interpretation of large amounts of textual data with the help of a machine-learning approach. The conceptual approach and the propositions emerging from it, imply a rich agenda for further research

First, it would be necessary to test the approach described in this book on different technology applications and compare the resulting classifiers. This can help understand the system universality. If a satisfactory system universality can be achieved, it would be interesting to test the approach on technologies outside of the "technology" working definition of this work in section 0. An example for technologies outside of this definition are "social technologies", such as abstract political concepts (socialism, capitalism, democracy), musical flavors (classical, hip-hop, electro), arts (naturalism, expressionism, graffiti), or sports trends (wrestling, skateboarding, parkour).

Second, a series of improvements could help increase the overall performance of the operationalized technology maturity model. One important improvement concerns the machine-learning approach. Instead of the LDA, more sophisticated and non-linear approaches such as (kernel) support vector machines should be tested to further increase classification performance. Another improvement would be to adjust the underlying indicators, for example, by implementing indicator specific time slice lengths to improve model accuracy or by using an exponential smoothing rather than the rolling linear regression to determine the activity slope in a given year. Moreover, instead of just relying on activity indicators, additional indicators could be included in the model to further improve the misclassification rates. For example, the slope indicators could be based on exponential smoothing rather than rolling linear regression. The slope could also be measured relatively to consider the level of aggregation of a technology better. Other indicators such as the meta data indicators presented by HAUPT et al. could be included into the model based on a thorough indicator selection (Haupt et al. 2007). Also, instead of just relying on information concerning the current maturity state, it would be helpful to develop a maturity speed indicator to hint towards how fast reaction times concerning the decision making process in respect to a certain technology needs to be. For a sound data basis of a monitoring, which could even improve itself automatically to a certain degree, it would be interesting to incorporate approaches for improved search strategies such as described in TEICHERT & MITTERMAYER (2002) with a supervised learning approach to enhance process automation (Teichert & Mittermayer 2002). A data warehouse infrastructure and approaches for an automated generation of such a maturity assessment could be defined to increase the speed of the operationalized model.

Third, it would be interesting to detach maturity states from any existing models by deriving maturity states from the data and check with experts whether the resulting classification makes sense. A suitable approach would be to cluster the indicator values with a suitable clustering algorithm to then apply an unsupervised machine-learning approach. The result would be a much more stable, data-friendly classification. A drawback that would have to be solved is that no strategic implications could be deduced directly, unless by a chance correlation with any existing technology maturity model. In any case, it would be helpful to align strategic implications from the theoretical models with industry experience, e.g. based on interviews or surveys.

The approach in this book looks at technology maturity from a firm-perspective. But after all, technology maturity is interesting for different groups in different institutions for timely initiation of different purposes. All of them can profit from the approach in this book to some extent. Some examples include, but are not limited to:

- social scientists (social technology impact assessment);
- macroeconomists, politicians (assistance measures, policy adjustments);
- investors, financial institutions (investment strategy);
- marketing professionals (target-oriented marketing);
- innovation managers (technology strategy; budget allocation);
- product managers (product development strategy)
- future researchers (forewarning, foresight, forecasting);
- HR departments/consultancies (timely expert recruitment)
- IP-professionals (property rights strategy)

In the long run, it is the vision of this book to enable inclusion of technology maturity as one value of many in a business intelligence technology monitoring framework useful for a number of different user groups.

Bibliography

Abernathy, W.J. & Utterback, J.M., 1978. Patterns of Industrial Innovation M. L. Tushman & W. L. Moore, eds. *Technology Review*, 80(7), pp.40–47.

Achelis, S., 2013. *Technical Analysis from A to Z* 2nd ed., New York: McGraw-Hill.

Akerberg, J., Gidlund, M. & Bjorkman, M., 2011. Future research challenges in wireless sensor and actuator networks targeting industrial automation. In *2011 9th IEEE International Conference on Industrial Informatics*. IEEE, pp. 410–415.

Albert, T., Moehrle, M. & Meyer, S., 2015. Technology maturity assessment based on blog analysis. *Technological Forecasting and Social Change*, 92(March), pp.196–209.

Albert, T., Moehrle, M.G. & Walde, P., 2011. Towards a Standardized Technology Intelligence Report - Technology Maturity Estimation Based on Blog Analysis. In *R&D Management Conference 2011 Norrköping - Proceedings*. Linköping, Sweden.

Amara, N., Landry, R. & Traoré, N., 2008. Managing the protection of innovations in knowledge-intensive business services. *Research Policy*, 37(9), pp.1530–1547.

Ambroise, C. & McLachlan, G., 2002. Selection bias in gene extraction on the basis of microarray gene-expression data. *Proceedings of the National Academy of Sciences of the United States of America*, 99(10).

Ames, E., 1961. Research, invention, development and innovation. *The American economic review*, 51(3), pp.370–381.

Anderson, P. & Tushman, M.L., 1990. Technological Discontinuities and Dominant Designs: A Cyclical Model of Technological Change. *Administrative Science Quarterly*, 35(4), pp.604–633.

Ansoff, H., 1980. Strategic management of technology. *Journal of Business Strategy*, 7(3), pp.28 – 39.

Ansoff, H. & McDonnell, E., 1990. *Implanting strategic management* 2nd ed., Englewood Cliffs, NJ, USA: Prentice-Hall.

Archer, K. & Kimes, R., 2008. Empirical characterization of random forest variable importance measures. *Computational Statistics & Data Analysis*, 52(4), pp.2249–2260.

Ashton, W.B., Campbell, R.S. & Levin, L.O., 1983. Patent Analysis As Technology Forecasting Tool. In *Chemical Marketing Research*. Richland, USA: Battelle Columbus Division, pp. 1–16.

Audi, R. ed., 1999. *The Cambridge Dictionary of Philosophy* 2nd ed., Cambridge University Press.

Backhaus, K. et al., 2003. *Multivariate Analysemethoden: Eine anwendungsorientierte Einführung (Springer-Lehrbuch) (German Edition)* 10th ed., Springer.

Balconi, M., Brusoni, S. & Orsenigo, L., 2010. In defence of the linear model: An essay. *Research Policy*, 39(1), pp.1–13.

Barnett, V. & Lewis, T., 1994. *Outliers in statistical data* 3rd ed., Chichester: Wiley.

Bass, F.M., 1969. A New Product Growth for Model Consumer Durables. *Management Science*, 15(5), pp.215–227.

Bauckhage, C., 2011a. Calibrating Google Insights. *July 5, 2011.* Available at: http://w-d-i-a-m.blogspot.de/2011/07/calibrating-google-insights.html.

Bauckhage, C., 2011b. Update on Calibrating Google Insights. *July 7, 2011.* Available at: http://w-d-i-a-m.blogspot.de/2011/07/update-on-calibrating-google-insights.html.

Benaroch, M., 2002. Managing information technology investment risk: A real options perspective. *Journal of management information systems*, 19(2), pp.43–84.

Berrueta, L.A., Alonso-Salces, R.M. & Héberger, K., 2007. Supervised pattern recognition in food analysis. *Journal of chromatography. A*, 1158(1-2), pp.196–214.

Beuckelaer, A. De, 1996. A closer examination on some parametric alternatives to the ANOVA F-test. *Statistical Papers*, 37(4), pp.291–305.

Bevilacqua, M., Ciarapica, F.E. & Giacchetta, G., 2007. Development of a sustainable product lifecycle in manufacturing firms: a case study. *International Journal of Production Research*, 45(18-19), pp.4073–4098.

Bewley, R. & Fiebig, D., 1988. A flexible logistic growth model with applications in telecommunications. *International Journal of Forecasting*, 4(2), pp.177–192.

Bichowsky, F.R., 1942. *Industrial Research*, Brooklyn, N.Y.: Chemical Pub. Co.

Bird, S., Klein, E. & Loper, E., 2009. *Natural language processing with Python* 1st ed. J. Steele, ed., Sebastopol, CA, USA: O'Reilly Media.

Björneborn, L. & Ingwersen, P., 2004. Toward a basic framework for webometrics. *Journal of the American Society for Information Science and Technology*, 14(55), pp.1216–1227.

Blankenstein, C., 1988. *Die Patentanmeldung in der Praxis.*, Freiburg: Haufe.

Bos, J., 2013. Innovation over the industry life-cycle: Evidence from EU manufacturing. *Journal of Economic Behavior & Organization*, 86, pp.1–236.

Brand, S., 1987. *The Media Lab: Inventing the future at MIT* 1st ed., New York, NY: Penguin Books Australia.

Breiman, L., 2001. Random forests. *Machine learning*, 45(1), pp.5–32.

Brookes, N. & Butler, M., 2014. The use of maturity models in improving project management performance: An empirical investigation. *International Journal of Managing Projects in Business*, 7(2), pp.231 – 246.

Brozen, Y., 1951a. Invention, innovation, and imitation. *The American Economic Review*, 41(2), pp.239–257.

Brozen, Y., 1951b. Research, technology and productivity. In L. R. Tripp, ed. *Industrial productivity*. Madison, Wisconsin: Industrial Relations Research Association, pp. 25–49.

Burgelman, R.A., Christensen, C.M. & Wheelwright, S.C., 2009. *Strategic management of technology and innovation* J. Mcgee & H. Thomas, eds., McGraw-Hill/Irwin.

Campbell, R.S., 1983. Patent trends as a technological forecasting tool. *World Patent Information*, 5(3), pp.137–143.

Campbell, R.S., 1983. Patenting the future. A new way to forecast changing technology. *Futurist*, 17(6), pp.62–67.

Carneiro, H.A. & Mylonakis, E., 2009. Google trends: a web-based tool for real-time surveillance of disease outbreaks. *Clinical infectious diseases: an official publication of the Infectious Diseases Society of America*, 49(10), pp.1557–64.

Carpenter, M., Narin, F. & Woolf, P., 1981. Citation rates to technologically important patents. *World Patent Information*, 3(4), pp.160–163.

Carrière-Swallow, Y. & Labbé, F., 2013. Nowcasting with Google Trends in an emerging market. *Journal of Forecasting*, 32(4), pp.289–298.

Cawley, G. & Talbot, N., 2010. On over-fitting in model selection and subsequent selection bias in performance evaluation. *The Journal of Machine Learning Research*, 11, pp.2079–2107.

Chang, Y.S., 2013. *Toward a Revised Theory of Technology Cycle for the Knowledge Economy - An Empirical Analysis of Microprocessor, Mobile Cellular and Genome Sequencing Technologies*,

Chen, D.-Z. et al., 2012. Technology Forecasting via Published Patent Applications and Patent Grants. *Journal of Marine Science and Technology*, 20(4), pp.345–356.

Chen, Y., Chen, C. & Lee, S., 2010. Technology forecasting of new clean energy: The example of hydrogen energy and fuel cell. *African Journal of Business Management*, 4(7), pp.1372–1380.

Chesbrough, H.W., 2005. *Open Innovation: The New Imperative for Creating And Profiting from Technology*, Boston, Mass.: Harvard Business Review Press.

Choi, D., Kim, J. & Kim, P., 2014. A Method for Normalizing Non-standard Words in Online Social Network Services: A Case Study on Twitter. In *Context-Aware Systems and Applications*. Springer International Publishing, pp. 359–368.

Choi, H. & Varian, H., 2012. Predicting the present with google trends. *Economic Record*, 88(Supplement S1), pp.2–9.

Christensen, C.M., 2013. *The innovator's dilemma: when new technologies cause great firms to fail* 3rd ed., Boston, Mass.: Harvard Business School Press.

Coase, R.H., 1937. The Nature of the Firm. *Economica*, 4(16), pp.386–405.

Cooper, R., 2009. How Companies are Reinventing Their Idea-to-Launch Methodologies. *Research-Technology Management*, 52(2), pp.47–57.

Coughlin, T., 2013. Declining Growth Projections For Hard Disk Drive Industry In 2013. *May 5th, 2013*. Available at: http://www.forbes.com/sites/tomcoughlin/2014/02/10/hdd-decline-expected-to-slow-and-reverse/.

Coughlin, T., 2014. HDD Decline Expected To Slow and Reverse. *Feb. 10th, 2014*. Available at: http://www.forbes.com/sites/tomcoughlin/2014/02/10/hdd-decline-expected-to-slow-and-reverse/.

Cox, W.E.J., 1967. Product Life Cycles as Marketing Models. *The Journal of Business*, 40(4), pp.375–384.

Crawford, J.K., 2010. *The Strategic Project Office, Second Edition (PM Solutions Research)*, New York, NY, USA; Basel, Switzerland: CRC Press.

Dalkey, N. & Helmer, O., 1963. An experimental application of the Delphi method to the use of experts. *Management science*, 9(3), pp.458–467.

Defernez, M. & Kemsley, E.K., 1997. The use and misuse of chemometrics for treating classification problems. *TrAC Trends in Analytical Chemistry*, 16(4), pp.216–221.

Deng, H., Runger, G. & Tuv, E., 2011. Bias of importance measures for multi-valued attributes and solutions. In T. Honkela et al., eds. *Artificial Neural Networks and Machine Learning–ICANN 2011*. Espoo, Finland, pp. 293–300.

Devezas, T. & Korotayev, A., 2011. Kondratieff Waves. *Journal of Globalization Studies*, 3(2).

Dhalla, N.K. & Yuspeh, S., 1976. Forget the product life cycle concept. *Harvard Business Review*, 54(1), pp.102–112.

Diamantopoulos, A. & Winklhofer, H.M., 2001. Index construction with formative indicators: an alternative to scale development. *Journal of Marketing Research*, 38(2), pp.269–277.

Dickinson, M.W., Thornton, A.C. & Graves, S., 2001. Technology portfolio management: optimizing interdependent projects over multiple time periods. *IEEE Transactions on Engineering Management*, 48(4), pp.518–527.

Docherty, M., 2006. Primer on open innovation: Principles and practice. *PDMA Visions Magazine*, XXX(2), pp.13–17.

Dror, I., 1989. Technology Innovation Indicators. *R&D Management*, 19(3), pp.243–249.

Dubarić, E. et al., 2011. Patent data as indicators of wind power technology development. *World Patent Information*, 33(2), pp.144–149.

Duijn, J. Van, 2013. *The long wave in economic life*, New York, NY, USA: Routledge.

Eisenhardt, K., 1989. Agency theory: An assessment and review. *Academy of management review*, 14(1), pp.57–74.

Eisenhardt, K. & Martin, J., 2000. Dynamic capabilities: what are they? *Strategic management journal*.

Enkel, E. & Gassmann, O., 2010. Creative imitation: exploring the case of cross-industry innovation. *R&D Management*, 40(3).

Erickson, T. et al., 1990. Managing technology as a business strategy. *MIT Sloan*, 31, pp.73–78.

Ernst, H., 1997. The Use of Patent Data for Technological Forecasting: The Diffusion of CNC-Technology in the Machine Tool Industry. *Small Business Economics*, 9(4), pp.361–381.

Erzberger, C. & Kelle, U., 2003. Making inferences in mixed methods: The rules of integration. In A. Tashakkori & C. Teddlie, eds. *Handbook of Mixed Methods in Social & Behavioral Research*. Thousand Oaks, CA, USA: Sage Publications, pp. 457–490.

European Space Agency, E.S.A., 2012. Strategic Readiness Level - The ESA Science Technology Development Route. Available at: http://sci.esa.int/sre-ft/37710-strategic-readiness-level/.

Fama, E. & MacBeth, J., 1973. Risk, return, and equilibrium: Empirical tests. *The Journal of Political Economy*, 81(3), pp.607–636.

Faulstich, W., 2004. *Grundwissen Medien* 5th ed. W. Faulstich, ed., Munich, Germany: Wilhelm Fink Verlag.

Fenn, J., 1999. Decision Framework: When to leap on the Hype Cycle. *Gartner ID: SPA-ATA-305*, p.2. Available at: http://www.cata.ca/_pvw522C275E/files /PDF/Resource_Centres/hightech/reports/indepstudies/Whentoleaponthehypecy cle.pdf [Accessed October 23, 2013].

Fenn, J. & Raskino, M., 2008. *Mastering the hype cycle: how to choose the right innovation at the right time*, Boston: Harvard Business Review Press.

Field, A., 2009. *Discovering statistics using SPSS* 4th ed., London: Sage Publications Ltd.

Fisher, J.C. & Pry, R.H., 1971. A simple substitution model of technological change. *Technological Forecasting and Social Change*, (3), pp.75–88.

Fisher, R., 1936. The use of multiple measurements in taxonomic problems. *Annals of eugenics*, 7, pp.179–188.

Floyd, S.W. & Wolf, C., 2010. Technology Strategy. In V. K. Narayanan & G. C. O'Connor, eds. *Encyclopedia of Technology and Innovation Management*. St. Gallen: Wiley-Blackwell, pp. 125–129.

Foden, J. & Berends, H., 2010. Technology Management at Rolls-Royce. *ResearchTechnology Management*, 53(2), pp.33–42.

Ford, D. & Ryan, C., 1981. Taking Technology to Market. *Harvard Business Review*, 2/1981, pp.117–126.

Foster, R.N., 1986. *Innovation: The Attacker's Advantage*, New York, NY, USA: Summit Books.

Foxcroft, C. et al., 2004. *Psychological assessment in South Africa: A needs analysis*, Pretoria.

Friedman, J., 1991. Multivariate adaptive regression splines. *The annals of statistics*, 19(1), pp.1–67.

Furnas, C., 1948. *Research in industry. Its Organization and Management*. C. C. Furnas, ed., Toronto, New York, London: Industrial Research Institute, Inc.

Gao, L. et al., 2013. Technology life cycle analysis method based on patent documents. *Technological Forecasting and Social Change*, 80(3), pp.398–407.

Garfield, E., 2006. The History and Meaning of the Journal Impact Factor. *Journal of the American Medical Association*, 295(1), pp.90–93.

Garson, D.G., 2013. *The Delphi Method in Quantitative Research*, Statistical Associates Publishers; Auflage: 2014.

Gasior, G., 2013. IHS iSuppli: HDD market to decline 12% in 2013. *February 5, 2013*. Available at: http://techreport.com/news/24317/ihs-isuppli-hdd-market-to-decline-12-in-2013.

Gassmann, O. & Bader, M.A., 2010. *Patentmanagement: Innovationen erfolgreich nutzen und schützen (German Edition)*, Berlin, Heidelberg, Germany: Springer.

Genuer, R., Poggi, J.-M. & Tuleau-Malot, C., 2010. Variable selection using random forests. *Pattern Recognition Letters*, 31(14), pp.2225–2236.

Gerken, J. & Moehrle, M., 2012. A new instrument for technology monitoring: novelty in patents measured by semantic patent analysis. *Scientometrics*, 91(3), pp.645–670.

Ginsberg, J. et al., 2009. Detecting influenza epidemics using search engine query data. *Nature*, 457(7232), pp.1012–1014.

Glass, G. V, Peckham, P.D. & Sanders, J.R., 1972. Consequences of Failure to Meet Assumptions Underlying the Fixed Effects Analyses of Variance and Covariance. *Review of Educational Research*, 42(3), pp.237–288.

Glohr, C., Kellermann, J. & Dörnemann, H., 2014. The IT Factory: A Vision of Standardization and Automation. In F. Abolhassan, ed. *The Road to a Modern IT Factory*. Berlin, Heidelberg: Springer, pp. 101–109.

Godin, B., 2006. The Linear Model of Innovation: The Historical Construction of an Analytical Framework. *Science Technology And Human Values*, 31(6), pp.639–667.

Gompertz, B., 1825. On the nature of the function expressive of the law of human mortality, and on a new mode of determining the value of life contingencies. *Philosophical Transactions of the Royal Society of London*, 115, pp.513–583.

Grantham, L.M., 1997. The validity of the product life cycle in the high-tech industry. *Marketing Intelligence & Planning*, 15(1), pp.4–10.

Grupp, H., 1997. *Messung und Erklärung des technischen Wandels: Grundzüge einer empirischen Innovationsökonomik; mit 26 Tabellen*, Berlin: Springer.

Guion, L.A., Diehl, D.C. & McDonald, D., 2011. *Triangulation: Establishing the Validity of Qualitative Studies*, Gainesville.

Guyon, I. & Elisseeff, A., 2003. An introduction to variable and feature selection. *The Journal of Machine Learning Research*, 3, pp.1157–1182.

Halfacree, G., 2013. Startup heralds 1TB ReRAM breakthrough. Available at: http://www.bit-tech.net/news/hardware/2013/08/06/crossbar/1.

Hall, B.H., Jaffe, A.B. & Trajtenberg, M., 2001. The NBER Patent Citation Data File: Lessons, Insights and Methodological Tools. , (8498). Available at: http://www.nber.org/papers/w8498.

Hamilton, J., 1994. *Time series analysis*, Princeton, N.J.: Princeton Univ.Press.

Han, B. & Baldwin, T., 2011. Lexical normalisation of short text messages: Makn sens a# twitter. In *Proceedings of the 49th Annual Meeting of the Association for Computational Linguistics: Human Language Technologies - Volume 1*. Stroudsburg, PA, USA: Association for Computational Linguistics, pp. 368–378.

Hansen, L., 1982. Large sample properties of generalized method of moments estimators. *Econometrica: Journal of the Econometric Society*, 50(4), pp.1029–1054.

Harrell, F., Lee, K. & Mark, D., 1996. Tutorial in biostatistics multivariable prognostic models: issues in developing models, evaluating assumptions and adequacy, and measuring and reducing. *Statistics in medicine*, 15(4), pp.361–387.

Harrison, S. & Rivette, K., 1998. The IP portfolio as a competitive tool. In P. H. Sullivan, ed. *Profiting from Intellectual Capital: Extracting Value from Innovation*. New York, NY, USA: John Wiley & Sons, Inc., pp. 119–128.

Harwell, M.R. et al., 1992. Summarizing Monte Carlo Results in Methodological Research: The One- and Two-Factor Fixed Effects ANOVA Cases. *Journal of Educational and Behavioral Statistics*, 17(4), pp.315–339.

Hastie, T., Tibshirani, R. & Friedman, J., 2009. *The elements of statistical learning* 2nd ed., New York, NY, USA: Springer Science+Business Media, LLC.

Haupt, R. et al., 2004. Der Patentlebenszyklus: Methodische Lösungsansätze der externen Technologieanalyse. *Friedrich-Schiller-Universität Jena, Wirtschaftswissenschaftliche Fakultät, Jenaer Schriften zur Wirtschaftswissenschaft*, (24/2004).

Haupt, R., Kloyer, M. & Lange, M., 2007. Patent indicators for the technology life cycle development. *Research Policy*, 36(3), pp.387–398.

Hawkins, D.M., 2004. The problem of overfitting. *Journal of chemical information and computer sciences*, 44, pp.1–12.

Henderson, R. & Clark, K., 1990. Architectural innovation: the reconfiguration of existing product technologies and the failure of established firms. *Administrative science quarterly*, 35(1).

Hermann, A., Huber, F. & Kressmann, F., 2006. Varianz- und kovarianzbasierte Strukturgleichungsmodelle: ein Leitfaden zu deren Spezifikation, Schätzung und Beurteilung. *Schmalenbachs Zeitschrift für betriebswirtschaftliche Forschung*, 58(1), pp.34–66.

Hirsch, J.E., 2005. An index to quantify an individual's scientific research output. *Proceedings of the National Academy of Sciences*, 102(46), pp.16569–16572.

Höft, U., 1992. *Lebenszykluskonzepte: Grundlage für das strategische Marketing- und Technologiemanagement*, Berlin: Erich Schmidt Verlag GmbH & Co.

Holzman, T. & Jamison, C., 2007. Vote verification system and method. *US Patent 7,178,730*. Available at: http://www.google.com/patents/US7178730 [Accessed October 31, 2014].

Höök, M. et al., 2011. Descriptive and predictive growth curves in energy system analysis. *Natural Resources Research*, 20(2), pp.103–116.

Howells, J. et al., 2003. Knowledge regimes, appropriability and intellectual property protection: a conceptual framework for services. In K. Blind et al., eds. *Patents in the Service Industries. Fraunhofer Institute Systems and Innovation Research.* Karlsruhe.

Hruska, J., 2013. ReRAM, the memory tech that will eventually replace NAND flash, finally comes to market. Available at: http://www.extremetech.com/computing /163058-reram-the-new-memory-tech-that-will-eventually-replace-nand-flash-finally-comes-to-market.

Hsueh, S., 2013. A Fuzzy Logic Enhanced Environmental Protection Education Model for Policies Decision Support in Green Community Development. *The Scientific World Journal*, 2013, p.8.

Huang, T.-M., Kecman, V. & Kopriva, I., 2006. *Kernel Based Algorithms for Mininig Huge Data Sets: Supervised, Semi-supervised, and Unsupervised Learning*, Berlin, Heidelberg, Germany: Springer.

Ihnen, J., 2000. A patent strategy for genomic and research tool patents: are there any differences between the USA, Europe and Japan? *Drug discovery today*.

Inaganti, S. & Aravamudan, S., 2007. SOA maturity model. *BP Trends*, p.23. Available at: http://bpmg.orgwww.bptrends.com/publicationfiles/04-07-ART-The SOA MaturityModel-Inagantifinal.pdf [Accessed January 7, 2015].

Intellogist, 2013. Patent Families. *10 July 2013*. Available at: http://www.intellogist. com/wiki/Patent_Families#Derwent_World_Patents_Index.

International Business Machines (IBM), 2011. Testing Homogeneity of Covariance Matrices - SPSS Statistics Information Center. Available at: http://pic.dhe. ibm.com/infocenter/spssstat/v22r0m0/topic/com.ibm.spss.statistics.cs/spss/tutori als/glmm_patlos_homcov.htm.

Irani, Z. & Love, P.E.D., 2010. The propagation of technology management taxonomies for evaluating investments in information systems. *Journal of Management Information Systems*, 17(3), pp.161–177.

Jaffe, 2000. Knowledge spillovers and patent citations: evidence from a survey of inventors. *American Economic Review, Papers and Proceedings*, 90(2), pp.215–218.

Järvenpää, H.M., 2009. In Technology Forecasting Using Bibliometrics What Information Source is Relevant When? In *PICMET Proceedings*. Portland, OR, pp. 2426–2432.

Järvenpää, H.M. & Mäkinen, S.J., 2008a. *Empirically detecting the Hype Cycle with the life cycle indicators: An exploratory analysis of three technologies*, Ieee.

Järvenpää, H.M. & Mäkinen, S.J., 2008b. The Sequence of Early Publishing Activity Communicating New Technological Innovations. In *International Conference on Management of Technology 2008*.

Järvenpää, H.M., Mäkinen, S.J. & Seppänen, M., 2011. Patent and publishing activity sequence over a technology's life cycle. *Technological Forecasting and Social Change*, 78(2), pp.283–293.

Järvenpää, H.M. & Tapaninen, A.S., 2008. An empirical study of the wood pellet publishing activity development. In *2008 4th IEEE International Conference on Management of Innovation and Technology*. Bangkok, Thailand: IEEE, pp. 81–86.

Jenkins, H., 2006. *Convergence culture: Where old and new media collide*, New York, NY, USA: New York Univ Press.

Kanellos, M., 2003. Moore's Law to roll on for another decade - CNET News. *February 10, 2003*. Available at: http://news.cnet.com/2100-1001-984051.html [Accessed January 24, 2014].

Kaplan, S. & Tripsas, M., 2008. Thinking about technology: Applying a cognitive lens to technical change. *Research Policy*, 37(5), pp.790–805.

Kapur, P. & Chanda, U., 2010. Innovation diffusion of successive generations of high technology products. In *2nd International Conference on Reliability, Safety and Hazard (ICRESH)*. Mumbai, India, pp. 505–510.

Kauffman, R.J., Liu, J. & Ma, D., 2013. Technology Investment Decision-Making under Uncertainty: The Case of Mobile Payment Systems. In *46th Hawaii International Conference on System Sciences*. Wailea, HI, USA: IEEE, pp. 4166–4175.

Keppel, G., 2004. *Design and analysis: A researcher's handbook* 4th ed., London: Pearson.

Khan, A. & Möhrle, M., 2012. Multi cross industry innovation–eine Herausforderung an das Innovationsmanagement. In C. Mieke & D. Braunisch, eds. *Innovative Produktionswirtschaft*. Berlin: Nomos, pp. 45–58.

Kim, B., 2003. Managing the transition of technology life cycle. *Technovation*, 23(5), pp.371–381.

Kim, J. et al., 2012. Technology trends analysis and forecasting application based on decision tree and statistical feature analysis. *Expert Systems with Applications*, 39(16), pp.12618–12625.

Kling, R. & McKim, G., 1999. Scholarly communication and the continuum of electronic publishing. *Journal of the American Society for Information Science*, 50(10), pp.890–906.

Knight, H., 2012. *Patent Strategy for Researchers and Research Managers* 3rd ed., Chichester: John Wiley & Sons.

Kondratieff, N., 1979. The long waves in economic life. *Review of the Fernand Braudel Center*, 2(4), pp.519–562.

Kotsiantis, S., Zaharakis, I. & Pintelas, P., 2007. Supervised machine learning: A review of classification techniques. *Informatica*, 31, pp.249–268.

Kraaijenbrink, J., Spender, J. & Groen, A., 2010. The Resource-Based View: A Review and Assessment of Its Critiques. *Journal of management*, 36(1), pp.349–372.

Kucharavy, D. & Guio, R. De, 2007. Application of S-shaped curves. In *Proceeding of the ETRIA World TRIZ Future Conference, Vol. 9*. Dublin, pp. 559–572.

Kucharavy, D. & Guio, R. De, 2008. Logistic substitution model and technological forecasting. In *TRIZ Future Conference 2008*. Enschede, Netherlands, pp. 65–73.

Kuhn, M., 2014. Recursive feature elimination rfe {caret}. Available at: http://topepo.github.io/caret/featureselection.html#rfe.

Kurzweil, R., 2005. *The singularity is near: When humans transcend biology*, New York, NY, USA: Penguin Group.

Lee, T.H. & Nakicenovic, N., 1988. Technology lifecycles and business decisions. *International Journal of Technology Management*, 3(4), p.16.

Leeds, M., 2012. Bollinger Bands Thirty Years Later. Available at: http://arxiv.org/abs/1212.4890 [Accessed July 30, 2013].

Legendre, P. & Legendre, L., 2012. *Numerical Ecology* 3rd ed., Amsterdam, Oxford: Elsevier.

Legendre, P. & Legendre, L., 1998. *Numerical Ecology* 1st ed., Amsterdam: Elsevier.

Lei, Z., Sun, Z. & Wright, B., 2009. Are Chinese Patent Applications Politically Driven? *oecd.org*, p.26. Available at: http://www.oecd.org/site/stipatents/4-3-Lei-Sun-Wright.pdf [Accessed September 16, 2013].

Li, T., Zhu, S. & Ogihara, M., 2006. Using discriminant analysis for multi-class classification: an experimental investigation. *Knowledge and Information Systems*, 10(4), pp.453–472.

Liaw, A. & Maitra, R., 2012. Box's M R code. Available at: http://www.public. iastate.edu/~maitra/stat501/Rcode/BoxMTest.R.

Linden, A. & Fenn, J., 2003. Understanding Gartner's Hype Cycles. *Analysis*, 2009(July), p.8.

Link, J., 1985. Phasenspezifische Organisation strategischer Projekte. *Harvard Manager*, 4, pp.17–20.

Lister, M. et al., 2008. *New media: A critical introduction* 2nd ed., New York, NY, USA: Routledge.

Livesey, F., 2012. Rationales for Industrial Policy Based on Industry Maturity. *Journal of Industry, Competition and Trade*, 12(3), pp.349–363.

Lix, L.M., Keselman, J.C. & Keselman, H.J., 1996. Consequences of Assumption Violations Revisited: A Quantitative Review of Alternatives to the One-Way Analysis of Variance F Test. *Review of Educational Research*, 66(4), pp.579–619.

Lizaso, F. & Reger, G., 2004. Linking roadmapping and scenarios as an approach for strategic technology planning. *International Journal of Technology Intelligence and Planning*, 1(1), pp.68–86.

Lou, Y., Fu, X. & Huang, L., 2009. An empirical study on the commercial prospect of emerging technology through bibliometrics. In *International Conference on Grey Systems and Intelligent Services (GSIS 2009)*. IEEE, pp. 1484–1489.

Maclaurin, W.R., 1953. The sequence from invention to innovation and its relation to economic growth. *The Quarterly Journal of Economics*, 67(1), pp.97–111.

Magdy, W. & Jones, G., 2010. PRES: a score metric for evaluating recall-oriented information retrieval applications. In *Proceedings of the 33rd international ACM SIGIR conference on Research and development in information retrieval*. New York, NY, USA, pp. 611–618.

Mankins, J., 2009. Technology readiness assessments: A retrospective. *Acta Astronautica*, 65(9-10), pp.1216–1223.

Mankins, J.C., 1995. Technology Readiness Levels - A White Paper. , 6(2), p.5. Available at: http://ehbs.org/trl/Mankins1995.pdf.

Mansfield, E., 1968. *The Economics of Technological Change*, New York, NY: Longman Publishing Group.

Martino, J.P., 2003. A review of selected recent advances in technological forecasting. *Technological Forecasting and Social Change*, 70(8), pp.719–733.

Meade, N. & Islam, T., 2006. Modelling and forecasting the diffusion of innovation – A 25-year review. *International Journal of Forecasting*, 22(3), pp.519–545.

Mees, C., 1920. *The organization of industrial scientific research* 1st ed., New York, NY, USA: McGraw-Hill Book Company.

Mees, C.E.K. & Leermakers, J.A., 1950. *The Organization of Industrial Scientific Research*, New York, NY, USA: McGraw-Hill Book Company.

Messick, S.J., 1992. Validity of test interpretation and use. *Alkin, M.C. (ed.) Encyclopedia of Educational Research*, pp.1487–1495.

Meyer, M., 2000. Does science push technology? Patents citing scientific literature. *Research policy*, 29(3), pp.409–434.

Moehrle, M. & Gerken, J., 2012. Measuring textual patent similarity on the basis of combined concepts: design decisions and their consequences. *Scientometrics*, 91(3), pp.805–826.

Moehrle, M., Isenmann, R. & Phaal, R., 2013. Basics of technology roadmapping. In *Technology Roadmapping for Strategy and Innovation*. Berlin: Springer, pp. 1–10.

Møller, S.F., von Frese, J. & Bro, R., 2005. Robust methods for multivariate data analysis. *Journal of Chemometrics*, 19(10), pp.549–563.

Moore, G.E., 1965. Cramming more components onto integrated circuits. *Electronics*, 38(8), pp.114–117.

Morrell, R., Mayhorn, C. & Bennett, J., 2000. A survey of World Wide Web use in middle-aged and older adults. *Human Factors: The Journal of the Human Factors and Ergonomics Society*, 42(2), pp.175–182.

Murphy, J.J., 1986. *Technical Analysis of the Futures Markets: A Comprehensive Guide to Trading Methods and Applications*, New York, NY, USA: Prentice Hall Press.

Myers, S. & Marquis, D.G., 1969. *Successful industrial innovations: a study of factors underlying innovation in selected firms*, Washington, DC: National Science Foundation.

Nacke, O., 1979. Informetrie: ein neuer Name für eine neue Disziplin. Begriffs-bestimmung, Wissensstand und Entwicklungsprinzipien. *Nachrichten für Dokumentation*, 30(6), pp.219–226.

Narin, F., Noma, E. & Perry, R., 1987. Patents as indicators of corporate technological strength. *Research policy*, 16(2-4), pp.143–155.

Norton, J. & Bass, F., 1987. A diffusion theory model of adoption and substitution for successive generations of high-technology products. *Management science*, 33(9), pp.1069–1086.

Nsoesie, E.O. et al., 2013. A systematic review of studies on forecasting the dynamics of influenza outbreaks. *Influenza and other respiratory viruses*, 8(3), pp.309–316.

Oliver, C. & Holzinger, I., 2008. The effectiveness of strategic political management: A dynamic capabilities framework. *Academy of Management Review*, 33(2), pp.496–520.

Östlund, U. et al., 2011. Combining qualitative and quantitative research within mixed method research designs: a methodological review. *International journal of nursing studies*, 48(3), pp.369–83.

Palm, W.I., 2014. *System Dynamics* 3rd ed., New York, NY, USA: McGraw-Hill.

Patton, A., 1959. Stretch your product's earning years - Top Management Stakes in the Product Life Cycle. *Management Review*, 48(6), pp.9–14; 67–79.

Paul, H. & Wollny, V., 2011. *Instrumente des strategischen Managements: Grundlagen und Anwendung*, Munich, Germany: Oldenbourg Wissenschaftsverlag GmbH.

Petersen, S. & Jaecks, H., 2005. Combination electronic and paper ballot voting system. *US Patent 6,951,303*.

Pillkahn, U., 2008. *Using Trends and Scenarios as Tools for Strategy Development* 1st ed., New York, NY, USA: John Wiley & Sons.

Pipino, L., Lee, Y. & Wang, R., 2002. Data Quality Assessment. *Communications of the ACM*, 45(4), pp.211–218.

Popper, E.T. & Buskirk, B.D., 1992. Technology life cycles in industrial markets. *Industrial Marketing Management*, 21(1), pp.23–31.

Porter, A.L. et al., 2011. *Forecasting and Management of Technology* 2nd ed., New York, NY, USA: John Wiley & Sons, Inc.

Porter, A.L. et al., 1991. *Forecasting and Management of Technology*, New York, NY, USA: John Wiley & Sons.

Porter, A.L., 2005. QTIP: quick technology intelligence processes. *Technological Forecasting and Social Change*, 72(9), pp.1070–1081.

Porter, A.L. & Cunningham, S.W., 2005. *Tech mining: Exploiting new technologies for competitive advantage*, Hoboken, NJ: Wiley.

Porter, M.E., 2004. *Competitive Strategy: Techniques for Analyzing Industries and Competitors*, New York, NY, USA: Free Press.

Porter, M.E., 1980. *Competitive Strategy: Techniques for Analyzing Industries and Competitors*, New York, NY, USA: Free Press.

Potts, G.W., 1989. Im Servicezyklus steckt Profit. *Harvard Manager*, 11(2), pp.100–104.

Puranam, P., Gulati, R. & Bhattacharya, S., 2013. How much to make and how much to buy? An analysis of optimal plural sourcing strategies. *Strategic Management Journal*, 34(10), pp.1145–1161.

Rai, L., 1999. Appropriate models for technology substitution. *Journal of Scientific and Industrial Research*, 58, pp.14–18.

Rao, C., 1948. The utilization of multiple measurements in problems of biological classification. *Journal of the Royal Statistical Society. Series B (Methodological)*, 10(2), pp.159–203.

Ricker, T., 2008. Official: HD DVD dead and buried, format war is over. Available at: http://www.engadget.com/2008/02/19/official-hd-dvd-dead-and-buried-format-war-is-over/.

Riera, A. & Brown, P., 2003. Bringing confidence to electronic voting. *Electronic Journal of e-Government*, 1(1), pp.14–21.

Rigby, R. & Stasinopoulos, D., 2005. Generalized additive models for location, scale and shape. *Journal of the Royal Statistical Society: Series C (Applied Statistics)*, 54(3), pp.507–554.

Roberts, E.B. & Liu, W.K., 2001. Ally or Acquire? How Technology Leaders Decide. *MIT Sloan Management Review*, 43(1), pp.26–34.

Rodriguez-Galiano, V. & Ghimire, B., 2012. An assessment of the effectiveness of a random forest classifier for land-cover classification. *ISPRS Journal of Photogrammetry and Remote Sensing*, 67, pp.93–104.

Rogers, E.M., 1962. *Diffusion of innovations* 1st ed., New York, NY, USA: Free Press of Glencoe.

Rogers, E.M., 1983. *Diffusion of innovations*, New York, NY, USA: Free Press.

Ruttan, V.W., 1959. Usher and Schumpeter on invention, innovation, and technological change. *The quarterly journal of economics*, 73(4), pp.596–606.

Ryu, J. & Byeon, S., 2011. Technology level evaluation methodology based on the technology growth curve. *Technological Forecasting and Social Change*, 78(6), pp.1049–1059.

Sadin, S.R., Povinelli, F.P. & Rosen, R., 1989. The NASA technology push towards future space mission systems. *Acta Astronautica*, 20, pp.73–77.

Sartor, F. & Bourauel, C., 2012. *Risikomanagement kompakt: in 7 Schritten zum aggregierten Nettorisiko des Unternehmens*, Munich, Germany: Oldenbourg Wissenschaftsverlag GmbH.

Schembri, P.J., 2007. The different types of scientific literature. , p.2. Available at: https://www.um.edu.mt/__data/assets/file/0006/42981/The_different_types_of_s cientific_literature.pdf.

Scherer, F., 1965. Invention and innovation in the Watt-Boulton steam-engine venture. *Technology and Culture*, 6(2), pp.165–187.

Schickedanz, W., 2000. *Die Formulierung von Patentansprüchen: deutsche, europäische und amerikanische Praxis*, Munich, Germany: Beck.

Schmookler, J., 1966. *Invention and economic growth*, Cambridge, MA: Harvard University Press.

Schumpeter, J.A., 1939. *Business Cycles - A Theoretical, Historical, and Statistical Analysis of the Capitalist Process*, New York, Toronto, London: McGraw-Hill Book Company.

Schumpeter, J.A., 1911. *Theorie der wirtschaftlichen Entwicklung* 1. ed., Leipzig: Duncker & Humblot.

Seawright, J. & Gerring, J., 2008. Case Selection Techniques in Case Study Research: A Menu of Qualitative and Quantitative Options. *Political Research Quarterly*, 61(2), pp.294–308.

Segal, M., 2004. Machine learning benchmarks and random forest regression. *Center for Bioinformatics & Molecular Biostatistics*. Available at: https://escholarship.org/uc/item/35x3v9t4.pdf [Accessed October 15, 2014].

Shareef, M. et al., 2011. e-Government Adoption Model (GAM): Differing service maturity levels. *Government Information Quarterly*, 28(1), pp.17–35.

Sharif, M. & Islam, M., 1980. The Weibull distribution as a general model for forecasting technological change. *Technological Forecasting and Social Change*, 18(3), pp.247–256.

Sher, P. & Lee, V., 2004. Information technology as a facilitator for enhancing dynamic capabilities through knowledge management. *Information & management*, 41(8), pp.933–945.

Shuen, A., 2008. *Web 2.0: A Strategy Guide: Business thinking and strategies behind successful Web 2.0 implementations.*, Sebastopol, CA, USA: O'Reilly Media.

Shuen, A. & Sieber, S., 2009. Orchestrating the New Dynamic Capabilities - Collaborative Innovation in Action. *Harvard Business Review*, 3, pp.58–65.

Sommerlatte, T. & Deschamps, J.-P., 1986. Der strategische Einsatz von Technologien. In *Management im Zeitalter der strategischen Führung*. Wiesbaden: Gabler, pp. 39–76.

Sood, A. et al., 2012. Predicting the Path of Technological Innovation: SAW vs. Moore, Bass, Gompertz, and Kryder. *Marketing Science*, 31(6), pp.964–979.

Specht, G., Beckmann, C. & Amelingmeyer, J., 2002. *F und E- Management. Kompetenz im Innovationsmanagement.*, Stuttgart: Schäffer-Poeschel Verlag.

Spink, A. et al., 2002. US versus European Web searching trends. *ACM Sigir Forum*, 36(2), pp.32–38.

Srivastava, T.N. & Rego, S., 2011. *Business Research Methodology (With Cd)*, New York, NY, USA: Tata McGraw-Hill Education.

stackoverflow.com, 2011. Classification functions in linear discriminant analysis in R. *Apr 12th 2011.* Available at: http://stackoverflow.com/questions /5629550/classification-functions-in-linear-discriminant-analysis-in-r.

Stammers, T. & Robinson, S., 2014. Would the real flash storage successor please stand up? Available at: http://www.computerweekly.com/feature/Would-the-real-flash-storage-successor-please-stand-up.

Stasinopoulos, D. & Rigby, R., 2007. Generalized additive models for location scale and shape (GAMLSS) in R. *Journal of Statistical Software*, 23(7).

Statistic Brain, 2013. Google Annual Search Statistics. , p.1. Available at: http://www.statisticbrain.com/google-searches/.

Steinke, I., 2004. Quality criteria in qualitative research. In U. Flick, E. von Kardorff, & I. Steinke, eds. *A companion to qualitative research*. London: Rowohlt, pp. 184–190.

Stevens, R., 1941. A Report on Industrial Research as a National Resource. *Journal of the Patent Office Society*, 23(6), pp.405–430.

Steyerberg, E. & Eijkemans, M., 2000. Prognostic modelling with logistic regression analysis: a comparison of selection and estimation methods in small data sets. *Statistics in ...*, 19(8), pp.1059–1079.

Steyn, P., 2013. Data Assumption: Homogeneity of variance-covariance matrices (Multivariate Tests). *Oct. 16, 2013.* Available at: http://www.introspective-mode.org/2012/06/data-assumption-homogeneity-of-variance_17.html.

Suhr, C., 2000. *Patentliteratur und ihre Nutzung: Der Leitfaden zu den Quellen technischer Kreativität* 1st ed., Renningen-Malmsheim: expert-Verl.

Svetnik, V. et al., 2004. Application of Breiman's random forest to modeling structure-activity relationships of pharmaceutical molecules. In *5th International Workshop, Multiple Classifier Systems, Cagliari, Italy, June 9-11.* Cagliari, Italy: Springer, pp. 334–343.

Tabachnick, B. & Fidell, L., 2001. *Using multivariate statistics,* Upper Saddle River, NJ, USA: Pearson PLC.

Tague-Sutcliffe, J., 1992. An introduction to informetrics. *Information processing & management,* 28(1), pp.1–3.

Tanner, J.M., 1990. *Foetus into man: Physical growth from conception to maturity* Revised., Cambridge, MA: Harvard University Press.

Taylor, M. & Taylor, A., 2012. The technology life cycle: Conceptualization and managerial implications. *International Journal of Production Economics,* 140(1), pp.541–553.

Teece, D., 2007. Explicating dynamic capabilities: the nature and microfoundations of (sustainable) enterprise performance. *Strategic management journal,* 28(13), pp.1319–1350.

Teece, D. & Pisano, G., 1994. The dynamic capabilities of firms: an introduction. *Industrial and Corporate Change,* 3(3), pp.537–556.

Teece, D., Pisano, G. & Shuen, A., 1997. Dynamic capabilities and strategic management. *Strategic Management Journal,* 18(7), pp.509–533.

Teichert, T. & Mittermayer, M.-A., 2002. Text mining for technology monitoring. In *IEEE International Engineering Management Conference.* IEEE, pp. 596–601.

Thompson, B., 1995. Stepwise Regression and Stepwise Discriminant Analysis Need Not Apply here: A Guidelines Editorial. *Educational and Psychological Measurement,* 55(4), pp.525–534.

Thompson, L.H. et al., 2014. Emergency department and "Google flu trends" data as syndromic surveillance indicators for seasonal influenza. *Epidemiology and Infection,* 142(11), pp.1–9.

Tiefel, T., 2008. Technologielebenszyklus-Modell - Eine kritische Analyse. In T. Tiefel, ed. *Gewerbliche Schutzrechte im Innovationsprozess*. Wiesbaden: Gabler, pp. 25–49.

Tseng, F.-M. et al., 2011. Using patent data to analyze trends and the technological strategies of the amorphous silicon thin-film solar cell industry. *Technological Forecasting and Social Change*, 78(2), pp.332–345.

United States Patent and Trademark Office & United States Department of Commerce, 2014. 2111.03 Transitional Phrases [R-08.2012]. In *Manual of Patent Examining Procedure (MPEP)*.

Utterback, J.M., 1974. Innovation in industry and the diffusion of technology. *Science*, 183(4125), pp.620–626.

Utterback, J.M. & Abernathy, W.J., 1975. A dynamic model of process and product innovation. *Omega*, 3(6), pp.639–656.

Valle, D., 1996. *Der sachliche Schutzbereich des europäischen Patents.*, Frankfurt am Main: Peter Lang Internationaler Verlag der Wissenschaften.

Veugelers, R. & Cassiman, B., 2013. Complementarity between technology make and buy in innovation strategies: Evidence from Belgian manufacturing firms. , p.40. Available at: http://www.econ.upf.edu/docs/papers/downloads/279.pdf [Accessed October 22, 2013].

Watts, R.J. & Porter, A.L., 1997. Innovation forecasting. *Technological Forecasting and Social Change*, 56(1), pp.25–47.

Weber, I. & Jaimes, A., 2011. Who uses web search for what: and how. In *Proceedings of the fourth ACM international conference on Web search and data mining*. New York, NY, USA, pp. 15–24.

Weiber, R. & Mühlhaus, D., 2009. *Strukturgleichungsmodellierung: Eine anwendungsorientierte Einführung in die Kausalanalyse mit Hilfe von AMOS, SmartPLS und SPSS (Springer-Lehrbuch) (German Edition)*, Berlin, Heidelberg, Germany: Springer.

Welte, S., 1991. *Der Schutz von Pioniererfindungen (Schriftenreihe zum gewerblichen Rechtsschutz) (German Edition)*, Heymann.

Wilbers, W., Albert, T. & Walde, P., 2010. Upscaling the Technology Intelligence Process. *International Journal of Technology Intelligence and Planning*, 6(2), pp.185–203.

World Intellectual Property Organization, 2014. FAQs: Patents. Available at: http://www.wipo.int/patentscope/en/patents/.

World Intellectual Property Organization, 2008. WIPO Intellectual Property Handbook: Policy, Law and Use. Available at: http://www.wipo.int/export /sites/www/about-ip/en/iprm/pdf/ch2.pdf [Accessed March 4, 2013].

World Intellectual Property Organization, 2011. World Intellectual Property Indicators - 2011 Edition. Available at: http://www.wipo.int/edocs/pubdocs/en/intproperty /941/wipo_pub_941_2011.pdf.

World Intellectual Property Organization, 2012. World Intellectual Property Indicators - 2012 Edition. Available at: http://www.wipo.int/ipstats/en/wipi/index.html [Accessed March 4, 2013].

Yin, R.K., 2013. *Case Study Research: Design and Methods* 4th ed., Thousand Oaks, CA, USA: Sage Publications Ltd.

Zahra, S., Sisodia, R. & Matherne, B., 1999. Exploiting the dynamic links between competitive and technology strategies. *European Management Journal*, 17(2), pp.188–203.

Zhao, S. et al., 2011. Human as Real-Time Sensors of Social and Physical Events: A Case Study of Twitter and Sports Games. Available at: http://arxiv.org/abs /1106.4300 [Accessed January 3, 2015].

Zivot, E. & Wang, J., 2006. *Modeling Financial Time Series with S-PLUS®*, New York, NY, USA: Springer.

Annex A: Delphi Questionnaire and Information Basis

**Umfrage – Technologische Reife
von Speichertechnologien**

Eichung der Trainingsdaten für einen
Machine Learning-Algorithmus zur
automatischen Reifeklassifikation.

Übersicht

Mit Ihrer Hilfe werden Trainingsdaten für eine
automatische Reifeklassifizierung beliebiger Technologien
erstellt. Sie legen mit Ihrer Erfahrung und einem
Regelsatz fest, in welchem Jahr eine bestimmte Reifestufe
zum ersten mal erreicht wurde.

Tabelle 1 ist die **Antworttabelle**. Sie enthält die zu
klassifizierenden Technologien aus dem Bereich
Informationsspeicher.

Tabelle 2 ist eine Übersichten gängiger Indikatoren zur
Einschätzung technologischer Reife.

Im *Anhang* befinden sich Daten und Quellenhinweise, die
Sie für Ihre Einschätzung zu Rate ziehen können

Tabelle 1 (Antworttabelle)

Tragen Sie für jede Technologie das Jahr ein, in dem zum
ersten Mal die entsprechende Reifephase erreicht wurde.

		Reifephase		
	Entstehung	Wachstum	Reife	Alter
Beispieltechnolgie	1990	1998	2006	-
Lochkarten				
DVD				
ReRAM				
Magnetband				
Disketten				
BluRay				
HD-DVD				
Festplatten				
NVRAM (Flash)				
Compact Disc				
Minidisk				
Lochstreifen				

(Zeilenbeschriftung links: Technologien)

Tabelle 1 (Antworttabelle)

Tragen Sie für jede Technologie das Jahr ein, in dem zum
ersten Mal die entsprechende Reifephase erreicht wurde.

		Reifephase		
	Entstehung	Wachstum	Reife	Alter
Beispieltechnolgie	1990	1998	2006	-
Disketten				
Lochstreifen				
ReRAM				
Minidisk				
Festplatten				
Lochkarten				
Compact Disc				
DVD				
NVRAM (Flash)				
HD-DVD				
BluRay				
Magnetband				

(Zeilenbeschriftung links: Technologien)

Tabelle 2 (Indikatoren)

		Reifephase			
		Entstehung	Wachstum	Reife	Alter
Indikatoren	Unsicherheit über technische Leistungsfähigkeit	hoch	mittel	niedrig	sehr niedrig
	Investitionen in Technologieentwicklung	niedrig	maximal	niedrig	vernachlässigbar
	Breite der potenziellen Einsatzgebiete	unbekannt	groß	etabliert	abnehmend
	Typ der Entwicklungsanforderungen	wissenschaftlich	anwendungsorientiert		kostenorientiert
	Auswirkungen auf Kosten-Leistungs-verhältnis der Produkte	sekundär	maximal	marginal	marginal
	Zahl der Patentanmeldungen	zunehmend (Konzeptpatente)	hoch (produktbezogen)	abnehmend (verfahrensbezogen)	
	Zugangsbarrieren	wissenschaftliche Fähigkeiten	Personal	Lizenzen	Know-How
	Verfügbarkeit	sehr beschränkt	Restrukturierung	marktorientiert	hoch

Hinweise zur Beantwortung

Nutzen Sie zur Recherche z.B. Google und die deutschen und englischen Seiten von Wikipedia.

http://de.wikipedia.org/wiki/Datenspeicher
http://en.wikipedia.org/wiki/Data_storage_device

Dokumentieren Sie unbedingt die von Ihnen genutzten Quellen!

Im *Anhang* finden Sie in alphabetischer Reihenfolge für jede Technologie eine Übersicht der Entwicklung einiger wichtiger Indikatoren samt Erläuterung.

Einige der Technologien in *Tabelle 1* sind Sammelbegriffe für Untertechnologien. Bewerten Sie in diesem Fall ausschließlich diese Sammelbegriffe und betrachten sie die entsprechenden Untertechnologien als Meilensteine für die Reife der Technologie.

Meistens ist neben der persönlichen Einschätzung nur ein kleiner Teil der Indikatoren zur Reifephasenbestimmung notwendig!

Eine jahres-exakte Einordnung der Phase ist insbesondere nach 1976 wünschenswert (davor ist eine Einordnung auf ca. 10 Jahre genau ausreichend – z.B. Entstehungsphase der Lochkarte).

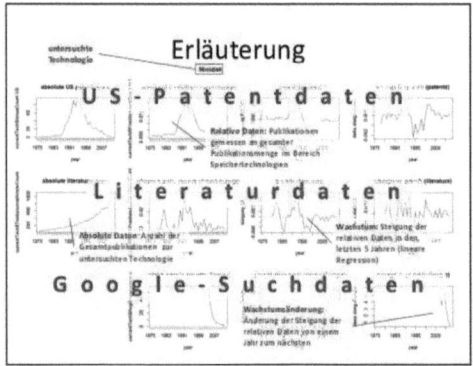

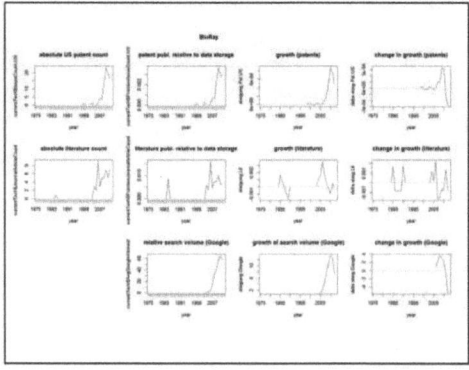

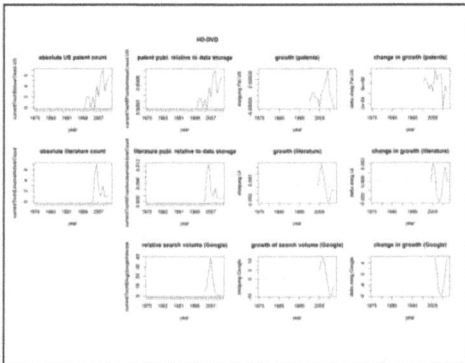

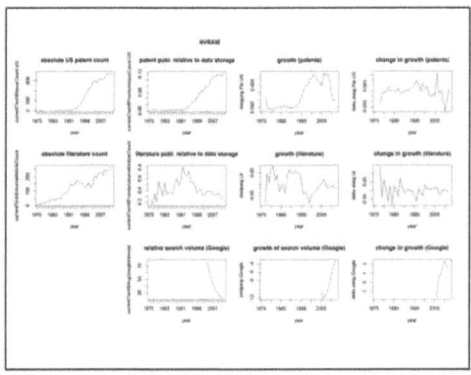

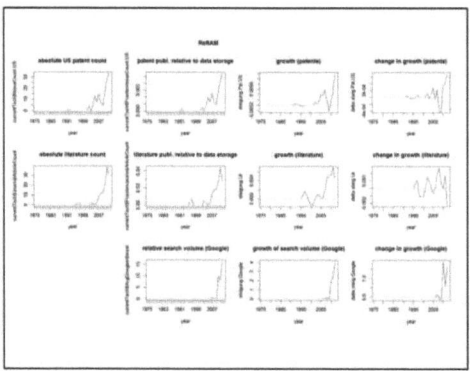

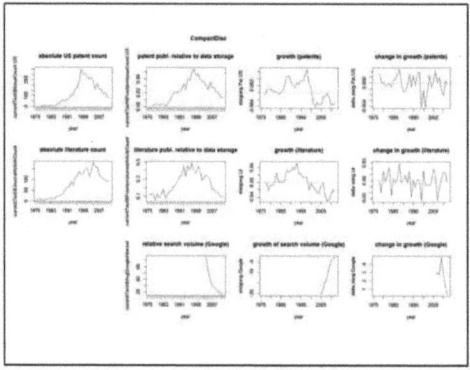

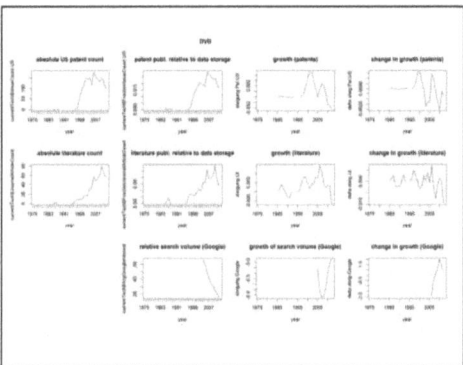

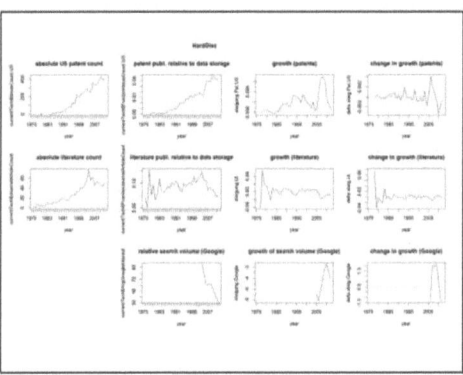

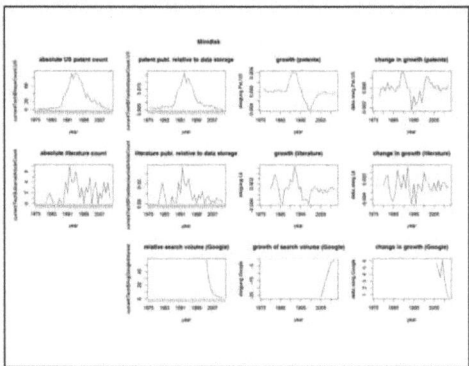

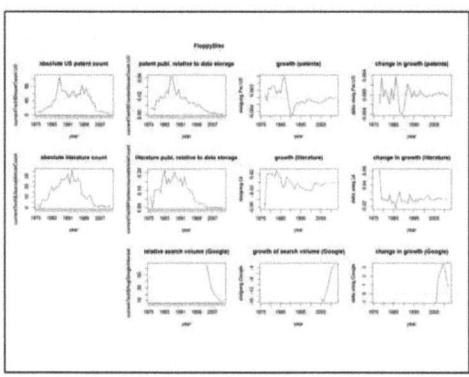

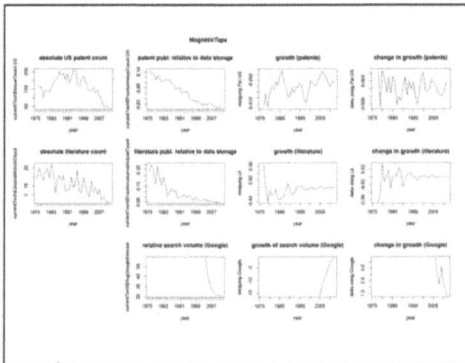

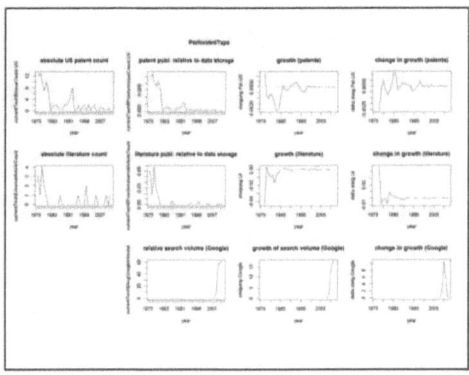

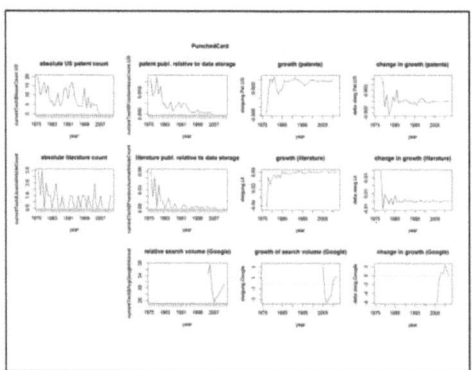

Results:

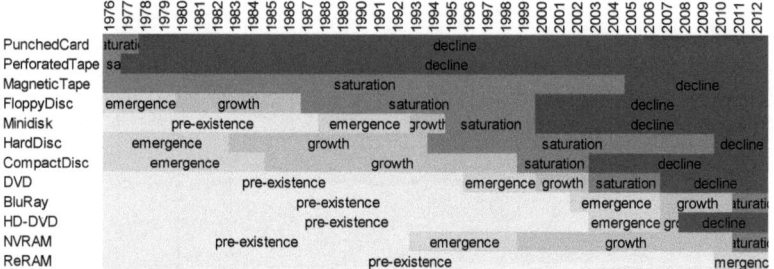

Detailed results (the table shows the first year of a given maturity state per technology by respondents P1 – 4 after the second round of the Delphi):

technology	maturity	P1	P2	P3	P4
PunchedCard	Emergence				
PunchedCard	Growth				
PunchedCard	Saturation	1976	1976		1976
PunchedCard	Decline	1978	1980	1976	1978
PerforatedTape	Emergence				
PerforatedTape	Growth				
PerforatedTape	Saturation		1976		1976

PerforatedTape	Decline	1976	1980	1976	1977
MagneticTape	Emergence				
MagneticTape	Growth				
MagneticTape	Saturation	1976	1976	1976	1976
MagneticTape	Decline	2005	2005	2003	2004
FloppyDisc	Emergence	1976	1976	1976	1976
FloppyDisc	Growth	1980	1979	1980	1980
FloppyDisc	Saturation	1987	1986	1987	1987
FloppyDisc	Decline	2000	2000	2000	2000
Minidisk	Emergence	1987	1988	1988	1988
Minidisk	Growth	1992	1993	1993	1993
Minidisk	Saturation	1994	1996	1996	1995
Minidisk	Decline	2000	2000	2000	2000
HardDisc	Emergence	1976	1976	1976	1976
HardDisc	Growth	1985	1980	1983	1983
HardDisc	Saturation	1995		1992	1994
HardDisc	Decline	2010		2010	2010
CompactDisc	Emergence	1976	1976	1976	1976
CompactDisc	Growth	1984	1983	1987	1985
CompactDisc	Saturation	1999	1997	2001	1999
CompactDisc	Decline	2005	2002	2003	2003
DVD	Emergence	1995	1995	1997	1996
DVD	Growth	2000	2000	2000	2000
DVD	Saturation	2003	2003	2003	2003
DVD	Decline	2007	2007	2008	2007
BluRay	Emergence	2002	2003	2002	2002
BluRay	Growth	2007	2006	2007	2007
BluRay	Saturation	2011	2011	2011	2011
BluRay	Decline				
HD-DVD	Emergence	2003	2003	2002	2003
HD-DVD	Growth	2007	2006	2007	2007
HD-DVD	Saturation			2008	2008
HD-DVD	Decline	2008	2008	2009	2008
NVRAM	Emergence	1993	1995	1992	1993
NVRAM	Growth	1998	1998	2000	1999
NVRAM	Saturation	2012	2012	2010	2011
NVRAM	Decline				
ReRAM	Emergence	2010	2010	2010	2010
ReRAM	Growth				
ReRAM	Saturation				
ReRAM	Decline				

Annex B: Technology Search Strategies for Different Text Media Databases

Technology	Google Trends Search	USPTO Patent search	Science Direct, Search in Journals, exclude books
Generation: Punched Card	punch card	TTL/("punch card" OR "punched card" OR "punchcard") OR ABST/("punch card" OR "punched card" OR "punchcard") OR ICL/G06K013/02 OR ICL/G06K013/04 OR ICL/G06K013/06$ OR ICL/G06K013/07$ OR ICL/G06K013/08 OR ICL/G06K013/16 OR ICL/G06K001/08 OR ICL/G06K001/16 OR ICL/G06K021/$	tak("punch card" OR "punched card" OR "punchcard")
Generation: Perforated Tape	perforated tape	TTL/("punch tape" OR "punched tape" OR "perforated tape" OR "perforation tape") OR ABST/("punch tape" OR "punched tape" OR "perforated tape" OR "perforation tape") OR ICL/G06K013/18 OR ICL/G06K013/20 OR ICL/G06K013/24 OR ICL/G06K013/26 OR ICL/G06K001/10	tak((punch OR punched OR perforated OR perforation) W/1 (tape))
Generation: Magnetic Tape	magnetic tape	TTL/("magnetic tape" OR "magnetized tape" OR "magnet tape") OR ABST/("magnetic tape" OR "magnetized tape" OR "magnet tape") OR ICL/G11B005/008 OR ICL/G11B005/584 OR ICL/G11B005/588 OR ICL/G11B005/592 OR ICL/G11B005/627 OR ICL/G11B005/78 OR ICL/G11B007/24009 OR ICL/G11B027/024 OR ICL/G11B027/032 OR ICL/G11B025/06	tak("magnetic tape" OR "magnetized tape" OR "magnet tape")
Generation: Floppy Disc	floppy disc	TTL/("floppy disc" OR "floppy disk" OR diskette OR "ZIPdisc" OR "ZIPdisk" OR "flexible magnetic disc") OR ABST/("floppy disc" OR "floppy disk" OR diskette OR "ZIPdisc" OR "ZIPdisk" OR "flexible magnetic disc" OR "flexible magnetic disk") OR ICL/G11B023/033	tak(((floppy OR ZIP OR "flexible magnetic") W/1 (disc OR disk)) OR diskette OR "ZIPdisc" OR "ZIPdisk")
Generation: Hard Disc	hdd	TTL/("hard disk" OR "hard disc" OR "harddisk" OR "harddisc" OR HDD) OR ABST/("hard disk" OR "hard disc" OR "harddisk" OR "harddisc" OR HDD)	tak("hard disk" OR "hard disc" OR "harddisk" OR "harddisc" OR HDD)
Generation: MiniDisc	minidisc	TTL/(minidisk OR minidisc OR "mini disc" OR "mini disk" OR "magneto optical disk" OR "magneto optical disc") OR ABST/(minidisk OR minidisc OR "mini disc" OR "mini disk" OR "magneto optical disk" OR "magneto optical disc") OR ICL/G11B013/04 OR ICL/G11C013/06	tak(minidisk OR minidisc OR ((mini OR "magneto optical") W/1 (disc OR disk)))
Generation: Compact Disc	compact disc	TTL/((CD AND (record$ OR music OR data OR information OR storage OR disk OR disc)) OR CD-R$ OR "compact disc" OR "compact disk") OR ABST/((CD AND (record$ OR music OR data OR information OR storage OR disk OR disc)) OR CD-R$ OR "compact disc" OR "compact disk")	tak((CD W/3 (music OR data OR information OR storage OR disk OR disc)) OR "CD R" OR "CD RW" OR "CD ROM" OR "compact disc" OR "compact disk")
Generation: Digital Versatile Disc	dvd	TTL/((DVD AND (record$ OR music OR data OR information OR storage OR disk OR disc)) OR DVD-R$ OR "digital versatile disc" OR "digital versatile disk" OR "digital video disc" OR "digital video disk") OR ABST/((DVD AND	tak(DVD OR "DVD R" OR "digital versatile disc" OR "digital versatile disc" OR "digital versatile disk" OR "digital video disc" OR

Annex 287

		(record$ OR music OR data OR information OR storage OR disk OR disc)) OR DVD-R$ OR "digital versatile disc" OR "digital versatile disk" OR "digital video disc" OR "digital video disk")	"digital video disk") AND NOT tak("HD DVD")
Generation: BluRay	bluray	TTL/(Bluray OR blueray OR "blue ray" OR "blu ray") OR ABST/(Bluray OR blueray OR "blue ray" OR "blu ray")	tak(Bluray OR blueray OR "blue ray" OR "blu ray")
Generation: HD-DVD	hd-dvd	TTL/("HD DVD" OR "high definition DVD" OR "high density DVD" OR "high definition digital versatile" OR "high density digital versatile") OR ABST/("HD DVD" OR "high definition DVD" OR "high density DVD" OR "high definition digital versatile" OR "high density digital versatile")	tak("HD DVD" OR ((HD OR "high density" OR "high definition") W/1 ("digital versatile disc" OR "digital versatile disk" OR "digital video disc" OR "digital video disk")))
Generation: NVRAM	nvram	TTL/("non volatile random access" OR NVRAM OR "flash drive" OR "thumb drive" OR "key drive" OR "flash memory" OR "compact flash" OR "smartmedia" OR "multimediacard") OR TTL/("MMC" OR "secure digital" OR "SD card" OR "memory stick" OR "xd picture card" OR "rs mmc" OR "minisd" OR "microsd" OR "intelligent stick" OR "nvSRAM" OR "FeRAM" OR "MRAM" OR "PRAM") OR ABST/("non volatile random access" OR NVRAM OR "flash drive" OR "thumb drive" OR "key drive" OR "flash memory" OR "compact flash" OR "smartmedia" OR "multimediacard") OR ABST/("MMC" OR "secure digital" OR "SD card" OR "memory stick" OR "xd picture card" OR "rs mmc" OR "minisd" OR "microsd" OR "intelligent stick" OR "nvSRAM" OR "FeRAM" OR "MRAM" OR "PRAM")	tak("non volatile random access" OR NVRAM OR "flash drive" OR "thumb drive" OR "key drive" OR "flash memory" OR "compact flash" OR "smartmedia" OR "multimediacard" OR "MMC" OR "secure digital" OR "SD card" OR "memory stick" OR "xd picture card" OR "rs mmc" OR "minisd" OR "microsd" OR "intelligent stick" OR "nvSRAM" OR "FeRAM" OR "MRAM" OR "PRAM")
Generation: ReRAM	reram	TTL/("resistive random access memory" OR RRAM OR ReRAM) OR ABST/("resistive random access memory" OR RRAM OR ReRAM)	tak(((resistive OR resistance) W/0 ("random access memory" OR RAM)) OR RRAM OR ReRAM)
Application: Data Storage	data storage	TTL/((information OR data OR media OR medium) NEAR (stor$ OR record$)) OR ABST/((information OR data OR media OR medium) NEAR (stor$ OR record$))	tak((data OR information OR file OR files) W/1 (archiv* OR save OR saving OR storage OR storing OR record*))

Annex C: R-Code of Statistical Analyses Performed in the Scope of the Approach in this Book

```
###################
# Step 1: Calculate meta data indicators
###################

# Results:

# largeTable2 (meta data indicator table, all indicators separate)

# largeTable3 (meta data indicator table, combined indicator X.backRefQ = patent backward
citations / non-patent backward citations)


###################
# Initialize Process
###################


# Install necessary libraries
install.packages('kernlab',dependencies=TRUE)


# Initialize database connection
library(RMySQL); drv <- dbDriver("MySQL"); con <- dbConnect(drv, user="PatentInfo", pass-
word="xxxxxxxx", dbname="uspto", host="xxxxxxxx"); dbListTables(con);


# Identify relevant Patents by Patent Number
library(XLConnect, pos=4); .workbook <- loadWorkbook("C:/Data/SelectedPatentsDataStorage-
USPTO.xlsx"); relevantPatents <- readWorksheet(.workbook, "Table1"); remove(.workbook)


# Initialize technology vector for row identification of current technology
technologie          <-          c("PunchedCard","PerforatedTape","MagneticTape","Flop-
pyDisc","Minidisc","HardDisc","CompactDisc","DVD","Blu-Ray","HD-DVD","NVRAM","ReRAM");
print(technologie);


# Initialize Variables


patCount <- matrix(); # Count of patents in year i

backRefP <- list(); # Count of backward patent citations (citations made)

backRefN <- list(); # Count of backward non-patent citations

Immediacy <- list(); # Average Backward Immediacy per patent (grant till grant)

ClaimsCountDep <- list(); # Dependent claims count per patent

PriorityCount <- list(); # Count of US Priorities (related applications)

ExamDuration <- list(); # Duration from application date until issue date

ForwardRefP <- list(); # Count of forward patent citations (citations received)

today <- Sys.Date()
```

```
year.start <- 1971
year.end <- format(Sys.Date(), format="%Y")


####################
# Add database location information (tablename) for each patent (necessary once at startup)
####################


tablename <- matrix() ; # Name (year) of matrix where to find Patent
for (p in 1:nrow(relevantPatents))
        {
        print(relevantPatents$PN[p]);
        query <- c("SELECT TABLENAME AS i FROM patentinfo WHERE PN = '",rele-
vantPatents$PN[p],"'");
        tablename[[p]] <- dbGetQuery(con, paste(query, collapse = ''));
        }
relevantPatents <- cbind(relevantPatents,unlist(tablename));
colnames(relevantPatents)[3] <- "tablename"
colnames(currentTech);
class(currentTech$tablename)
length(tablename)
####################
# Calculate meta data indicators for each year
####################


# Initialize output variables
labels        <-        c("backRefP","backRefN","Immediacy","PriorityCount","ForwardRefP","Claim-
sCountDep","ExamDuration");


X.backRefP <- matrix(NA);

X.backRefN <- matrix(NA);

X.Immediacy <- matrix(NA);

X.ClaimsCountDep <- matrix(NA);

X.PriorityCount <- matrix(NA);

X.ExamDuration <- matrix(NA);

X.ForwardRefP <- matrix(NA);

largeTable <- data.frame()

largeTable <- head(cbind(tablename,relevantPatents,X.backRefP,X.backRefN,X.Immediacy,X.Claim-
sCountDep,X.PriorityCount,X.ExamDuration,X.ExamDuration,X.ForwardRefP))


for (p in 1:nrow(largeTable)) # Collect data from all relevant rows
{
# 1. Count of Cited Refs - Patent (REF)
```

```
        query  <-  c("SELECT  LENGTH(REF)  -  LENGTH(REPLACE(REF,  '\n',  ''))  as  Count  FROM
patft_",as.numeric(as.character(largeTable$tablename[p])),"   WHERE   PN   =   '",largeTa-
ble$PN[p],"'"); # generate SQL query: Count = count us citations.

        largeTable$X.backRefP[p] <- dbGetQuery(con, paste(query, collapse = '')); # send SQL-
query
```

1. Count of Cited Refs - Non-patent (OREF)

```
        query  <-  c("SELECT  LENGTH(OREF)  -  LENGTH(REPLACE(OREF,  '\n',  ''))  +1 as  Count  FROM
patft_",as.numeric(as.character(largeTable$tablename[p])),"   WHERE   PN   =   '",largeTa-
ble$PN[p],"'"); # generate SQL query: Count = count us citations.

        largeTable$X.backRefN[p] <- dbGetQuery(con, paste(query, collapse = '')); # send SQL-
query
```

2. Average Backward Immediacy

```
        query <- c("SELECT AvgBackImmediacy FROM REFTable WHERE PN = '",largeTable$PN[p],"'");

        if (nrow(dbGetQuery(con, paste(query, collapse = ''))) > 0)

        {largeTable$X.Immediacy[p] <- dbGetQuery(con, paste(query, collapse = ''))}; # send SQL-
query
```

3. Count of Priorities

```
        query  <-  c("SELECT  LENGTH(RLAP)  -  LENGTH(REPLACE(RLAP,  ',',  ''))  as  Count  FROM
patft_",as.numeric(as.character(largeTable$tablename[p])),"   WHERE   PN   =   '",largeTa-
ble$PN[p],"'"); # generate SQL query: Count = Count of Related Prior US Applications

        largeTable$X.PriorityCount[p] <- dbGetQuery(con, paste(query, collapse = '')); # send
SQL-query
```

4. Count of Citing Patents

```
        query  <-  c("SELECT  COUNT(referencesTable.Source)  AS  Count  FROM  patft_",as.nu-
meric(as.character(largeTable$tablename[p])),"  JOIN  referencesTable  ON  patft_",as.nu-
meric(as.character(largeTable$tablename[p])),".PN=referencesTable.Target WHERE PN = '",largeTa-
ble$PN[p],"' GROUP BY patft_",as.numeric(as.character(largeTable$tablename[p])),".PN"); # gen-
erate SQL query

        if (nrow(dbGetQuery(con, paste(query, collapse = ''))) > 0) # Prevent error if no patents
in one year i

        {

                largeTable$X.ForwardRefP[p] <- dbGetQuery(con, paste(query, collapse = '')); #
send SQL-query

        }
```

5. Dependent Claims Count (Approximation: Claims Count - # Terms hinting towards independent claim ("comprising")

```
        query   <-   c("SELECT   LENGTH(REPLACE(ACLM,   'comprising',   'comprisin'))   -
LENGTH(REPLACE(ACLM, '\n', '')) as Count FROM patft_",as.numeric(as.character(largeTable$table-
name[p])),"  WHERE PN = '",largeTable$PN[p],"'"); # generate SQL query

        largeTable$X.ClaimsCountDep[p] <- dbGetQuery(con, paste(query, collapse = '')); # send
SQL-query
```

5. Dependent Claims Count (Approximation: Claims Count - # Terms hinting towards independent claim ("comprising")

```
        query   <-   c("SELECT   LENGTH(REPLACE(ACLM,   'comprising',   'comprisin'…))   -
LENGTH(REPLACE(ACLM, '\n', '')) as Count FROM patft_",as.numeric(as.character(largeTable$table-
name[p])),"  WHERE PN = '",largeTable$PN[p],"'"); # generate SQL query

        largeTable$X.ClaimsCountDep[p] <- dbGetQuery(con, paste(query, collapse = '')); # send
SQL-query

        ClaimsCountDep.j <- as.relistable(largeTable$X.ClaimsCountDep[p])

        ClaimsCountDep.k <- unlist(largeTable$X.ClaimsCountDep[p]);
```

```
    ClaimsCountDep.k[which(ClaimsCountDep.k<0)]=NA; # counting lines containing "compris-
ing" is an approximation. patents that return a negative dependent claims count become "NA".

    largeTable$X.ClaimsCountDep[p] <- relist(ClaimsCountDep.k, ClaimsCountDep.j);

# 6. Duration Examination Process

    query <- c("SELECT DATEDIFF(ISD,APD) AS Count FROM patft_",as.numeric(as.character(lar-
geTable$tablename[p]))," WHERE PN = '",largeTable$PN[p],"'"); # $generate SQL query

    largeTable$X.ExamDuration[p] <- dbGetQuery(con, paste(query, collapse = '')); # send
SQL-query

}


####################
# Finalize tables, delete unnecessary information
####################


# largeTable2: all indicators separately
keeps         <-         c("maturity.expert","X.backRefP","X.backRefN","X.Immediacy","X.Claim-
sCountDep","X.PriorityCount","X.ExamDuration","X.ForwardRefP")

largeTable2 <- largeTable[keeps]


# largeTable3: combined indicators according to Haupt Kloyer Lange-indicator hypothesis
keeps         <-         c("maturity.expert","X.backRefQ","X.Immediacy","X.ClaimsCountDep","X.Priori-
tyCount","X.ExamDuration","X.ForwardRefP")

largeTable3 <- largeTable2[keeps]

X.backRefQ <- largeTable2$X.backRefP / largeTable2$X.backRefN

largeTable3 <- cbind(largeTable3,X.backRefQ)

####################
# Step 2: Calculate activity indicators
####################

# Results:
# bigTable1 (activity indicators table with web search query data) and
# bigTable2 (activity indicators table without web search query data)


# Load alleTech-table -> All other relevant information has been loaded or generated in step 1!
.Workbook <- loadWorkbook("C:/Data/TimeSeriesRollingRegression-ThomsonData.xlsx"); alleTech <-
readWorksheet(.Workbook, "allTech"); remove(.Workbook);


# Initialize variables
# Final variables
steig.Pat.US.s <- list();

steig.Pat.PCT.s <- list();

steig.Lit.s <- list();

steig.Google.s <- list();

delta.steig.Pat.US.s <- list();
```

```
delta.steig.Pat.PCT.s <- list();

delta.steig.Lit.s <- list();

delta.steig.Google.s <- list();

# Intermediate variables

slope.Pat.US <- c(NA)

slope.Pat.PCT <- c(NA)

slope.Lit <- c(NA)

slope.Google <- c(NA)


bigTable <- cbind(subset(alleTech, X.Year >= 1976 & X.Year <= 2012, select=c("X.Year","Technol-
ogy","maturity.expert","Fraction-
FamCount.PCT","FractionIssueCount.US","FractionJournalArticleCount","AvgGoogleInterest")),slop
e.Pat.US, slope.Pat.PCT, slope.Lit, slope.Google);

        # intermediate variables containing slope information for all technologies instead of
just one

steig.alle.Pat.US <- vector(mode="list", length=12)

steig.alle.Pat.PCT <- vector(mode="list", length=12)

steig.alle.Lit <- vector(mode="list", length=12)

steig.alle.Google <- vector(mode="list", length=12)

delta.steig.Pat.US.mat <- vector(mode="list", length=12)

delta.steig.Pat.PCT.mat <- vector(mode="list", length=12)

delta.steig.Lit.mat <- vector(mode="list", length=12)

delta.steig.Google.mat <- vector(mode="list", length=12)

head(alleTech)

for (s in 1:12)

{ # This loop runs through all technologies s one after another

        select <- s; # Select desired technology: 1.PunchedCard 2.PerforatedTape 3.MagneticTape
4.FloppyDisc 5.Minidisc 6.HardDisc 7.CompactDisc 8.DVD 9.Blu-Ray 10.HD-DVD 11.NVRAM 12.ReRAM

        currentTech <- subset(alleTech, Technology == technologie[select] & X.Year >= 1976 &
X.Year <= 2012);

        par(mfrow=c(3,4),oma=c(0,0,2,0)); # initialize graphs


        ##################
        # Fraction, slope, and slope change
        ##################


        for (j in 2)
        { # j is the regression window size in years
                ######### Initialize variables
                jahr.start = 1976;
                jahr.end = 2012;
                jahr.start.Google = 2004;
                # patents US
                steigung.Pat.US = matrix();
```

```
delta.steig.Pat.US = matrix();

steig.max.Pat.US = 0;

steig.max.jahr.Pat.US = jahr.start;

steig.null.Pat.US = 0;

steig.null.jahr.Pat.US = jahr.start;

steig.min.Pat.US = 0;

steig.min.jahr.Pat.US = jahr.start;

# patents international

steigung.Pat.PCT = matrix();

delta.steig.Pat.PCT = matrix();

steig.max.Pat.PCT = 0;

steig.max.jahr.Pat.PCT = jahr.start;

steig.null.Pat.PCT = 0;

steig.null.jahr.Pat.PCT = jahr.start;

steig.min.Pat.PCT = 0;

steig.min.jahr.Pat.PCT = jahr.start;

# scientific publications

steigung.Lit = matrix();

delta.steig.Lit = matrix();

steig.max.Lit = 0;

steig.max.jahr.Lit = jahr.start;

steig.null.Lit = 0;

steig.null.jahr.Lit = jahr.start;

steig.min.Lit = 0;

steig.min.jahr.Lit = jahr.start;

# web search queries

steigung.Google = matrix();

delta.steig.Google = matrix();

steig.max.Google = 0;

steig.max.jahr.Google = jahr.start.Google;

steig.null.Google = 0;

steig.null.jahr.Google = jahr.start.Google;

steig.min.Google = 0;

steig.min.jahr.Google = jahr.start.Google;


######### Regression

for (i in jahr.start:jahr.end) # i is the current year

{

# calculate activity slope and slope change

        RegModel.Pat.US <- lm(formula = FractionIssueCount.US ~ X.Year, data=cur-
rentTech[currentTech[,1] >= i-j & currentTech[,1] <= i,]);
```

```
                    RegModel.Pat.PCT <- lm(formula = FractionFamCount.PCT ~ X.Year, data=cur-
rentTech[currentTech[,1] >= i-j & currentTech[,1] <= i,]);

                    RegModel.Lit  <-  lm(formula  =  FractionJournalArticleCount  ~  X.Year,
data=currentTech[currentTech[,1] >= i-j & currentTech[,1] <= i,]);

                    if (i >= jahr.start.Google) # web search data is only available for some
years

                        {

                            RegModel.Google  <-  lm(formula  =  AvgGoogleInterest  ~  X.Year,
data=currentTech[currentTech[,1] >= i-j & currentTech[,1] <= i,]);

                            steigung.Google[[i]] <- coef(RegModel.Google)[[2]];

                            delta.steig.Google[[i]]          <-          steigung.Google[[i]]-
steigung.Google[[i-1]];

                        }

                    steigung.Pat.US[[i]] <- coef(RegModel.Pat.US)[[2]]; # 1:Intercept (Y-
axis); 2:Slope

                    steigung.Pat.PCT[[i]] <- coef(RegModel.Pat.PCT)[[2]];

                    steigung.Lit[[i]] <- coef(RegModel.Lit)[[2]];

                    delta.steig.Pat.US[[i]] <- steigung.Pat.US[[i]]-steigung.Pat.US[[i-1]];
# slope change equals b(t) - b(t-1)

                    delta.steig.Pat.PCT[[i]] <- steigung.Pat.PCT[[i]]-steigung.Pat.PCT[[i-
1]];

                    delta.steig.Lit[[i]] <- steigung.Lit[[i]]-steigung.Lit[[i-1]];

                    for (g in 1:(nrow(bigTable))) # This loop writes the slope information
into bigTable

                        {

                            if (bigTable[g,]$X.Year == i & bigTable[g,]$Technology == tech-
nologie[select])

                                {

                                    bigTable[g,]$slope.Pat.US <- coef(RegModel.Pat.US)[[2]];

                                    bigTable[g,]$slope.Pat.PCT          <-          coef(Reg-
Model.Pat.PCT)[[2]];

                                    bigTable[g,]$slope.Lit <- coef(RegModel.Lit)[[2]];

                                    if (i >= jahr.start.Google)

                                        {

                                            bigTable[g,]$slope.Google          <-          coef(Reg-
Model.Google)[[2]];

                                        }

                                }

                        }

                }

        }


###################
# Calculate Variables for curve discussion
###################
```

```
# initialization
maturity.year <- list();

steig.Pat.US.mat <- list();

steig.Pat.PCT.mat <- list();

steig.Lit.mat <- list();

steig.Google.mat <- list();

delta.steig.Pat.US.mat <- list();

delta.steig.Pat.PCT.mat <- list();

delta.steig.Lit.mat <- list();

delta.steig.Google.mat <- list();


for (m in 0:5) # m is the maturity
{
        if (nrow(subset(alleTech,(alleTech$Technology == technologie[s]) & (alleTech$ma-
turity.expert == m))) > 0) # check, whether for technology at least one entry for maturity m
(otherwise no need for this loop)
        {
# write maturity indicator data for each maturity phase m into a vector list
                maturity.year[[m+1]] <- subset(alleTech,(alleTech$Technology == technol-
ogie[s]) & (alleTech$maturity.expert == m))$X.Year;

                steig.Pat.US.mat[[m+1]]                        <-                un-
list(steigung.Pat.US[maturity.year[[m+1]]]);

                steig.Pat.PCT.mat[[m+1]]                       <-                un-
list(steigung.Pat.PCT[maturity.year[[m+1]]]);

                steig.Lit.mat[[m+1]] <- unlist(steigung.Lit[maturity.year[[m+1]]]);

                steig.Google.mat[[m+1]]           <-         unlist(steigung.Google[matu-
rity.year[[m+1]]]);

                delta.steig.Pat.US.mat[[m+1]]                  <-                un-
list(delta.steig.Pat.US[maturity.year[[m+1]]]);

                delta.steig.Pat.PCT.mat[[m+1]]                 <-                un-
list(delta.steig.Pat.PCT[maturity.year[[m+1]]]);

                delta.steig.Lit.mat[[m+1]]        <-         unlist(delta.steig.Lit[matu-
rity.year[[m+1]]]);

                delta.steig.Google.mat[[m+1]]     <-         unlist(delta.steig.Google[matu-
rity.year[[m+1]]]);
        }
}
# write the data from above for each technology s into a vector list
        steig.Pat.US.s[[s]] <- steig.Pat.US.mat;

        steig.Pat.PCT.s[[s]] <- steig.Pat.PCT.mat;

        steig.Lit.s[[s]] <- steig.Lit.mat;

        steig.Google.s[[s]] <- steig.Google.mat;

        delta.steig.Pat.US.s[[s]] <- delta.steig.Pat.US.mat;

        delta.steig.Pat.PCT.s[[s]] <- delta.steig.Pat.PCT.mat;

        delta.steig.Lit.s[[s]] <- delta.steig.Lit.mat;
```

```
        delta.steig.google.s[[s]] <- delta.steig.google.mat;
    # Calculate Variables for curve discussion END


    }


    ##################
    # Create activity indicator tables with web search queries (bigTable1) and withough (bigTable2)
    ##################


    ### bigTable1: with web search queries (2004-2012)
    bigTable1 <- subset(bigTable, !is.na(AvgGoogleInterest) & !is.na(slope.Google), select=c("ma-
    turity.expert","Fraction-
    FamCount.PCT","FractionIssueCount.US","FractionJournalArticleCount","AvgGoogleInterest","slope
    .Pat.PCT","slope.Pat.US","slope.Lit","slope.Google"))

    # Delete rows from bigTable1 which contain technologies that don't change maturity between 2004-
    2012
    bigTable1        <-        subset(bigTable1,as.numeric(rownames(bigTable1))>=344   |   (as.nu-
    meric(rownames(bigTable1))>=256 & (as.numeric(rownames(bigTable1))<=263))) # hand-picked rows
    with technologies, which change maturity state between 2004 and 2012


    ### bigTable2: without web search queries (1976 - 2012)
    bigTable2 <- subset(bigTable, !is.na(slope.Pat.US) & !is.na(slope.Pat.PCT) & !is.na(slope.Lit),
    select=c("maturity.expert","Fraction-
    FamCount.PCT","FractionIssueCount.US","FractionJournalArticleCount","slope.Pat.PCT","slope.Pat
    .US","slope.Lit"))

    ####################
    # Step 3: Conduct necessary pretests
    ####################
    # Results:
    # pretest information


    # Load necessary libraries
    library(car)
    library(MVN)


    # Box's M-test for testing homogeneity of covariance matrices
    # Written by Andy Liaw (2004) converted from Matlab
    # Andy's note indicates that he has left the original Matlab comments intact
    # Slight clean-up and fix with corrected documentation provided by Ranjan Maitra (2012)


    ####################
    # define Box's M as R function
    ####################


    BoxMTest <- function(X, cl, alpha=0.05) {
```

```
## To cite this file, this would be an appropriate format:

## Trujillo-Ortiz, A., R. Hernandez-Walls, K. Castro-Morales,

## A. Espinoza-Tenorio, A. Guia-Ramirez and R. Carmona-Pina. (2002).

## MBoxtest: Multivariate Statistical Testing for the Homogeneity of

## Covariance Matrices by the Box's M. A MATLAB file. [WWW document].

##        URL        http://www.mathworks.com/matlabcentral/fileexchange/loadFile.do?ob-
jectId=2733&objectType=FILE

##

## References:

##

## Stevens, J. (1992), Applied Multivariate Statistics for Social Sciences.

## 2nd. ed., New-Jersey:Lawrance Erlbaum Associates Publishers. pp. 260-269.


if (alpha <= 0 || alpha >= 1)

        stop('significance level must be between 0 and 1')

g = nlevels(cl) ## Number of groups.

n = table(cl) ## Vector of groups-size.

N = nrow(X)

p = ncol(X)

bandera = 2

if (any(n >= 20))

        bandera = 1

## Partition of the group covariance matrices.




covList <- tapply(as.matrix(X), rep(cl, ncol(X)), function(x, nc) cov(matrix(x, nc =
nc)),ncol(X))

deno = sum(n) - g

suma = array(0, dim=dim(covList[[1]]))

for (k in 1:g)

        suma = suma + (n[k] - 1) * covList[[k]]

Sp = suma / deno ## Pooled covariance matrix.

Falta=0

for (k in 1:g)

# NEU

{

#       print(paste("Falta viejo: ", Falta)); # added later

#       print(paste("det(covList[[",k,"]])        =",        det(covList[[k]]),"        and
log(det(covList[[",k,"]])) =",log(det(covList[[k]])))); # added later
```

```
                    Falta = Falta + ((n[k] - 1) * log(abs(det(covList[[k]]))))  # Problem:
det(covList[[k]]) produces a negative value and therefore its log() doesn't exist --> NaN

      #       print(paste("Falta nuevo: ", Falta)); # added later

      }

      # ENDE NEU

      # ORIGINAL

      # Falta = Falta + ((n[k] - 1) * log(det(covList[[k]])))

      # ENDE ORIGINAL


      MB = (sum(n) - g) * log(det(Sp)) - Falta ## Box's M statistic.

      suma1 = sum(1 / (n[1:g] - 1))

      suma2 = sum(1 / ((n[1:g] - 1)^2))

      C = (((2 * p^2) + (3 * p) - 1) / (6 * (p + 1) * (g - 1))) * (suma1 - (1 / deno)) ##
Computing of correction factor.

      if (bandera == 1)

      {

            X2 = MB * (1 - C) ## Chi-square approximation.

            v = as.integer((p * (p + 1) * (g - 1)) / 2) ## Degrees of freedom.

            ## Significance value associated to the observed Chi-square statistic.

            P = pchisq(X2, v, lower=FALSE)  #RM: corrected to be the upper tail

            cat('----------------------------------------------\n');

            cat(' MBox Chi-sqr. df P\n')

            cat('----------------------------------------------\n')

            cat(sprintf("%10.4f%11.4f%12.i%13.4f\n", MB, X2, v, P))

            cat('----------------------------------------------\n')

            if (P >= alpha) {

                  cat('Covariance matrices are not significantly different.\n')

            } else {

                  cat('Covariance matrices are significantly different.\n')

            }

            return(list(MBox=MB, ChiSq=X2, df=v, pValue=P))

      }

      else

      {

            ## To obtain the F approximation we first define Co, which combined to
            ## the before C value are used to estimate the denominator degrees of
            ## freedom (v2); resulting two possible cases.

            Co = (((p-1) * (p+2)) / (6 * (g-1))) * (suma2 - (1 / (deno^2)))

            if (Co - (C^2) >= 0) {

                  v1 = as.integer((p * (p + 1) * (g - 1)) / 2) ## Numerator DF.

                  v21 = as.integer(trunc((v1 + 2) / (Co - (C^2)))) ## Denominator DF.

                  F1 = MB * ((1 - C - (v1 / v21)) / v1) ## F approximation.
```

```
                          ## Significance value associated to the observed F statistic.
                          P1 = pf(F1, v1, v21, lower=FALSE)
                          cat('\n----------------------------------------------------------------\n')
                          cat(' MBox F df1 df2 P\n')
                          cat('----------------------------------------------------------------\n')
                          cat(sprintf("%10.4f%11.4f%11.i%14.i%13.4f\n", MB, F1, v1, v21, P1))
                          cat('----------------------------------------------------------------\n')
                          if (P1 >= alpha) {
                                  cat('Covariance matrices are not significantly different.\n')
                          } else {
                                  cat('Covariance matrices are significantly different.\n')
                          }
                          return(list(MBox=MB, F=F1, df1=v1, df2=v21, pValue=P1))
                   } else {
                          v1 = as.integer((p * (p + 1) * (g - 1)) / 2) ## Numerator df.
                          v22 = as.integer(trunc((v1 + 2) / ((C^2) - Co))) ## Denominator df.
                          b = v22 / (1 - C - (2 / v22))
                          F2 = (v22 * MB) / (v1 * (b - MB)) ## F approximation.
                          ## Significance value associated to the observed F statistic.
                          P2 = pf(F2, v1, v22, lower=FALSE)

                          cat('\n----------------------------------------------------------------\n')
                          cat(' MBox F df1 df2 P\n')
                          cat('----------------------------------------------------------------\n')
                          cat(sprintf('%10.4f%11.4f%11.i%14.i%13.4f\n', MB, F2, v1, v22, P2))
                          cat('----------------------------------------------------------------\n')

                          if (P2 >= alpha) {
                                  cat('Covariance matrices are not significantly different.\n')
                          } else {
                                  cat('Covariance matrices are significantly different.\n')
                          }
                          return(list(MBox=MB, F=F2, df1=v1, df2=v22, pValue=P2))
                   }
            }
     }
}


#####################
# Conduct necessary pretests
#####################
# Order of tests:
```

```
# Box's M (equal variance-covariance matrices)

# Shapiro-Wilk (univariate normality)

# Kruskal-Wallis (homoscedasticity, non-parametrical test)

# Levene (Homogeneity of variance, pairwise)

# visual comparison of boxplots of separate maturity states


### Box's M (equal variance-covariance matrices)

# activity indicators with web search query data (2004-2012)
```

BoxMTest(X=bigTable1[,2:ncol(bigTable1)], cl=as.factor(bigTable1[,1]), alpha=0.05) # Use F test for period 2004-2012, because insufficient data (less than 20 observations per group at least once). Currently problem with F test!

```
# activity indicators without web search query data (1976-2012)
```

BoxMTest(X=bigTable2[,2:ncol(bigTable2)], cl=as.factor(bigTable2[,1]), alpha=0.05) # Use Chi square test for period 1976-2012, because sufficient data (20 observations per group)

```
# meta data indicators
```

BoxMTest(X=largeTable2[,2:ncol(largeTable2)], cl=as.factor(largeTable2[,1]), alpha=0.05) # Use Chi square test for meta data indicators, because sufficient data (25120 are too many observations to use boxM, which is intended for max 8000)

```
### Shapiro-Wilk (univariate normality)

# activity indicators with web search query data (2004-2012)

for (i in 2:ncol(bigTable1))

{

        print(colnames(bigTable1[i]))

        print(shapiro.test(bigTable1[,i]))

}

# activity indicators without web search query data (1976-2012)

for (i in 2:ncol(bigTable2))

{

        print(colnames(bigTable2[i]))

        print(shapiro.test(bigTable2[,i]))

}

# meta data indicators (separately)

for (i in 2:ncol(largeTable2))

{

        print(colnames(largeTable2[i]))

        print(shapiro.test(largeTable2[,i]))

}


### Kruskal-Wallis (homoscedasticity, non-parametrical test)

# activity indicators with web search query data (2004-2012)

for (i in 2:ncol(bigTable1))

{
```

```
        print(colnames(bigTable1[i]))
        print(kruskal.test(bigTable1[,i] ~ bigTable1[,1]))
}
# activity indicators without web search query data (1976-2012)
for (i in 2:ncol(bigTable2))
{
        print(colnames(bigTable2[i]))
        print(kruskal.test(bigTable2[,i] ~ bigTable2[,1]))
}
# meta data indicators (separately)
for (i in 2:ncol(largeTable2))
{
        print(colnames(largeTable2[i]))
        print(kruskal.test(largeTable2[,i] ~ largeTable2[,1]))
}


### Levene (Homogeneity of variance, pairwise)
# activity indicators with web search query data (2004-2012)

for (i in 2:ncol(bigTable1))
        {
        print(colnames(bigTable1[i]))
        print(leveneTest(bigTable1[,i], bigTable1[,1]))
        }

# activity indicators without web search query data (1976-2012)
for (i in 2:ncol(bigTable2))
        {
                print(colnames(bigTable2[i]))
                print(leveneTest(bigTable2[,i], bigTable2[,1]))
        }


# meta data indicators (separately)
for (i in 2:ncol(largeTable2))
{
        print(colnames(largeTable2[i]))
        print(leveneTest(largeTable2[,i] ~ largeTable2[,1]))
}


### Visual comparison of boxplots of separate maturity states
# activity indicators with web search query data (2004-2012)
```

```
dev.new()
par(mfrow=c(4,2), mar=c(4.1,4.1,0.5,0.5),oma=c(0,0,2,0))
for (plots in c(2,7,3,6,4,8,5,9))
{
        boxplot(bigTable1[,plots]~bigTable1[,1], ylab=colnames(bigTable1[plots]))
}
title("BOXPLOTS activity indicators with web search query data (2004-2012)", outer=TRUE)


# activity indicators without web search query data (1976-2012)
dev.new()
par(mfrow=c(3,2), mar=c(4.1,4.1,0.5,0.5),oma=c(0,0,2,0))
for (plots in c(2,3,4,5,6,7))
{
        boxplot(bigTable2[,plots]~bigTable2[,1], ylab=colnames(bigTable2[plots]))
}
title("BOXPLOTS activity indicators without web search query data (1976-2012)", outer=TRUE)


# meta data indicators (separately)
par(mfrow=c(4,2), mar=c(4.1,4.1,0.5,0.5),oma=c(0,0,2,0))
for(plots in c(2,3,4,5,6,7,8))
{
        boxplot(largeTable2[,plots]~largeTable2[,1],          ylab=colnames(largeTable2[plots]),
ylim=c(0.9,50000), log="y") # log-scale for readability!
}
title("BOXPLOTS meta data indicators (1976-2012)", outer=TRUE)
##########################################
# Step 4: Feature Selection
##########################################


##########################################
# Data Preparation
##########################################
# Load necessary libraries
library(MASS); library(car); library(klaR); library(kernlab); library(caret); library(random-
Forest); library(mlbench)


# load data: uncomment necessary line


 inputData <- subset(na.omit(bigTable1[,c(1,2,3,4,5,7,6,8,9)])) # bigTable1 = activity 2004-
2012
# inputData <- subset(na.omit(bigTable2[,c(1,2,3,4,6,5,7)])) # bigTable2 = activity 1976-2012
# inputData <- subset(na.omit(largeTable2)) # largeTable2 = meta data 1976-2012
```

```
#   inputData   <-   subset(na.omit(largeTable,   as.numeric(as.character(largeTable$table-
name))>2003))[,4:11] # largeTable2 = meta data 2004-2012 (by publication year)



#############################################
# Correlation and Near Zero Variance
#############################################


# determine near zero variables
nzv <- nearZeroVar(inputData, saveMetrics = TRUE)
nzv # here, all should be FALSE


# Identifying correlated predictors
descrCor <- cor(inputData)                          # creates a correlation matrix of
the predictors; Pearson correlation coefficient
highCorr <- sum(abs(descrCor[upper.tri(descrCor)]) > 0.75)   # counts the number of highly
correlated predictors (above 75% correlation)
highCorr
descrCor


#############################################
# Ability to Distinquish Between Maturity States
#############################################
# define function to calculate effect data

rFromWilcox<-function(wilcoxModel, N){
        z<- qnorm(wilcoxModel$p.value/2)
        r<- z/ sqrt(N)
        cat("Effect Size, r = ", r,"; z = ",z)
}


# requires data to be loaded in inputData


sapply(inputData, mean, na.rm=TRUE)
for (i in 2:ncol(inputData)){ # i = indicators
for (j in 0:3){ # j = maturity state to be compared
        for (k in j+1:4){ # k = other maturity state
                if(k < 5){
                        #   test<-t.test(subset(inputData,maturity.expert==j)[,i],subset(input-
Data,maturity.expert==k)[,i]) # t.test calls Welch's t-test
                        test <- wilcox.test(subset(inputData,maturity.expert==j)[,i],subset(in-
putData,maturity.expert==k)[,i], conf.int=TRUE) # Wilcoxon rank-sum test pairwise, non-paramet-
ric
                        rFromWilcox(test, nrow(inputData))
```

```
                          # test <- kruskal.test(inputData[,i]~inputData[,1]) # Kruskal Wallis
(non-parametric ANOVA)

                          # test <- pairwise.wilcox.test(inputData[,i]~inputData[,1], p.adj="bon-
ferroni", exact=F)

                          # print(paste(colnames(inputData)[i], j, k, test$conf.int, test$esti-
mate, test$null.value, test$p.value, test$parameter, test$statistic)) # conf.int, estimate,
null.value, p.value, parameter, statistic results

                  }

              }

          }

}


for (j in 0:4){

      print(summary(subset(inputData, maturity.expert==j)))

}



#############################################

# Reverse Feature Elemination (Random Forests)

#############################################


# variable initialization

reducedModel <- list()


# center and scale indicators

      normalization <- preProcess(inputData)

      training <- predict(normalization, inputData)

      training <- as.data.frame(training)


# Add dummy data

      p <- 40 # number of dummy indicators

      bogus <- matrix(rnorm(nrow(inputData) * p), nrow = nrow(inputData))

      colnames(bogus) <- c(paste("random", 1:p, sep = ""))

      training <- cbind(inputData, bogus)



# Perform random forest reverse feature elemination

  # Default ntree is 500 trees per forest and cannot be changed: http://stackoverflow.com/ques-
tions/13956435/setting-values-for-ntree-and-mtry-for-random-forest-regression-model

  # Default mtry is, as proposed by Breiman, sqrt(mdim = number of indicators including dummies)

  # Default information gain metric is entropy

      selectControl <- rfeControl(functions = rfFuncs, # random forest approach

                                              method = "repeatedcv",

                                              p=.75,
```

```
                                                         number = ifelse(method %in% c("cv",
"repeatedcv"), 12, 25),    # Either the number of folds or number of resampling iterations,
depending on method chosen

                                                         repeats   =   ifelse(method   %in%
c("cv", "repeatedcv"), 100, number), # For (repeated) k-fold cross-validation: the number of
complete sets of folds to compute

                                                         saveDetails = TRUE,

                                                         verbose = TRUE,

                                                         returnResamp = TRUE

                                                         )

        rf1 <- rfe(x=as.matrix(training[,2:ncol(training)]) , # x = input data

                        y=as.factor(training[,1]),              # y = group information

                        sizes=c(3:10),

                        rfeControl = selectControl             # import function settings,
e.g. cross validation

                        )

# Store data in list

        reducedModel <- rf1

#      reducedModel3 <- reducedModel # 1: first try 2004-2012; 2: second try 2004-2012; 3:
1976-2012

rf1 <- reducedModel2

reducedModel # determine best result of all runs


# show statistics on results

rf1        # shows best indicator combination and top 5 indicators

rf1$fit    # shows final model which performed best incl. confusion matrix and misclassification
rate

rf1$resample # shows

trellis.par.set(caretTheme()); plot(rf1, type = c("g", "o")) # plots the performance profile
for increasing numbers of indicators

predictors(rf1) # shows, which indicators were used in the best model

rf1$pred # best predictions within all branches of all decision trees in the random forest


##############################################
# Produce Random Forest Classifier
##############################################

rf1Model <- randomForest(as.factor(inputData[,1]) ~ ., data=inputData, ntree=1000, keep.for-
est=FALSE, proximity=TRUE, importance=TRUE)

plot(rf1Model, log="y")

varImpPlot(rf1Model)

MDSplot(rf1Model, as.factor(inputData[,1])) # plots resulting classification across two dimen-
sions

getTree(randomForest(as.factor(inputData[,1]) ~ ., data=inputData, ntree=10), 3, labelVar=TRUE)


#####################
```

```
# Step 5: Conduct ANOVA and LDA

####################

# Results:

# classifiers for all operationalized technology maturity models (activity indicators with and
without web search query data; meta data indicators separately and combined)


# Initialize process

require(MASS)


############
# Added Info for LDA
############


legendre.lda <- function(x, groups){
        x.lda <- lda(groups ~ ., x)


        gr <- length(unique(groups))    ## groups might be factors or numeric
        v <- ncol(x) ## variables
        m <- x.lda$means ## group means


        w <- array(NA, dim = c(v, v, gr))


        for(i in 1:gr){
                tmp <- scale(subset(x, groups == unique(groups)[i]), scale = FALSE)
                w[,,i] <- t(tmp) %*% tmp
        }


        W <- w[,,1]
        for(i in 2:gr)
                W <- W + w[,,i]


        V <- W/(nrow(x) - gr)
        iV <- solve(V)


        class.funs <- matrix(NA, nrow = v + 1, ncol = gr)
        colnames(class.funs) <- paste("group", 1:gr, sep=".")
        rownames(class.funs) <- c("constant", paste("var", 1:v, sep = "."))


        for(i in 1:gr) {
                class.funs[1, i] <- -0.5 * t(m[i,]) %*% iV %*% (m[i,])
                class.funs[2:(v+1) ,i] <- iV %*% (m[i,])
        }
```

```
        print(class.funs)
        x.lda$class.funs <- class.funs


        return(x.lda)
}



###########
# Conduct ANOVA
###########


### Activity indicators
# with web search query data (2004-2012)
curve.aov.with.google = aov(maturity.expert ~.,data=bigTable1)
print(curve.aov.with.google)
summary(curve.aov.with.google)


# without web search query data (1976-2012)
curve.aov.without.google = aov(maturity.expert ~.,data=bigTable2)
print(curve.aov.without.google)
summary(curve.aov.without.google)


### Meta data indicators
# indicators separately
classic.aov = aov(maturity.expert ~.,data=largeTable2)
print(classic.aov)
summary(classic.aov)


# Calculated indicator: patent backward citations divided by non-patent backward citations
(closer to original Haupt Kloyer Lange-hypothesis)
classic.aov = aov(maturity.expert ~.,data=largeTable3)
print(classic.aov)
summary(classic.aov)


###########
# Conduct LDA
###########


### Activity indicators
# with web search query data (2004-2012)
curve.lda.with.google = legendre.lda(x=bigTable1[,2:9], groups=bigTable1[,1]) # this generates
a table of the group discriminant functions. A new observation will be classified according to
which group scores the highest.
```

```
print(curve.lda.with.google)


# without web search query data (1976-2012)
curve.lda.without.google = legendre.lda(x=bigTable2[,2:7], groups=bigTable2[,1])
print(curve.lda.without.google)


### Meta data indicators
# indicators separately
classic.lda = legendre.lda(x=largeTable2[,2:8], groups=largeTable2[,1])
print(classic.lda)


# calculated indicator: patent backward citations divided by non-patent backward citations
(closer to original Haupt Kloyer Lange-hypothesis)
classic.lda = legendre.lda(x=largeTable3[,2:7], groups=largeTable3[,1])
print(classic.lda)
############################
# Step 6: LDA cross validation
############################
# Results:
# confusion matrices of all classifiers
# misclassification rates of all classifiers


####################
# define v-fold cross validation as R function
####################
vlda = function(v,formula,data,cl)
{
        require(MASS)
        grps = cut(1:nrow(data),v,labels=FALSE)[sample(1:nrow(data))] # sample function ensures
random sample, grps variable determines order of sample values
        pred = lapply(1:v,function(i,formula,data){
                        omit = which(grps == i)
                        z = lda(formula,data=data[-omit,])
                        predict(z,data[omit,])
                    },formula,data)

        wh = unlist(lapply(pred,function(pp)pp$class))
        table(wh,cl[order(grps)]) # here, grps is used to make sure that the predicted and actual
values line up properly.
}


####################
# Perform v-fold cross validation and print confusion matrix and misclassification rate
```

```
####################


### activity indicators
# with web search query data (2004-2012)
crossval.curve.with.google        =        vlda(v=12,formula=(as.integer(maturity.expert)
~.),data=bigTable1,cl=as.integer(bigTable1$maturity.expert))

print(crossval.curve.with.google)

# error rate of the classifier (the lower the better)
error.curve.with.google  =  sum(crossval.curve.with.google[row(crossval.curve.with.google)  !=
col(crossval.curve.with.google)]) / sum(crossval.curve.with.google)

print(error.curve.with.google)


# without web search query data (1976-2012)
crossval.curve.without.google        =        vlda(v=12,formula=(as.integer(maturity.expert)
~.),data=bigTable2,cl=as.integer(bigTable2$maturity.expert))

print(crossval.curve.without.google)

# error rate of the classifier
error.curve.without.google    =    sum(crossval.curve.without.google[row(crossval.curve.with-
out.google) != col(crossval.curve.without.google)]) / sum(crossval.curve.without.google)

print(error.curve.without.google)


### Meta data indicators
# indicators separately
crossval.classic    =    vlda(v=12,formula=(as.integer(maturity.expert)    ~.),data=largeTa-
ble2,cl=as.integer(largeTable2$maturity.expert))

print(crossval.classic)

# error rate of the classifier
error.classic  =  sum(crossval.classic[row(crossval.classic)  !=  col(crossval.classic)])  /
sum(crossval.classic)

print(error.classic)


# Calculated indicator: patent backward citations divided by non-patent backward citations
(closer to original Haupt Kloyer Lange-hypothesis)
crossval.classic    =    vlda(v=12,formula=(as.integer(maturity.expert)    ~.),data=largeTa-
ble3,cl=as.integer(largeTable3$maturity.expert))

print(crossval.classic)

# error rate of the classifier
error.classic  =  sum(crossval.classic[row(crossval.classic)  !=  col(crossval.classic)])  /
sum(crossval.classic)

print(error.classic)


####################
# Step 7: Conduct entire analysis on stratified sample of meta data indicators
####################
# Results:
```

```
# pretest information for stratified sample
# classifier for stratified sample
# confusion matrices of stratified sample
# misclassification rates of stratified sample


####################
# Drawing a stratified sample from the data to perform tests
####################


# choose how many records to sample per unique maturity value
sampleMax <- nrow(subset(largeTable2, largeTable2[,1]==0)) # max size of sample due to smallest
group, i.e. pre-existence


# draw the sample
my.sample    <-    largeTable2[unlist(tapply(1:nrow(largeTable2),largeTable2[,1],sample,sample-
Max)),]


####################
# perform pretests on stratified sample
####################


# Box's M
BoxMTest(X=my.sample[,2:ncol(my.sample)], cl=as.factor(my.sample[,1]), alpha=0.05)


# Shapiro-Wilk (Univariate normality)
for (i in 2:ncol(my.sample))
{
       print(colnames(my.sample[i]))
       print(shapiro.test(my.sample[,i]))
}


# Kruskal Wallis Test (parameter free homoscedasticity)
for (i in 2:ncol(my.sample))
{
       print(colnames(my.sample[i]))
       print(kruskal.test(my.sample[,i] ~ my.sample[,1]))
}


# Levene Test (univariate homoscedasticity)
for (i in 2:ncol(my.sample))
{
       print(colnames(my.sample[i]))
```

```
        print(leveneTest(my.sample[,i], my.sample[,1]))
}


####################
# Analysis of Variance
####################
classic.aov.stratified = aov(maturity.expert ~.,data=my.sample)
print(classic.aov.stratified)
summary(classic.aov.stratified)


####################
# Linear Discriminant Analysis
####################
classic.lda.stratified = legendre.lda(x=my.sample[,2:8], groups=my.sample[,1])
print(classic.lda.stratified)


####################
# Cross Validation
####################
crossval.classic.stratified = vlda(v=12,formula=(as.integer(maturity.expert) ~.),data=my.sam-
ple,cl=as.integer(my.sample[,1]))
print(crossval.classic.stratified)


# error rate of the classifier
error.classic.stratified = sum(crossval.classic.stratified[row(crossval.classic.stratified) !=
col(crossval.classic.stratified)]) / sum(crossval.classic.stratified)

print(error.classic.stratified)
```